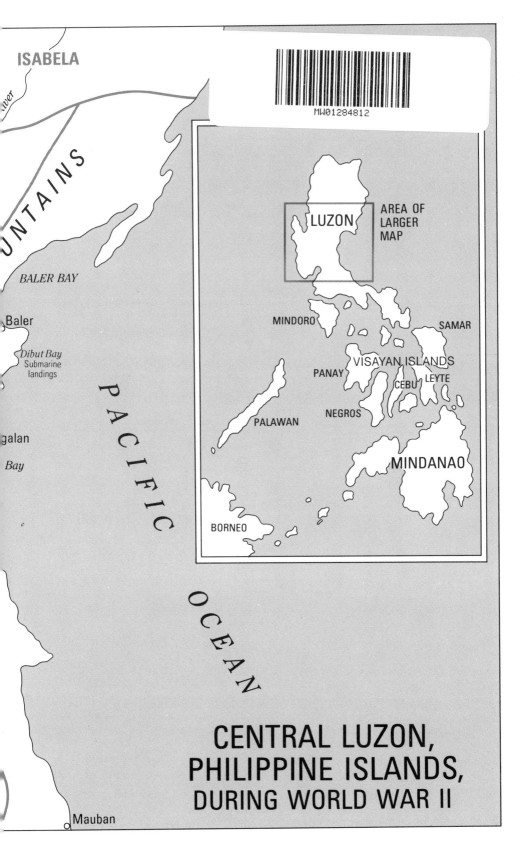

ISABELA

MOUNTAINS

BALER BAY

Baler

Dibut Bay
Submarine
landings

galan

Bay

PACIFIC

OCEAN

Mauban

LUZON · AREA OF LARGER MAP

MINDORO

SAMAR

VISAYAN ISLANDS

PANAY

CEBU · LEYTE

NEGROS

PALAWAN

MINDANAO

BORNEO

CENTRAL LUZON, PHILIPPINE ISLANDS, DURING WORLD WAR II

LAPHAM'S RAIDERS

LAPHAM'S RAIDERS

Guerrillas in the Philippines 1942-1945

ROBERT LAPHAM & BERNARD NORLING

THE UNIVERSITY PRESS OF KENTUCKY

Scholarly publisher for the Commonwealth,
serving Bellarmine College, Berea College, Centre
College of Kentucky, Eastern Kentucky University,
The Filson Club, Georgetown College, Kentucky
Historical Society, Kentucky State University,
Morehead State University, Murray State University,
Northern Kentucky University, Transylvania University,
University of Kentucky, University of Louisville,
and Western Kentucky University.

Editorial and Sales Offices:
The University Press of Kentucky
663 South Limestone Street
Lexington, Kentucky 40508-4008

Library of Congress Cataloging-in-Publication Data
Lapham, Robert, 1917-
   Lapham's raiders : guerrillas in the Philippines, 1942-1945 /
Robert Lapham and Bernard Norling.
      p.   cm.
   Includes bibliographical references and index.
   ISBN 0-8131-1949-9 (alk. paper)
   1. Lapham, Robert, 1917-   .   2. World War, 1939-1945—Underground
movements—Philippines—Luzon.   3. World War, 1939-1945—Personal
narratives, American.   4. Guerrillas—United States—Biography.
5. Guerrillas—Philippines—Luzon—Biography.   6. Luzon
(Philippines)—History, Military.   I. Norling, Bernard, 1924-
II. Title.
   D802.P52L896   1996
   940.53'599—dc20   95-20719

Contents

Foreword

Skeptics sometimes allege that it is close to impossible to write accurate history based on the memories of those who participated in events that took place decades ago. The claim has some substance, for we have only to try to recall precisely long past happenings in our own lives to realize the pitfalls that abound. Nonetheless, the difficulty is easily exaggerated.

Douglas Clanin, who worked for years collecting information from Americans and Filipinos who had been guerrillas on Luzon during World War II, and who got to know many of them quite well in the process, did not despair of extracting the essential truth about their activities and purposes from 1942 to 1945. It is possible, after all, to compare the memories of each man with those of the others as well as with numerous official records, private papers, and published materials.

Clanin does remind all concerned with research on this subject that we must remember the kind of men the Americans among them were, and the circumstances in which they lived and toiled. They were widely varying human types, from quite different civilian backgrounds, and had served in many different military units. They had all been thrown together in a situation that was both chaotic and extremely dangerous and for which they had had no training whatever. In the spring of 1942 most of them were sick, starved, frightened, and anxious about their own survival, but also initially overwhelmed by the magnitude and complexity of the problems they faced. The remarkable fact is not that many of them lost their lives and that most of the others bickered among themselves but that a considerable number of them did survive to form guerrilla organizations, badger the Japanese occupation forces persistently, and contribute appreciably to eventual Allied victory in the most extensive land campaign in the Pacific war, that on Luzon in 1945.

While it is virtually certain that this book contains some errors and distortions because parts of it are based on personal memories of events of half a century ago, we have tried to distinguish certitudes from likelihoods and both from mere possibilities. We do not think we have seriously misled readers about anything important; certainly we have not done so purposely.

The book is based on several major sources: (1) the personal recollections of Lt. Col. (as he was at war's end) Robert Lapham, augmented by many letters, clippings, personal records, and official papers he either saved during the war or acquired afterward; (2) copies of materials from the National Archives, some of which are in Robert Lapham's possession and many more in the archival section of the Ernie Pyle Museum in Dana, Indiana; (3) an extensive array of written statements by several dozen American and Filipino guerrillas from World War II, records of interviews with them by Wayne Sanford and Douglas Clanin, and materials relating to them, all in the Pyle Museum; (4) personal memoirs of participants in the Philippine sector of the Pacific war; and (5) secondary sources of the usual sort.

For many reasons, Robert Lapham's memoirs can contribute importantly to a clearer, more detailed, and more accurate picture of Philippine guerrilla activity in World War II. First, of the dozens of irregular groups that existed all over the Islands, his LGAF (Luzon Guerrilla Armed Forces) was the fourth largest, and the third largest on Luzon, where the most fighting took place for the longest time. Second, of all the Luzon guerrillas, none performed better under fire than those of LGAF. Third, there are many indications that Robert Lapham managed his sphere of influence on Luzon more capably than any of his peers managed theirs. Some of his colleagues praised the general efficiency with which LGAF was run and compared it favorably with what they had observed about other organizations. For instance, few aspects of guerrilla affairs gave rise to more controversy than military rank, and no other guerrilla chieftain handled it as wisely as Lapham. In this narrative a reader may well be irritated to encounter the same individual as "Lieutenant" on one page, "Captain" on another, and "Colonel" somewhere else. All I can do is plead lamely that it cannot be helped. American regular army officers had a permanent grade, a temporary (and usually higher) wartime grade, and those who became guerrillas usually bestowed on themselves or were given by others some still higher grade. Thus the woods were soon full of "colonels" and, among Filipino guerrilla officers in the south islands, even some "generals." It says much for Lapham's judgment and sense of proportion that in his organization the highest rank was "major," his own. His discretion was properly rewarded at the end of the war: LGAF was the only organization of irregulars in which nobody was reduced in rank by military higher authorities, and Lapham himself was promoted to lieutenant colonel. It is also noteworthy that of the numerous unflattering comments Luzon guerrillas directed at one another, fewer were aimed at Lapham than at anyone else of comparable stature.

Finally, and most significant, when Robert and Scharlott Lapham traveled to the Philippines in 1986 to visit the area where he had kept his headquarters from 1942 to 1945, he not only received a warm welcome from the local inhabitants but found that his old wartime followers had raised money by public subscription to erect in the town of Umingan a fine memorial to the LGAF guerrillas. Under a statue of a Filipino guerrilla was a bronze plaque on which was engraved a special tribute to (then) Major Lapham and a notation that here he had founded his guerrilla organization in 1942. Thus had Robert Lapham been honored by those who knew him best: the men he had led in resistance to the Japanese enemy, and the ordinary civilians he had endeavored to protect. It was these people, many of them poor, who had emptied their pockets to raise a memorial to his deeds, his example, and his memory, forty years after the event.

What such people themselves contributed to the Allied cause by their loyalty, their labor, and their suffering has been recorded in print by a fair number of Americans, many of whom owed their own lives to Filipinos, but too many others have been either unappreciative or forgetful. Quite apart from the terrible physical devastation Japan wrought in their country, the Filipinos suffered twice as many casualties in the war as did Americans, and that from a population only one-tenth as large. We hope this book will lead more Americans to remember this.

While I (B.N.) "wrote" this book, in the usual sense of organizing and putting it on paper, it has been a joint effort throughout. We have gone over the same source materials and read, reread, and revised the text several times. Thus what appears in print may be justly imputed to both of us. Since it is Robert Lapham's story, however, it is told in first person. Exceptions (in the notes, for example) are indicated by my initials, B.N. Further, there are scattered references throughout the text to events, circumstances, and situations in other places and at other times—ancient, medieval, and modern. Most of these observations and comparisons are my own. They have been inserted to link Robert Lapham's experiences, deeds, and thoughts to those of others comparably situated in the past. We hope this will make our narrative both more interesting and more meaningful to most readers. Chapter 13 too is mostly of my own composition. It is intended mainly to emphasize what many books on war slight: that victory is the product of enemy mistakes quite as much as of one's own planning and endeavors.

Anyone who produces a book based on research incurs debts to others along the way. I thank those in the University of Notre Dame Interlibrary Loan Office for securing many books for me; Sherry Reichold and Cheryl Reed for typing the manuscript; the staff of the Ernie Pyle Museum for allowing me uncontrolled access to the varied and valuable materials in their archives; Albert Hendrickson, Vernon Fassoth, and Clyde Childress, who expanded my knowledge of things Philippine; Morton "Jock" Netzorg, who once let me use his extensive private library of books and source materials on Philippine history and who generously added much from his extensive personal knowledge; Ray Hunt, with whom I spent much time and effort discussing and eventually writing a book similar in many ways to this one, and whose experience of guerrilla existence in the Islands quickened my interest in that subject.

Last and most, I thank Wayne Sanford and Douglas Clanin. Since the early 1980s Sanford has both published and written extensively for The *World War II Chronicle*, a newspaper that appears several times a year and carries articles about the deeds, designs, and thoughts of the middle- and lower-ranking men and women who waged and experienced World War II, especially in the Pacific theater. Sanford and Clanin (of the Indiana State Historical Society) have also sponsored conventions of survivors of Bataan, Corregidor, and guerrilla warfare in the Philippines. They have queried scores of veterans of these campaigns by letter, telephone, questionnaire, and personal interview to collect as much information as possible about guerrilla activity, then sorted and arranged their voluminous findings. These have since been deposited in the Pyle Museum for the use of scholars and others. Those of us who spend our time writing either conventional academic history or "popular" accounts of the deeds of mankind easily forget how much we owe to the compilers, bibliographers, archivists, and enthusiastic students who do so much to seek out, collect, and preserve historical source materials. Published histories owe at least as much to the labors of these spadeworkers as to the individuals who wield the pen—or, in our age, the word processor.

BERNARD NORLING

Preface

I was born in 1917 and so grew up in the 1930s, the difficult and troublesome time of the Great Depression. We were fortunate that my father always had a job, though like many families we had little left over after securing life's necessities. In a way this was good, for it brought people closer, taught us to work together and help one another, and made us recognize the value of things other than money.

In that decade the Depression spread worldwide, bringing dissatisfaction and discontent in its wake. Mussolini, already long in power in Italy, began to build a big army. In September 1931, Japan invaded Manchuria; in 1937, China proper. Italy conquered Ethiopia in 1935–36. Hitler began the ominous rearmament of Germany in 1935. Although Americans felt sorry for the Manchurians and Chinese because they suffered Japanese atrocities, that whole part of the world still seemed remote. To my college friends and me "the Philippines" was some vague place where Admiral Dewey had once sunk a Spanish fleet. We did recognize more immediately the danger that Hitler and Mussolini represented, and found the thought unsettling that somehow our country might have to fight them someday.

In my junior and senior years (1938–39) at the University of Iowa, I enrolled in advanced ROTC and graduated with a commission as a second lieutenant in the Army Reserves. We ROTC cadets, as well as many of my other friends, were uneasy at the visibly increasing tension in Europe. Hitler revealed his belligerence clearly by occupying Austria in 1938 and Czechoslovakia in stages in 1938–39. When Germany invaded Poland in 1939, England and France at last abandoned "appeasement" and declared war on the Third Reich. All these developments were topics for serious discussion in our ROTC classes, for we were of prime "cannon fodder" age. Congress had enacted neutrality laws in 1936 and 1937, but President Franklin Roosevelt called for us to give all "aid short of war" to the Allies, for which many called him a warmonger.

After graduation in June 1939, I was employed by the Burroughs Corporation in Chicago as a sales trainee. I worked hard familiarizing

xi

myself with the company's products and how to sell them. Eventually I was proud to be assigned a territory of my own. Always in the back of my mind, though, was the threat of war. Throughout 1940 the uncertainty increased. More reserve officers were being called to active duty all the time. With the introduction of selective service in September my friends and I were sure it was only a matter of time before we would be drafted or called to active duty. France had already surrendered, and the British had barely escaped at Dunkirk.

By spring of 1941 it was growing difficult for me to concentrate on my work. Reserve officers were required to keep in touch with Reserve Headquarters, and when not enough volunteered, some were being ordered to active duty. Should I go into service or wait to be summoned?

In early May of 1941 I was told I could expect to be ordered to active duty in the near future. Almost certainly this would mean maneuvers in the swamps of Louisiana. If I cared to volunteer, however, there were many attractive foreign assignments available: Hawaii, Puerto Rico, Panama, Alaska, and the Philippines. I talked this over with two of my buddies at Burroughs, and we all decided we should get in and get it over with. The next day my two friends enlisted, and I signed up for active duty. I indicated my preference for assignments in the order listed above. As anyone familiar with the U.S. Army might have predicted, I was shortly put aboard the USS *President Pierce*, along with about 400 other similarly gullible souls, and sent to the Philippines.

I want to dedicate this book to the memory of my mother, Alberta, and my father, C.E. Lapham, for their patience and understanding, for teaching me the value of family love and loyalty, for instilling in me the will to fight and not surrender to adversity, and for their faith. When friends would say, "Won't it be wonderful *if* Bob returns," my mother would reply, "Not *if*—*when* he returns!"

I also dedicate this book to the many fine Filipinos, too numerous to name, who served with me in the war. They are men like Father Gabriel, the parish priest in Umingan, and the Anolin brothers Leo and Des, who have remained close personal friends. To all my Filipino comrades, my sincere thanks for your friendship, your loyalty, and your love.

ROBERT LAPHAM

— 1 —

The Philippines, 1941

The military unpreparedness of the United States in the Pacific in 1941 can only be called appalling. It is difficult to say whether American folly exceeded Philippine, but U.S. folly was more serious in its consequence because of our vastly greater potential might. At the top, American policy was hopelessly inconsistent. Officially, we were committed to the defense of the Philippines, but we kept there mere token forces that could not mount a serious defense against a determined enemy. The Roosevelt administration harassed Japan by word and deed, but Congress, ever mindful of the next election, pandered to voters who were sunk in emotional isolationism. Washington even refused to appropriate funds to make Guam a major naval base. Caught in the middle, the flamboyant, spendthrift Philippine president, Manuel Quezon, talked disconsolately of his nation's helplessness, ostentatiously paid a visit to Japan, and cut his military budget—though he did not neglect to pour money into showy public works projects whereby he glorified himself.[1]

Before World War II, the major purpose of Philippine military activity was to train a citizen army prepared to defend the archipelago once it became an independent nation in 1946. Philippine reserve officers in training at that time knew they needed more instruction and practice before full responsibility fell to them, but they expected to have time to acquire it. On the eve of the war the Philippine army had about 500 officers on active duty (though 10,000 were needed), supplemented by 5,000 reserve officers who had only ROTC training.[2] The nucleus of this army was potentially good, and some of those in it were actually so, but both regulars and reserves included legions of political appointees of indifferent competence. To remedy this crucial deficiency, in 1941 several shiploads of American officers, of whom I was one, were sent to expand, advise, instruct, and train this existing army. Largely by default, many of us soon became de facto commanders of many units in the Philippine army.

Contrary to what some might think, this was not an innately undesirable situation, nor one without precedents. Most of the time during World War II military cooperation between Americans and Filipinos (always excepting the Hukbalahaps) was better than that which usually prevails between allies. One reason was that most Filipinos were glad to see Americans around and habitually deferred to us. More important, it seemed to me, was that nearly all high-ranking officers were American. Thus we managed everything, and there were few Filipino military egos to get in the way of planning. It was one more demonstration that in war the nation with the fewest allies may not be the best off, but it is almost always the one with the least trouble.

It was also a state of affairs reminiscent of that in the old German army, where major units were often formally commanded by members of royal or great aristocratic families, but the decisions that counted in war were customarily made by the General Staff officers of lower rank attached to these units. In our case we were charged with creating many new units and pumping both these and the old ones full of zeal for war. Some writers have alleged that we lacked a sense of urgency—indeed, that we bore more than a passing resemblance to the British who were preparing lackadaisically for the defense of Singapore at about the same time. Some charge that the slackness extended all the way to the top, to General Douglas MacArthur himself, then a field marshal in the Philippine army.[3]

Such contentions are hard to evaluate. In regard to the middle and lower levels they are unjust: all the younger officers I knew soon realized the dangers we faced, were intelligent enough to worry about them, and worked hard to try to improve our situation and prospects. Higher up, sadly, the allegations contain some truth. It had long been a common practice in the U.S. Army to send to the Philippines for their final tour of duty officers who were full of years and high in rank. There they and their wives could warm their aging bones the year around, enjoy inexpensive food and liquor, buy luxury goods at bargain prices, hire servants for a pittance, and prepare themselves to slide pleasantly into retirement. Few such men were renowned for zeal in pursuit of their professional duties.[4]

The Philippine army had many problems more basic than mere military slackness. In the 1940s the Philippines were a collection of many peoples of varied races, religions, and languages but hardly a true "nation." Though I thought their similarities increasingly exceeded their differences, it was undeniable that different groups lived at different stages of historical evolution and were frequently at odds among themselves. The Negritos, tiny, primitive black people who lived in the mountains of Luzon, often not far from Manila, seemed more central African than Asian. Among other early inhabitants were the Illongots and Igorots. The latter, of Indonesian extraction, are thought to have been the first invaders of the Philippines and to have driven the native Negritos into the mountains. Subsequent Indonesian invaders are assumed to have pushed the Igorots themselves into the mountains to live a primitive life thereafter. In modern times many Igorots had come out of the highlands, accepted Christianity, learned English, gotten used to Americans, and become "civilized." I thought they and the Illocanos were the toughest people and best soldiers among Filipinos. One such was Tom Chengay, a smart, brave Igorot who became one of Ray Hunt's most valuable commanders in my eventual guerrilla organization. Another was Esteben Lumyeb, who was to be my companion when I established my first guerrilla headquarters. Not long thereafter he saved my life.[5]

Farther south in the Islands, the Moslem Moros of Mindanao and Jolo got on badly with Christian Filipinos and were often on the edge of revolt. Further evidence of cultural cleavage was the rapidity with which the Hukbalahap (Philippine Communist) movement made headway among people who spoke Pampango but generally failed to attract those who spoke Tagalog. In 1941 Manila was "the Pearl of the Orient," one of the world's great cities. Its educated and affluent residents resembled their counterparts in the big cities of Europe and America, yet portions of several of the larger islands were still unexplored.

In most Philippine army units many men could not understand the languages of most of the others; moreover, they had been together so briefly that they had not had time to learn one another's names, much less develop mutual confidence or a collective esprit de corps. More than a few units had first sergeants and company clerks who could not read or write. Vehicles of every type were notable mainly by their absence, and the available rifles were mostly ancient British Enfields, in some of which the steel extractors had deteriorated so badly in tropical heat and humidity that they broke when used.[6] The only ammunition for these relics dated from 1917 or before.

In general, men in the Philippine army were brave enough, but their idiosyncrasies created difficulties and produced exasperation. In civilian life most of them had been simple farmers. They liked routine and disliked unfamiliar tasks. Few of them knew much about mechanical equipment or how to take care of it. Some drove vehicles at whatever the speedometer said was the highest possible speed rather than what was sensible in given circumstances. Their English vocabulary was often so inadequate that it was difficult to be sure they understood commands, doubly so when their pride forbade them to admit that they did not understand. Steve Mellnick, a Coast Artillery officer, said he got the best results by speaking slowly and carefully, considering only one topic at a time, avoiding slang, and supplementing his verbal orders with written instructions.[7] My men were all Philippine Scouts who could speak English. With them I "followed the book": that is, I gave an order and then had the man give it back to me.

These Philippine Scout units, which had been authorized by Congress in the 1920s and were part of the American army, were better prepared than the rest of their countrymen. Because much prestige adhered to being a Scout, many aspired to fill the few openings that existed in the corps, making it possible to select recruits with care. As a result the Scouts were the cream of Filipino soldiery, real professional troops who had undergone long training. They were familiar with their vehicles and equipment and took pride in maintaining them. Still, there were only about 10,000 Scouts, and their supplies were frequently inadequate. It indicates much that their Twenty-Sixth was still a horse cavalry unit.[8]

The overall command of the U.S. forces in the Philippines was called the Philippine Department. Under its jurisdiction was the Philippine Division, consisting of three infantry regiments, a field artillery regiment, and support troops. The only completely American regiment was the U.S. Thirty-first Infantry; the other two were the Forty-fifth Infantry (Philippine Scouts), of which my own Scouts were a part, and the Fifty-seventh Philippine Infantry (also Scouts). All the Philippine Scout units had mostly American officers and Filipino enlisted men. Also reporting to the Philippine Department were the Twenty-sixth Cavalry and three Philippine Scout Coastal Artillery regiments. There was also a Scout regiment in Mindanao. In all these units the men were armed with 1903 Springfield rifles until a month or two before the war began. At that time we were issued fine new Garands and new ammunition, but officers and men alike got only one opportunity to fire the new weapons on the range.

The strictly American army was in better shape than the forces of our Philippine allies, but not much better. Our Far Eastern Air Force consisted of 35 Flying Fortresses and 107 P-40 Pursuit planes. The latter were much inferior to the Japanese Zeroes they would soon have to face. On the ground we had National Guard tanks and (usually) old Stokes mortars from World War I whose ammunition had deteriorated in storage. Sometimes we had new 60 mm mortars with no ammunition at all[9] or, what was nearly as bad, ammunition that had become so defective from storage in the tropics that about two-thirds of the shells were duds. This wretched state of affairs brought about the defeat, with heavy casualties, of Philippine Scout units around Matabang-Abucay in mid-January 1942, where they would likely have stopped a Japanese attack at much lower cost to themselves had they had proper ammunition.[10] One National Guard tank regiment arrived in November 1941. Its members were promptly issued oil company road maps and a few compasses, vital for movement in the jungle.[11]

Perhaps the worst American deficiency was psychological. It derived directly from one of our notorious national shortcomings: lack of interest in and consequent ignorance of other peoples. Its fruit was gross overconfidence throughout American society. From chairborne warriors at Olympian heights in Washington to the humblest KPs and latrine orderlies in army camps around the United States, it was taken for granted that any piece of American equipment must be of better quality and construction than its Japanese counterpart, that U.S. soldiers were naturally superior as well, that Japanese pilots were shortsighted and lacked a sense of balance, that soldiers from an authoritarian society lacked the intellectual flexibility of defenders of democracy, that (presumably) some celestial source had decreed Yankee ingenuity to be the unique property of Americans forever, and that the unprepossessing little men from Japan knew these eternal truths just as well as we did and so could never drive U.S. troops out of the Philippines.

By contrast, American officers like me who had been in the Islands for a while had become aware of how vulnerable we were militarily. No matter. The neglect of years could not be remedied in a few months by any person or any process. Few of us, civilian or military, stopped to reflect that the enemy had several million veterans of many years of war in China. We knew of Japanese cruelty to the Chinese but seemed to think that white people would always be treated humanely.[12] Most of us did not know that virtually every Philippine town of any size harbored Japanese spies, masquerading as tourists or businessmen, who spent much of their time gathering information and making maps for the Nipponese soldiers who would follow them. If America's famed Orange Plan for the defense of the Philippines, which called for a last stand on the Bataan peninsula, was familiar to all U.S. officers, it was equally well known to all these "travelers" and "merchants," not to speak of those Japanese officers who had gone to West Point, where the Plan had been taught for years as a classic withdrawal procedure.

To be sure, both General MacArthur and his superiors in Washington did begin to address these problems in the last half of 1941. Army and navy transports regularly unloaded officers at Manila. There was much war talk aboard these ships as they crossed the Pacific and a lot more in the Islands themselves. Blackouts were rehearsed, convoys appeared periodically, and great numbers of bulldozers and other supplies were unloaded. In December alone thirty ships were scheduled to arrive in Manila. Rapid departures by day and by night became common; by the fall of 1941 departing ships had taken away most of the dependents of servicemen. Ashore, every effort was being made to cram months of training into mere weeks. Clearly, major developments were anticipated soon. MacArthur's headquarters expected to have about 100,000 men reasonably ready for them by February.

The intensity of my own regimen likewise increased steadily. For the first two or three weeks after debarking in Manila on June 25, 1941, I trained half-days and attended numerous lectures but still found plenty of time to play golf and baseball, go to movies, and socialize in the evenings. But life changed in the middle of July. There was much hard marching, which improved my physical condition and put a few pounds of muscle on my lean frame. Military field problems grew more complex, took more time, and—to me, anyway—became more interesting. By September I had been chosen to referee some of them, a duty that enabled me to learn a good deal more than I had as a participant. By then I had also assumed several additional duties, the most pleasant of which was to coach the Third Battalion basketball team. Fortunately, there were several good players in the outfit, so we were able to savor an undefeated season without excessive dependence on the genius of the coach.

Most important to me personally, four months of hard training markedly bolstered my self-confidence. On November 1 I wrote to my parents that whereas I had previously felt inadequate as an officer and often suffered stage fright when I had to give a lecture, I had now grown accustomed to lecturing and had seen enough other officers botch their assignments on field problems to convince me that I must be at least as capable as the rest of them. Moreover, I now positively enjoyed field problems. It was a good thing. I would have plenty of them in the next three and a half years, though most would not be of the sort posed in army manuals.

Someone once said that confusion is the first weed to grow on the field of battle. True—but confusion comes in many forms and degrees. I certainly *felt* confused when the war began, but, looking back, I think I was probably less so than many. Immediately, I became part of an effort to manage an orderly retreat in the face of a mobile, aggressive enemy. This is one of the most difficult of all military operations. It requires competent leaders, careful timing, coordination of all units, and obedience and good morale among those backpedaling. Generally speaking, the U.S. withdrawal in the face of Japanese landings at Lingayen Gulf was managed well. The defeated American and Filipino forces dropped back down the central plain of Luzon and into the Bataan peninsula without undue losses or disorder. Some historians have claimed that, by contrast, the retreat from southern Luzon and Manila around the north end of Manila Bay into Bataan was more of a headlong rush. Some blame this on General MacArthur, alleging that his mind was paralyzed by the unexpected, rapid flow of events, that he "behaved like an old-time fighter recalled from retirement and suddenly thrust into the ring against a young and hard hitting opponent whose lightning reflexes left him dazzled."[13] This seems to me much overstated. First of all, the supreme commander's own plan for the defense of Luzon had not included withdrawal into Bataan. It was the surge of events that compelled him to fall back on the old Orange Plan, part of which did call for such a retreat. It then took about two weeks to commandeer all the civilian cars, trucks, and buses we could find, change everybody's orders, and put the old plan in motion. Finally, we had to retreat as rapidly as possible around the north end of Manila Bay and into Bataan while the road was still open and bridges over the rivers were still intact. This was carried out successfully in the main, without panic, and with Filipino troops who had little or no training in maneuver or counterattack. It was no mean achievement.

One would suppose that the events of the two or three weeks following December 8, 1941 (December 7 in the States), would be indelibly imprinted on my memory until the day of my death. Certainly they were by far the most important and traumatic days of my life up to that point. Yet when I try to recall them, more than half a century later, the details are dim.[14] I remember a great deal of bombing in and around Manila, not only at Clark Field but at Cavite Naval Base and Nichols Field as well. I don't remember any bombs falling at Fort McKinley, where I was then stationed, though planes flew back and forth overhead, and there were dogfights and probably some strafing. It was clear, though, that the troops there were grievously vulnerable, so it was soon decided to move the two regiments away from the fort. My friends departed with them, while I was left behind with two regimental bands whose musicians were to do sentry duty and other routine tasks, as well as with some military police and a few others. We were soon joined by a number of retired Philippine Scouts who lived nearby and who rushed over to volunteer and were reenlisted.

On December 8 I was executive officer of "I" Company, one of the few companies that happened to have two American commissioned officers, so I fell heir to much extra duty. When the war began I was officer of the guard: that is, commander of sentries from several companies. Then, abruptly, I was detached from my own company and assigned to head the MPs.

Edwin Ramsey, later to become a guerrilla leader as I did, said he was much impressed by the randomness of war, of events taking place quite unconnected with any rational design or deliberate intention.[15] Ed had a point. Here I was, hitherto an officer of the guard, suddenly in command of a detachment of MPs and Filipino musicians, with orders to bolster the efforts of units of the Philippine army who were trying to resist a Japanese landing at Mauban, southeast of Manila. One recollection of these first days of the war was that the night before my units departed I hosted a distinctly premature Christmas party. The reason was that in my group of friends I was the only one who had (thus far) received a Christmas box from home. I gave each man a present to open in hope of providing a bit of relaxation and enjoyment before what looked to me like extremely tough days ahead.

We moved off southward and exchanged desultory gunfire with the enemy for a day or so, then began a gradual withdrawal back north toward Manila alongside the main body of Philippine army forces. We had to take a long detour around Manila because General MacArthur had declared the metropolis an open city. I have never forgotten the sight of Filipino civilians who had stood by the roads, cheered us, and given the "V for Victory" sign when we marched south. Now they stood in silence as we hastily backtracked. It was a portent of much to come. The retreat itself was fast and continuous: north to San Fernando, then south into Bataan, with few stops on the way. I was in charge of the rear guard. Fortunately, our withdrawal was rapid enough that the Japanese following behind could do no more than provoke an occasional skirmish. To my great surprise, they did not bother to bomb us. Perhaps they thought that later they would be able to overrun us at their leisure.

Before World War II the U.S. Army took it for granted that infantrymen were supposed to walk. Thus there was insufficient transportation not merely for the Philippine army but for the Scout regiments as well, not to speak of my nondescript supplementary forces. There was not even adequate transport for our arms and supplies, even when we commandeered all the civilian conveyances we could find. As a consequence, many supplies had to be abandoned—though not as many as by the troops retreating southward after the Lingayen Gulf landings, for we had not taken a lot with us when we had gone south to Mauban. Most of what we left behind on our retreat northward was ammunition, much of which we buried in an effort to keep it from the enemy. Filipino civilians later retrieved many of these caches and sold or gave them to guerrillas.

Though our "retrograde movement" was undeniably hasty, it was not a rout. The Filamerican defensive line above San Fernando held and enabled us to move into Bataan in good order. I believe we were the last units to go into the peninsula. One side effect of this hurried operation was that any soldier who could not catch a ride on some wheeled vehicle soon found himself cut off from his unit and left behind. Inevitably he then looked like a deserter. Sometimes he really was; more often he was merely lost and confused.

During the retreat the only troops that offered the Japanese any serious resistance were Philippine Scouts. Most of the ordinary, untrained Philippine soldiers were terrified by falling bombs and difficult to control—though discipline did not collapse among them. General MacArthur wisely ordered that these men be used in the immediate future only to harass the enemy and saved for the decisive struggle that would come months—or years—later.[16] Once in Bataan, where they had a chance to rest and regroup, they settled down and performed creditably.

Nonetheless, reverberations from this retreat illustrate the truth of Napoleon's contention that the moral aspects of war are often more important than the material ones. Some American officers and men were disgusted by the seeming cowardice (which was really only lack of training) of their allies and treated Filipino soldiers with condescension afterward. Filipinos naturally resented their attitude. Fortunately, the Japanese, habitually blind and deaf to the feelings of others, failed to exploit either this potential hostility between allies or resentment of another type: the widespread feeling of betrayal among American servicemen in the spring of 1942, when political leaders in Washington and their lackeys in the press persisted in promising American rescue fleets that never arrived and tried to pass off U.S. defeats as "previously planned retrograde movements." I felt bitter about this myself for a time but gradually got over it when I became an active guerrilla. Others were plunged into a mixture of rage, gloom, and despair for a much longer period.[17] The Japanese could have used such feelings to great advantage in their propaganda, but they never did so effectively. Victory in war often owes as much to the enemy's maladroitness as to one's own power or virtue.[18]

— 2 —
Flight From Bataan

There has long been controversy about who first conceived the idea of fomenting guerrilla resistance to the Japanese in the Philippines and who actually organized the first bands of irregulars. Many writers, both American and Filipino, have asserted that General MacArthur devised elaborate plans for guerrilla operations well before the war began.[1] They point to what the general wrote in his memoirs;[2] to the rapidity with which small units of Filipino guerrillas, all much alike, sprang up while the struggles for Bataan and Corregidor were still going on;[3] and, after the fall of Corregidor, to MacArthur's order to Gen. William F. Sharp to break the USAFFE (United States Armed Forces, Far East) troops on Mindanao into small groups so they could undertake irregular resistance to the invaders.

Vernon Fassoth, who was in a position to know, maintains that Cpl. John Boone, later to become a noteworthy guerrilla leader, began to organize such resistance while he was still being treated for a variety of medical problems in the Fassoth camp.[4] On a far larger scale, before the war began, MacArthur and some associates had begun to develop an extensive network of prominent businessmen, plantation owners, miners, and newspaper people to gather information about Japanese movements and plans and to form the nucleus of an Allied underground in case the Japanese overran the whole archipelago.[5] Many of those involved in this enterprise did valuable work in the first months of the war, but some were captured and tortured to death, so the whole effort gradually disintegrated after the fall of Bataan and Corregidor in the spring of 1942.[6]

General MacArthur believed that the mass of the Filipino people were so loyal to the United States and hated their Japanese conquerors so fiercely that they would never cease guerrilla operations against the invaders. Though this faith was not shared in Washington, events were to prove him substantially correct. As remarkable as anything was the boundless faith that multitudes of ordinary Filipinos had in MacArthur himself. For instance, when the dogged Filipino and American resistance on Bataan became generally known, all sorts of wild tales began to circulate and gain credence among Filipinos. According to one, the Americans had developed bombs that they rolled down mountains, bringing death to thousands of Japanese soldiers below; another had it that an electromagnetic force, by some mysterious process akin to immense suction, drew thousands of enemy soldiers to their doom as soon as they entered the Bataan battle area; still another told of some supernormal power, like that of the storied Bermuda Triangle, over Corregidor and the Bataan peninsula which drew Japanese planes inexorably to annihilation whenever they flew into a certain circle. Many Filipinos believed that the Americans had bored vast tunnels through the mountains of both Bataan and Corregidor to provide impregnable fortresses for themselves. Others declared that Japanese attackers on Bataan sometimes encountered walls of fire that caused them to see horrible visions of all the Filipino civilians they had harmed. These drove them mad, or caused them to desert or to kill their officers or to commit suicide. In all cases these wonders had been devised by or installed at the behest of that superhuman universal genius, Douglas MacArthur.[7] Still another rumor had it that the Japanese had loaded time bombs on ponies and driven them toward Allied lines, only to have the omniscient MacArthur order his men to fire just ahead of the horses and thus panic the animals, which then turned and ran back into Japanese lines, where the bombs exploded and killed thousands of Japanese soldiers.[8] Though faith in such marvels waned after the fall of Bataan, great numbers of ordinary Filipinos long remained confident that an American invasion to rescue them would come soon.

In the more prosaic world, near the end of the Bataan campaign MacArthur wanted Gen. Johnathan Wainwright, then in command of Allied forces on Bataan and Corregidor, to stage a massive artillery assault as a feint and then try to break through the Japanese lines in a different area. If that succeeded, U.S. and Philippine troops could stream out into the central Luzon plain, where food was plentiful, and protect the northern approaches to Bataan and Corregidor. Even if their efforts failed, he thought, survivors could flee into the Zambales Mountains to the north and west and support the few guerrillas already organizing there.[9] The fact that *some* of us, both Americans and Filipinos, did get through Japanese lines and become guerrillas shows that MacArthur's design was *plausible*, his admirers have said; surely a major attack would have allowed many more like us to get through, and then surely something noteworthy could have been accomplished. Even if many had been killed in the process, their fate would have been less grim than that of those who endured the Death March, followed by disease, starvation, and brutality in Japanese prison camps.

In fact nothing came of this enterprise and I, at least, am convinced that nothing could have. The Filamerican troops on Bataan in late March 1942 were too starved, weak, sick, and dispirited to attack anyone. Even had they not been so debilitated, the whole scheme was impracticable because the Philippine army had not had time to absorb serious training, much less gain experience, in attacking an enemy or even conducting an organized campaign, in Bataan or anywhere else.

As for the other schemes to wage guerrilla warfare, whether they were already under way or merely gleams in somebody's imagination, all I can say is that in January 1942 I had never heard of any of them. I began to think about the subject only after I met Maj. Claude A. Thorp, then in his early forties and a veteran of many years in the regular army. He had served under Pershing in Mexico and had fought in France in World War I, rising to sergeant. After that war he moved from one routine assignment to another and eventually received a commission. In 1940 he was made provost-marshal at Fort Stotsenberg. On Bataan he had the same job under Gen. Edward P. King. Since I was still assigned as an MP officer, I soon had Thorp for my commanding officer.

In my first week or two on Bataan I went on a couple of patrols that resulted in exchanges of fire with the enemy. Such patrols ordinarily had two purposes—training, and to see how far American troops could penetrate the jungle before encountering serious Japanese resistance—but ours had a different purpose: to practice working our way through enemy lines. During a sharp engagement with the enemy about January 15, Thorp was shot in the left leg. Laid up with his wound, he talked enthusiastically about an idea he had broached to me before his injury, and which had obviously been on his mind for some time: to organize a raiding party that would slip through Japanese lines, pick up some supplies he had cached before retreating into Bataan, and then proceed to Clark Field, where we would blow up Japanese planes and commit other acts of sabotage. I was all for it and had already agreed, since staying on Bataan looked more and more unpromising.

When Thorp had approached General Wainwright with this scheme, Wainwright was not interested. Neither was USAFFE Chief of Staff Gen. Richard Sutherland, who feared Japanese reprisals against

Filipino civilians. But Thorp had managed to get to Corregidor to see MacArthur and his adjutant, Col. Hugh Casey. Both approved the plan enthusiastically and authorized Thorp to proceed. His main business, apart from the immediate objective of sabotaging Clark Field, would be to gather intelligence.[10] Thus my guess would be (and it *is* a guess) that MacArthur and Thorp had quite independently conceived similar plans for guerrilla warfare before the war began.

I volunteered to go with Thorp, as did perhaps a dozen other people. We were a motley array. There was Ralph McGuire, once a civilian engineer but now a captain in the Philippine army. He was supposed to be well acquainted all over Luzon (certainly he was well acquainted with bottles there) and was also said to know several Philippine dialects. Among others I remember were noncommissioned officers, both American and Filipino, whom Thorp had known at Fort Stotsenberg: Sgts. Alfred Bruce, Fred Sladky, Everett Brooks, and Malacoli; and Cpls. Daniel Cahill, George McCarthy, and Young (a Moro); and two Filipinas, one of whom was Herminia Dizon, generally known as "Minang."[11] She had been Thorp's secretary at Fort Stotsenberg before the war. That the two were also lovers, was obvious to the rest of us. This would have been a purely personal matter had not the men made jokes about it, thereby visibly reducing the respect some of them had for Thorp. It is sometimes said that one mark of intelligence is the capacity to learn from the experience of others as well as one's own. One thing I learned from this episode, and heeded strictly when I became a guerrilla, was to avoid "shacking up." I was convinced that I would be regarded with greater respect and be better able to enforce necessary discipline if I demonstrated some personal discipline. Otto von Bismarck, hardly a lovable man but certainly a perceptive one, once remarked that in human affairs the "intangibles," factors that cannot be weighed, counted, or measured, are frequently more important than those that are subject to precise computation.

As for Minang, she knew several Filipino dialects, so her official position with us was "interpreter." Our ragtag force was soon augmented by some two dozen *cargadores* (Filipino porters). When Thorp was wounded, we all worried that our plans would have to be abandoned, or delayed so long that they would become irrelevant. But Claude Thorp was a tough, determined man. Despite a decided limp from his half-healed wound, he was eager to leave only a few days later.

On January 27, 1942, armed with our favorite weapons—tommy guns for some, Garands for others—we slipped through enemy lines and disappeared into the Zambales Mountains, the rough, jungle-covered range that runs 130 miles along the west coast of Luzon from Lingayen Gulf southward to the tip of the Bataan peninsula. Our destination was Mount Pinatubo, less than forty miles away in a straight line. It would take us more than forty days, and several fights as well, to get there.

From the first day we were assailed by troubles of every sort. It soon became painfully evident that far from being a mountain man of vast knowledge and unerring instinct, Ralph McGuire couldn't find a porcupine in a telephone booth. He was lost half the time and repeatedly led us around in circles. We were lucky that we never met any Japanese while wandering in the mountainous jungle of northern Bataan, though we did find Japanese cigarette packages, ashes from their fires, and other evidence that we had not missed them by much. One bright moonlight night I became separated from the rest of the group and was sure I heard two Japanese nearby. They heard me at about the same time. Both they and I leaped off the trail (on opposite sides, fortunately) into the stygian blackness of jungle undergrowth and stayed quiet for some time. Gradually I became aware of a potentially lethal development. I was seated at the dark end of a fallen log, but a shaft of moonlight shining through a break in the trees was lighting the log. It was some distance from me and moving inexorably in my direction. I had to do something soon. Abruptly I leaped to my feet, shouted as loudly as I could, fired my tommy gun where I thought the Japanese might be, then jumped back on the trail and ran off down it. Maybe they ran off too. I never saw them, but we were fairly sure they were stray Japanese; we killed one such the next day.

Meanwhile, the hard going every day was wearing us out, and we were running so short of food that our daily rice ration was smaller than it had been on Bataan. We simply had to go down into the lowlands, risk or no. West of Orani, near the head of Manila Bay, we came to a main road that ran westward through the mountains to Olongapo on Subic Bay. We began to hike along it. Soon we met some civilians, who told us that the Japanese trucked food and supplies over that road every afternoon. The thought occurred to us that we might replenish our depleted larder by hijacking their supply trucks. We went about it carefully. We camped back away from the road a bit and watched it. Sure enough, that afternoon some supply trucks went by. We decided to set an ambush the next afternoon.

We chose some high ground on the north side of the road. The area provided good cover. It was wooded but not dense jungle. Major

Thorp divided us into three groups. I was sent with four Philippine Scouts to the left flank, about 150 yards east of the main body of our small force. Sgt. Everett Brooks guarded the right flank about 150 yards west of our main body. Thorp, with the rest of the men, stayed in the center to launch the main attack. McGuire, who proved more able as an explosives specialist than he had as either a guide or a linguist, buried some dynamite in the road.

It is unlikely that what happened will ever be described with real accuracy. Years after the event Sgt. Fred Sladky penned a colorful description: he said the ensuing battle lasted maybe forty minutes and ended in a sweeping Allied victory.[12] Minang, who stayed back in our camp throughout and wrote about the shootout only four years after the event, must have been either unconscious or badly confused, since she said the fighting lasted two hours.[13] I am sure it was all over in half an hour, probably less.

The best I can do now is recount what I can remember of an event that took place some fifty years ago. After waiting for quite a while, we heard motors coming from the east. A command car went by me, then a truck, then another truck, and then—to my mounting amazement, another and still another. As far back as I could see there were trucks. We hadn't intercepted a mere food shipment; we had "ambushed" a Japanese troop convoy! Just as the thought flooded my mind, "Don't attack *this* convoy!" the dynamite exploded. It blasted the Japanese staff car, killing the colonel in charge.[14] Abruptly, a whole string of trucks piled in close together and stopped. My men and I were supposed to rush down to the road and attack the truck nearest us when the dynamite went off, but I could see at once that this would be suicidal, so the five of us stayed in the underbrush and began to shoot at the *several* trucks opposite us instead.

I can still see the faces of the Japanese soldiers in the one directly in front of us. They were staring straight ahead to see what had happened when our bullets began to strike around them. At once they turned toward us, then poured out of their trucks and scrambled under them or leaped into a ditch across the road to return our fire. They weren't good targets for us in either of those locations, so we continued to shoot at the trucks as we crawled through the undergrowth down toward the road.

We got there just as Thorp and his men decided it was time to withdraw from their central position because some of the more distant Japanese had set up mortars and were beginning to drop shells near us. Somebody went off to alert Brooks, after which all of us pulled back to our camp, perhaps a kilometer north of the road. Everybody was excited, laughing and talking about his personal role in the mini-battle. We were all sure we must have killed several high-ranking Japanese officers. That the colonel we did get was riding in the lead vehicle indicates how secure the Japanese already felt in an area they had so recently conquered. They would be more cautious thereafter.

Was the Battle of Olongapo Road a victory? In a sense. We killed a number of Japanese soldiers, threw a scare into a lot more, and shot up some of their vehicles while getting away unscathed ourselves. Looked at from another angle, however, it had been a fiasco: we had gotten neither food nor supplies. Hungry as ever, we had to get out of the area and walk all night through the jungle to escape the far more numerous enemies we had just "vanquished." Next morning we were all so exhausted that we had to leave the two weakest of our party in the care of friendly civilians.

The whole adventure did have one tragi-comic feature. Some days earlier we had run into a lone American in the jungle. He gave us a name, but his account of how he happened to be there was neither coherent nor plausible. After a time Major Thorp, perhaps tired of listening, abruptly told the fellow that he would not be charged with desertion if he joined our party. He accepted, but when we attacked the Japanese convoy he vanished. None of us ever saw him again.[15] It is thought that he joined John Boone's guerrillas and then committed suicide near Olongapo.

After this terrible month in the mountains we came down into the lowlands at the north end of Manila Bay and began to work our way northward toward Floridablanca in Pampanga province. On our journey and afterward, Thorp often spoke of his "original orders." Now, in 1995, I don't doubt that he had them, but I sometimes wondered then if he was, as the rest of us had to be at times, just a good improviser. In any case, he claimed that his orders empowered him to enlist in our ranks anybody, American or Filipino, who was willing to help us carry on our private war behind Japanese lines. As we moved along, we gradually accumulated such people. One was an American sergeant who had never left the area when Fort Stotsenberg was abandoned. We suspected him of having sold the supplies that Thorp had hidden near the fort weeks earlier and that we were now unable to find. Our luck with Filipino recruits was better. At Floridablanca the mayor was persuaded to become a guerrilla leader under Thorp's command, and the man's nephew, a doctor, was made medical officer of this new unit.

A few miles farther on, the mayor of Porac, with his wife, came out to see us on March 6. They brought with them a true Philippine patriot, Col. Mario Pamintuan. Nearly a year earlier Pamintuan had written to General King, then commandant of Fort Stotsenberg, offering the services of himself and four of his sons to the U.S. Army. He said he knew a good deal about Filipinos whose primary loyalty was either to Japan or to the Soviet Union and that he was willing to provide as much information about them to American authorities as he was able. He concluded by saying that whether he was paid or not was immaterial: his motive was to serve the United States.[16] Nothing had come of Pamintuan's offer in 1941 but when he now appeared before us and renewed it, Thorp immediately welcomed him and commissioned him to raise guerrillas and to collect supplies and donations.[17] Pamintuan soon became Major Thorp's confidant and in a few months succeeded Ed Ramsey as commander of guerrillas in northwest Pampanga. He received several official commendations later in the war for his valor, loyalty, and service.[18]

The next day Pamintuan added two of his associates, Tomas Lumanlan and Francisco Ocampo. All three brought us arms and supplies while we stayed in the vicinity. Ocampo eventually became Pamintuan's chief of staff and, like his mentor, proved an able recruiter and leader of guerrillas.[19] In Timbo we recruited still another eventual guerrilla leader, Eugenio Soliman, who had formerly had a government job dealing with local Negritos.[20]

Disappointed at failing to get the expected cache of arms and supplies at Fort Stotsenberg, we camped briefly near the foot of Mount Pinatubo in an area that had seemingly been used for picnics before the war. A well-defined horse trail led up the mountainside. Thorp decided that we should follow it up to a large plateau. There we established our headquarters, known variously as Camp Four and Camp Sanchez.

We soon had some welcome visitors. When we left Bataan we had only a radio receiver. We could get information but could not send any in return. Authorities on Bataan tried to rectify this situation on March 20 by sending Major Llewellyn Barbour and five men in a PT boat up the west coast of Bataan to make contact with us and to bring us a radio transmitter and other supplies. After a thrilling all-night ride that included firing two torpedoes into a Japanese ship, the party landed near Botolan, about seventy-five miles northwest of Mount Pinatubo. Employing some of the $5,000 given them by General Wainwright for just such emergencies, Barbour hired two guides to lead his group through the Zambales

Mountains to our newly established headquarters. Along with him came Sgt. Bill Brooks to set up the transmitter, a soldier named Garrison to operate it, demolitions specialist Sgt. Albert A. Short, and two Philippine Scouts. Not the least interesting aspect of our visitors' journey was that they brought along a promotion to lieutenant colonel for Thorp, who immediately donned his new silver oak leaves.[21]

As soon as regular two-way communication with Bataan was established, Barbour went back. Thereafter, we gathered information picked up by Thorp's scouts, added the daily departure times of Japanese planes from Clark Field, and sent these reports for a few weeks—until Bataan fell on April 9.

The headquarters that now-Colonel Thorp established at Camp Sanchez clearly reflected considerable advance planning. Years before, the cavalry had erected several buildings on the site for use on maneuvers and perhaps for weekend camping trips as well. The main one was a roomy stone cottage into which Thorp now moved along with Minang and another secretary. This became his headquarters. Minang presided over the place as our cook. The location gave us a good view of Clark Field and any Japanese activity that went on there. Thus comfortably established, Thorp reorganized his staff. He made McGuire his adjutant, me his supply officer, and Colonel Pamintuan his unofficial adviser-for-all-purposes. Three of Pamintuan's sons became couriers and personal bodyguards for our commandant.

It is sometimes said that regular army officers do not make good guerrillas because they are trained to fight like gentlemen. Guerrillas, from the nature of their calling, spend most of their time collecting information, setting ambushes, undertaking sabotage, intimidating civilians, and engaging in other activities that are distinctly ungentlemanly. It is not without interest that Philippine Scouts, who had been trained by regular army officers, seldom joined the scores of thousands of their countrymen who became guerrillas. Some have asserted that as a regular army officer of the "old school," Thorp was not planning either to fight or to descend to skulduggery. They contend that he was really not much interested in guerrilla activity at all but intended simply to dig in, avoid the Japanese, enjoy his "secretaries," and wait out the war.[22]

I do not think this appraisal of Thorp is accurate or its implications fair. The colonel was not an imaginative man, but he was tough, fearless, and well liked both by his fellow officers and by enlisted men. If he seemed less zealous than I to strike blows at the

Japanese in April–May 1942, it must be recalled that at that time I knew next to nothing about the practical side of guerrilla warfare. After he and I parted, he tried to activate and manage a guerrilla organization all over Luzon and to negotiate a working alliance with the Hukbalahaps (Philippine Communists) to resist and harass the Japanese more effectively. If he seemed to move slowly at times, his critics should recall how difficult it became for any of us to communicate with any others. How successful Thorp might have been in the long run, nobody can ever know because there was no long run; a few months later he was captured by the Japanese. James Boyd, a guerrilla who knew him, described him as "one of those rugged individualists who always come through."[23] Maj. Bernard Anderson, a level-headed man himself, characterized Thorp as a real leader: a serious officer devoid of vanity or pretense.[24] Col. John E. Duffy, a Catholic chaplain, footloose on Luzon like the rest of us, praised Thorp for the vexations he visited on the Japanese.[25]

I too respected Thorp, even though I did not always agree with him. For instance our numbers expanded steadily as escapees drifted in, yet we stayed in the mountains where our food supply was chronically low and could easily be cut off. Worse, our locale left us no place to hide and no place to retreat. With every day that passed it seemed increasingly clear to me that if we were going to live in proximity to the Japanese, we must always make sure we could escape from any given place. Moreover, if we stayed together, we would attract the attention of the enemy and tempt him to undertake some massive raid that might catch all of us, whereas if we divided into small groups and scattered, it would be impossible to catch us en masse—and probably easier for us to contact and recruit Filipino followers as well. Finally, I was restless and believed that it really wasn't any safer to hide out in the mountains than to try to resist the enemy more actively. That Thorp intended to undertake some action against the Japanese was shown by his later deeds, but at that time I thought we should try to do more—and sooner.[26]

By late March 1942 nearly a hundred assorted Filipinos and Americans had attached themselves to us. Since Thorp had made me supply officer, he now sent me along with Sgt. Everett Brooks down into the lowlands to arrange for the regular collection and transportation of food and supplies to support this assemblage. We soon found ourselves a small nipa hut near a barrio outside the town of Angeles and settled down. The place was not bad for comfort, but it was hell for noise. We were almost in a direct line with the takeoff and landing pattern at Clark Field. Day and night, planes roared directly overhead—about ten feet so, it seemed. Sometimes we could even see the faces of the pilots. Fortunately, they had more important things on their minds than staring straight down during take-off, so we remained undetected.

Securing supplies did not prove difficult. Though Americans around Clark Field had been the commonest of sights to Filipinos before the war, nearly all of us had vanished soon after December 8. Now, nearly four months later, we had become a novelty again. They sorely missed us as living assurances that the venerated Douglas MacArthur had not forgotten them, that he would return soon, and that all would be well once more. Consequently, most of them were anxious to help us. Sergeant Brooks and I did not think it wise to let a lot of people go up the path to Camp Sanchez, or see how many or which persons were living there. Instead, we usually employed one squad of Filipino soldiers to carry supplies from Angeles to the bottom of the trail, and another squad from the camp to relay the stuff on up the mountain to our hideout. A third squad from the camp would then come down, and the process would be repeated. Sometimes one of the Americans would get bored and come down the horse trail with them. One who did this often was Sergeant Sladky, an old regular army man who was nearing retirement. An unredeemed traditionalist, he was regarded with some amusement because he loved the feel of his old Springfield rifle and refused even to think about trading it for a new Garand. On one of his sojourns he gave Brooks and me a scare by coming into our hut and relating how he had barely missed being captured by a Japanese patrol.

Another time we ought to have been more frightened than we were. Four or five armed, tough-looking Filipinos arrived abruptly and said they wanted to meet Thorp. They were Hukbalahaps. One of them, I am reasonably sure, was their overall leader, Luis Taruc, though Minang identifies the man as Casto Alejandrino, one of Taruc's confidants.[27] I sent a runner on ahead to alert Thorp, then escorted the visitors up the mountain to headquarters, where they were treated to lunch. Much conversation followed, replete with pledges of good will and cooperation, all of which were ignored soon after. Then I led the visitors back to the lowlands. It was the first, and least violent, of my many contacts with the Huks between that time and the end of the war.

Other events in the lowlands were a good deal more pleasant. One evening Brooks and I were invited to a dance in a nearby barrio. The orchestra consisted of three guitar players who strummed a lot of currently popular American songs, interspersed with occasional

Filipino ballads. We were expected to dance with the local girls, a social obligation we fulfilled with enthusiasm.

April 9, 1942, began auspiciously but ended quite differently. In midday Brooks and I were in a barrio near Fort Stotsenberg arranging a pickup of food for Camp Sanchez when a runner arrived with a message from Thorp that Bataan had surrendered. The note directed us to return immediately to camp and to say nothing of this news to Filipinos lest they be shocked or panicked. Of course, *we* were shocked, and disappointed as well, since we had been invited to a dinner party that night. We decided we should to go and try to act as if nothing had happened. We succeeded—sort of. We did finish a fine dinner, only to have a Filipino rush in from town bearing a proclamation from Japanese authorities that Bataan had fallen. The messenger added that the "benevolent Japanese" were inviting all people who had guns and all "stray Americans" to turn themselves in. We hurriedly assured all present that the message was just Nipponese propaganda, then slipped away as soon as we decently could and hurried up the mountain to the camp.

It has been alleged that at this juncture Colonel Thorp simply gave up. That is not what happened. We had a general discussion about various possible actions, and at length Thorp brought it to an end by announcing that we could all do as we liked: surrender to the Japanese, stay with him, or strike out on our own. In the three weeks since the arrival of the PT boat crew with our transmitter, I had become friends with Sgt. Albert Short, one of the crewmen who had stayed behind with us. He and I had talked a good deal about what we could or should do in the days ahead. Now we were the first to ask Thorp if we might leave. Most of the others then also chose to leave, seemingly in hope of making their way through mountains and jungle to join Filipinos who, they had heard, were already undertaking irregular action up north. A day or two later Thorp bade amiable farewells to each of us and wished us all good luck.

Sergeant Short, a young Philippine army sergeant named Esteban Lumyeb, and I set off together. None of us—or, so far as I could tell, anyone else in Camp Sanchez—had any clear idea of what guerrilla war was or what it might entail. Our position was not unlike that of Christopher Columbus on August 3, 1492. Like him, we were in for a lot of surprises.

— 3 —
An Independent Guerrilla

Perhaps my comparison with Columbus is inapt, even unfair to the great Genoese navigator. Columbus at least *thought* he knew where he was going, and he knew *how:* he would sail to his destination. He also took the precaution of insisting that he be named viceroy of whatever he might discover along the way. I lacked comparably clear ideas of any kind.[1]

Seargents Short, Lumyeb, and I had heard that the Philippine Fourteenth Infantry was still in existence some two or three hundred miles to the north across broad, rough mountains. We thought idly of trying to go there. We had also heard that by going almost directly east across the lowlands and then over a different mountain range, one could reach Baler Bay, home of outstanding sailors with small boats capable of traveling great distances, perhaps to Mindanao or even to Australia. That alternative seemed more attractive, especially since it was only about half as far.

In fact, the two sergeants and I didn't pursue either objective. We just walked down the mountain trail from Thorp's camp, picked up some rice and other food from friends in local barrios, and started northward through the Zambales foothills. We stayed near the mountains to avoid civilians, for we did not yet know whether they could be trusted, but this route proved so arduous that we gradually abandoned it. After three or four days we came to a graveled road that stretched eastward across flatlands. Since sooner or later we had to go east and also mingle with civilians, we abandoned some of our caution and walked uneasily down the road, tommy guns in hand—safeties off. I felt simultaneously ready for anything and scared half out of my wits. Before long we came to a village, which we later learned was the town of O'Donnell. Had we kept going, we would have walked right into the O'Donnell prison camp. Filipinos gawked out their windows in amazement mingled with horror. One young fellow recovered his composure sufficiently to rush up to us and warn us not to go any farther because of what lay immediately ahead. He and other Filipinos hurriedly took us to a house on the

23

south side of town where we were given our first good meal in several days and then guided around the town so we could continue off northward for a few more days. Once more we went back into the Zambales foothills.

When we could avoid the plains no longer, we decided to compromise: we would walk at night and hide by day because we still felt uncertain about how many civilians could be trusted. Both Short and I were too tall and light complexioned to have any chance to pass ourselves off as Filipinos. The first day he and I took a siesta in a dry creek bed, while Lumyeb looked over a nearby barrio. We soon had the feeling that somebody was watching us. Standing up slowly, we saw two little boys on the bank above us, peering down inquisitively. We spoke to them, but they scurried away. We hurriedly collected our gear and prepared to move out, only to have a whole group of people show up, along with Sergeant Lumyeb. Fortunately, some of them spoke English.

The experience forced us to face facts at last: it was impossible to hide from Filipino civilians; we had to trust them. Thereafter, we tried to find someone reliable in each town who could provide us with a trustworthy guide to the next town, and so on. In this way we quickly crossed the plain to what proved to be our destination. It was the town of Lupao in northern Nueva Ecija province, just east of its border with Pangasinan to the west. When we arrived in Lupao toward evening, we were immediately led to the public square where a fiesta was in progress. Filipinos love fiestas and seize upon any pretext to start one. At this one we were treated like visiting royalty. I sat with the mayor in the place of honor, and all three of us were invited to dance with the local girls.

What promised to be a splendid evening was soon dampened. A man sidled up to the mayor and spoke quietly to him. Soon after, the mayor relayed the information to me that Corregidor had fallen. Though he and I were saddened and discouraged, he decided not to spoil the people's fun and so said nothing to them.

After the party we were taken to a safe house on the eastern edge of town. There Short and I again discussed our future, which now looked even more dismal than before. Next morning a Sergeant Estipona from the Twenty-Sixth Cavalry appeared abruptly, accompanied by four or five other soldiers. In proper Philippine Scout fashion he announced that he was reporting for duty. Short, Lumyeb, and I concluded that a council of war with our new supporters was needed. It proved to be a good deal like the one with Thorp some days earlier. I was covered by whatever orders (which I had never seen) Thorp had from MacArthur, but none of my fellow escapees had any orders at all. Should we try to hide out indefinitely? Make our way to some coastal town in the faint hope of somehow escaping to somewhere in some kind of boat? Become guerrillas and organize a resistance movement until the arrival from the United States of the reinforcements that we all still confidently expected? I cannot imagine what we might have decided had we known that the "reinforcements" would not arrive for nearly three years. Sometimes ignorance really *is* bliss. To be sure, General Wainwright had already broadcast an order for all Americans to surrender, but we so hated the prospect that we easily convinced ourselves that he had been forced by the Japanese to issue the surrender order, from which it followed that it was our duty to continue the war as best we could. Perhaps our conclusion vindicates the nineteenth-century German philosopher Arthur Schopenhauer, who believed that the mind is but the instrument of the will.

We spent most of the rest of the day considering what should be our next specific move. Lupao seemed a promising place to settle. The area was attractive and the people seemed friendly. I suggested that we might attract followers faster if we divided our group and undertook operations in two localities. Accordingly, it was decided that Short and Estipona would stay in Lupao, while Lumyeb and I would continue north to seek another similar location. The decision to divide our meager numbers was actually a good one for a personal reason. Albert Short was a sound man, but he and I had been cheek by jowl day and night ever since we had left Mount Pinatubo and this proved to be more "togetherness" than either of us could bear easily. Once we began to see each other only intermittently, we got along fine.

No mode of communication on this earth transmits news faster than a Philippine "bamboo telegraph." By the time Lumyeb and I reached Umingan, about ten miles away, a delegation of Filipinos had assembled to meet us. They all urged me to organize a body of guerrillas and offered to serve in it. There is an old adage that some are born great, some attain greatness, and some have greatness thrust upon them. My career as a guerrilla chieftain began with leadership being thrust upon me.

I do not say this jokingly. Most Americans have merely assumed that guerrilla activity in the wartime Philippines must have been initiated by U.S. escapees like me and that we then coaxed or bullied Filipinos into supporting us.[2] This was not the case at all. Most Americans who managed to evade the Japanese in 1942 wanted to get back to their units some time, some way, or just to escape from the Philippines and get to Australia or China or somewhere safe. Overwhelmingly, Filipinos came to us and begged us to lead them and help them fight their oppressors. Major Anderson said he became a guerrilla for the same reason I did: Filipinos entreated him to lead them, which led him to conclude that he did not have to look further to find something useful to do.[3] The earnestness and persistence with which some Filipinos sought aid and guidance was sometimes little short of heartrending. Alejo Santos relates that he and a few others somehow learned early in 1942 that Thorp had led a party of American officers through Japanese lines in order to form guerrilla organizations. Santos and his friends wanted desperately to organize a guerrilla band of their own but did not know how to go about it. For several months they wandered aimlessly over half of Luzon trying to find Thorp, then *any* American officer, who could either provide guidance or, better still, take them into his own organization, since more prestige attached to having an American as commander. They had little luck: Ramsey and Anderson seemed always to be either on the move or in hiding; other USAFFE officers seemed more bewildered than anything else;[4] still others appeared to be preoccupied with their personal survival.[5] When they were at last able to link up with Anderson in Bulacan province (in BMA, the Bulacan Military Area north of Manilla), their arsenal consisted of one rifle plus a pistol they had managed to steal from a municipal building.[6]

With all due respect to Alejo Santos, who subsequently became a captain in Anderson's organization and served capably, I am skeptical about some aspects of his lament. After all, Harry McKenzie, Al Hendrickson, Criscenzio Hipolito, and a runner from Ray Hunt did not have undue trouble finding me in 1942–43 when they sought me out. That Santos wanted either to join an existing guerrilla organization or to form one of his own, I do not doubt, but I wonder how hard he looked for guidance. Always an independent man, he may have been most concerned to form an organization that *he* could command.

Among the local men who volunteered immediately to serve under me, only one had any sort of military experience: Juan Desear, who had retired as a sergeant from the Philippine Constabulary (PC, the national police force). Of the others, Juan Marcos and Emilio Casayuran had small farms, and Filadelfo Macaranas ran a small grocery store in Umingan. Training or no, they were all willing, even eager, to risk their lives to badger the Japanese invaders, and they assured me that they knew at least ten or fifteen others who would join us and bring rifles with them. I simply could not turn away men so obviously loyal, courageous, and eager to do something. Within a couple of days I had about twenty five men and rifles. I set up my headquarters in a small barrio a mile or so from town and went to work organizing. I also wrote at once to Thorp to explain what was happening and to ask for orders.

That was how Umingan and environs became my "home" for the rest of the war. Physically and scenically it was an attractive locale. Immediately to the west lay extensive rice paddies. To the east and northeast there was rolling, hilly country covered with short grass interspersed with some trees, giving it a pleasant pastoral appearance. Farther off, real mountains covered with jungle began.

In my first days I was overwhelmed. People poured in from every direction, often laden with food and other gifts, all offering good wishes and support, and many volunteering to fight as well. I had to explain that we would need a little time to collect weapons and get ourselves organized before we could use any more recruits. Organization proved a good deal easier than weapons collection. I began by appointing Juan Desear a sergeant and putting him to work training riflemen. Juan (Johnny) Marcos was a natural "boss" and so was made a patrol leader. Macaranas, thoroughly acquainted with Umingan, was the logical choice to become our official liaison with town authorities. Casayuran was convinced that only he truly understood how to look after the commander in chief, so he appointed himself my personal aide.

Although visitors continued to flock to our headquarters what I really wanted was not more volunteer cheerleaders but a serious meeting with the more influential townspeople, especially the mayor. This suggestion encountered immediate resistance from my new staff. They warned me that the mayor was pro-Japanese, which indeed proved to be true and soon led to a grisly showdown with that dignitary. We did arrange a meeting with the chief of police, several town councilmen, some prosperous businessmen, and a few owners of local haciendas. Two concerns were of vital importance to them: first, we should not fight with the Japanese near Umingan, for they might take reprisals against civilians; second, something decisive had to be done about roving bands of former soldiers and outlaws who were terrorizing local civilians. I agreed at once on both points and asked for their help in locating the bandits.

By the end of May 1942 my local Squadron 111 (to use its later designation) had attained company strength, as had Sergeant Short's

Squadron 300 in Lupao. The two together were the nucleus of what would become the Luzon Guerrilla Army Forces, (LGAF). With their backing I would eventually dominate the northern half of the fertile central plain of the largest Philippine island.

These beginnings fit in well with what had been going on at Southwest Pacific Area (SWPA) headquarters, then in Australia. Just before leaving Corregidor for Australia in March 1942, General MacArthur had divided his Philippine forces into four distinct commands, leaving himself as overall commander. This arrangement was intended to allow each commander to surrender only his own troops, thereby compelling the Japanese to conquer them in turn. This was an ideal setup for the development of guerrilla operations. Unhappily, since the supreme commander failed to notify his superiors of what he had done, Washington appointed General Wainwright overall commander in the Islands. When Corregidor was about to collapse, the enemy demanded that Wainwright surrender all U.S. and Filipino forces. He acceded—most unwillingly—for fear that the alternative would be massacre of the whole Corregidor garrison.

Most local unit commanders heeded Wainwright's orders. A few did not, believing either that they were answerable only to MacArthur or that Wainwright must have been coerced by the Japanese. Others, like Thorp, indicated—without giving explicit orders—that each man under their authority might do as he pleased. How many American soldiers chose to disappear into the jungle rather than surrender to the enemy nobody can ever know; the number was in the hundreds. Some had managed, as I did, to get through Japanese lines before Bataan fell. Others took to the jungle when Bataan surrendered. Still others escaped during the Death March or managed somehow to get away from internment camps.[7] More than a hundred such fugitives were in and out of the Fassoth camp during 1942, though more of us never saw that establishment.

Many American escapees soon died from starvation, disease, jungle accidents, or the bullets of Japanese soldiers or Filipino outlaws. Some became guerrillas and died fighting. Japanese patrols captured others, and more eventually surrendered. A few holed up in the mountains or were successfully hidden by Filipino families and so survived the war. Only a handful of us became guerrillas, actively vexed the Japanese throughout the war, and survived to tell about it. The number of Filipinos who did so was vastly greater.

In the latter part of May 1942 I began seriously to take stock of my situation. Edwin Ramsey says he did so as well, at about the same time. For ten months before the war he had lived the life of a playboy polo player in Manila, oblivious to much beyond personal enjoyment. Now he was defeated, dispirited, half starved, cut off from others, convinced that he had been betrayed by both Mac-Arthur and Washington, hoping only to survive, and having no idea how long his plight might last. Then he began to think of how many Filipinos had already helped him and other Americans too, in various ways, often at the risk of their own lives. Reflecting that the war was by no means over for them, he resolved—to some degree from remorse and shame—to become a guerrilla. He says Capt. Joe Barker agreed with him.[8] I shared some of these sentiments, but my basic mind-set was somewhat different. Like Ramsey, I still felt disgusted and disillusioned at how little support we had gotten from our government since December 8, 1941. But since I had oral authority from Thorp to organize guerrillas and make use of them, it seemed my duty to do so.[9]

My decision to stay down in the lowlands near Umingan highlighted a quandary that many guerrillas faced: which kind of terrain was safer? Early in the war the invaders, still unacquainted with the country, got nearly all their specific information from Filipino spies and sympathizers, who were mostly in the flatlands and so numerous there that many Americans thought it impossible to survive anywhere out of the mountains.[10] It was also true that Japanese patrols seldom ventured into the mountains, partly because they disliked the rough country and jungle, partly because their troops were more sorely needed in other war theaters than for patrolling lands already conquered. On the other hand, when occasional enemy patrols did penetrate the uplands they found it easier to stage surprise raids there than in open country. Moreover, food was far more plentiful down in the lowlands.

So what was the better choice? The answer depended mostly on individual taste. Both Maj. Bernard Anderson and Col. Russell Volckmann, two men with whom I had quite different dealings, preferred the seemingly greater safety of hideouts far back in the mountains. Harry McKenzie and Ray Hunt, who eventually became two of my ablest and most trusted subordinates, were like me: they wanted to take their chances in or near towns and barrios in the flatlands where it was not difficult to move about. At Camp Sanchez with Colonel Thorp I had been impressed with how much food any considerable number of men consumed and how difficult it was to move these supplies into the mountains on the backs of other men. On my journey to Umingan I had also gradually become convinced that life in the mountains wasn't safer than on the plains anyway. For one thing, if the Japanese could see us from a long distance across rice fields, we could also see *them*.

Then there was nature itself. The mountains of Luzon may look green and attractive from a distance, but they are in fact rough and jagged. Worse, they are covered either with jungle that is only semi-penetrable or, in many areas, with terrible sawgrass that grows ten to fifteen feet high and is so sharp it lacerates clothing and flesh impartially. The grass also hides numerous boulders, holes, cliffs, and steep gullies. Moreover, at high elevations it is often uncomfortably cold. When the wet season comes, on high ground or low, rain falls in blinding torrents, after which the ravines and valleys fill up with vast clouds of malarious mosquitoes.[11]

Russell Volckmann said that he had to learn the business of organizing, training, and leading irregular troops by trial and error.[12] So did I. When the war began, many well-off Filipinos were not crushed by the thought of surrendering to the Japanese because they expected to keep their businesses or public offices and to live as they had always done, though a few of them were truly pro-Japanese and anti-American. Most ordinary folk, by contrast, liked Americans, disliked the idea of surrendering to invaders, and were so accustomed to a hard life that they did not blanch at the thought of forcibly resisting enemies. A considerable number of people merely sat on the fence for a time, waiting to see who was likely to win. To point this out is in no way to denigrate Filipinos. The lot of small countries and groups caught up in the quarrels of stronger neighbors has never been enviable. One thinks at once of the Poles, trapped for a thousand years between Germans and Russians and with Turks on their southern frontier for five hundred of those years; of Rumanians caught in the middle for centuries among Russians, Turks, and the Hapsburg Empire; of Belgium located athwart the only easy invasion route between France and Germany. In 1942 it was as true as ever that "when the elephants dance it is unsafe for chickens." The position of the Philippines, between the United States and Japan, was that of the chickens.

If I could organize and arm a body of dependable followers, I would have at least a chance to kill several birds with one stone. I might be able to do oppressed Filipino civilians a great favor by suppressing the roving bands of merciless robbers who preyed on them. In the process my forces might come to dominate a considerable area and improve our own prospects for the future. We could give peasants a reason to be grateful to us, we could stimulate their loyalty to their own government and to the United States, and we could cause them to fear us more than our foes.

To say that I needed to instill fear must make me appear to some a monster of ingratitude, since many ordinary Filipinos then regarded Americans with near-veneration. For instance, everywhere I went I was regarded as something like a folk hero. Filipino families were obviously pleased and proud to have me stay at their houses, even though this put them in grave danger of Japanese reprisal. Incredible though it may seem, more than once I awoke to find my bedroom full of Filipinos who had been standing there for who knows how long, just watching me sleep.

Of course, such conduct was not typical of all Filipinos—certainly not of educated people from the cities—and American guerrillas soon became aware of how many natives anywhere in the islands were either actively anti-American or secretly untrustworthy. But most of the rural folk among whom I spent most of my time regarded me much as loyal peasants regarded their kings centuries ago. The American journalist H.L. Mencken used to maintain that most people are natural monarchists. The eagerness of multitudes to lavish hero worship on actors, athletes, musicians, and other "celebrities" certainly lends substance to his contention. So does the open disdain of scores of millions, even in "advanced" countries, for politicians who talk and debate endlessly but seldom do anything. In crises, notoriously, people everywhere look not for more discussion but for leaders who will reassure them and then act. It is not coincidental that most government throughout recorded history has been authoritarian.

It salved my ego to be the object of so much hero worship, of course, but it also laid an extra burden on me to try to be at least somewhat worthy of it when I confronted my first serious tasks. The most immediate of these was to quell local gangs of outlaws. This was sometimes dangerous, but usually not difficult. Every barrio contained people who had been robbed or injured by brigands. They were only too glad to tell us where such scoundrels were currently residing.

We had been in Umingan only a few days when we got a tip that a band of half a dozen "soldiers" of some sort would be spending the night in a certain barrio. The barrio *teniente* (head man or village representative) offered them supper and a place to sleep, ostensibly as an act of hospitality but actually to give our men time to get there. Juan Marcos and I led our tiny force on its first mission.

We waited at the outskirts of the village until everyone was asleep; then a local man guided us to the house where the unwanted guests were ensconced. Some of our men surrounded the house while Marcos and I and two others rushed inside and awakened the inmates at gunpoint. They proved to be Filipino soldiers who had never surrendered to the Japanese. They were still in uniform, still had their weapons, and insisted that they were only trying to find a guerrilla organization they could join. I offered to enlist them in my forces on the spot. They accepted with alacrity and served faithfully thereafter. A few days later I undertook a similar raid with similar results except that several of the men captured chose to surrender their rifles and return to their homes. After this success Marcos, whom I had promoted to sergeant, asked to undertake further raids on his own.

I would like to report that all encounters with unauthorized gangs went off as smoothly as these first efforts, but in fact they did not. What usually happened was that our night patrol would catch a number of bandits asleep. When they awakened, a fight would ensue; the leader would be killed, as would anyone else who resisted; and the rest of the band would be disarmed. The survivors would then be "weeded." Some would simply be sent home but those who seemed potentially loyal and useful would be invited to enroll in our organization. After a few sorties of this kind our rivals were much diminished in number. Many erstwhile outlaws hastily reformed and became irregular soldiers, often quite good ones. Other vanquished freebooters, fearing our reprisals, hurriedly disbanded and left the area. Civilian confidence in us soared.

As our success mounted, however, life grew more complex. It is impossible to keep anything secret for long in the Philippines, and the Japanese soon heard rumors that an American officer was in the area. They responded by sending in more troops and increasing the frequency of their patrols. Meanwhile, more and more of my time was taken up with meetings and organizational problems, and I was growing steadily weaker from repeated attacks of malaria and dysentery.

In one of our war councils it was suggested that for greater security we should establish a hideaway back in the mountains as a command post. Scouts dispatched to follow streams up toward their headwaters found a level spot several kilometers up a large creek. It was cleared to make a small parade ground, a few huts were built, and we had a new headquarters. Feeling our oats a bit and wishing to defy our enemies, we named the place Camp Manchuria, an allusion to the Japanese invasion of Manchuria in 1931.

Soon after we settled in I had one of my many strokes of good luck during the war. One day there appeared at the camp a Filipino who said his name was Federico Doliente. He was accompanied by ten other men. They asked to be taken into my organization. Like so many others, Doliente had no formal military training, but far more important, as things turned out, he was shrewd, tough, fearless, and a natural leader. He even looked and acted the way I thought a guerrilla should. If Johnny Marcos was our best recruiter and trainer in 1942, Doliente proved to be the best fighter. Soon he became my most trusted companion on patrols.

One of the things Doliente impressed upon me was that "firmness" was just as efficacious when dealing with troublesome town officials as it was with bandit gangs. As news spread of our success at suppressing brigands and expanding our own numbers, our reputation swelled well beyond our actual accomplishments or capabilities. Though I am reasonably sure that there were no spies in our organization, everybody in Umingan talked about us. The pro-Japanese mayor soon had a good idea which townspeople were our supporters. To get information from them he threatened to turn them in to the Japanese, which of course terrified many. He was also known to be using his Japanese connections for personal gain. He seemed to think that he could do as he pleased, that his Nipponese friends could protect him against any enemies. After considerable deliberation we decided that it was necessary to disabuse him of that illusion, to make an example of him, to "terminate him with extreme prejudice," as the U.S. Central Intelligence Agency would phrase it a generation later. Sergeant Doliente, new to our group and eager to make a good impression, volunteered to deal with him.

The task would not be easy, since the mayor kept a number of Japanese soldiers around him most of the time, but Doliente's men watched him for several days and noticed that he always returned from a nearby barracks to his home, alone, about dawn. A few mornings later I was awakened by a commotion on our little parade ground. I thought to myself, "Doliente must have gotten his man" and went to ask him. "Yes, Sir," he replied, and promptly pulled the mayor's head out of a gunnysack. I am not especially squeamish, but that experience was a shock. One thing I did learn from it and from lesser episodes was that Filipino subordinates, suffused with hatred for the Japanese or for collaborators among their own countrymen, would sometimes do things no American commander could approve, much less authorize. Members of a patrol sent out with orders to gather intelligence and avoid trouble often returned with long faces and a sad tale about having accidentally run into a few Japanese troops—whom, of course, they had been compelled to shoot, arousing the whole neighborhood in the process.

— 4 —
Getting Organized

The last half of 1942 was a period of general disaster for Col. Claude Thorp and all his plans. Conversely, despite some close brushes with death for me, it was six months of rapid growth and consolidation for my guerrilla organization.

Thorp's endeavor to establish a centrally directed system of irregular operations all over Luzon was both stimulated and complicated by men who came out of the Fassoth camp. The camp was a collection of bamboo buildings erected in the foothills of the Zambales Mountains by locally prominent rice and sugar planters William and Martin Fassoth. Initially, it was built as a refuge for William's family, but the brothers soon rebuilt it farther back in the mountains to hide American soldiers who might manage to escape the Japanese. By late April and early May of 1942 many such escapees from Bataan and from the Death March, augmented by stragglers of various sorts, had drifted into the Fassoth camp. Some soon died, but most eventually recovered from starvation, exhaustion, injuries or illness.

Quarrels broke out among them from the first. Some wanted earnestly to organize and keep fighting the Japanese, but others appeared content to sit and wait for an American army to rescue them. Many escapees, particularly lower-ranking officers and enlisted men, argued that since regular American military organization had broken down, everybody should be equal again, as though all were back in civilian life. Another faction, in which Maj. Bernard Anderson, Capt. Jack Spies, and Col. Gyles Merrill figured prominently, tried to persuade William Fassoth to make the place a military camp and put senior officers like themselves in charge. Mr. Fassoth flatly rejected this proposal. He insisted that the camp belonged to him, not the U.S. armed forces, and that he had built it as a combination refuge and hospital rather than a military cantonment. Squabbles about these and other matters were numerous, heated, and protracted. Gradually, most of the discontented departed.[1]

One of the most energetic and ambitious men in the camp was Capt. Joseph Barker, a West Pointer from Alabama. He was convinced that some kind of guerrilla organization should be formed in order at least to harry the Japanese. Knowing of Thorp's presence in that general area, in mid-June he led a group from the Fassoth camp and soon found Thorp. When I had left Camp Sanchez more than a month earlier, I was under the impression that Thorp did not have many specific plans for the future. Whether he abruptly developed some or whether he was persuaded to do so by Barker, I do not know for sure, but he soon worked out on paper a complete reorganization of all the guerrillas under his shadowy command.[2] He made Capt. Wilbur Lage his own adjutant and retained radioman Bill Brooks, then divided Luzon into four parts and named a commander for each one. Joe Barker was given the East Central Luzon Guerrilla Area (ECLGA), with Edwin Ramsey as his adjutant and Bernard Anderson as his chief of staff; Barker in turn appointed Charles Cushing as district commander of Pangasinan province. Thorp made Col. Ralph Praeger commander in northern Luzon, Ralph McGuire in western Luzon, and Jack Spies in southern Luzon. A few weeks later I was designated inspector general of Thorp's entire domain,[3] an exceedingly vague assignment. By then, too, I was already building my own virtually independent guerrilla force. Thorp followed up with Order No. 1 to all his subordinates, specifying their responsibilities and duties.

Some of Thorp's appointments were wise and some were not, but most proved temporary. Barker was an excellent choice. He did a fine job but was captured by the enemy in January 1943.[4] Anderson was his logical successor, but he had no orders from General MacArthur, and he lacked both personal ambition and ruthlessness. Moreover, he stayed holed up in the mountains and thus out of contact with the rest of us much of the time. Consequently, his real authority was limited to Bulacan and Tayabas provinces. I gradually became de facto commander farther north, and Ramsey went off to pursue varied objectives around Manila. Praeger made a good start in the far north but was eventually captured by the Japanese. In western Luzon, Ralph McGuire managed to seize many guns and much ammunition left on and around Bataan. He also liquidated spies and collaborators energetically and undertook some sabotage. Otherwise, he was a poor choice on several counts, but it mattered little: disloyal Negrito guerrillas succumbed to the lure of Japanese money and beheaded him before the end of the year.[5] Jack Spies did not get along with Filipinos and was killed before he ever assumed his command.[6]

Confusion was universal in Luzon in the last half of 1942. Even memories of it half a century later are garbled. A trivial example relates to rank. Ramsey says Thorp issued promotions to all his appointees; Wayne Sanford says Ramsey simply declared himself a major;[7] and my memory of it is that I assumed the rank of major, then told Ramsey what I had done, after which he made himself a major too. A more important contretemps involving substance rather than form concerns Col. Gyles Merrill. A memorable character who had recently escaped from Bataan, Merrill was fifty and looked older. He had been in the regular army all his adult life and was a stickler for regulations but generally liked by his peers and his men. Long service in the tropics had made his skin so tough that he simply ignored the trillions of mosquitoes that swarmed over every square foot of Luzon and bit everyone in relays. During the summer of 1942 he left the Fassoth camp and moved into a fishing shack in a swamp, then into the home of a Filipino family. Along the way he attracted to himself several other footloose Americans, among whom were Col. Peter Calyer, Captains Crane, Kadel, and Volckmann, Lieutenant Blackburn, and that free spirit who never totally joined any organization, Pvt. Leon Beck.[8]

Merrill then began to put together a staff and to make some tentative plans. About August 20 he gave Volckmann and Blackburn a sealed letter and sent them to Thorp's camp. Thorp burst into a rage because the letter seemed to assume that Merrill was the supreme commander of guerrillas on Luzon. The cause of the trouble was really quite simple: Merrill did not know that Thorp had orders from MacArthur or that Thorp himself had forbidden the formation of freelance guerrilla units. Once these matters were clarified, Thorp simmered down and extended official recognition to Merrill's embryonic unit.[9] Merrill then established his headquarters in Zambales province. Three months later Thorp was captured by the enemy, and only Merrill's ramshackle organization was left on that part of the island.

Colonel Merrill's outfit was less active than most of the other USAFFE guerrilla groups, a consideration that caused some to claim that there was little difference between its members and those American escapees who wanted to do nothing but sit out the war as permanent guests of Filipino families. Both Beck and Anderson have remarked about how many such men they encountered while traveling about Luzon; Beck claims that he knew one such "evader" who eventually turned traitor, which so enraged Beck that after the war he traced the reprobate back to Texas and publicly spat in his face.[10] Ed Ramsey also records that early in the war, when he was a weak, sick, hungry, would-be guerrilla slinking about in the jungle, he went to the hacienda of some wealthy Filipino planters and discovered half a dozen Americans there. They were clean and healthy, living comfortably in hiding, and obviously uninterested either in his condition or in becoming guerrillas themselves.[11]

Sgt. (later Maj.) Alfred Bruce lends support to the view that Merrill's organization stressed personal safety above an aggressive attitude toward the enemy by remarking of Col. Peter Calyer and Capt. Winston Jones, two of Merrill's subordinates, that they lived so far back in the mountains "we even had to pipe sunshine back to them."[12] Still, Merrill and associates had a reason, or at least an explanation, for their frequent inactivity: they were obeying orders. MacArthur wanted all guerrillas primarily to gather intelligence and convey it to his headquarters, not to pick fights which they had no chance to win and for which the Japanese would surely retaliate savagely against Filipino civilians. The inactivity itself, moreover, was relative, for Merrill did establish a body of guerrillas who periodically collected useful information, and in 1945 joined the regular army to fight the Japanese.

Whereas Thorp's general guerrilla enterprise encountered rough weather from its inception, my own portion of it grew steadily throughout the summer and fall of 1942. In May, Capt. Charles Cushing, one of three brothers who had come to the Philippines as mining engineers and lived on to lead guerrilla bands during the war, came to San Nicolas, a few miles north of Umingan. Barker had appointed him district commander of Pangasinan province, and Cushing began at once to organize what would ultimately be ten squadrons of irregulars. Unlike many guerrilla leaders who lived near each other, he and I were never rivals. I paid him a visit promptly and we got along well. I hoped and expected to cooperate closely with him, and in fact I had no trouble doing so because he was not forceful or personally ambitious.

Soon afterward I acquired several men of great value. The first of them was Jeremias C. Serafica, who arrived on July 1 at the head of some fifty to a hundred armed men. I made him a captain and gave him command of Squadron 207 in the Cuyapo-Guimba-Munoz sector of central Luzon, a few miles southwest of my headquarters. An even better stroke of luck came in August when I fell heir to Harry McKenzie, the first American to join my force. Harry was a tough man in his early forties. Before the war he had been superintendent of a mine in north Luzon. After the fall of Corregidor he had thrown in his lot with Major Anderson. Anderson proclaimed him a second lieutenant, took him off south to the barrio of Biak-na-Bato on the western slopes of the Sierra Madre in Bulacan province, and soon thereafter sent him north into Nueva Ecija to attempt to form new guerrilla units.

Early in August he arrived at the camp of Lt. Juan Pajota, an intelligent and resourceful independent guerrilla who had already formed several squadrons of his own in central Nueva Ecija. Pajota understood the Japanese well and had recently annihilated one of their patrols. He staged the ambush along a jungle trail down which seven Japanese were passing single file. Pajota put himself at the far end of his own line in the underbrush, then opened fire when the last Japanese came even with him. At once the rest of his men fired and killed all the others at no loss to themselves.

It was not long after this that MacKenzie met Pajota, who fed Harry and his companion, informed them at length about what he had been doing, and sent them on their way to see me. Mac and I had a long talk. He had been impressed with Pajota and recommended that I offer to appoint him a captain and invite him to bring his guerrillas into my organization. Pajota was agreeable, so I gave him a "jungle promotion." He then dubbed several of his own ablest followers lieutenants, and they all became a valuable part of my forces.[13]

Meanwhile, I dispatched several runners with various messages for Anderson, but they could not find him; he had gone east over the Sierra Madre into a mountain hideout in Tayabas province even more isolated than the one he had left in Bulacan. Consequently, McKenzie, who disliked mountains as much as I did, asked if he could stay with me. He seemed like a potentially valuable fellow, so I agreed. Anderson, always a reasonable, conciliatory man, accepted his envoy's defection without complaint when he got word of it. Harry was a proverbial diamond in the rough: he had little formal education but much common sense; he liked a few drinks now and then, but was faithful and dependable. I soon made him district commander of Nueva Ecija as well as my executive officer—in effect, my right-hand man.

Unlike most guerrillas, McKenzie was married; indeed, he had been remarkably fortunate in life's matrimonial sweepstakes. His wife, Mary, was an altogether admirable Filipina: kind, patient, good-humored, and a woman who knew how to manage both her husband's occasional vagrant impulses and other practical problems. She and their son, who was perhaps six years old in 1942, spent part of their time with friends in Manila and part of it with her husband. When she was with us, she would at once become chief cook for our headquarters people and any visitors we might have. Not the least of her services was inducing her cousin Manuel Bahia to throw in his lot with us and become, in effect, Harry's adjutant. Manuel spoke excellent English, was a capable administrator, and proved an exceptionally valuable aide to me shortly after the war.

We added new units regularly, four of them under Maj. Emilio Hernandez in Pampanga during the summer. In September Capt. Gemeniano de Leon, with whom I had been in informal contact since July, was incorporated into the LGAF and his unit christened Squadron 206.

On September 20 I elevated Sgt. Albert Short to lieutenant, appointed him district commander of northeastern Nueva Ecija and southern Nueva Vizcaya provinces, and instructed him to negotiate with various guerrillas in far northern Luzon to establish respective spheres of influence that would not overlap. Sadly, Short's luck was not nearly as good as mine. Both of us were soon pursued by sizable Japanese forces, but reliable information about enemy movements from friendly Filipinos enabled me to evade the enemy by moving frequently. Short decided simply to withdraw some twenty-five miles eastward over part of the Central Cordillera to Pantabangan, a town on a large lake of the same name. There he stayed until the Japanese stopped looking for him. Then, after returning to the lowlands to spend a week with me, he withdrew again to Pantabangan because he liked it better than the area around Umingan. What happened next was tragic. Short was shot in the arm during a skirmish with a rival band of Filipino guerrillas, and while he was still weak from his wound the Japanese renewed their pursuit. In attempting to escape from them, he was shot and killed.

Short's last important act for us was to contact an independent leader, Capt. Carlos Nocum, and his guerrillas, who were soon incorporated into our growing LGAF force as Squadron 311. Meanwhile, I appointed Abdon Aquino to replace Short. One of his men, Esteben Alipio, eventually played an important role in securing arms and supplies from Australia, as well as protecting Capt. Robert Ball, who brought us our first radio transmitter from Australia in 1944.

All these transactions required several trips to Pantabangan. One of them in particular I have never forgotten. The general area is distinctly more pleasant than much of Luzon, covered not with horrible sawgrass but with extensive stretches of "buffalo grass" not unlike what once covered vast areas of the Great Plains in the United States. It is only about a foot high and not difficult to travel through. The town itself is on a plateau that abuts the lake and stands well above lowlands to the east, south, and west. To approach it other than by an open road (which was too dangerous to risk when Japanese patrols were about), one had to clamber up a steep hill. One evening, just at dusk, I arrived at the top of the hill with a patrol and stopped to rest. As I gazed down at the towns and barrios far below, darkness fell and lights came on from horizon to horizon. The spectacle was overwhelming, and my thoughts turned irresistibly to prewar life at home without fear or the prospect of some sudden new crisis. Never in my life have I felt so alone, so misplaced, so utterly estranged from normal human existence.

On August 8, 1942, before my promotion of Short and his subsequent death, Thorp elevated me to inspector general of all he surveyed. Capt. Ray Hunt, who was eventually to become my area commander for Pangasinan province, has said this was the "most inspired" appointment Thorp or his subordinates ever made.[14] It was kind of Ray to say this, but in fact, I did not know what my imposing new title meant or implied. Moreover, everything was still so disorganized in the late summer of 1942 that there was little to inspect, and I was sick for so much of the time that I could not have inspected anything beyond the room where I happened to be housed. My "inspections" therefore consisted mainly of sending periodic instructions to my own unit commanders: gather intelligence, harass the Japanese, catch fifth columnists and traitors, protect people from Japanese and bandit predation, treat civilians fairly and humanely, try to keep up the morale of all Filipinos, and behave yourselves.

Mingled with my organizational concerns and recurring illnesses were occasional mere bizarre incidents. One of the most memorable of these had semicomic overtones. A relatively wealthy townsman, who may genuinely have wanted to be helpful or perhaps hoped mostly to score some points with me, tried to give me a huge white horse. Now most Philippine horses are like Filipinos themselves, small and dark. When I, tall, blond, and Caucasian, mounted this enormous white beast I could not have been more conspicuous to a sharpshooter if I had put a neon bull's-eye on my back. I refused the present as tactfully as I could.

A far worse threat to the success of my plans was the state of my health. Many historians have long been convinced that few considerations could better improve our understanding of historical

June 10, 1942

TO ALL UNIT COMMANDERS:

I would like to talk to all of you personally but the time it would require makes this impossible. Therefore I am taking this means of communicating with you.

It seems that some of the units are not operating quite as they should, some complaints have been received. So I am passing on to you a few observations I have made.

First of all: What is our mission?

1. To hinder and harass the Japanese troops.
2. To apprehend 5th Cols. and Traitors.
3. To keep up the moral and spirit of the people.
4. To protect the people as far as possible from cruel tratment.

Now, how is the best way to carry out our mission?

As to fighting with the Japanese we can do little of that at the present time. First of all, because the Japanese take revenge on the civilians and since they are not engaged anywhere else at the present we can do them no damage which would have any great effect. So most of our activities against the Japanese will have to wait until our reenforcements arrive. Then we can cause them serious damage. We can make our plan now, though, as to what we are going to do so we will be ready when the reenforcements lands.

Our main activity now centers around the stopping and capturing of persons engaged in pro-Jap activities. Common sense tells us the ones to get are the leaders and the ones doing the most harm, not the persons who are forced to work for the Japanese and the ones on whom we have only suspicions. Too many innocent persons are being arrested and treated harshly and in some cases even killed. Only those who we have definite proof on should be arrested. Do not listen to rumors spread by someone who does not know what he is talking about. Find out for yourself. Actually make a thorough investigation before you capture the man not after. You must be able to back up your arrest with evidence, I could cite many incidents where innocent men have been taken from their homes in the middle of the night. This terrorizing of innocent civilians must stop.

Some of the soldiers have started confiscating the personal belongings of civilians. This is in reality looting. The only equipment we have a right to confiscate is government equipment. If your soldiers are guilty of terrorizing, threatening and looting, you had better see that it is stopped for you know as well as I the seriousness of these charges.

Be on the lookout for small groups of soldiers who have turned outlaws and are looting and terrorizing the people. These men must be captured. They are giving all our troops a black name. If you hear of any of these men and are unable to capture them. Report them to other units can look for them, too.

Furthermore many civilians are already becoming angered by the actions of some of our soldiers. If this situation continues to grow worse the people will no longer support us and might even go to the Japanese for aid. We cannot exist without the help of the people.

In conclusion let me caution you commanders that you are responsible for the actions of your men and will have to answer for them after the war. Therefore it is important that you exercise close control over your men. See to it personally that they do not loot, threaten, or arrest innocent persons. If you do this you will have a record you will be proud to turn in.

Here's to victory

R. B. Lapham
1st Lt. 803rd MP

A combined collection of orders, admonitions, and advice that I sent to all the officers in my then-fledgling LGAF organization soon after it began to take shape. This was mostly an effort to establish discipline and order.

causation than greater knowledge of the influence of plagues and diseases on entire peoples and especially on the thoughts and actions of individuals in key positions at crucial times. For instance, the surrender of Bataan was more a medical disaster than a battlefield defeat narrowly defined. When the physical resources of troops have been sapped by chronic disease and protracted semistarvation, their will to fight declines along with their ability to do so. For me, the first eight or nine months of the war were by far the hardest because I was sick so much of the time. Like many others, I was already beset by malaria and dysentery when I came out of Bataan in February. Fighting off these maladies wasn't easy. There were doctors in Philippine towns in 1942, but they often lacked both equipment and essential medicines; most soon ran out of quinine in one of the most malarious areas on the globe because the Japanese had conquered the Dutch East Indies, then the world's number one source.

Malaria is a dreadful disease by any reckoning. When an attack is imminent, one has an insatiable thirst, but the first swallow of water is immediately followed by alternating chills and fever. One shivers and shakes, then breaks into a sweat. At the height of the sickness these cycles repeat frequently until the sufferer either recovers or dies. If the crisis passes, the period between attacks lengthens, and the victim is usually discommoded for only a day or two at a time. Quinine breaks an attack promptly, but there was no quinine where I was in the summer of 1942.

Dysentery, a wearing disease in itself, complicates and intensifies the crisis stage of malaria. In the absence of proper medicine and treatment, one can only endure the ailments until they subside. One never really recovers from them; I continued to suffer from both for a considerable time after the war was over. Leon Beck, a freelance guerrilla who was often a messenger for Colonel Merrill in the Zambales Mountains, said the only things he could consume when beset with malaria were lemon juice and salt.[15] I tried boiling cinchona bark, from which quinine can be extracted, but the infusion was so bitter I could not drink it. Millard Hileman and Clay Conner were offered *dita*, a remedy used by Philippine aborigines but potentially lethal to Western patients.[16] In any case, I had never heard of it in 1942.

I became seriously sick in May and gradually got worse at precisely the time I was laboriously wending my way across central Luzon to Umingan and making my first efforts to recruit and organize guerrillas. About the end of June, when we were all elated at having eliminated the hostile mayor of Umingan, I grew so sick that most of my time was spent either in bed or at the latrine. A doctor who was called from town had no medicine and could treat me only with words of optimism. Even these he did not mean: I eventually found out that he had told his friends I would die in a few days.

In fact, something quite different happened. We got wind that the Japanese were planning to raid Camp Manchuria to avenge the dead mayor. This was no surprise in itself, but the scale of their anticipated raid was. Many truckloads of Japanese troops were pouring into Umingan and would soon move up into the mountains, our informants said. This was a mortal threat, for the only way either in or out of Camp Manchuria was along the stream on which it was located. We had to get downstream and out before the enemy could intercept us.

By then I was so weak I could walk only a few steps. Hurriedly, my men made a hammock and slung it on a long bamboo pole. All night pairs of men took turns carrying me through the jungle near the stream. My faithful friend Sergeant Lumyeb did more carrying than anyone else, and by morning we had managed to get far enough south to slip away. The Japanese continued to look for us for three or four days before finally giving up. I might add that I never returned to Camp Manchuria. My preference for the open plains over the dense forest and mountains around the camp we had left so hastily was firmly reinforced by this harrowing escape.

Ed Ramsey says that while he was languishing in the Fassoth camp he saw a young officer grow so obsessed with the belief that the American government had deserted him that the man lost his will to live, refused to eat, and soon expired.[17] Ramsey adds that on one occasion he himself—wet, cold, hungry, sick, and alone in the mountains with an infected foot—went crazy. He screamed and yelled at the cruelty and injustice of his lot and drew out his .45 to shoot himself—but recalled his rage at the Japanese just sufficiently that he could not quite pull the trigger.[18] My spirits never sank quite that low but many times during that terrible day I did ask my men simply to put me down beside the trail and let me die in peace. They refused, and insisted upon struggling along with me even at the peril of their own lives. Though I did not realize it at the time, they were wiser than I. They either knew or sensed what Ramsey and some other Americans had learned from hard experience but I did not yet know: that many sick people really die not from their illnesses, however genuine, but from giving up. Anderson says he often sent sick men on missions just to keep their minds off their ills, and he found that most of the time they felt better when they returned.[19] Pierce

Wade, who also had much experience with life in the jungles of Luzon, lamented that he had seen too many men get sick, become depressed, and thus pass beyond the power of their buddies to nurse them back to health.[20] As for me, even now, half a century later, I can still hear Esteban Lumyeb answering my entreaties: "Not now, sir. We can make it. You will see, sir." I owe my men undying gratitude, for they surely saved my life.

Shortly after daybreak we emerged from the mountains and arrived at a comfortable farmhouse in a secluded spot in the foothills. Doubtless in utter desperation, one of my men came to me and asked sheepishly if I would allow a native witch doctor to treat me. Not caring much one way or the other, I acquiesced. Now there is one thing to be said unequivocally for witch doctors: they have specific medical plans. This functionary looked me over carefully, then produced an egg-shaped stone, some corn, and a few coins or small medallions over which he muttered incantations. Next, he sat back and stared fixedly into space for perhaps fifteen minutes, as though in a trance. Then he began to give instructions to about fifteen men in a local dialect I did not then understand. They hurried off and eventually returned with an impressive array of leaves and herbs. The doctor put these in a pot and boiled them until they were reduced to a nondescript mass resembling a mixture of spinach and cauliflower. When this substance had cooled somewhat, the doctor put poultices of it in the crooks of my knees and elbows and on the middle of my back. He repeated this procedure daily for three days. On the fourth day the men prepared a feast featuring all sorts of local delicacies. The witch doctor carried a great tray of this food to the top of a hill where he shouted and chanted for a quarter-hour or so. My men said he was calling on evil spirits to leave my body and come to the fine food. Then he picked up the tray and rushed down the hill, whereupon the *men* ate the food with gusto to kill the evil spirits. They must have succeeded, for I soon began to get well.

What to make of it? I don't know. Many others have reported instances of witch doctors' ministrations producing cures that seem miraculous to Occidentals, or of "absurd" Filipino superstitions leading to predicted results. An example reported by Millard Hileman is typical. He once slipped in a mountain stream and thought he had broken his knee. Some Negritos procured an old female witch doctor to examine the injury. Armed with banana leaves, sea shells, coconut oil, a large candle, and a necklace of garlic, she peered learnedly at his ailing limb and muttered incomprehensibly. Then she heated the oil in a sea shell, dipped in a rag, and bathed his knee with it. Next, she rubbed garlic on the knee, chanting all the while. This medical debauch reached its climax when she poured more hot oil on a banana leaf, added some mashed garlic, and wrapped the leaf around Hileman's knee. Late that night she came and repeated the procedure, with more mumbling and chanting. By morning both the pain and the swelling were gone.[21] Both Russell Volckmann and his aide Donald Blackburn reported comparable wonders worked by Igorot magicians and witch doctors in the mountains of northern Luzon.[22]

Western rationalists would say that experiences like these, including my own recovery, were likely mere coincidences. Perhaps so, but medical knowledge is not the exclusive possession of people of any one nationality, race, culture, or geographical locality. Even in the Western world medical "science" is still an art to a considerable degree. Moreover, it was only a few generations ago that many European and American medical ideas and practices were quite as bizarre as those of the Philippines. No one fully understands all the nuances of our bodily processes, much less their relationship to those quintessentially inexact entities the human "mind," "spirit," "will," and "soul."

Maybe it is all relative anyway. Hileman relates that an American escapee from Bataan, Hank Winslow, once dealt with a painful cavity in a Filipino boy's tooth by heating a wire red hot and sticking it into the cavity. The victim jumped, but the pain stopped.[23] The deed itself and its aftermath must have seemed as marvelous to the Filipino lad as the performances of the witch doctors did to us. Doyle Decker was once marooned in the jungle with his buddy, Bob Mailheau, who had a severe case of tonsillitis. Decker recalled that when he was a child, his own father had treated him with iodine for the same affliction. Decker happened to have some iodine, so he daubed Mailheau's infected tonsils liberally with it. He never knew that his own father had diluted the iodine for this purpose, so he used it full strength on his friend. It literally burned out Mailheau's tonsils, but the patient lived, and when he underwent a physical examination back in the States after the war, a doctor remarked that his tonsillectomy was the cleanest the physician had ever seen.[24]

Quite as interesting as their unorthodox medical practices were a lot of quasi-superstitions and mere odd ideas cherished by numerous Filipinos. One such was that pythons in the grass or along the edge of the jungle would keep pace with humans walking. Hileman believed it; he claimed that he had once been stalked by a twelve-foot python.[25] If so, it was no joke, for a python that size could crush the life out of a grown man. The most memorable tale I used to hear about these huge snakes was that they would sometimes lie on low limbs in trees and swing their hard heads downward to knock passersby unconscious. I always suspected that this claim was a yarn to pull the leg of someone unfamiliar with pythons. In Civilian Conservation Corps camps in the Pacific Northwest during the 1930s there were many boys from eastern cities who knew little or nothing about the outdoors. Local rangers would sometimes regale them with harrowing tales of encounters with "mallet cats." These creatures were said to be about the size of cougars, to possess hard, bony masses on the ends of their long tails, and to lie in wait on low tree limbs. When forest animals or human beings passed underneath, a "mallet cat" could switch its lethal tail and knock the victim unconscious, thus supplying itself with dinner for the day. Many of the CCC boys were led to believe in "mallet cats" and became wary of venturing into the woods alone because of them. To me, Philippine pythons kayoing their prey by swinging their hard heads sounded suspiciously like the old "mallet cat" stories.

More interesting was a tale that accompanied a sheriff to whom I was once introduced. He looked about sixty years old. His neighbors swore that earlier in his life he had remained the same age for several decades because he possessed a certain *anting anting* (a Philippine charm). Then, unhappily for him, he lost the miraculous amulet and suddenly became his true age, thirty to forty years older.

I nearly lost my life on one more occasion, not from disease but from a peripheral development. By September 1942 I had recovered from most of my maladies and had just left Umingan, intending to make my way cross-country to see Thorp again. About an hour out of a barrio where I had spent the night I had a sudden recurrence of malaria. I already knew there was a price on the head of any guerrilla—for those of us who were leaders, a high price—and that thousands of poor Filipinos would have been less than human had they not been tempted to turn us in for the reward money. Consequently, I seldom stayed at the same place on successive nights. But now, the sudden illness drove me back to where we had been the previous night. Sure enough, the enemy had discovered this too and so decided to raid the village. Everybody was asleep. Guards were supposed to be on duty, but they were not. Most Philippine houses do not have back doors, but providentially, the one where I stayed did.

Just before dawn we were startled by shots, and a couple of my men saw Japanese trying to get into the house. They began to shoot and awakened everyone, but especially my bodyguard Lalugan.

I had several bodyguards who watched over me from time to time, but he was the most persistent and faithful. All the other Filipinos I ever knew had at least two names, but for reasons unknown to me everybody called this man simply "Lalugan." One name or two, he was a formidable fellow. Tall for a Filipino, he was slim but extraordinarily strong. More than once I saw him lift two heavy Enfield rifles by their muzzles and hold them straight out from his body. Before the war he had been a judo instructor; fortunately, he was also a good shot. He bagged one Japanese climbing a ladder into the house. A couple of others were killed by our men who were shooting out the windows, but one of my auxiliary bodyguards was shot in the arm and another got a bullet in his hip. The whole uproar gave me time to jump up from the sleeping mat on the floor and grab a gun. We all ran out the back door without stopping to don shoes or even pants. Fortunately, the enemy had not had time to surround the house, and several of us bounded into the underbrush, leaped into an irrigation ditch, kept going, and escaped. It was the last time during the war that I took off my pants before going to bed. (That was also when I finally lost the dollar bill I had brought from Bataan.)

Shocking as this experience was, it was no more so than the news in November that Colonel Thorp had been captured. I really should not have been surprised. The Japanese regarded him as a formidable foe and had pursued him relentlessly ever since they had learned of his existence and endeavors. They had almost gotten him two months earlier. Thorp had scheduled a conference of his district commanders and squadron leaders for August 29 at his headquarters in Timbo. The Japanese raided the place the night of August 28, but the alarm sounded in time, and they caught only a few servants. Minang, who in 1946 wrote a six-page account of Thorp's activities, says they were betrayed by a Tagalog runner named Rodriguez and were saved only because the fellow gave the Japanese the wrong date.[26]

Thorp and his small band of American and Filipino followers had then headed north into Tarlac province, intending either to make contact with rumored American "reinforcements" at Lingayen Gulf or to pursue what Minang calls his "obsession" to negotiate with the Huks.[27] Despite warnings from Colonel Pamintuan, his chief aide, Thorp led his party to Santa Juliana, where they were met by the former mayor, named Frias, and Marcos Laxamana, who was Minang's uncle and Thorp's most trusted contact man.[28] More important, he was part Negrito and had much influence with the tribes who lived in the mountains of western Tarlac. Laxamana found the party a guide who led them to a hideout he had specially prepared for them. Minang says she was suspicious of the place at once. It was surrounded by mountains, and there was no way to escape, but her uncle assured her that he had "connections" with the Japanese and could always learn of any planned raid well in advance. A few days later she received a letter from a Captain Salangsang warning her that the Japanese had just captured Laxamana. She told Thorp, who prepared at once to leave but Japanese raiders caught the whole party on October 29, 1942.

There seems no doubt that Laxamana had betrayed them, and from the simplest of motives: love of money.[29] The guide he had chosen for Thorp, Andres de la Cruz, was released at once by his captors and given back his gun, though the others remained "hog-tied," as Minang put it. Laxamana himself received a handsome reward for his treachery. Afterward, he was protected by the Japanese and helped to invest in real estate from which he made a great deal more money,[30] though he may have eventually ended his inglorious career buried alive by guerrillas.[31] Meanwhile, Thorp and associates were marched to the O'Donnell prison camp and then to Fort Stotsenburg. On January 22, 1943, Thorp was transferred to Old Bilibid prison in Manila, sentenced to death after a brief show trial, and eventually executed by the Japanese.

Minang fared better. She was released from confinement in only two weeks, then put through a brief course of "spiritual rejuvenation" to prepare her for a career of making propaganda speeches for her former jailers. Since she spoke English well and knew several Philippine dialects—which most Japanese did not—she says she soon became adept at sabotaging her sponsors by telling Filipino audiences in one dialect to disregard what she had said in another, and by using words with double meanings.[32] This was not impossible. Other daring Filipino interpreters are known to have fooled the Japanese in the same way.[33] But it was extremely dangerous, for it would have required only one of her constant Japanese attendants to know one of the dialects she spoke to penetrate the sham. Yet not only was her perfidy never detected, but several of her Nipponese keepers were quite taken with her; one high-ranking officer even offered to take her along on their anticipated conquest of Australia. Wily, resourceful, and fearless as the devil himself (not to say luckier, too, for Lucifer fell from Heaven to Hell forever, whereas Minang died a Philippine lieutenant), she managed to put off her importunate would-be patron long enough to make her escape and throw in her lot with my organization. Eventually she became Ray Hunt's girlfriend. Understandably, he esteemed her highly.[34]

— 5 —
Growing Pains

In the last half of 1942 I had my share of problems both within my own organization and with my immediate neighbors, but whether from good management or mere good luck none of them got out of hand. The kinds of situations I often had to deal with are reflected in correspondence from that period. A letter dated October 24, 1942, concerns a jurisdictional dispute between two of my subordinates; I told them to settle it by treating the Agno River as the boundary between their respective domains. Each should stay on his own side and not interfere with the other, I wrote, and both should remember that our main business was to *sock it to the Japs* (original emphasis).

A letter to me dated January 1, 1943, from Capt. Wilbur Lage, who had been Thorp's adjutant, highlights how uncertain we all still were about just who was or should be in charge of what. Lage congratulated me on doing some sort of "great work" (which I have long since forgotten); informed me that I had become the most wanted man on Luzon; and assured me that if Volckmann and Blackburn tried to give me orders, I should tell them to consult him, since he had sent me "authorization" for central Luzon. Lage was a friend and most likely was just trying to cheer me up, but his wording implied that I was a member of his command, whereas I was not aware that I had any official connection with him.

Other letters from me to Lt. Charles Cushing and Captain Barker offered advice about the best ways to deal with three Filipino officers, Lieutenants Soniega and Benito and Major Acosta, who had either been arrested or accused of wrongdoing but had been able officers in the past. In general, I urged leniency in such cases.

Of greater importance was the issue of how to deal with Visayan troublemakers. When the war began, there was a unit of the Philippine army composed of soldiers drawn from the Visayan Islands, which lie in the center of the Philippine archipelago between the two big islands of Luzon to the north and Mindanao to the south. This unit fought against the Japanese when they landed at Lingayen Gulf in December 1941. Like the other USAFFE troops they

51

were defeated and scattered about Luzon as the triumphant invaders pushed southward. Some joined one or another of the guerrilla forces gradually taking shape; others formed small bands that roamed the countryside. The men usually spoke dialects different from those of Luzon. Many of them, far away from home for the first time in their lives, were homesick, and most of them eventually went back to their islands when transportation became available. Meanwhile, like idle men anywhere, they were restless and often got into trouble of various sorts. Several letters of mine to my squadron commanders in the summer and fall of 1942 admonished them to avoid stirring up ill feeling between the Visayans and local people. I reminded them that men accused of crimes should be treated as innocent until proven guilty, and that lenience was advisable toward persons whose misdeeds were not heinous and who stayed out of trouble after a first offense. I insisted, however, that nobody known to want to join the Japanese should be released, and that the rifles of offenders should be given back not to the miscreants themselves but only to their first sergeants. Though the Visayan problem was troublesome for several months it gradually evaporated as the men were able to return to their homes.

Another vexatious business involved a dismal mixup that began in September when I started to receive reports that a rash subordinate of Charles Cushing's named Telesforo Palaruan had been forcibly disarming guerrillas from my units around Umingan, San Quintin, Rosales, and Balungao, places not within his jurisdiction. I penned stern warnings to both Cushing and Captain Barker that this practice interfered with my efforts to consolidate new units in these areas and that it created much bad feeling among my men toward Cushing's. I warned that if it was not stopped promptly it would soon cause real trouble, perhaps even a mini-war between the outfits concerned. I concluded that we should be fighting Japanese and "Ganaps" (pro-Japanese Filipinos), not wasting the lives of valuable men in a stupid intramural war among Filipinos.[1]

I soon found out, however, that I was being deceived in my own organization. Several of my men, as well as some civilians in Umingan, had told me glowing stories about a Filipino captain named Edades who had once attended West Point and had been an officer in the Philippine army before the war. Unfortunately, none of them knew him personally. One day a stranger showed up claiming to be Captain Edades and speaking authoritatively about military matters. In retrospect, it is obvious that I should have been more skeptical and vigilant, but I was new at the game then and had no reason to disbelieve the man, so I took him into my organization. At once he set to work collecting food and money—most of which he kept for himself, I discovered later.

I gave him command of some men and sent him to clean out a nest of Ganaps. He did a good job, so I wrote him a letter of congratulation on October 27 and promised that I would ask Cushing, who was also troubled by Ganaps, to turn over to him all such Fifth-Column and Ganap cases in the future. In the same letter I urged him to have Lieutenant Doliente and another patrol ambush some Japanese, and assured Edades that Juan Marcos, recently promoted to lieutenant, would also be sent to help fight the Japanese north of Umingan.

Soon thereafter I heard that Edades had ordered Doliente not to ambush Japanese but to attack Palaruan. Fortunately, Doliente knew his own countrymen better than I did. Suspicious about the order, he sent a runner to tell me about it. I left at once and caught up with Doliente about two miles from Palaruan's camp. Then I sent another runner to Palaruan to ask if Doliente and I could have a talk with him in a nearby schoolhouse. The conversation was highly productive. Palaruan was friendly and reasonable. He had actually disarmed only one patrol of ours and had done so in the belief that the men had encroached on his territory. Most of the trouble had been fomented—or invented—by Edades. We quickly came to an understanding with Palaruan about jurisdictions and separated on terms of respect, even friendship.

Even before this episode I had had fleeting suspicions that all was not what it seemed with Edades. Now Doliente and I confronted him. It was soon evident that he was not the real Captain Edades at all but a mere con man. When Doliente and I gave him the old western movie order to get out of town by sundown, he faced facts without comment and departed forthwith. Unhappily for him, he did not reform but only changed his base of operations. Soon he was busy, only a few towns distant, collecting money—to support guerrillas, he said, but actually to line his own pockets. This time we brought his career to a sudden end, which so outraged his wife that she threatened to take the whole story to the Japanese. Whether she would have done so, nobody knows, for she abruptly disappeared and was never seen again. The whole repellent business was reminiscent of a similar case with which Al Hendrickson and Ray Hunt once had to deal. They had executed a man whom they believed to be a Japanese spy, only to be confronted by his outraged wife. She—eight months pregnant, to make the whole affair more poignant—half convinced them that he had been innocent. Filled with doubts, they deluged her with dire warnings and threats, then took a long chance and let her go.[2] War is full of excruciating choices.

Incidentally, Palaruan died a hero. Though only twenty-three, he was a charismatic leader, a skilled resistance fighter, and brave to the point of recklessness. The last quality led to his doom. He ambushed some Japanese and in the ensuing fight was wounded in the upper leg. The only way he could secure treatment where he happened to be was to surrender to the Japanese, but they would treat him only if he signed pro-Japanese propaganda materials. He refused; infection set in, and they let him die.[3]

Amid all the trouble of this period I could claim one small triumph for "system." I once suggested to Captain Barker that guerrilla affairs might be clarified somewhat if we would all designate our squadrons numerically by province. He must have thought it was a good idea and bucked it up the line to Thorp, since an order to this effect eventually came from the colonel. Thereafter, squadrons in Pangasinan were given numbers starting with 100; in western Nueva Ecija, numbers in the 200s; in eastern Nueva Ecija, 300s; Tarlac, 400s, and so on.

Overall, as 1943 dawned, prospects for Luzon guerrillas looked dim. Japanese patrols had increased steadily for months. The Fassoth camp had been raided and burned the preceding September. Thorp and Bill Brooks had been captured a month later, Barker in January 1943. By February, Thorp and Barker were in Fort Santiago awaiting execution, and Bill Brooks was on his way to Rabaul, New Britain, where his captors nearly starved him to death. McGuire had been beheaded by Negritos. Spies had been killed by somebody. Far off to the west Colonel Merrill was barely hanging on in isolation up in the Zambales Mountains. In the distant north turmoil prevailed; nobody knew where Praeger was, and Volckmann had begun to supplant Cols. Martin Moses and Arthur Noble, the top commanders there, but had not yet succeeded.

My domain was still beset by problems and uncertainties, and Major Anderson was still holed up in the mountains of Bulacan and Tayabas. Yet compared to those who had been our colleagues and compatriots only a few months before, Anderson and I were thriving. Best of all, though we did not know it at the time, the worst of our travail was over. Most (but not all) of the guerrilla leaders who died in the war were killed or captured in its first year while we were all learning how to operate. Those of us who had managed to eliminate or chase off spies and collaborators, who had learned how to win the support and trust of civilians, who had succeeded in establishing effective spy systems of our own, who had learned when to hide out and when to show ourselves, and who had been lucky were still alive early in 1943—and most of us then made it to the end of the war.

Progress throughout the LGAF was general in 1943 and 1944. Though there were occasional setbacks, our numbers grew steadily until we had about 13,000 men who were sufficiently active guerrillas that after the war I certified them as deserving official recognition and pay for their services. We intensified all our normal activities during this midwar period, in particular harassing the Japanese more than we had in 1942. The rampant jealousy and animosity among guerrilla leaders and their units never vanished entirely, but it did subside somewhat in 1943 and 1944, at least where I was.[4]

Nonetheless, 1943 did not begin promisingly. One of the most dispiriting experiences for a guerrilla is to learn that somebody in circumstances like his own has surrendered to the enemy. In March, Capt. Charles Cushing, who commanded our units in eastern Pangasinan, went over to the Japanese. The ostensible reason was that a month earlier they had imprisoned his wife in Santo Tomas in Manila, then released her so that she could entreat her husband to surrender. Supposedly, he was promised that he would be allowed to see her and that she and their children would be treated well.[5]

The news was no great surprise to me. Charles was a nervous man and, unlike his brothers Walter and James, had never seemed to me to be cut out for guerrilla life. When Volckmann and Blackburn made their way north after visiting me in the late summer of 1942, they had also stopped to see Cushing, and they too thought he showed little enthusiasm for guerrilla warfare. They were more impressed by two former gold miners, Herb Swick and Enoch French, who had become his subordinates.[6] A couple of months later a coded directive was sent from Colonels Moses and Noble to Cushing. He decoded a little of it, then sent the letter on to me, saying he was "too busy" to struggle further with it. In the message itself Moses and Noble complained that Cushing's own code was hard to decipher and advised him that some (unspecified) criticism of him in an earlier letter had been "necessary" but was not to be taken personally.[7] It was at about this same time that I had reproached Cushing about Palaruan's actions.[8] After that he remained inactive until the time of his surrender.

MacArthur's headquarters in Australia believed that Cushing had promised to cooperate with the Japanese army,[9] and Al Hendrickson

always suspected the same thing, for Cushing had spent the night of
March 6, 1943, with Al and had told him that he was going to surrender the next day. A few days later Al's camp was raided by a Japanese patrol.[10] The truth is impossible to know for sure. Sometimes
those who were captured or who surrendered to the enemy cooperated willingly, sometimes the Japanese were able to induce them to
do so or to torture them until they cooperated.

The surrender of Americans or Filipinos to the Japanese (or
their capture) often posed some pressing problems: it was usually
necessary to move at once any headquarters or units known to the
defecter before he could lead the enemy against his old comrades.
Cushing's case, however, presented fewer such difficulties. He had
always been impressed by my title of inspector general and for some
time before his defection had accepted me as his commanding officer and reported directly to me. Thus, when he left behind a couple
of well-trained units that had been commanded by Palaruan and Feliciano Nobres, they readily accepted incorporation into the LGAF
command. His other units evaporated.

The reasons men defected to the enemy varied widely. Capt.
Manuel Enriquez surrendered because his children were ill, and the
Japanese kept them from receiving medical attention.[11] Rufino Bald-
win was turned in to the Japanese by his ex-fiancée because he had
dumped her for a new girlfriend. The Japanese tortured him every
day for two weeks at Baguio, then sent him on to grim Fort Santiago
in Manila. It was a sharp reminder that he who lets himself be distracted by romance during a war can pay a high price.[12] Millard Hileman, who never became a guerrilla, said he eventually surrendered
to the enemy partly because he felt betrayed that U.S. forces had
never come to rescue soldiers like himself, partly because he was re-
morseful at the thought that many Filipinos who were feeding and
hiding him would be tortured and murdered by the Nipponese if he
was discovered.[13]

In the spring of 1943 I heard that Edwin Ramsey was not far away in
Pangasinan province. I hadn't seen an American other than McKenzie for many weeks, and I had a little business to clear up with Ed
anyway. It had all begun some time before when Joe Barker, not content to rely on information collected for him by Filipinos and probably from a sheer desire to defy the Japanese as well, had disguised
himself as a priest and gone down to Manila.[14] There he had been
promptly captured. Almost at once Ramsey assumed command of
the domain that Barker had inherited from Thorp only a few months

before. Some of Ramsey's agents then began to form guerrilla organizations in Tarlac and northwest Pangasinan, immediately south of Lingayen Gulf. In March, Ramsey himself started off to take physical possession of his new realm. Around the first of May I decided that a conference with him was needed, so Harry McKenzie and I set off westward. We met and conferred for a few days on matters of mutual interest, as diplomats say, after which McKenzie returned to LGAF headquarters. I had never met Ramsey before. He proved so easy to get along with and talk to, at least on a personal basis, that we walked around for a few more days looking over our existing guerrilla forces, recruiting new men, and discussing our possible future relations. One day somebody had the wit to observe that the Agno River was in flood stage and would float a good-sized boat nicely. Since that stream flows southward out of the Cordillera, then west and northwest right through the territories whose fate we were discussing, we decided that we might as well ride as walk. We soon found a sizable boat with a willing captain. The boat had a nipa roof rather like that of a covered wagon over its center, which would keep off the sun and also afford cover from prying eyes. So we got aboard and drifted down the river like tourists at ease until we came to its mouth at Lingayen Gulf. Here we met, for the first time, Capt. Charles Putnam, still another of the numerous American mining engineers who had come to the Philippines in the 1930s and been caught in the war. Like many others, he had been awarded an "emergency" commission and had begun to recruit guerrillas locally after the fall of Bataan. He was an interesting character: big, boisterous, and a hard drinker. He had lived long among Filipinos, obviously liked them, and understood them well. He behaved toward them like an amiable despot and was extremely popular with his "subjects." Not overcome by humility, he advised us to heed his example if we wanted to save our skins.[15] On that score I could not follow him. I too liked most Filipinos, usually got along with them easily, and, like Putnam, thought they responded well to affection. But it seemed to me even more important to be dignified around them and to treat them with respect.

One pleasant feature of this whole expedition involved an admirable lady named Ramona (Mona) Snyder. She was a member of the Escoda Group, a clique of young Manila socialites who were ideological and temperamental opposites of those wealthy Filipinos who either collaborated with the Japanese or tried to remain uncommitted. These fine (from our viewpoint) young people were ready, even anxious, to risk their money and their lives to aid guerrillas in any way they could. Late in the preceding summer I had been "close enough to death to smell smoke," as someone once put it. At that time Mona Snyder happened to be nearby visiting relatives, one of whom was a lieutenant of mine. Though she had never seen me before, she showed up one day well supplied with money, medicine, and provisions and began to try to nurse me back to health. This was especially reassuring, since she arrived just after my treatments by the witch doctor. Mona was a naturally cheerful woman who actually seemed to enjoy danger. In short, she was exactly the tonic I needed at that time. She stayed a short while, and intermittently over the next two months she mailed me two suits of clothes, a can of brown bread, and a razor and some blades—always accompanied in standard motherly fashion by admonitions to gain weight and take care of my health.[16]

Now, half a year later, Mona was in our neighborhood once more, visiting her friends and relatives. During that phase of the war civilians whom the Japanese felt no reason to mistrust could travel freely if they had the means to do so. Mona happened to remember that it was my birthday, so one day she arrived with a big birthday cake, and we all repaired to the home of a local sympathizer to commemorate the occasion suitably. The most notable aspect of the whole soiree was that Ramsey was immediately smitten with Mona.[17] In rapid succession she became his girlfriend, then an intermediary between him and Manuel Roxas. This turned out to be a coup of the first order, for Roxas not only had been one of the most prominent prewar Filipino politicians but would become president of the independent Philippines in 1948. At the moment he was the chief adviser of José Laurel, whom the Japanese had installed as puppet president of their wartime "Philippine Republic." Roxas, who was secretly sympathetic to the guerrillas, was in a position to pass invaluable information to Mona, thence to Ramsey.

Ed acknowledges that Mona sometimes awed him. Though he was a professional soldier, he was frequently nervous and apprehensive, whereas she—a mere "society lady"—was habitually relaxed and optimistic, even though she would have been torn to pieces by the Japanese had they ever discovered what she was doing.[18] Ray Hunt confessed to a somewhat similar feeling about Minang Dizon.[19] Perhaps the main difference between the two women was that Mona was basically calm and composed, whereas, as Ray put it, if he had been allowed only one word to characterize Minang it would have been "fierce."[20] If there is a moral anywhere here, surely it is that courage is an individual attribute, not the exclusive property of one sex or of people of a certain temperament.

After several weeks of discussion with Ramsey interspersed with social events, I returned to Umingan in June. In his book Ed says we agreed that he should be overall commander of the entire area and that I should be second in command.[21] That is not how I would describe it. Though we got along well and separated amicably, I did not think his designs were any more realistic than those entertained by Colonels Moses and Volckmann. Ed wanted to form a great host of guerrillas, with many officers, whether enough weapons were available to arm them or not. He believed that would elevate Filipino morale and tie many people to us. I thought it wiser to build a small, better-armed force capable of gathering intelligence, maintaining law and order, and repelling bandits and Japanese.[22] It seemed to me obvious that each area had special problems that would be best dealt with locally, not to mention that the modes of communication and transport then available to us made close central direction of our activities physically impossible. In practice, what either of us thought had been agreed upon made little difference. Ed soon went south to Manila; I quietly resumed my former activities and seldom heard much from him thereafter.

Ramsey says he underwent something like a spiritual transformation at about this time. He claims that by the summer of 1943 many Filipinos had succumbed to a malaise of the spirit; they had grown weary of the war with its shortages, burdens, and cruelties and were beginning to doubt that American "reinforcements" would ever arrive. This convinced Ramsey that guerrilla strategy must change: that deceit, intimidation, and force as practiced by the Huks[23] and often by USAFFE guerrillas as well should be abandoned, that we should struggle simply to free the Philippines when the war was finally won. He adds that this conviction was intensified by an experience he had on his way to his conference with me. He had stopped at the home of his bodyguard, who was regarded as a hero by all the members of his family except his wife. She, by contrast, was so scared that she urged her husband to try to save the lives of all of them by surrendering to the Kempeitai, the Japanese secret police. He replied that if she ever did this, he would kill her. Ramsey was profoundly impressed, for Filipinos (like many Mediterranean Europeans) tend to revere their families a great deal more than they do governments, parties, or ideologies. He realized for the first time, he says, that for Filipinos the war had truly become a crusade, and this new comprehension transformed him. Where he had formerly plunged into guerrilla activity because he hated the cruel Nipponese and longed for revenge, and because it was his duty as an American officer to continue to resist, now for the first time he fully appreciated how much the Filipinos had done for Americans. Consequently, he had become a Philippine patriot, convinced that his primary duty was to help Filipinos win the war and achieve their freedom.[24]

I understand how Ramsey felt. I had always been impressed by the Filipinos' near-deification of General MacArthur and was frequently amazed that so many of them had remained loyal to us even though we had so signally failed to protect them. I often wondered, too, if Americans would have been as kind and generous and would have risked as much for Filipinos as millions of them did for us had the situation been reversed. Yet it was also true that Japan had attacked their country more directly than ours and that they were fighting for their own freedom quite as much as for American causes and interests. In war all serious members of an alliance contribute what they can to the common cause, and many factors—not the least of which are geography and mere luck—determine what forms that contribution must take. In World War II the Filipinos gave their full share.

What I don't agree with is Ed's allegation that the Filipinos lost faith and spirit in 1943–44. Maybe I fooled myself; maybe I saw mostly what I wanted to see. But I don't think so. Maybe more people were despondent around Manila, but I traveled extensively throughout my domain for two and a half years and most of the peasants I saw were so obviously overjoyed to see an American that they could hardly have been sunk in gloom over the way the war was going.

An important spinoff from my extended meetings with Ed Ramsey was that I acquired a new American subordinate, Capt. Albert Hendrickson. It is bound to seem strange for me to say this, but I am not sure just when or how I got Al. A private first class in the Signal Corps, he had undergone an incredible array of harrowing experiences and close brushes with death early in the war. Early in 1943, as he recalled it, he had hiked southward out of the mountains, dodged Japanese patrols along the way, and managed to find my headquarters. I had taken him in, given him quinine to combat his malaria, and then made him commander of Tarlac province.[25] Maybe this is entirely accurate, though I suspect that Al's memory may have grown cloudy as years passed into decades. It is possible that I secured Al as part of a deal of some sort with Ramsey. In 1946 when my memory of wartime events was far fresher than it is now, I wrote a thirteen-page outline history of the LGAF in which this passage appears: "By agreement between Major Lapham and

Ramsey, Capt. Albert Hendrickson . . . was ordered to Tarlac in the latter part of May 1943 to act as District Commander of Ramsey's Tarlac units."[26] To muddy the waters further, Criscenzio Hipolito offers still another version of what happened, but in order to evaluate that, I must say something about the talents and proclivities of "Captain Cris."

Early in 1943 Lt. Col. Criscenzio Hipolito was intelligence officer of the Tarlac Military Area. He knew English well as a *learned* language, but the shades of meaning that differentiate basically similar words still baffled him. Even more pertinent here, Hipolito had the soul but not quite the talent of a poet. He loved ornate phraseology, and he liked to please people by praising them. When these various influences on his language were expressed on paper, the result was often hilarious. For instance, Cris once described me as "a sort of legendary hero" whom the Japanese regarded as "superhuman." On my "trail blazed incredible tales of heroic exploits and valiant deeds." Cris was sure "that Fate had destined this lanky, low-voiced, devil-may-care blond and boyish Iowan to cause more trouble and headache in four provinces to the Japanese than an Army put together." I should hasten to add that such an accolade did not turn my head in the 1940s any more than it does in the 1990s. Now, it makes me think of a prosperous cattle-raising area of western Montana where, along Interstate 90, I once saw a large sign bearing the legend "Welcome to Drummond, Montana. Home of World Champion Bull Shippers." I don't suppose Cris had ever been to Drummond, Montana, but the general flavor of his prose could lead one to suspect that he might have had a remote ancestor or two from there. Worse for my semicelestial grandeur, Cris habitually showered comparable compliments on many others with whom he came into contact. Nor did he spare himself. He described his own G-2 (intelligence) units as the best in Tarlac "and perhaps in the entire LGAF command." He added that various of his American colleagues were so "appalled" by the excellence of his organization that they said such things as "It was amazing"; "It works like a magician"; "The best outfit I ever saw"; and "Holeproof and foolproof." Cris was a loyal man and a good fellow, but he fell easily into rapture in front of a typewriter.[27]

According to Hipolito (to return to my narrative), Ramsey asked *him* to look for Hendrickson—"a tough guy from Montana who does not know the word surrender."[28] In a mere two days Cris found his man. He was overwhelmed. Hendrickson was strong, healthy, robust, athletic, full of life, and "looking more of a screen actor than a hunted guerrilla." What a dramatic contrast he was to us other American guerrillas who, sick, half-starved, emaciated, and disfigured by scraggly beards, looked like hermits or fugitives from a mortuary. Small wonder that he and Hendrickson immediately admired one another, cooperated enthusiastically, infiltrated both the Philippine Constabulary and the Japanese Kempeitai, and caused the spirits of local Filipinos to soar heavenward. In Tarlac "from thenceforward the names Capt. Hendrickson and Capt. Cris became household words. To the oppressed we stood for liberty and justice; to our people, hope eternal; to the spies and quislings, their nemesis; and to the Japs, defiance."[29]

Winnowing the truth from this baroque phraseology presents some problems. Al Hendrickson was "a tough guy from Montana" all right, but even so, the task he faced in southern Tarlac was extremely daunting. The place was a Huk stronghold, and nobody from LGAF was powerful enough to reorganize it in the face of adamant Huk opposition. In northern Tarlac Al was reasonably successful in forming effective units, though Japanese patrols were so numerous and active that he was kept on the move almost constantly. Much of his success was due to several able and aggressive Filipinos. The most important was Capt. Diosdado Aganon, commander of Squadron 403, Al's strongest unit. Aganon was later promoted to sector commander in eastern Tarlac. (His career ended tragically in the spring of 1945 when he was killed in savage fighting along the Villa Verde Trail.) Another able officer was a Captain Ramos, who commanded Squadron 401 in western Tarlac. Al also especially esteemed "Captain Cris" for his skill as a recruiter and organizer, and Minang Dizon, whom he called his most valuable courier and spy.[30]

As for Hendrickson himself, I must admit that I sometimes found him rather hard to take. He was brusque, short-tempered, and not one to refuse a drink or three. Like several other people in my command, I would not have picked him for his position had I possessed perfect freedom of choice. But what does that prove? Guerrillas, in the nature of their pursuits, seldom have "perfect freedom of choice" about anything. For that matter, why should I suppose that General MacArthur would ever have picked me to oversee a guerrilla enterprise had *he* possessed "perfect freedom of choice?" Fate throws us into close association with lots of people. You like some, prize some, and view some with reservations, but you have to try to get along with all of them and to get something out of them and they have to make comparable adjustments to you. In this world, anyway, we play the cards we are dealt.

Major Ramsey had sound reasons for moving his central head-quarters away from Bayambang down to the vicinity of Manila. He would be the sole legitimate authority in the area, and more information about the Japanese came through Manila than elsewhere. According to his account he next reorganized all east-central Luzon guerrilla forces into five districts, replaced several American officers with Filipinos, worked his way into an influential position in Philippine politics, and began to negotiate with a respected Filipino general, Vincente Lim, about what seemed by then an obsession of his: the unification of all the guerrillas in the Philippines.[31] All I can say about his professed absorption in all these endeavors is that a lot of it I never heard about and none of it affected me. All his units, real or claimed, across Nueva Ecija, Pangasinan, and Tarlac gradually became permanent elements of the LGAF under my control. I would emphasize here that there was no controversy over this evolution. Ed and I had been on friendly terms before and during our lengthy spring conferences and we remained so afterward. Our unresolved difference of opinion about the best way to pursue objectives that both of us desired did not make us enemies.

The latter months of 1943 were punctuated by the sad news that Thorp, Col. Hugh Straughn, and several others had been executed by the Japanese.[32]

One of the narrowest escapes I had in the whole war also occurred that fall, near the town of San Nicolas, about ten miles north of Umingan. I went there to break up a racket that had been organized by some officers and men of the U.S. Fourteenth Infantry. Originally, this outfit had been commanded by Capt. Guillermo Nakar, subsequently by Capt. Manuel Enriquez, then by Maj. Romulo Manriquez. The last two were subordinates of Russell Volckmann, who does not appear to have realized what was taking place in this branch of his command. What his minions were doing was taking steel cables, acid used in mining, and other scrap materials out of mines in the mountains and selling these commodities to the enemy. The long cables were especially coveted by the Japanese navy. The excuse advanced for doing this was that the perpetrators were making money to support their guerrilla activities. Actually much of the money was going into their own pockets.

I first heard about this operation from Esteban Lumyeb, by then a lieutenant, who told me that Lieutenants Langley, French, and Jagoe had already issued orders to end the sales. About a week later I learned from Capt. Tom Chengay that Langley and Jagoe had been murdered and that cable sales were thriving again. Tom asked me to come north to deal with the situation. I took forty men and moved swiftly into San Nicolas. We spent a day talking to agents there, one of whom was the mayor, Felipe Ortiz. It appeared that Nicholas Sali, Cipriano Alles, and the commandant of the Fourteenth Infantry, Major Manriquez, were the ringleaders in the operation. Most likely the two civilians were the main profiteers, paying Manriquez a small percentage for his cooperation. In any case, after dark that evening, we slipped into Manriquez's camp, and a local Filipino pounded on the door of the house where he was staying. When the sleepy major opened the door, there I was with my .45 pointed at his midsection.

An extended discussion followed. At first Manriquez insisted that selling the mine supplies was not wrong because the money was going to support his guerrillas. Eventually he came around to accept my insistence that the enemy needed the cables and scrap steel a lot more than he needed their "Mickey Mouse" money. His conversion seems to have been genuine because he helped me suppress the whole operation before going back north to his old haunts in the Cagayan Valley, where he stayed out of trouble thereafter.

Actual destruction of the cables was carried out by Tom Chengay's troops. Of course, most of those who had been profiting from the thievery were enraged. Years after the war some of them wrote a pack of lies to the U.S. Veterans Administration in an effort to secure revocation of Chengay's veteran status and consequent rights to veteran's benefits.[33] At the time, all they could do was tip off the Japanese that I was in the vicinity.

A whole regiment of enemy troops must have been brought into the area, for it was soon overrun by Japanese intent on trapping us against the nearby mountains. Our prospects were not bright. We could not return to Umingan the way we had come. The only way out was a pass through the mountains toward the Cagayan Valley. The Villa Verde Trail was aptly named, for only at its near end was it even a rude dirt road; the remainder was a mere track through the mountains (where much hard fighting would take place in the spring of 1945). The Japanese knew as well as we did that it was our last resort, so a spirited race ensued to be first to seize this primitive pathway. At the foot of the mountains it crossed a river. We beat our foes there by just enough to get across and around a bend in the road before we heard the first of their trucks on the side we'd just left. Of course, this did not slow us down any. On their part, as soon as they had crossed they set up a road block, not knowing that we were already over. Fearful of pursuit, we slogged upward and onward all night and most of the next day, well beyond where the road turned into a mere trail. At last we arrived, exhausted, at a tiny Igorot barrio that boasted four huts.

I happened to know that at this time another American, an MIT graduate and prewar mining engineer, Enoch French, was living in a larger Igorot barrio some five hours' hike farther on through some of the wildest mountain country in Luzon. At once I sent an Igorot runner, bearing news of our location and circumstances, to look for him. The next day a runner from French came back to suggest that we move to his more commodious abode in the town of Aritao. Most of us were utterly exhausted, so I decided to remain where we were to rest for a day. Then a couple of my men told me that they knew the mayor of Aritao was not to be trusted, so I sent another runner to take this news to French. Too late—just short of his destination he met a fellow Igorot runner headed our way with word that French and six of his men had been captured by the Japanese. When our runner returned, we realized there was only one thing to do: pack and get out. French and associates knew all about us, and nobody could ever be sure how much torture any human being could endure.[34] In fact, the Japanese raiders of Aritao were already so close behind the runner that they were beginning to lob mortar shells around our tiny barrio just as we left it.

We were in a most unenviable position. We had no food and no prospect of getting any, since there were no barrios within miles of us. Enemy soldiers were closing in on one side, and there were impenetrable mountains on two others. We could only backtrack even though we knew that other Japanese had blocked that rude mountain trail somewhere between us and San Nicolas. We hiked all night. Sometime before dawn we stopped maybe five hundred yards above and away from the river. We slipped into the underbrush and slowly climbed down a steep ridge in the dark until we came to a small creek that ran off toward the river. There we halted and sent out scouts. They returned to report that enemy troops appeared to be watching the mouth of every creek that ran into the river and that there were troops in every barrio they could see. (We discovered later that if we had not left the road when we did, we would have run into an enemy roadblock around its very next curve.)

The only course left was to head southward over successive jungle-covered ridges in the hope of outflanking our foes. We struggled onward all day on empty stomachs. After nightfall we decided to try again to come back out of the mountains. By then we were south of Natividad. Scouts were sent out again and brought back the news that Japanese patrols were active in the area but that there were no Japanese troops stationed there for the moment. We decided to keep struggling along in the dark through the hellish mountain jungle, relying on barking dogs—of which there must have been 100,000,000 in the Philippines—to warn us of Japanese patrols. If there was one constant in the Philippines, it was that at any given time and place one to a dozen dogs would be barking. Most Filipinos like dogs, and rural families usually had one or two, but why they howled so relentlessly I never knew.

At dawn we stopped outside San Quintin to rest and get food. Barrio people assured us that there had been no Japanese there for some time and began to rustle some chow for us. Whether pride goes before a fall or not, complacency surely does. The civilians whom we carelessly set out as guards proved to be the sort of people who couldn't see lightning or hear thunder. We had just begun to eat when one of my men spotted a small Japanese patrol approaching the house we were in. It is hard to say whether we or they were more astounded; certainly we took them by surprise when we thrust our rifles out the windows and began to blaze away at them at virtual point-blank range. We killed three or four, but the rest escaped and fled back to San Quintin. Of course, many more Japanese were soon on our trail again. Back into the mountains we went, but being only a few miles from Umingan we made it there without further incident. I disbanded most of my men, then sneaked into town and stayed at a private house about half a mile from the permanent Japanese barracks while its occupants industriously searched the countryside for me.

During the aftermath of this episode I experienced what was for me probably the most interesting sideshow of the war. It had all begun many months before when Japan had conquered what is now Indonesia. The Japanese now in and around Umingan had brought back with them perhaps twenty soldiers from the island of Celebes, apparently with the intention of using them as laborers. The Celebians were several hundred miles across the sea from their homeland and gave their captors no trouble, so before long the Japanese allowed them to go into barrios to make small purchases, accompanied only by a bored guard or two. On these expeditions they would often run into various of my guerrillas off duty or going about their regular civilian activities as farmers. My men soon learned that some of the men from Celebes would like to escape and join guerrilla units. My men encouraged them, so one day when their guards were especially lax, about fifteen of them simply walked away.

Though most of them joined Captain Doliente's unit, a few split off from the rest and ended up in Tarlac. Al Hendrickson once recounted with deep disgust that one had deserted his new benefactors and gone back to the Japanese, thereby making a lot of trouble for Al and the local Filipinos who had fed him.[35] Two others west of Tarlac City, where Cris Hipolito happened to be, did the same thing. "Captain Cris" described the subsequent deliverance of himself and his men in his customary colorful fashion: "The moment our yellow-bellied traitors Franz Callalo and John Sampo, reached their yellow-skinned masters every agency supposed to be Jap-controlled had been alerted not on the side of the Japs but on our side."[36] LGAF men scattered in all directions, with the Japanese in hot pursuit.

I met the Celebians only after the affair of the stolen cables and the ensuing chase through the mountains. I had a number of interesting talks with some of them, especially their leader, Lt. Adolph Lembong, who would live on to become a lieutenant colonel in the Indonesian Revolutionary Army that expelled the Dutch from the old East Indies after World War II. Lembong was the only one who had known English when they escaped from the Japanese, but some of the others gradually picked up a little English and rather more of the Illocano dialect, which somewhat resembled their native tongue. Thus, if we had plenty of time at our disposal we were able to fashion conversations of sorts.

One of the most interesting things Lieutenant Lembong told us was that numerous Indonesians claimed to be mediums and that séances were popular events in his homeland. For a long time the Dutch had refused to believe that natives could speak to the dead, but some of them eventually came to think it was possible. So the Dutch colonial government forbade the practice, seemingly because those under the spell of the leader during a séance would occasionally utter anti-Dutch sentiments, or because they feared that the leader might induce them to rebel or otherwise behave in ways contrary to Dutch interests. Human nature being what it is, the prohibition merely stimulated the zeal of the natives to hold more séances.

Lembong once took me to one of these performances. The leader put one of the others into a trance. The man gesticulated wildly, then fell to the floor and began to speak in perfect Illocano, even though none of the Celebes men had yet mastered that dialect. He said he had been killed by guerrillas three days earlier because they believed he had been a spy for the Japanese. He added that he had deserved to be killed because he had indeed been a spy. Afterward the Celebians assured me that the easiest time to contact the dead was three days after their demise, since one fell into a deep sleep immediately after death but then awakened in the new life three days later. I found the whole performance strange—and thought-provoking, especially the three-day effort of the dead soul to come back to life. This motif recurs in various forms in the religions and folklore of people widely scattered over the globe, most notably in the resurrection of Christ on the third day after his crucifixion.

In December 1943 I acquired my last American refugee: Ray Hunt, who had begun the war as an aircraft mechanic with the Twenty-First Pursuit Squadron. Since then, his array of experiences had rivaled those of Al Hendrickson and Edmund Ramsey. During the battle for Bataan he had been pressed into service as an infantryman. Later, though weak from sickness and semistarvation, he managed to escape from the Death March and had the good luck to fall into the hands of friendly Filipinos who took him to the Fassoth camp. There he lingered close to death for months but was one of the few who escaped when the Japanese destroyed the camp in September 1942. For nearly a year he had wandered in the mountains and lowland barrios, always hidden and fed by compassionate Filipinos, as he gradually recovered his health. In the middle of 1943 a combination of restlessness and a desire to do something useful impelled him to begin to organize a guerrilla outfit of his own. He acquired a handful of followers and became still another of the free spirits then at large in Luzon. From others he heard about my organization and eventually sent a runner to my headquarters bearing his offer to join LGAF. At that time Al Hendrickson was trying to cope with the Huks and subdue various embattled factions in Tarlac. I thought he could use all the help he could get, so I sent a message to Hunt to look for Al and join his unit and another to Hendrickson notifying him to expect Ray.

Ray finally located his new commander. They seemed to hit it off well together and Al soon made Ray his executive officer. But on this side of heaven, nothing in human affairs proceeds placidly for long. Soon Al requested that Ray be promoted from staff sergeant, his rank in the regular army, to captain. The request was received at my headquarters by Harry McKenzie. Unfortunately, Harry and Al were not fond of each other. They had once had a dispute about Al's desire to set a trap for a collaborator, and Al also mistakenly believed that Harry had once killed a fifteen-year-old boy whom he thought was a Huk. What had actually happened was quite different: Mac had begun questioning a suspected Huk when his gun went off accidentally, inflicting a flesh wound in the man's side. I questioned the man later. He was not a Huk at all, and he realized that the gunshot had been accidental. All three of us had parted without hard feelings.

Anyway, McKenzie now protested that second lieutenant should be sufficient rank for somebody not well known to us and thus far untested. Eventually, though, we all acceded to Al's request, since none of us was a good bet to survive the war, and if Ray died a captain his family would receive larger survivor's benefits. The fate of nations was not always the determining factor in the decisions we made.

In June 1944 I decided to reorganize my command somewhat. At about the same time I received a request from Captain Hunt, whom I had still not met, for another assignment. Though Ray always said, as long as Al was alive, that he had not wanted to leave him, the two had actually begun to irritate each other. To say this is not to put down either of them. Lots of people simply get on one another's nerves if they are constantly together. As mentioned earlier, one reason I had separated from Sergeant Short in 1942 was that we were both getting restive from too much of each other's company. I avoided the problem with Harry McKenzie by visiting him regularly, since he commanded a large number of troops, but seldom staying with him long. With Hunt and Hendrickson, however, there was an additional difficulty: Ray had actually become afraid of Al. There was no indoor plumbing in guerrilla camps; anyone who felt an urge of nature at night had to get up and go somewhere out in the underbrush. Inevitably, a little noise often accompanied such excursions. Al was both a light sleeper and jumpy from his many narrow escapes from the Huks and Japanese, and Ray grew increasingly fearful that some night Al would suddenly spring up half awake and shoot him for an enemy raider.

I decided to try to solve two problems with a single decision. Some of the units formed by Ramsey in Pangasinan had lost contact with him after he left for Manila and had broken up under Japanese pressure. In addition, with the arrival of radios and other equipment from Australia in mid-1944, plus steadily increasing Japanese pressure, I was growing too busy to be both overall commander of LGAF and personal chief in Pangasinan. Antonio Garcia, acting commander of the Third Provisional Pangasinan Regiment, tried to hold the remnants together, but he clearly needed help. Thus the presence and availability of Ray Hunt just then was most opportune, so I did some hurried rearranging of designations and jurisdictions. Ray was made area commander for all Pangasinan, and Garcia was given command of a reconstituted and renamed western sector of Pangasinan. Being an American made Ray an ideal candidate for the new position too. Several Filipinos had the ability to fill the position, but selecting one of them would have aroused the jealousy of the others who regarded themselves as equally qualified. An American of respectable ability, by contrast, would be looked up to by most Filipinos. Moreover, Ray had no prior ties with any of the Filipino alternatives. Overall, then, he seemed the most promising choice. He performed his duties well; in particular, his intelligence operation, headed by a bright Filipino, Juan Utleg, did outstanding work in collecting valuable information for transmission to MacArthur's headquarters.[37]

In July 1944 my domain reached its organizational apex when Maj. Bernard Anderson voluntarily ceded to me his southeastern Nueva Ecija sector, then under the command of Capt. Dioscorro de Leon. This really changed nothing, since de Leon had been reporting to me as one of my own for many months; nonetheless the action was typical of Andy.

Near Manila there was a troop called Marking's guerrillas after their leader, a former boxer and cab driver named Marcos Augustin. The "brains" of this outfit was Marking's mistress, a prewar mestizo (half-American) journalist named Yay Panlilio. Marking's group enjoyed close relations with Anderson's followers, and Panlilio especially admired Andy himself. He was not moody or given to fits of uncivilized conduct like so many guerrillas, she said, but was a quiet, considerate man who did not carry tales or criticize other outfits, and who stayed away from towns so that Japanese would not punish civilians who might have seen him but failed to turn him in.[38]

I had a similarly good opinion of him. Andy was an especially generous man, phenomenally so for one in our straitened circumstances. When a submarine from Australia brought him forty-seven tons of supplies in mid-1944, he promptly apportioned forty tons among his Filipino aides and supporters.[39] In December of that year a detachment from the Hunters, another guerrilla band operating near Manila, came to Anderson's camp to ask for arms and supplies. He gave them seventy tommy guns, twenty-five new carbines, five .45-caliber pistols, some medicine, and many cigarettes—all followed by what was, for them, a sumptuous Christmas party.[40] No wonder Panlilio liked him!

My whole organization now consisted of thirty-eight squadrons in Nueva Ecija, fifteen in Pangasinan, and six in Tarlac. I no longer tried to recruit; there were always more volunteers than were needed. Our practical problem was to keep the enlisted strength of units commensurate with their armed strength. Even when I began to expand our numbers again in the fall of 1944, in anticipation of an American invasion, I could have added many more units than I did. But mere numbers are of little use if one lacks the food, arms, and supplies necessary to sustain them.

— 6 —
Guerrilla Life

Some American guerrillas have emphasized how worried they were about their lack of official status and what their fate might be if they were ever hailed before American, or even Filipino, military or civil authorities after the war. Even Gen. Charles Willoughby describes us as "desperate men" gravely in need of having our legal positions regularized by MacArthur's headquarters in Australia.[1] I do not say this in a spirit of bravado, but he must have worried about it a lot more than I ever did. I knew the Japanese would almost certainly execute me if they ever caught me, but that my own country might punish me after the war for fighting the enemy I simply could not imagine. I thought about a lot of things from 1942 to 1945—survival, my possible contribution to eventual victory, day-to-day practical problems—but never about my hypothetical legal status. It could not have worried Filipino guerrillas much either; otherwise, there would not have been scores of thousands of them.

Once I began to acquire some followers, my immediate tasks were obvious: I must organize, feed, supply, and train them. When I began to form my first units I decided to call them squadrons. The word, drawn from the old horse cavalry, had a more romantic, Hollywood ring to it than conventional U.S. Army unit designations. In practice, a squadron was often formed by persuading someone who was prominent locally to bring in a couple of dozen of his friends and neighbors. He would then be made an officer or a noncom, and his entourage would serve under him. It was a system much like the ancient Roman one of enlisting Germanic chieftains and their tribal followers as *foederati*. The chief would be made a general in the Roman army, and all his tribesmen would be given Roman citizenship after twenty years of military service. (The Roman Empire collapsed after three hundred years of this practice. Fortunately, my enlistment procedures were never put to such a stern test.)

The LGAF squadrons were about the size of a prewar Philippine army company: around a hundred men (a Philippine company comprised 250 men on paper, but it was seldom up to strength). Each one did whatever routine tasks its officers thought best, but all were expected to follow my general directives and to ask permission before undertaking any enterprise that was unusual or of notable importance. District commanders coordinated the activities of several squadrons. Over them were three area commanders, all ultimately responsible to my personal staff: Capt. Harry McKenzie in Nueva Ecija, Capt. Al Hendrickson in Tarlac, and, after June 1944, Capt. Ray Hunt in Pangasinan. As our organization grew, especially in Nueva Ecija and Tarlac, sector commanders had to be created to aid their area chiefs. Some guerrilla groups in other parts of the Philippines actually established regular schools modeled on American Officer Candidate Schools to provide semiformal training for their officer corps.[2] I never even considered trying that. My officers were mainly natural leaders in their native localities and usually had good instinctive organizational and leadership capacity. I had lots of troubles during the war, but I never lacked capable officers and men.

If a squadron grew large enough to be unwieldy, it was divided into two. As the numbers of squadrons increased, rivalries and disputes over jurisdiction began to appear. I sought to deal with the problem promptly by making each squadron responsible for a certain town or other specific area and forbidding units to enter each other's territory without obtaining permission. This headed off trouble for the moment. As time passed and the men became better acquainted with those in other units, friendliness spread, a spirit of cooperation developed, and most of the regulations were eventually revoked. One was not: if a joint operation was undertaken, the top commander must always be the squadron leader in whose district the action was to take place.

Despite these arrangements, which generally worked well, my men remained reluctant to let other units enter their home territory. In part, this reflected mere pride of possession, but it was also distinctly practical. A squadron's food was ordinarily secured from civilians in its own locality, and visiting units placed an additional burden on local farmers. Moreover, Filipinos are like everybody else in that they tend to be more frolicsome away from home than around their families and friends. Those who were carrying guns for the first time in their lives and thought of themselves as intrepid warriors often did not play gently. Hence, enthusiasm for visits by boisterous outsiders, even if they were loyal allies, was always tepid. I insisted that my own men must treat civilians respectfully and tried to impress on them that much of our standing with civilians always depended on our ability to protect them from gangs of outlaws.

We gradually developed a regular system of runners to carry instructions back and forth between units. The runners also brought intelligence back to my headquarters and carried my messages routinely to Manila; from there, still others took the information on to southern Philippine islands for relay to Australia. At least that was what was supposed to happen. I never knew for sure whether information I despatched southward actually reached its intended destination. The runners' main importance was quite different anyway: since I always had more volunteers than I knew what to do with, making runners of a considerable number gave them a chance to do, and feel they were doing, something useful.

Around Manila, guerrillas were also sometimes used as guides, chaperons, or bodyguards for civilians.[3] I never let my men perform such services; rather, civilians were guides for *us*. One thing all my followers learned from hard experience, though, was never to disclose our ultimate destination to native guides—not because they were disloyal but because they might be captured by the enemy and compelled to talk.

That the exchange of directives and intelligence was reasonably efficient, at least among our own LGAF units, gradually became evident and recognized. In late 1944 several Americans managed to get to Australia via submarine. They had to proceed from Umingan over the Sierra Madre to the east coast, through territory infested with Japanese patrols. Accurate intelligence had to be secured in advance to get them safely to their point of embarkation. All went off as planned. Capt. Wilbur Lage, the ranking officer among the evacuees, wrote a report in Australia praising our forces for their industry and efficiency.

Throughout 1943 and 1944 our numbers grew steadily. By the latter part of 1944 we had combat capability in Tarlac, Pangasinan, and Nueva Ecija provinces, a single unit on coast-watcher duty at Baler Bay in Tayabas province on the east coast, two others near Carranglan and Pantabangan, an intelligence unit in Nueva Vizcaya, and even one combat unit off to the southwest in Pampanga. (The last was commanded by Emilio Hernandez. He and his brother Tony were able officers and two of my closest friends throughout much of the war.) The evolution of an effective guerrilla force had proceeded remarkably since that distant day back in April 1942 when Sergeants Short, Lumyeb, and I had bade Colonel Thorp goodbye and set off without even a definite destination in mind.

One of my organizational inspirations turned out much less impressively. We once accumulated a considerable number of small

Philippine horses, so I decided to form a headquarters cavalry unit. I was not under any illusion about winning twentieth-century wars by cavalry charges, but who could tell? A band of horsemen might be useful out in the countryside where we were located, and certainly such a troop would impress local civilians. Alas! the project had to be abandoned because the piles of manure the horses left behind immediately tipped off the Japanese that guerrillas were in the vicinity. Though I hate to think so, perhaps those heaps were a silent commentary on the worth of the whole scheme.

As for training, the limitations that nature and circumstances imposed prevented its becoming elaborate or arduous. Cloth and military insignia were never available in sufficient quantity for uniforms and close-order drill is of little use to men who will spend much of their time hiding from the enemy, or in operations after dark, or pretending to be ordinary farmers at work in their fields. We did far more patrolling and cross-country hiking, pursuits that served several purposes. They improved the physical condition of the men, disciplined them a bit, gave them useful training in scouting and gathering intelligence, increased a feeling of comradeship and interdependence among them, and got them accustomed to going at once to a predetermined position in the line of march or if a skirmish developed. Not least, it kept them busy.

Weapons training was minimal. We had no heavy or complex weapons, but many Filipino farmers had rifles or small arms before the war. Quite a few had been hunters, and most Filipinos *like* guns. Thus the main thing they needed to be taught was proper care of the weapons they had or that we could acquire.

A more difficult matter was simulating a military appearance. Ray Hunt describes his habitual garb as what might have been worn by a Mexican bandit in a Hollywood movie, but I tried to look at least slightly military by wearing denim, if I could find any, with epaulettes or some such, again if I could find any. Shaving was another problem. Filipino men have little facial hair and were usually content to pick out individual whiskers with bamboo tweezers or occasionally to scrape their faces nonchalantly with a rusty razor blade. I was convinced that I needed to shave regularly in order to look like a proper commanding officer. Once I let one of Al Hendrickson's men assail me with his razor, but the experience was so memorable that I always shaved myself thereafter. When my razor blades became so dull that I couldn't stand to use them any longer, I got a straightedge razor and gradually learned to hone it and keep it sharp. If necessity requires it people can learn to be content with many processes they would ordinarily spurn or regard as "impossible." For instance, I had no toothbrush until a submarine brought some in mid-1944. But Filipinos knew how to cut a stick off a certain bush, chew on one end of it until it was half-soft, and then use it to clean their teeth. I tried the technique and found that it worked quite as well as a conventional toothbrush. In fact, the first time I went to a dentist after the U.S. landings on Luzon in 1945, he was surprised that after three years in the jungle and underbrush I had no cavities.

Professional soldiers have traditionally scorned guerrillas as rude, untrained, undisciplined, and unreliable; likely to be poachers, smugglers, convicts, or bandits more interested in plunder than victory; frequently more terrorists than soldiers; corrupted by personal and political ambitions—in short, mere murderous outlaws rather than gentlemen who wage war in at least a semichivalrous fashion.[4] Although this attitude displays neither understanding nor appreciation of the valuable services guerrillas can often provide to regular troops, it is not surprising; guerrilla war does have vile aspects, and a lot of unsavory people are often involved in it. This was as true in the Philippines of 1942–45 as in most other places where guerrillas have operated in modern times.

First off, to be successful a guerrilla leader must become, in one way or another, the de facto ruler of the territory in which he operates. Failure to achieve authority will defeat all his plans and hopes. From this it follows that he must maintain the loyalty of local officials and local people, making it safer for them to give him such loyalty than to pursue any other course. That, in turn, requires that spies, collaborators with enemies, and anyone else who breaks down trust between himself and the local population must be eliminated or neutralized without pity. Nothing less will suffice. Russell Volckmann made the point bluntly by remarking that his number one priority in northern Luzon was always to kill all the Filipinos who spied for the Japanese or collaborated with them.[5] One of his subordinates, Maj. George Barnett, once fitted deed to word by hanging a pro-Japanese mayor of San Fernando in La Union province right next door to a Japanese garrison.[6] Nobody in LGAF ever acted with quite that degree of flamboyance, but Federico Doliente's beheading of the mayor of Umingan came close.

On occasion, too, one had to set an example. My worst case of this sort was our experience with the con man "Captain Edades" and his wife. More distasteful was the periodic need to be remorseless with some ordinary civilian collaborator. Once a former guerrilla of ours betrayed some of his erstwhile comrades to the Japanese and then, fearful for his life, fled to Manila. Fortunately, some of our men knew friendly fellow guerrillas there who promptly located the culprit and executed him for us.

As always, some cases were more equivocal. We had little trouble with spies in our immediate locality, but occasionally some outsider, perhaps posing as a rice buyer, would ask a lot questions of local people. Because most Filipinos like to talk, and many like to impress others with the extent and depth of their knowledge, a smooth operator could sometimes get considerable information from unsuspecting civilians about LGAF numbers, locations, resources, plans, and the like. If some abnormally talkative stranger showed up near me, I was usually content to have him questioned closely. Our village police were often less patient; a visitor who seemed to one of them to be unduly inquisitive about matters that were none of his business sometimes "disappeared" soon afterward.

Some writers have complained, after the fact, that we guerrillas were inhumanly hard on barrio and town officials who were caught in excruciating dilemmas.[7] I cannot deny it; I can only remind them that guerrilla warfare is not a sporting contest among gentlemen who observe Marquis of Queensberry rules. It is a mean, dirty, brutal struggle to the death, devoid of any principle or sentiment save to survive and win.[8]

Actually, after 1942 matters were not as grim and bloody where I was ruling as the foregoing examples might indicate. Probably 90 percent of ordinary Filipinos, both farmers and local officials, in their hearts preferred Americans and American ideals to their Japanese counterparts. This did not mean that all of them were brave enough to risk the lives of themselves and their families to feed and shelter us openly; it did mean that if I managed my affairs with reasonable capability, gradually added to my authority and influence, did not blunder in some ostentatious way, and treated people with respect, I could count on their sympathy and cooperation.

The respect factor must be emphasized in justice to most American guerrilla leaders. The people I controlled knew well enough that my men and I could be just as tough as we needed to be to gain their compliance, but we never relied primarily on compulsion to secure civilian support. We performed many valuable services for ordinary people. We rid their localities of the bandit plague and provided them with the police protection they seldom got from the Japanese. If we assassinated or, more commonly, chased out or otherwise removed disloyal (and often dishonest) local officials, we filled their positions as mayors, police chiefs, and barrio lieutenants with the ablest and most reliable pro-American replacements we could find. We then consulted these functionaries regularly and stood behind them while they performed their duties.

"Fence-sitters" were more difficult to manage. Many of them were, understandably, frightened. With the future so highly uncertain, and knowing that they would almost surely be punished by *somebody* (Japanese, Americans, or fellow Filipinos) if they backed a loser, they wanted to stay uncommitted as long as possible.[9] Some people of this sort could be won over by propaganda; more were impressed as we grew visibly in armed strength and public support. With wavering town officials, there were ways of pressuring them into supporting us. For instance, the Japanese often judged the loyalty and effectiveness of officials by the amount of guerrilla activity in their areas. If we expanded into a new locality and found that a mayor or his subordinates or the townspeople were cool to us, we might raid some nearby Japanese installation, or ambush enemy soldiers in the vicinity. The invaders, with their habitual brutality, would then punish the officials. On at least one occasion they executed a mayor who had been, in fact, loyal to them.

A mixture of appeals, threats, and persuasion would usually bring an official around. A good illustration was the manner in which guerrillas managed the Philippine Constabulary—and the PC allowed themselves to be so "managed." In June 1943 Chick Parsons, who had lived in the Islands for years before the war who was currently employed by General MacArthur to coordinate submarine contacts between Australia and Philippine guerrillas, made a formal report to Gen. Willoughby, MacArthur's Chief of Intelligence. He asserted that a small percentage of the PC were true Quislings who spied on both their fellows and guerrillas for the benefit of their Japanese masters, but that a large majority of PC men stayed at their posts merely to make a living and would turn against the Japanese if the Americans ever returned.[10] The PC chief, Gen. Guillermo Francisco, was a Filipino officer who had served on Bataan. He had been captured, then put through a de-Americanization program by the Nipponese. They half-trusted him to do their will thereafter. Francisco had his men pursue bandits and cutthroats, which was good in itself and which allowed them to look good to their Japanese overlords, but it was known among many of his officers and some outsiders as well that he and most of his men were just waiting for an opportune time to change sides.

It was not the least valuable of the many contributions we guerrillas made to the ultimate victory of the Allies that as we grew visibly in strength and public support, more and more Filipinos who had either been fence-sitters or, like the Constabulary, forced into impossible positions began to drift in our direction and to look for opportunities to change sides openly. For instance, early in the war many Filipinos would brag about their membership in or connection with the Huks, or with the Sakdals or the Kalibapi (groups of "patriots" who were of considerable use to the Japenese). But as the months lengthened into years and the guerrillas became better organized and clearly more powerful, they gradually fell silent. Late in 1944 the Japanese at last faced up to what was taking place before them. They successively disarmed, then disbanded, the Constabulary—after which most of its members openly defected to the LGAF or other guerrilla organizations.

A policy of calculated frightfulness was impracticable for us. Terrorism alone will not cow people unless it is used without restraint, after the fashion of Stalin, Mao Tse-tung, and Adolf Hitler. Even then it does not cow them totally. Worse, it leaves behind a residue of ill will that destroys the possibility of winning *willing* support.[11] More fundamentally, any civilized guerrilla leader is unwilling to disgrace the principles he professes to represent; unless he is content to be a mere bandit himself, he will try to lift the reputation of his followers above that of mere pillagers and robbers.

Inevitably, then, I had to concern myself with lawmaking and law enforcement. This was no easy task. No code of law anywhere governs the activities of guerrillas, and where we were, there were no effective courts or judges either. As one writer sums it up, "We may define guerrilla law, in the last analysis, as the will of the sector commander, tempered by his private sense of right and wrong and his fear of later punishment."[12] I would add "and by what circumstances compel him to do." Some crimes of moderate seriousness in ordinary peacetime civilian society cannot be tolerated by guerrillas in wartime, while others that are even more serious in peacetime have to be overlooked or dealt with lightly during wars. As an example of the former, stealing from civilians—as both Huks and guerrilla gangs of the outlaw type often did—could not be tolerated in our LGAF forces if we expected civilians to support us. Most Filipinos are generous; if approached properly they freely gave much of what they had to deserving guerrillas. Thus to steal from them was both unconscionable in principle and idiotic in practice, since it would turn them from friends into enemies. Hence, looting was absolutely forbidden in LGAF territory.

Other tough practical considerations seriously affected the administration of justice too. We had no jails; we could not afford to waste time, men, food, and money paying jailers to look after prisoners; and nobody ever joined a guerrilla band because he wanted to guard prisoners anyway. Consequently, punishments for misdeeds had to assume forms other than confinement. For some minor offense a man might be punished by being put on KP or assigned to look after the horses, but for something serious there was usually little real choice between setting an accused free (with perhaps a stern lecture) and executing him.

Elmer Lear observes with some acerbity that every guerrilla leader said the administration of justice *in his area* was fair and regular, irregular and cruel only somewhere else. All I can reply is that I did what I thought was necessary but still could be called civilized.[13] Early on, I specified three offenses for which no excuse would be accepted and which would be punished by execution: looting, rape, and giving aid and comfort to the enemy. In 1942 I issued an undated directive titled "Military Regulations to Follow." It reminded officers and NCOs to keep a record of all volunteers who were to be discharged and to make sure that we kept their guns; to arrest anyone who actively opposed us; and to restore to their former positions any town officials who had been removed by the Japanese. Other provisions warned against plundering or mistreating civilians, and directed that every patrol had to be led either by an officer or a competent noncom. Our food was to be acquired through a purchasing agent and the seller given a U.S. credit slip redeemable after the war. Anyone not heeding the directive was threatened with a court-martial, flagrant violators with execution.

Such a list of regulations and the draconian punishments that could follow their violation may seem—as the formal recitation of the Articles of War often does to a U.S. Army inductee—like an endless litany of threats, failure to heed which will result in "death, or such other punishment as the court-martial may direct." In practice, there was less to worry about than met the eye. Rulers of all sorts discovered many centuries ago that it was often convenient to possess a vast array of laws commanding this and forbidding that, not to impose on everyone every day but to hold in reserve as a legal armory to which they might have recourse when it seemed necessary to make an example by "legally" getting rid of some troublesome person or "legally" exerting pressure on some group whose conduct or attitude the government wished to change.

Actually, I did not have a difficult time either developing a well-disciplined organization or earning the loyalty and cooperation of most of the civilian population in territory I controlled. Whenever I could, I talked to our men about the reasons for so many and such ominous-sounding regulations. I hoped thereby to elevate their conduct, improve our public reputation, and avoid having to mete out severe punishments for noncompliance. Usually such warnings were sufficient, but not always.

I never kept records of the uglier cases we had to deal with. In our century humanity seems to have been seized by a collective mania to preserve every imaginable bit of information and to publicize it without concern for its impact. Historians and media operatives have an occupational interest in furthering this practice; others seem to think that maximum publicity above virtually anything will, by some magical process, prove constructive and helpful in the long run. It is one of the derivatives of the faith of the eighteenth-century Enlightenment that knowledge is the path to virtue. I will say only that the dark side of human nature is evident enough without keeping careful records of all its manifestations. The long-standing rules of some governments about keeping much state business secret for fifty or 2 hundred years, until all those concerned with it have died, is based on a sound instinct. It avoids needless trouble.

As for the larger question of unpalatable deeds themselves I would have to agree with Cardinal Richelieu (d. 1642), no candidate for canonization but one of the ablest of French statesmen and a great state builder of early modern times. In politics, he said, it is sometimes necessary to do things that no honorable private individual would do willingly. Anyone unable to face up to this necessity, he thought, should stay out of public life.[14] The observation is equally applicable to guerrilla life.

Arming guerrillas sufficiently was never achieved until the American landings in 1945, but from the first it was always possible to find *some* weapons. Those of us who did not surrender to the Japanese usually brought a rifle or hand gun with us. Many Filipino families had guns of some sort which they would sell or give to USAFFE forces. Other weapons could be confiscated, or those stolen by bandits could be taken them back when we broke up outlaw gangs. Former outlaws who willingly joined our LGAF forces of course brought their weapons with them. Occasionally, wealthy Filipinos would give guerrillas money to buy guns. When our relations with the Philippine Constabulary grew increasingly cordial, they sometimes gave us guns or told us where we could find some.[15]

One problem we had with the minority of our guerrillas who had been full-time soldiers was that they became bored easily. Armies through the centuries have had to contend with this fact of military life. The usual response of leaders has been to find some activity or invent some make-work to keep the men busy and out of trouble. Men busied in these ways have usually resented what they perceived, often correctly, as useless labor imposed upon them when they could have spent the time more interestingly, or at least more restfully. One thing I sometimes did, and I am sure other guerrilla leaders did also, was to undertake small raids on Japanese patrols or installations, mostly to let my men work off surplus energy. A side benefit was that enemy weapons, ammunition, and supplies of various sorts could often be taken in such operations. For a time, a curious circular trade in such materiel grew up. The Japanese occupation forces acquired large quantities of military supplies from defeated American and Filipino troops in the first months of the war; guerrillas then raided Japanese outposts and took much of this booty back. Before long the imaginations of many guerrillas expanded. They attacked the Japanese not merely to get useful equipment but also clothes, shoes, wristwatches, and money. Then they and civilians even took to fishing the bodies of dead soldiers from rivers to retrieve personal belongings.[16]

In fact, however, more arms were acquired by simple salvage than by any other method. War is the supreme waster of resources as well as human lives. It did not take brigands, Huks, USAFFE guerrillas, or ordinary civilians long to realize that much of western and central Luzon, especially the Bataan peninsula, was strewn with the flotsam and jetsam of battle. All these groups, including my own, soon had agents scouring the battlefields to salvage anything of value. A common procedure was to look for anything white in the jungle. Often it proved to be the bleached bones of someone who had died in the early campaigns, especially on Bataan. Often there might be a gun or two and sometimes ammunition nearby. For many a poor Filipino family, scavenging for guns became a supplemental source of income when these weapons began to command high prices from guerrillas who happened to have some money. In a report to SWPA in 1944, before arms from Australia began to reach us by submarine, Capt. Wilbur Lage credited LGAF with 1,500 rifles and an undetermined number of small arms. Since his report did not include all our units, my own count of 3,000 rifles was closer to the actual number. Overall, we were approaching a level of armament that would make us a significant factor in real fighting if we could make contact with contingents of the U.S. Army.

Other supplies were secured in similar ways, but most of the time they were either contributed freely by civilians or purchased. The production, acquisition, and distribution of food and supplies was always more complex than might appear on the surface. If civilians contributed frequently, liberally, and willingly they thereby demonstrated that they were anti-Japanese, pro-American, and trustworthy. Meager donations given in a niggardly spirit seemed to show the reverse. But what should a truly pro-guerrilla family do when a mob of known or suspected bandits claimed to be guerrillas and demanded a contribution? or when the supplies requested seemed to have little military value? or if the Japanese were tightening up just then, making it dangerous to give anything to anyone who was not Nipponese? We guerrillas considered that we had a right to civilian support, since we were risking our lives against common enemies and of course could not operate without food and equipment. Yet civilians had only so much to give anyone; if pressed too hard they might starve. That was the primary reason for the decentralization of my whole command. My headquarters, the several area headquarters, and various LGAF squadrons all undertook frequent patrols and traveled about considerably to spread the burden of supporting us as equally as we could among all the Filipino families on whom we relied.

If what we needed was to be requisitioned, how was this to be done? A central command might have managed it and issued currency to pay the providers, but this process had little appeal without an organized central government to back it. Another possibility was to ask for or demand contributions in money and then simply buy what we needed. Still another was to leave methods to the discretion of local commanders, who would likely have a better idea than did central headquarters of what local people might expect and could tolerate. Some municipalities gave certain guerrilla groups lump sums at regular intervals; some landlords contributed to guerrillas as an "insurance policy" against assassination. The Huks wanted to use requisitioning and pressure as a way of systematically ruining the wealthy, but all the other guerrilla groups were pragmatists who would request, purchase, or simply seize whatever they needed from anyone. If a landlord was driven off his estate to the safety of Manila or elsewhere, guerrillas would sometimes keep his tenants working on his land and simply take the owner's usual share of the produce. Others encouraged loyal Filipinos in cities to farm small plots on abandoned plantations to feed both themselves and guerrillas, with the understanding that the lands would be given back to their original owners when the war was over. Most landowners in LGAF territory were absentees or people who had gone to Manila during the war. Their usual policy was to leave their own overseers in charge with instructions to cooperate with us.

We and the Japanese alike wracked our brains to devise ways to deny each other food and supplies, but neither of us enjoyed much success. Before the war a quasi-government agency operating much like a cooperative had purchased, transported, stored, marketed, and distributed peasants' rice. During the war the Japanese allowed the system to continue but watched over it closely and set its prices low enough that they were assured of getting all the rice they needed at bargain rates. All we could do was urge farmers to hold back some of their rice, both for patriotic reasons and because Japanese paper money was likely to become worthless. Since most Filipino peasants had tiny farms of three to five acres and marketed little rice at any time, they could usually hold back small amounts with minimal danger of being caught. Perhaps they thus prevented the shipment of surplus Philippine rice to Nipponese troops outside the Islands.

Those pinched hardest by the hoarding of rice were Filipino urbanites in meager circumstances, especially in Manila. The wealthy or the better placed could come out into the countryside to buy rice (usually at inflated prices), and absentee landlords could usually get some from their tenants, but even they found transporting the vital food back to Manila precarious. The Japanese had spies everywhere, and many a purchaser lost his precious rice when he ran into a roadblock abruptly thrown up by occupation troops.

Questions related to modes of payment for food were always knotty. I never had much money, and what I did get now and then was generally used to buy arms, shoes, clothing, and other "hard essentials." When I bought food, I tried to purchase fairly large amounts at once and pay for it with receipts that were really promissory notes, though of course the recipients and I both knew that these would be redeemable only if the United States won the war. The receipts ordinarily specified only the commodities purchased (ten kilos of rice, five chickens), not their monetary value. I did not keep formal records of such "sales," or of contributions either, because I thought it dangerous to write the names of benefactors in record books that might be seized by the enemy. If a civilian accepted a receipt of some sort and wanted to keep it in hope of post-war redemption, it was up to him to figure out how to conceal it: perhaps bury it in a glass jar or hide it in a bamboo tube.

Now and then I did issue a receipt for some trifling purchase such as a chicken or a couple of eggs, but the recipient in such a case was usually more interested in getting my autograph or just chatting for a few minutes than in the sale itself. People frequently brought us presents of some delicacy just to have an excuse to socialize, without expecting payment at all. On the whole, I believe I collected food with less trouble than most of my fellow guerrillas. Rice especially was plentiful nearby, and most local people supported us enthusiastically whether they were paid in American IOUs, Japanese invasion notes printed on cheap paper that lacked even serial numbers, or nothing at all.[17]

Our formal, regular supply system was more systematic than this. It was managed by "special agents" who had been appointed during my first weeks in Umingan in 1942, when far more men had volunteered to serve as guerrillas than I could possibly arm or find any regular use for. Because I did not want to turn away anyone who was eager to serve and who might be useful some day, I gave many of them official enlistment papers and such titles as special agent. They were authorized to spy and collect food for us, and told to return to their communities to pursue these vital activities under our direction. This arrangement kept the number of my regular troops small enough that we would not be an undue burden on peasant farmers, at the same time enabling me to build up a sizable body of reserves and sympathizers. Most were proud to be selected for these tasks and performed their duties faithfully.[18]

It may be wondered why, in the midst of a war in which we and the Japanese seldom showed each other any mercy, we did not emulate the mercenary captains of fifteenth- to seventeenth-century Europe who dealt with their supply problems crudely and directly: if the inhabitants of a given locality failed to provide stipulated amounts of food and other desired commodities by a certain time, the captain would turn his men loose to rape the women, torture the men, steal whatever they wanted, and often burn whatever was left. The last and most formidable such buccaneer, Albrecht Wallenstein (d. 1634), was especially ruthless and efficient. During the Thirty Years War (1618–48) he would draw up his army before the walls of a town and offer the local magistrates a deal: if they raised a huge sum of money, he would move his troops elsewhere (usually to repeat the performance); if not, he would quarter his men in the town and let them "take what they needed."

Considered abstractly, our LGAF forces and other guerrilla groups had sufficient physical force to do the same thing. But most guerrillas were operating in their home areas and under such a policy would have had to plunder and oppress their own friends, neighbors, and relatives. Moreover, conduct that might have been at least explicable if inflicted on enemies could not possibly be excusable if the victims were our own allies. Finally, such action would have been stupid, since we wanted to keep the Filipinos friendly rather than multiply enemies, of whom we had more than enough already.

As for the food we got from farmers, it was plain but nourishing and plentiful: rice mainly, supplemented with ground corn, squash, *camotes*, and sometimes chicken. Now and then there might be some beef as well. If a cow or carabao was killed, accidentally or on purpose, the event was sometimes followed by a general feast, since there was no refrigeration and meat spoils rapidly in the tropics. More often we cut the meat into strips and put it in the sun to dry and become jerky, which would keep for a long time. Thus, unlike my compatriots in the mountains, if I was ill it was from malaria or dysentery rather than a poor diet.

Chick Parsons's biographer says that some guerrilla outfits had well-trained doctors and nurses among their personnel and were able to establish hospitals that served both guerrillas and neighboring civilians, though he acknowledges that they usually lacked sufficient medicines or proper equipment.[19] Maybe such medical care existed somewhere in the Visayan Islands or elsewhere to the south, but the only place it could be found on Luzon to my knowledge was up north in Volckmann's organization. He ran a regular army camp with barracks, close-order drill, homemade uniforms, and a field hospital staffed by doctors, nurses, dentists, and seventy enlisted men who worked as aides.[20] Still, I had to wonder what sort of a "hospital" it actually was, since Volckmann once asked me if I could send him some soap, cornstarch, a toothbrush, and insulin.[21] Panlilio says the only doctor that Marking's guerrillas ever had was Marking himself; he had once taken a correspondence course in nursing and had passed on what little he had learned to her and a few of their men.[22] In the Fassoth camp Mrs. Catalina Fassoth—already a harried cook and housekeeper for dozens of starved and ailing Americans—had tried to care for the sick and the injured in elementary ways. And, as noted earlier, Mona Snyder and a Philippine witch doctor had once cared for me. All these varied cases were typical of "medical treatment" in our part of the world.

Around my own headquarters we treated ourselves most of the time. If anyone was too badly injured to do so, we took him to a local medic who was thought to be trustworthy. In almost every unit there would be somebody who knew at least one such practitioner, some of whom were as brave as any guerrilla. In Cabanatuan City, for instance, Drs. Antonio and Nicolas de Guzman, Pedro Jimenez, Eli Ballesteros, and Juan Lazaro, along with their wives and other family members, gave Capt. Juan Pajota and his men medical attention for thirty-two months at constant risk to their own lives. In December 1944, shortly before our raid on the Cabanatuan prisoner-of-war camp, Pajota persuaded still another doctor, Carlos Layug, and his wife, to be available to treat anticipated casualties from the impending action.[23]

Of the two commonest ailments in the Philippines, malaria never seemed to worry young Filipinos, since most of them were healthy and had been used to malaria since birth. Likewise, dysentery was a terrible scourge to Americans, but Filipinos seemed virtually immune to it.

Some guerrillas obviously hated the lives we led. Panlilio records that Marking had never wanted to be a guerrilla but became one out of a sense of duty, quickened by intense hatred of the Japanese. When things went badly, he would sometimes fall into furious rages, really semihysterical fits, in which he would denounce guerrilla life and threaten to leave all his followers so he could murder Japanese on his own, alone. Some of his men either caught the contagion or, succumbing to bravado or boredom, would play Russian roulette.[24] Charles Cushing plainly disliked the life and had contemplated surrendering to the enemy for some time before he did it. Robert Arnold, sick much of the time, perpetually chased by the Japanese, and often feeling abandoned or betrayed by his compatriots, thought guerrilla activity was useless and came to hate the life.[25] Donald Blackburn complained that the most onerous part of his existence was mere tedium, lying around for days with nothing to do. I don't think it is coincidental that all these people except Cushing spent most of their time isolated up in the mountains. Down on the fertile plains there were always lots of people around and usually some sort of activity taking place. I was miserable when I was ill, sometimes scared during dustups with enemies, periodically burdened by the responsibility I bore, and occasionally sickened by the frightful things that had to be done, but overall I did not dislike the life I led in those years.

The town of Umingan was my headquarters and the place to which I could usually retreat to safety if the Japanese embarked on one of their periodic efforts to put the heat on me, but I lived there only in a general sense. Actually, I managed my dominions in much the same fashion as did the kings of late medieval Europe. That is to say, I did not try to rule systematically like a master bureaucrat in a permanent office-residence, such as the American president from the White House or a ruler of Russia in the Kremlin. Instead I emulated Carlos I, Spain's last "medieval" king. Carlos (who was also Charles V, Holy Roman Emperor, 1519–56) traveled about his widely scattered dominions throughout his life, seldom staying more than two weeks in any one place, all in an effort to oversee everything personally, if casually.[26]

I always thought one of my main tasks was to bolster civilian morale, so as I moved from town to town I gave lots of speeches, talked to local people, dispensed what passed for justice, and took part in fiestas. On public occasions I thought it important to look as good as possible and to have my bodyguards also dress neatly and act circumspectly. Maybe we fooled ourselves and impressed nobody, but I don't believe it.

Every week or two I went off for a time to Cuyapo, Muñoz, Lupao, Rosales, or some other place ten to twenty-five miles distant, and now and then still farther afield. This unscheduled roaming kept people from learning too much about me and my movements, news that had a way of getting to the Japanese. On a typical jaunt I might spend a few days visiting, say, a squadron commanded by Jeremias Serafica. I would examine his roster of enlistees, inspect his troops, question him about any patrols he had recently undertaken, and perhaps accompany him on a patrol. Then we would talk over his problems and exchange information and advice. Often the visit would end with a feast, a dance, and some speeches in a nearby barrio. My travels allowed both my various units and civilians to see and talk to me with some regularity and to be reminded afresh that America was still in the war, unconquered. It was also useful to me to see in person how matters were proceeding away from headquarters, and for my officers and men to remain aware that I was keeping an eye on them.

Moving around did not present major problems. I did not need a lot of people with me, since my main task was to observe my units and keep from getting captured. I had an entourage of about fifty men whom I could summon quickly if they were needed, but I regularly traveled with only ten to fifteen—enough to ward off a Japanese patrol and get me a few miles to the next town or barrio where another squadron was stationed. Of course, once we got radio transmitters in mid-1944 and my most important task became the dispatch of information to Australia, I needed to do less wandering.

Security was less of a problem for me than for many others. The Japanese disliked going into the jungle at night so nocturnal ambushes were rare. In town an attempted enemy search would always awaken either people or dogs, so we were less concerned with security guards than many guerrilla outfits had to be. Now and then the Japanese, who usually knew in general where I was but never exactly, would move into an area in battalion strength and systematically comb the whole district for several days to see if they could flush me out. Their maneuvers were broad, general sweeps, often appearing to be field exercises for green troops fresh from Japan. If I happened to be close to Umingan on such an occasion, I would simply slip into town and stay out of sight in some private home until the Nips tired of looking for me. Lieutenant Doliente and his wife lived in town too, unmolested, and we both derived considerable perverse pleasure from being virtually under the noses of the Japanese while they vigorously searched the countryside for us.

Enemy operations of this sort were oddly different from our own in one respect. Most American and Filipino guerrillas tried to be quiet on patrols to avoid alerting foes and perhaps getting ambushed, though there were times, especially when we carried certain kinds of equipment, when silence was impossible. The Japanese, by contrast, were chronically noisy. We could often hear their conversations and their clanging equipment long before we encountered them. Why? I never knew exactly, but I suspected that they wanted us to hear them, that they thought (or hoped) we would then flee and leave them alone.

Much of our traveling was positively enjoyable. On one occasion I performed a wedding. The aspiring groom, a well-known Filipino guerrilla, feared for his own and his bride's safety if they were married in their town, and the priest he had asked to preside refused to come to the barrio the groom proposed. So the man came to me and said something like "You are the captain of our ship so you should be the one to marry us." After the ceremony there was a big party to celebrate the occasion. Years later I used to joke about my varied roles as quasi-feudal lord over my "subjects" in the land of the LGAF: "I've judged them, sentenced them, married them, and buried them."

What moved me a good deal more than this isolated wedding was the frequency with which pregnant peasant women would approach me shyly and ask if they might touch me; they hoped thereby to bear a "whiter" baby than would otherwise be the case. It is easy to laugh at such actions as both superstitious and trivial, but I never felt like laughing at the time. To have such obviously good women regard me with awe invariably made me feel both proud and humble.

If we came to a village where we intended to stay overnight, or if local authorities told us that a Japanese garrison had just left town, it was not hard to predict what would happen next. Somebody would rush out to greet us and give us some fruit and cakes. Others would come out to talk, ask some small favor, or just bask in the sunlight of celebrities. In a few minutes a small crowd would gather. Soon wine bottles would circulate, the conversation would grow animated, village belles would show up in twos and threes, somebody would find a guitar, and the older women would prepare a lavish dinner. After supper there would be more wine (*miding*, usually),[27] music, speeches, exchanges of mutual admiration, optimistic speculation about the war, and much dancing with the girls. When the festivities were over, villagers would give us their best living quarters for the night. I must admit that I thoroughly enjoyed being treated as the biggest dog in the neighborhood.[28]

Even such fiascos as my effort to organize a Philippine cavalry unit were not totally worthless, because local Filipinos derived much amusement from the whole endeavor. Many great soldiers have insisted that morale is more important in war than materiel. In our century one could immediately reinforce the point by citing the French collapse before Germany in 1940, the failure of the French colonial wars of 1946-58, and the American defeat in Vietnam. Certainly high morale is absolutely vital for success in partisan warfare.

In the general area of lightening one's cares by devising celebrations, Harry McKenzie was the unquestioned champion among us. Somehow he managed to discover a Swedish priest living in Carranglan, in the mountains northeast of us. Given that modern Sweden is one of the most secularized countries in the world, and that its predominant Christian church since the sixteenth century has been Lutheran, finding a Swedish Catholic priest in the mountains of Luzon was about as likely as finding a fan dancer in a convent. More to the point, at some time in the past the clergyman had laid in an ample supply of good liquor. Whenever he could find a plausible excuse, Harry would pay a visit to his new-found spiritual adviser and fill up on Spanish brandy.

Overall, I believe day-to-day life went somewhat more smoothly for me than for many other guerrilla leaders, though I would not push this claim unduly. I did have periodic cases of individual guerrillas shooting, robbing, or raping civilians, though no instance of a whole unit descending to such misconduct. Some of my officers were cocky and forgot that no guerrilla can ever afford to grow careless, with the result that one would now and then become too conspicuous, be picked up by the enemy, and usually tortured and killed. Since many human beings could not withstand determined Nipponese interrogation, if an officer was captured the rest of his outfit usually packed up hurriedly and moved away for a while.

Of all my officers, Federico Doliente, was the one I trusted the most in combat, but even he was once picked up by the enemy. That he not only survived his arrest but lived to foil his captors is a tribute to the man's practical intelligence, quick wits, and icy nerves. He told the Japanese he had quarreled with me, had left me in disgust, and was now ready to collaborate with them. Somehow they not only believed him but made him a local police chief. Regularly thereafter he fed them false information about my location and activities, which caused them to waste a lot of effort trying to find me. When one of his new employers' spies came to town to report, Doliente would question the man, treat him to a sumptuous dinner, and then take him on a short journey from which the agent would never return. Once when he was talking to a Japanese in his home, his small son suddenly came into the room carrying his father's .45. Though the Nipponese had trusted Doliente considerably their confidence was not boundless: they had never given him any gun, much less an American .45. Federico had to do a lot of fast talking about how essential it was for him to have procured such a weapon to protect himself and his family from the USAFFE guerrillas who hated him for having deserted them and who were now seeking any opportunity to kill him. Once more, the Japanese eventually swallowed the story. Lots of Filipinos are accomplished con artists. Doliente might have been national champion.

Federico wanted to desert his new employers and rejoin us in the field, but I was convinced that having a "mole" among our enemies was invaluable and so was able to persuade him to remain a "Japanese police chief."

Of all the activities in which we guerrillas engaged, much the most important was collecting intelligence. President Manuel Quezon was adamant that this should always be the main function of Filipino guerrillas. He had striven for many years to weld the disparate peoples of the Islands into a nation, and one of his greatest fears was that if different groups of them got to fighting Japanese, they would soon be fighting one another to punish domestic rivals for real and fancied wrongs. The result would be the undoing of much of his own life's work. General MacArthur also insisted upon the primacy of intelligence collection, for all sorts of commonsense reasons.[29] A band of guerrillas ambushing a dozen Japanese soldiers now and then would gratify the ambushers and delight Filipino civilians, but it could have no discernible effect on the eventual outcome of the war. Even supposing some guerrillas proved able to wrest control of some town from the Nipponese, what then? The enemy would simply bring reinforcements by sea, bomb or shell the town, land some troops, strengthen a local garrison, and retake the place at their leisure. Most likely they would then kill or torture a lot of civilians and hunt down the offending guerrillas with greater zeal than before. Meanwhile, neither guerrillas in the Islands nor Americans elsewhere could do anything about it until U.S. forces gradually grew strong enough to undertake an outright invasion of the archipelago. In 1942 that eventuality seemed dismally remote.

How much better to maintain a low profile, hoard our weapons and ammunition until we were more numerous and our proper objectives clearer, and then try to act decisively, a time that came, in fact, only when the Allied invasion was imminent. Meanwhile, however, we could collect information about enemy troop concentrations and movements, beach defenses, air base sites, and changes in his habits or morale. Such intelligence would surely be useful to MacArthur in planning and executing his island-hopping campaigns to the south and might well prove invaluable once the invasion of the Philippines actually began. It would also be extremely important then that most Filipino civilians be friendly toward American troops, and *that* would be a lot more likely if guerrilla activities had not brought mass Japanese reprisals down on them in the interim. It was also desirable to keep the enemy ignorant of guerrilla strength. Their estimates of our numbers were often wildly inaccurate, usually on the low side. If we avoided combat with them they would find it difficult to correct their misapprehensions.

A broader consideration, though Washington did not want to draw attention to it at the time, was that the highest levels in the British and American civilian and military establishments had decided to give primacy to the European war. Thus Washington wanted to keep Far Eastern activities from being publicized unduly.

Our job was to collect information, reassure the Filipino people, make plans, and stockpile resources for eventual all-out war there, but to do so unobtrusively until the European war was well in hand. A lot of small-scale but losing battles with the Japanese would, if publicized, get the whole American public excited about Pacific events and distract everybody from the first Allied objective: the defeat of Germany in Europe.

Response to SWPA's known desires on this score varied widely from one unit to another. Walter Cushing, who liked to ambush the Japanese (perhaps because he once did so with marked success in the first month of the war), abandoned the practice after the fall of Corregidor because the enemy then held some 40,000 American POWs against whom they could take reprisals.[30] Leyte's guerrillas, perpetually mired in intramural feuds, contented themselves with trying to make the interior of that island unsafe for the Japanese: to harass them sufficiently to confine them to a few coast towns but not goad them so much that they would land reinforcements and strengthen their garrisons.[31] Ed Ramsey instructed his subordinates to attack enemy patrols or otherwise badger them only when success was certain and reprisals against civilians unlikely.[32] That was roughly my policy, too, or at least my aspiration.

On Luzon the only major guerrilla organization that repeatedly ignored these wise guidelines was the Hunters. This outfit, which operated in the mountains east of and close to Manila, was more reckless than any other band of irregulars. Its members fought repeatedly among themselves and against their rivals, Marking's guerrillas, but especially against the Japanese. They once succeeded in ambushing a large Japanese convoy and killing 127 of the enemy. Of course, this got them much favorable publicity in Manila and stimulated their recruiting,[33] but they purchased such "victories" at a far higher price to themselves and to their civilian supporters than less openly agressive organizations had to pay.

Other outfits experimented with tactics that allowed them to feel as if they were doing something but, at the same time would not (they hoped) provoke major Japanese reprisals. Visayan guerrillas sometimes tried to work ambushes in reverse against the Japanese. Nothing delighted the invaders more than to set traps for guerrillas. If the Visayans got wind of one they would pretend to take the bait but would content themselves with firing a few shots from the underbrush until local civilians could flee into the hills. Then the guerrillas would withdraw and try to lead their Japanese pursuers into an ambush of their own.[34]

One of the most spectacular ambushes of Japanese by guerrillas was supposedly the work of a decidedly unorthodox American and his private army of Negritos. Of the many different peoples in the Philippines in the 1940s, the most primitive were the Negritos, shy pygmies seldom over four feet tall but fine hunters and fishermen. They were also good guides, scouts, and packers. If given guns, they would use them, but they really preferred to hunt and fight with bows and arrows. Sometime in their distant past they had learned how to make a fearsome double-barbed arrowhead that was notably effective for hunting. Its first barbs pointed away from the head; other barbs pointed in the opposite direction. Thus the arrow would penetrate far enough for the first barbs to become embedded, but the opposite barbs prevented it from going deep enough to be pulled out on the far side. Only surgery could remove such an arrow.[35] The Japanese especially feared these lethal weapons and hated the Negritos for using them.

American experiences with Negritos and opinions of them varied widely. I had none in my immediate outfit and had only occasional dealings with them. Cpl. Wilbur Jellison mistrusted them and once wrote to Thorp a long, semicoherent account of how some Negritos bought a rifle from a Sergeant Stafford, an American, then became dissatisfied with their pay as *cargadores*, and one dark night murdered Stafford with the new weapon.[36] Alfred Bruce wrote a lurid description of their unappealing side: according to him, when a Filipino accused of stealing carabaos was turned over to Negritos for punishment, the little tribesmen hacked the miscreant to pieces and thereafter embarked upon an orgy of superstitious barbarity that included cannibalism.[37]

Most other Americans had a much better opinion of Negritos, and some positively liked them. Doyle Decker deplored their dirtiness and a culinary unconcern that led them to regard anything that flew as "chicken," but he otherwise esteemed them as generous people, good travelers, and good companions.[38] Millard Hileman sometimes traded food with them, mostly rice for *camotes*, and often found them amusing individuals. When they brought him food, they wanted to eat their return rice right from the pot in which it had been cooked, especially savoring the crisp toasted rice that clung to the sides. Clinton Wolfe, an American fugitive who wore dentures, would sometimes take out his teeth and clack them together, to the Negritos' invariable amazement.[39]

The most enthusiastic admirer of Negritos was Henry Clay Conner, himself one of the strangest of all the Luzon guerrillas.

Conner lived among Negritos for nearly three years, during which he shared their existence and organized them into a personal army of several hundred men. He regarded them as ideal guerrillas. Not only were they enthusiastic fighters who hated the Japanese, but it was impossible to put spies among them because no other people looked like them. He thought they had much more intelligence than others gave them credit for, and said they were remarkably loyal to him once he learned their language and treated them as equals. Overall, their good qualities vastly outweighed their primitive habits and unconcern with sanitation.[40]

According to Conner, he once threatened to let his half-wild followers raid the lowlands. Word of this incited the Japanese to pursue them into the mountains, where an ambush had been prepared. While enemy soldiers wasted much machine gun ammunition firing at everything that moved, the nimble little Negritos skipped from one rock or tree to another, picking off individual Nips with rifles or arrows at considerable cost to their foes and none to themselves.[41]

I have always had misgivings about the accuracy of this tale. Conner himself was, at the very least, a memorable man, one of those complex, impulsive characters about whom colorful stories accumulate and circulate. In this instance, Conner says he was amazed at how readily a primitive people responded to organization; he attributed it to their desire to show the world what they could do after having been so long repressed. To me, this sounds like a typical case of an educated Occidental projecting his own state of mind onto primitive people of an entirely different culture. But whether this episode took place as he described it or not, there is no denying that the Negritos did fight enthusiastically on occasion.

A chronic problem that inhibited guerrilla projects everywhere was inadequate resources. Once on Mindanao, when some irregulars had the good luck to trap about a hundred Japanese in a stone schoolhouse, they lacked not merely the guns and ammunition to blast out their adversaries but even enough food for themselves to lay siege and starve out the enemy.[42]

I don't recall receiving any specific orders in 1942 or 1943 to lie low and avoid the Japanese, though mere common sense counseled that strategy most of the time. This was especially the case on Luzon, where there were more Japanese and more roads than on any other Philippine island, making it easier for the enemy to hunt us down and force combat on us. The Japanese attempted several major raids against LGAF units that their spy system had located. Occasionally, our counterintelligence warned us in time to move the targeted units to a quieter location until the Japanese maneuver was over; more often we were saved by our policy of moving at least once a week anyway. Sometimes enemy raids came only a day or two after we had shifted locales, and once or twice we had just begun to move when we were alerted that we needed to speed up our change of address because the Japanese were only one barrio behind. In 1943 they staged such a raid in embattled Tarlac at a time when our forces there were still so disorganized and inadequately equipped that the best they could do was resort to some hit-and-run delaying actions as they withdrew in all directions.

Not long afterward I was nearly caught in a Japanese raid. It was late January 1944, in the middle of the dry season. I had spent a week at Serafica's headquarters a few miles east of Cuyapo and intended to leave that evening to visit a generous financial supporter of Serafica's. In the social structure of the rural Philippines then he would have been roughly "upper middle class": that is, he owned considerable land that was worked by tenant farmers and hired hands, but he was not so wealthy that he could live at his leisure in Manila or some other city; he still had to work alongside his tenants and employees. Many of our officers were sons of men like him. Below him in the social scale were independent small farmers who owned a few acres, and below them were the tenant farmers. Most of our rank-and-file guerrilla soldiers came from these latter two groups. Atop the rural hierarchy were the *hacienderos*, or great landowners, who owned from half a dozen to scores of farms and might live either in a hacienda in the country or, more commonly in wartime, in a city home in Manila.

I was looking forward to visiting Serafica's friend, partly because he lived in "luxury"; he had a "real" house with wooden walls and floors and a corrugated steel roof rather than a nipa hut with the bamboo sides and floors and thatch roof we had grown used to. About suppertime, one of Serafica's runners came in with the news that several truckloads of Japanese had arrived in Cuyapo and would likely soon be searching for us. We decided to leave promptly to visit our friend, who lived perhaps ten miles away and probably outside the normal Japanese search area. We arrived uneventfully, stayed overnight, and were eating breakfast when another runner from Serafica brought word that additional truckloads of Japanese had arrived in Rosales and Guimba. Since these places were in opposite directions from where we were, it appeared that the enemy might well be sending troops into other surrounding towns as well and that a major sweep would soon be under way. Our host had a nice house perched on a little hill overlooking extensive rice paddies on every side. There was no cover and no escape route.

We packed up at once and set off to the east where in the distance trees lined a currently dry stream. We could at least hide there. When we got to the trees, several of Serafica's scouts who had accompanied us were sent off to barrios on either side to seek information. They reported none of the enemy nearby, so we set out along the stream bed toward Lupao. Along the way various villagers offered to go on ahead and seek news in other barrios. Soon they were back to report that the Japanese were indeed sending out patrols all over the area and that one of them was already searching the house where we had just spent the night. We moved rapidly to the next barrio, to be told that an enemy patrol was just then going through the one immediately behind us. So it went the rest of the day: we proceeded towards Lupao always about one barrio ahead of our pursuers. We knew this state of affairs had to end soon because the Japanese had a road block near the point where our dry stream bed crossed the main highway to Lupao. At last night came to our rescue. We were able to slip off in the dark, make our way back to Umingan, and get into my favorite "safe house" before daylight. There I stayed for the next few days while Japanese tramped all over the neighborhood asking everyone, "Where Rappham?" The query invariably delighted my men, who could never understand why the Nipponese had so much trouble pronouncing the letter L.

Sometimes I sent out patrols merely to let people know we were still around and able to act. Now and then one of them would run into a Japanese patrol, and a brief fight would ensue. Otherwise, I seldom sought contact with the enemy, though that was not always true of my Filipino lieutenants. Most of them were "tough hombres"; indeed, they would not have been any good as guerrillas had they not been tough, but they tended to become restless and did not relish long periods close to me where I could keep an eye on them. Out in the field with their own units they would sometimes raid a garrison in some pro-Japanese town, such as San José or Bongabon in Nueva Ecija, just to have something interesting to do.

Problems of this sort were rarer than one might suppose, though, thanks to the climate of the Philippines. Weather on Luzon consisted of two seasons: too wet and too dry. All our operations were heavily influenced by whichever dispensation we happened to be in. At times during the wet season the rain would pour down relentlessly for a week to ten days without ever stopping. Not only did this make life dismally boring for the duration of the "shower"; it created innumerable pools of water and vast seas of mud. When we considered it unsafe to travel openly on the roads, we would often walk along the top of the dikes that separated the rice fields, and in the wet season these became so slick and slithery that it was close to impossible to avoid repeatedly falling into the paddies. Still, we generally felt safer during the rainy season because the Japanese disliked the wet and the mud as much as we did and seldom tried to make any trouble for us then. Moreover, if we did think it necessary to move in the middle of a rainstorm, it was hard for anyone to see us. Once in a while the enemy tried to surprise us with a raid during a monsoon, but nature usually turned such efforts into fiascos.

During the dry season, by contrast, we and the Japanese could both move around easily, and once the rice was harvested and the paddies dried out, everybody could see what was going on for miles around. This compelled both sides to travel mostly at night and provided many more opportunities for each side to try to raid or ambush the other.

Early in the war we spent as much time fighting the Huks and various pro-Japanese individuals and groups as we did combatting the Japanese themselves.[43] This problem was never entirely resolved, but it declined markedly in importance in 1943 and thereafter as many of the collaborators were silenced, others left the area, and still others covertly changed sides. In the first year or more of the war, though, these groups were not trivial foes. They were organized into various parties, some of which had already been in existence for several years before the war.

The Sakdalistas were one such association. Originally discontented farmers with the same sort of grievances as those who supported the Huks,[44] the Sakdals in the 1930s came under the leadership of Benigno Ramos, a disgruntled Tagalog poet who hated the flashy Manuel Quezon and the grafters who surrounded him in Manila. Ramos denounced government corruption, demanded the abolition of taxes, urged distribution of lands to the peasants, and called for immediate and complete independence from the United States. After a brief uprising in 1935 his followers were repressed harshly by Quezon. Deeply embittered, Ramos fled to Japan, where he gave his new friends Sakdalista membership lists. Once in the Philippines, the Japanese were able to compel those listed to help them under threat of revealing their names to USAFFE guerrillas. In the first days of the war Ramos and his followers aided the invaders considerably by cutting communications in Luzon behind Allied lines.[45] Later they acted as spies for the conquerors, pointing out prewar American store-houses, pro-Americans in the military police, Filipino escapees from Japanese prison camps, anti-Japanese civilians who possessed fire-arms, and the like.[46] Gradually, these people came to be called Ganaps, a general term for anyone who was pro-Japanese.

Closely akin to the Sakdalistas were the Kalibapi, a pseudo-patriotic organization put together at the behest of the Japanese to serve José Laurel's puppet "Philippine Republic." By 1943–44 its membership may have reached 400,000. The movement was headed by Benigno Aquino, a fiery pro-Japanese orator and prewar Common-wealth official who was thought by the Japanese to be a more im-pressive leader than Ramos.[47] Nominally, the Kalibapi constituted a spying service for the Japanese of a type common in many twentieth-century dictatorships: the leader of a neighborhood group is made re-sponsible for watching ten households and reporting any suspicious words or actions to his superior, who supervises ten larger groups and reports to *his* superior, who presides over ten still larger groups, and so on. In the LGAF we quickly reached "understandings" with the Kalibapi, just as we did with the Philippine Constabulary, and they often became quite useful to us. Sometimes they were almost laugh-able as well. For instance, civilians in the Kalibapi were supposed to set out guards at night to inform the Japanese if any guerrillas were at large; in fact, the guards kept *us* apprised of nocturnal adventurers and so saved us the trouble of putting out guards of our own.

Rather different were the Makapili, simple, out-and-out indi-vidual collaborators with the Japanese. Organized late in the war by Gen. Artemio Ricarte and several other prominent pro-Japanese Fili-pinos, they made no pretense to be Philippine patriots.[48] Their activi-ties included disguising themselves from head to foot in flowing robes with only slits cut for eye-holes. Thus safely garbed, they pub-licly pointed out to their Nipponese masters any guerrillas or no-tably pro-American Filipinos, who were then usually forced to dig their own graves before being bayoneted to death. The Japanese eventually issued rifles to the Makapili hoping to use them as sol-diers to resist the American reinvasion of the Philippines. I never ac-tually saw any hooded Makapili but heard much about them, and they were active for a time in Tarlac. Understandably, they terrified many Filipinos, though overall they accomplished little because per-haps no more than 5,000 Filipinos ever joined up, and the Japanese began to arm them only a month before the American invasion.[49]

Finally, the Japanese pressured General Capinpin and General Francisco (chief of the Philippine Constabulary) to appeal to Filipino soldiers and civilians alike to recognize the Nipponese conquest and cooperate in the formation of the new "Greater East Asia Co-Prosperity Sphere."[50] They also tried to indoctrinate Filipino soldiers captured after the fall of Bataan and use them to infiltrate guerilla groups. This effort enjoyed some success; it was probably one of its graduates who managed to penetrate Anderson's unit in November 1943. One of Andy's officers had made contact with a man who said General MacArthur had sent him to coordinate the activities of various intelligence gatherers in Manila. He displayed extensive knowledge of the situations of all the guerrillas on Luzon and seemed zealously anti-Japanese. Anderson was impressed and took him in. Before long the fellow was seized by the Japanese, who, he said later, had tortured him until he gave them information about Anderson's outfit, plans, and prospects. Andy never did find out for sure who the man was, who he was working for, whether or not he had really been tortured by the Nips, or how he had previously managed to live grandly without visible income. Nonetheless, to be on the safe side Anderson felt compelled to reorganize his own intelligence apparatus and to become considerably more wary thereafter.[51]

By the turn of 1944 I was the real ruler of much of Nueva Ecija and Pangasinan in the sense that I had greater influence on day-to-day events there than did either the Japanese army or local officials. Yet my power had definite, albeit intangible, limits. I might dominate the northern half of the central plain of Luzon but I certainly did not control the southern half. Tarlac was part of my LGAF command, but my hold there was clearly less secure than in Pangasinan and Nueva Ecija. As in medieval Europe, there were no surveyed borders anywhere. One "realm" merely extended outward indefinitely until it first merged with and then was superseded by another center of "authority."

Of course, one of the most obvious tasks of any serious guerrilla was to maintain the loyalty that so many Filipinos already felt for us. I have already described my efforts toward this end, but there is indeed more than one way to skin a cat. Other guerrillas sometimes won and kept the affection and support of Filipinos by means far different from any that ever occurred to me. One such was Clay Conner. Doyle Decker, who stayed with him throughout the war and knew him well, said Conner had a dual personality and character. Perhaps this was due, in part anyway, to his having undergone the same harrowing experience as Leon Beck: being abandoned to die in the jungle by most of the companions with whom he had escaped from Bataan. Only one man in the party, Frank Gyovai, had stayed with Conner; he saved his life and remained with him for the rest of the war.[52] Robert Mailheau, who was also close to Conner throughout the war, has called him, variously, a salesman, a slicker, one of the most unselfish persons he had ever seen, and a man for whom he had great respect.[53] Conner had a religious streak in his complicated makeup too, and sometimes he wrote emotional, patriotic poetry. Always, he seems to have felt deeply grateful to the Filipinos who fed, supplied, and hid him and his followers.[54] Typical of his quixotic character, Conner usually regarded Ramsey as his superior officer, even though Ed was down near Manila much of the time, and Conner, far away in Tarlac, generally did as he pleased.

Before the war Mailheau had been stationed at Clark Field. One of his favorite diversions then had been to rent a horse, ride off into the mountains, and trade various commodities from the Post Exchange for fruit or homemade jewelry and the like offered by the Negritos. He had thus become well acquainted with them.[55] Whether for this reason or some other, he and Conner and their associates Gyovai and Decker simply moved in with the Negritos in 1942. Conner called the whole experience one of the great adventures of his life.[56]

Shrewd and persuasive, Conner was above all a man receptive to unusual ideas. As American prospects began to look hopelessly bleak to him—in part, at least, because he and his companions were so isolated that they heard only Japanese war news—he proposed to the others one day that he surrender to the Japanese just to see how they would treat an American. If they dealt with him decently, he promised to get word back to his buddies so they might surrender too. Mailheau, who had survived the Death March and distrusted all Japanese, says that he and the other Americans talked Conner out of the scheme.[57] But Conner remained sunk in gloom, convinced that the war would last for many years yet and that they could survive only by staying in the jungle. But life there would be possible only if they had absolutely loyal friends bound to them by the closest of ties. So, to save his own life and that of his American friends, he offered to marry the sister of Kodario Laxamana, the chief of the Negrito tribe they were living with. The Negritos felt honored and were jubilant. The wedding took place, ties with Negrito friends and allies were strengthened, the new wife bore Conner a son, and the four Americans survived the war.

In old folktales, all concerned would then have lived happily ever after. In this instance, that was not quite the outcome. When the U.S. invasion force landed in 1945 and American guerrillas rushed off to join them, Conner went with the rest. The Negritos, who had been loyal to Americans throughout, looked sorrowful—or so it seemed to Doyle Decker.[58]

Conner's desertion of his pygmy wife was not in itself so remarkable, for a fair number of American guerrillas deserted Filipina wives or girlfriends at the end of the war and returned to the states to live "normal" lives. The genuinely intriguing feature of the whole episode was that Conner, mercurial as ever, went back to Luzon in the early 1960s, found his erstwhile brother-in-law Kodario, and gave him a considerable sum of money to support and educate the son borne to Kodario's sister (now dead) and Clay Conner.[59]

— 7 —
Chronic Discord

In a famous passage in *Leviathan,* the seventeenth-century English philosopher Thomas Hobbes described the State of Nature as a realm where life was "solitary, poor, nasty, brutish, and short." In 1942, life in central Luzon fit that description closely save only for "solitary." It was not solitary at all. Luzon was inhabited by numerous Filipino farmers and their families, Japanese occupation troops, American and Filipino escapees from Bataan, Corregidor, and elsewhere, Allied soldiers who had never surrendered, aspiring guerrillas, Communist guerrillas, and mere roving gangs of outlaws. The same was true nearly everywhere else in the archipelago. Within six months to a year every sizable Philippine island had from one to a dozen guerrilla "armies." Some such bands were led by Americans, but an overwhelming majority in all of them were Filipinos whose motives were varied: hatred of the Japanese enemy, a sense of duty, personal ambition, pursuit of private grudges, a desire to plunder, sheer fear, or some combination of these.

Unhappily, all such groups were vexed by internal turmoil and were at odds with other groups, for the human propensity to quarrel with and try to dominate others is universal. Further, all Philippine guerrillas were fed and supplied by native farmers and so were convinced that they had to defend their sources of sustenance against potential rivals.[1] Finally, guerrilla activity is by nature rent with factionalism. It ordinarily develops slowly and unevenly. Considerable time is needed to organize units, establish regular procedures in them, and develop a sense of unity and loyalty among their members. Communications between different groups are often poor. In the Philippines, geographical barriers separated most groups from most others, and different bands and their leaders often had quite different ultimate objectives.

In this atmosphere quarrels over jurisdiction, prestige, food, and a thousand other matters became endemic. Units would rise, thrive briefly, then collapse with the death of their leaders. Sometimes they were replaced by new bands, sometimes not. Many small guerrilla gangs of the outlaw sort were forcibly suppressed by organizations like my own. Often, many of their surviving members were co-opted into stronger organizations. Often they consolidated willingly, even eagerly. All such groups wanted to harass the Japanese in some way, but in 1942 most were so weak that their real problem was to keep the enemy from harassing them.

Many Filipinos, like most of us, were simply dazed for a time by the magnitude of the American defeats and the cruel aftermath for both peoples. For Americans the discomfort, danger, and sheer squalor of life were extremely disheartening. Most of us were physically sick much of the time. Many were semistarved, and others felt so because even when Filipino food was plentiful and tasty, it was less "solid" and seemed less nourishing than the "meat and potatoes" meals they were used to. Many had only tattered remnants of GI clothing; some were barefoot. It was wet and hot in the lowland jungle, wet and cold in the mountains. Everybody's nerves were on edge from fear of capture by the Japanese or from frightful memories of things seen and endured during the battle for Bataan, on the Death March, or in the jungle afterward. Leon Beck, for instance, had undergone the shattering experience of listening to one member of his escape party urge the others to leave him in the jungle to die because he was too sick to travel at their accustomed pace.[2] Another U.S. escapee acknowledges that when an American soldier met his group in the jungle and asked to join them, they drove him off by threatening to shoot him.[3] Even after guerrilla bands were organized, many of them had to be on the move almost constantly because they were not yet well known or accepted in a given community and were too weak to do anything but try to hide from the enemy.

Long afterward, Alfred Bruce remarked that these circumstances quickly peeled away the veneer of soft comforts that characterize modern American civilian life, "leaving the flint-like hardness of the true American soldier."[4] More accurately, these conditions produced selfishness,[5] pessimism, despondency, and listlessness among some; a grim determination to avenge themselves on the Japanese in others; and increased testiness and unreliability on the part of nearly everyone.[6] According to Donald Blackburn, he and Volckmann kept their balance in the mountains of northern Luzon by sheer hard labor, notably chopping wood.[7] Ed Ramsey says he did not expect to survive the war but maintained his sanity by plunging into the endless work of organizing resistance to the enemy and maintaining his faith that somehow General MacArthur would get him through.[8] Ray Hunt did not expect to survive the war either, but he was a man of natural high spirits who took adversity in stride and so did not succumb to gloom and despair.[9] As for me, I had no particular reason to expect that I would live through the war, but except for that once when I begged to be allowed to die, I just *assumed* I would survive.

In our stressful circumstances, small matters often provoked major temperamental outbursts. Once when Colonel Calyer came into his room and found two enlisted men, Raymond Herbert and Johnny Johns, sitting on his bed picking off crab lice, he flew into a memorable rage.[10] When Leon Beck caught the man who had once wanted to abandon him in the jungle now sleeping on his blanket, a major row followed. Beck grabbed his rifle, but others intervened and wrestled the gun from him, tearing a gash in his hand in the process. In the same group merely the way a certain man smoked cigarettes irritated everyone else intensely.[11] Millard Hileman, an enlisted man in the 698th Ordnance who escaped with several others after the fall of Bataan, toyed with the idea of becoming a guerrilla but eventually surrendered to the Japanese instead. He may have been exceptionally touchy, or perhaps he was just more candid than most; either way, he relates numerous instances of his snarling quarrels with Bill Main and Paul Vacher. The trio had been friends in peacetime but got on each other's nerves constantly when they were fellow fugitives in Luzon's jungles. Hileman admits that he periodically hated them and resented the fact that Main had greater resistance to disease than he did. He also mistrusted the Filipinos who risked their lives to bring him food and medicine, then realized the absurdity and unworthiness of such an attitude and was filled with remorse.[12] Volckmann and Blackburn were personal friends as well as close associates, but even they irritated each other and fell out periodically.[13] Nobody with whom I was associated ever flew into wild rages, though it was not uncommon for somebody to get drunk to let off steam. As for me, I traveled around a lot, saw many different people regularly, and so was buoyed up. It was those who were holed up alone back in the mountains who seemed most susceptible to the strain.

Much of the trouble between guerrilla units resulted from personal animosities, rivalries, and idiosyncrasies. Hostility between two all-Filipino groups often built on some prewar enmity between their leaders. Among Americans there was considerable ill feeling between those who wanted to organize active guerrilla resistance and others who wanted merely to wait out the war quietly.[14] Romantic attachments sometimes caused trouble: leaders and whole units were betrayed to rival units or to the Japanese by "other women," outraged wives, vengeful husbands, or disgruntled boyfriends.[15] Finally, the old regular army contained many rough characters who may have been capable soldiers when organized and disciplined but were unreliable and hard to get along with once they escaped the tutelage of superiors. Some were merely troublesome, such as one known as "Major Bottle," whose "supreme qualification was his ability to empty bottles of whiskey."[16]

Some Americans and some Filipinos, all far more important than mere incompetents like "Major Bottle," were cruel, sinister men. When Japan conquered the Philippines, the capacity of native authorities to maintain ordinary law and order was much diminished. This situation was extremely tempting to certain Filipinos with criminal tendencies, who were not minded to heed Japanese authority in any case. Many of these outlaw types began to commit crimes of every sort, mostly against their own people. Many of them sought material gain, or wanted to defy hated authority, or just liked to show everyone how tough they were. Worse, some were true monsters. In Illocos Norte, Capt. Emilio Escobar and his guerrilla band raided villages, robbed and plundered, kidnapped girls, committed numberless horrifying personal crimes, and are thought to have murdered some three to four thousand civilians. So generally hated was Escobar that in the battle for Bessang Pass in the spring of 1945, most of his men were killed by other guerrillas rather than by the Japanese.[17]

Some Americans were nearly as savage and just as troublesome. One officer, not content with killing a suspected collaborator with the Japanese, also carried off the best-looking women in the culprit's family.[18] On the island of Cebu, Col. James Cushing's guerrilla unit was disgraced by the conduct of one of his subordinates, Capt. Harry Fenton. Fenton's brutality and dissoluteness led to a series of plots, arrests, and executions that destroyed the morale of the whole outfit.[19]

Most devastating was the savagery of the Japanese. The degree to which they raped and otherwise brutalized legions of women led to the frequent remark that the Spaniards had built churches in the Philippines, the Americans had built schools, and the Japanese had built brothels. They also arrested, maimed, and murdered Filipinos by the tens of thousands and did so in myriad horrible ways: whipping them, starving them, setting fire to the hair in their armpits, pulling out their fingernails, giving them showers of boiling water, abusing and killing their children in front of them, and chaining them to slabs of iron in the burning midday sun so that they slowly fried to death. Perhaps most bestial of all, they forced the stomachs of men and women full of water until they were about to burst, then stomped on the victims until water spurted from all their bodily orifices.[20]

Such actions poisoned the whole atmosphere in the wartime Philippines and provoked countercruelty on the part of both Filipinos and Americans. When one of Ralph Praeger's lieutenants in the north discovered who had been responsible for Praeger's death, he rounded up all the pro-Japanese local officials and killed almost everyone involved. A Filipino priest admitted to an American friend that he had killed a countryman who was an informer for the Japanese even though he wasn't sure such action could be reconciled with the teachings of his church.[21] In 1942 a Japanese patrol was ambushed by a small band of Filipino guerrillas, led by a Chinese woman who had been maimed by the Japanese. She gained her revenge by supervising the killing of seventeen of the eighteen Japanese soldiers ambushed.[22] In 1944 a Japanese ship was sunk near a small offshore island. Those aboard tried to swim ashore. American officers ordered Filipino guerrillas to take as many prisoners as possible so they could be interrogated, but the Filipinos grabbed their bolos, rushed out in boats, and beheaded most of the Japanese before they could get ashore.[23]

Another source of trouble, within and between guerrilla units, was bickering over rank. To people who have only a casual interest in the theatrical world, the spectacle of actors and actresses wrangling bitterly over top billing seems petty and childish, indicative of bloated egos and withered brains. To many civilians, squabbles over rank among professional military people looks much the same. But, as a Marxist might say, this is "objectively untrue." Armies exist to fight wars. In war some men must send others to their deaths, and the men so sent must go without question. If they refuse, the army soon becomes hopelessly ineffectual. Nobody has ever figured out an entirely satisfactory way to deal with this circumstance, but requiring men of lower rank to obey orders from those of higher rank is the least troublesome procedure developed so far. Very early in my guerrilla career it became evident to me that I needed rank if I expected my orders to be obeyed; it was not mere egoism that caused me to declare myself a "major" in mid-1942. I elevated Sergeant Short to lieutenant in September of that year for the same reason. The higher rank would improve his chances of clearing up gangs of outlaws around Pantabangan.[24] Another consideration obtained as well: as the plain-spoken Leon Beck put it, in the eyes of ordinary Filipinos anybody as exalted as a colonel was "next to Jesus Christ."[25]

One thing I will say for myself in this connection is that I retained a sense of moderation. The highest promotion I bestowed on anybody in LGAF was major, my own rank, and at the end of the war none of my officers were reduced in rank by American authorities. This was true of few other organizations; in most, jokes circulated about having "more colonels on the loose than we had privates,"[26] or so many high dignitaries in "our outfit" that it took four colonels to sign one letter.[27] Many enlisted men and lower ranking officers did not hide their disdain for the ordinary privileges of rank when all of us were out in the jungle. Donald Blackburn, then a lieutenant, took an immediate dislike to Colonel Thorp because the latter seemed to him cold, brusque, arrogant, and condescending.[28] Hileman says he was on the brink of joining Merrill and Calyer's guerrillas but found the two colonels so cool and haughty that he decided, "To hell with guerrilla life."[29]

Even more damaging than disagreements and feuds inside guerrilla organizations were those between rival outfits. Major Bernard L. Anderson was not at all a quarrelsome man by nature, yet he was at least peripherally involved in many of the squabbles that went on all over Luzon throughout the war. Forty years after the events he attributed most of the trouble to the circumstances of our existence. Colonel Thorp had tried to assign specific areas to certain individuals, but he had little real control over any of us once we were over the nearest hill and out of sight. Moreover, he was captured by the Japanese within a few months. After that, all of us just staked out our claims to what seemed to us suitable areas, even though these usually overlapped the claims of others. To protect our turf, most of us kept informants in the domains of our neighbors without telling them so. This anarchic situation was constantly aggravated by the paucity of reliable communications at any time before mid-1944. Anderson said that when he was able to sit down and talk to another American guerrilla face to face they could usually settle their mutual problems in half an hour, but this seldom happened. Most messages went by runners, a hit-or-miss procedure at best—and always slow.[30]

In the main I agree with Andy; my own lengthy negotiations with Ed Ramsey in 1943 support his general contention. But lack of communication was not the only cause of trouble. The fiercest feud between rival guerrilla groups on the whole island of Luzon was between the Hunters and Marking's guerrillas, who operated very close together near Manila yet hated each other so intensely that gun-fights, kidnapping, and even executions frequently followed the desertion of disgruntled individuals from one group to the other. Perhaps the most basic source of their problems was social. The Hunters were very young, most of them in their teens or early twenties. A high proportion came from the Philippine upper class or prosperous middle class; and many had been students in ROTC programs when the war began. Most of Marking's followers were older men from lower social strata. Each group regarded the other with undisguised contempt. Because both established their first base camps in the mountains of Rizal province, they drew supplies and support from the same civilians, used the same trails to transport these commodities up from the lowlands, tried to recruit in the same area, killed each other's cattle for food, listened to the same civilians who ran to them with complaints, and were rivals for the same girls.[31] An American officer says that the leader of the Hunters, Eleuterio "Terry" Adeviso, once tried to persuade him to take a unit of the Hunters, raid Marking's camp, and wipe out the whole Marking leadership.[32]

Nothing more complex than personal ambition and mutual hatreds caused much trouble in other parts of the island as well. Up in Illocos Norte there was a troop of irregulars commanded by a former Brooklyn policeman, John O'Day. I saw O'Day once and thought him a decidedly peculiar fellow. His main interest seemed to be pursuit of a vendetta with another group headed by Capt. Fermin Bueno. The feud was resolved only when O'Day raided Bueno's camp, captured Bueno and some of his men, and had them flogged. Then Bueno and some of his lieutenants mysteriously disappeared, after which the rest of his men joined O'Day's outfit from abject fear.[33] Also in the north Walter Cushing, the most flamboyant of the three Cushing brothers, got a few of his miners together and joined forces with Lt. Robert Arnold and thirty American soldiers who had been cut off when the Japanese first landed in December 1941. Arnold trained Cushing's men, and the two contingents cooperated in the highly successful ambush of a Japanese truck convoy. Afterward, Cushing claimed all the credit for the operation and commandeered Arnold's men for good measure. The outraged Arnold left him and joined the outfit of Capt. Guillermo Nakar, one of the earliest guerrilla chieftains to establish himself in northern Luzon.[34]

It is tempting to ascribe some of this incessant squabbling to ignorance of the facts in Australia, since writings emanating from

MacArthur's headquarters as late as October 26, 1944—less than three months before the American invasion of Luzon—make it clear that SWPA headquarters still had only hazy impressions about what was going on in Luzon.[35] But SWPA had established both radio and submarine contact with the southern Philippine islands long before doing so with us, yet internecine animosities and fighting remained as common in the south as on Luzon. From the island of Negros a Colonel Abcede tried to extend his authority to other islands. On Leyte there were usually more than half a dozen mutually hostile groups, the most important of them led by Lt. Col. Ruperto Kangleon and Brig. Gen. Blas E. Miranda. When Col. Wendell Fertig, who commanded the Tenth Military District (Mindanao), and Col. Macario Peralta, who commanded the Sixth (Panay), got permission from SWPA to organize guerrillas on nearby islands as well, each laid claim to Leyte, Peralta backing Miranda and Fertig supporting Kangleon. The upshot was that Kangleon and Miranda each regarded the other as a usurper. They eventually fought a pitched battle in which two hundred men died. Miranda was routed and many of his supporters went over to Kangleon.[36] Meanwhile, Fertig had plenty of trouble at "home," where Luis Morgan, his nominal subordinate, was plotting to supplant him. Fertig finally got rid of his rival by persuading Lt. Samuel Grashio, an American pilot who had escaped from the Davao prison camp, to lure Morgan to Australia with him via submarine.[37] Fertig got on badly with two of his other lieutenants as well, Capts. Ernest McClish and Clyde Childress. They thought him paranoid and consumed with personal ambition, not to speak of ungrateful and discourteous to them after they had made it possible for him to move his headquarters to a safe location on the eastern part of the island.[38]

Given this general atmosphere, which extended from north Luzon to southern Mindanao, it was surely inevitable that strong or merely ambitious leaders should strive to assert their authority over their contentious colleagues and establish larger, more centralized organizations. Thorp had assumed a semblance of authority over Luzon guerrillas until his capture in late October 1942. Colonel Gyles Merrill had sent around a circular letter to all American officers in rest camps such as Fassoth's, directing them to report for guerrilla duty if they were physically able, but few had done so, and Merrill soon consented to allow his own small following to become part of Thorp's larger domain.[39] I replied dutifully to Thorp's and Merrill's occasional directives but otherwise did nothing at all.

It was a tactic I would employ regularly with aspiring empire builders thereafter, as my dealings with Cols. Martin Moses and Arthur Noble demonstrate. They had escaped from Bataan, spent some time in the Fassoth Camp, and then headed north, stopping briefly in my camp. Though it did not seem to me that they had any clear intention of undertaking guerrilla activity, they soon did begin to organize in the north. Supposedly, they eventually assembled some 6,000 volunteers in a ragtag force armed mainly with machetes.[40] Supposedly, also, they sabotaged the Japanese industriously and seized impressive stocks of enemy arms and ammunition. But one wonders. Guerrilla numbers were notoriously elastic, always depending on whether the totals referred to active, full-time resisters, occasional helpers, or mere sympathizers. Moreover, if so many Japanese arms were seized, why did most of Moses's guerrillas still fight with machetes? In any case, Moses and Noble were like Merrill in one respect: they were expansionists. In October 1942, Moses directed me to proceed to his headquarters for a conference. At that time I was planning to attend a conference called by Thorp, so I sent Harry McKenzie. When Moses expressed his desire to incorporate the LGAF into his command, I replied evasively that the LGAF was still under the command of Colonel Thorp and that he and I deemed it best to continue that association. Not wishing to add to my troubles, however, I and assured Moses that I desired good relations with the North Luzon Command and that he (Moses) could always count on full cooperation from the LGAF. There the matter stood for several months.

Following the capture of Thorp in October, Capt. Joseph Barker assumed command of Thorp's shadowy realm. When Barker himself was seized by the enemy on January 14, 1943, and the whole paper edifice collapsed, Maj. Edwin Ramsey at once proclaimed himself Thorp's heir. Ramsey was both ambitious and persuasive.[41] Arriving at the Fassoth camp July 5, 1942, he had soon quarreled with the Fassoth brothers over his attempt to sign up their "guests" for his projected guerrilla outfit. He finally induced forty-three of them to promise to join him. He also worked hard to enlist Cpl. John Boone, who had assembled a small group of his own. Finally, he created a unit near Orani in northern Bataan. Among its members were Pierce Wade and Frank Gyovai, with Lt. Clay Conner as commander, but it was barely organized when the Japanese broke it up.[42] Ramsey and Conner then tried to reorganize near Olongapo, but the Japanese routed them again in August. Undiscouraged by these setbacks, in

January 1943 Ramsey simply *asserted* his authority over most of Luzon, and in his book he wrote of his plans, orders, and directives as if everyone had accepted all his claims without demur.[43] I negotiated amicably with Ed some months after this but ended, like most others, by paying little attention to him.

One who did, however, was Major Anderson. He and Ramsey did not get along well, and during much of 1943 they carried on an intermittent exchange of assertions and directives about who was rightfully the supreme commander on Luzon. This worried Alejo Santos a good deal because he repeatedly received conflicting orders from Ed and Andy and, being a conscientious sort himself, feared that the Huks and other troublemakers would exploit the division to their own advantage.[44] John Boone was at least equally perplexed, since he was receiving the same contradictory orders plus an additional array from Colonel Merrill, who still reasserted his own evanescent pretensions from time to time.[45] Ultimately, nothing serious came of the feud. Anderson was never a "good hater," and since he seldom stirred from his mountain stronghold, which was both distant from the rest of us and difficult to find, he could not control others effectively. Ramsey soon became preoccupied with other matters, and by 1944 their whole "struggle" had evaporated.

A more persistent sort was Colonel Russell Volckmann. He and his sidekick Lt. Donald Blackburn, like Moses and Noble, had come north late in the summer of 1942. They stopped at my camp for a few days. Since they were unarmed, I gave them a couple of rifles when they resumed their journey. Both of them say in their books that my camp was better organized than others they had seen. Several months later it became apparent that Volckmann himself was energetic, ambitious, and possessed of exceptional talent for recruitment and organization. Back in August I had guessed that he and Blackburn were no more anxious to undertake serious guerrilla operations than Moses and Noble had seemed to be, but I was more seriously wrong about Volckmann and associates. Maybe I was just a poor judge of people then? But maybe it was because the bitterness at having been seemingly abandoned and betrayed by our own government—a feeling that consumed so many of us in 1942—tended to subside as memories of Bataan receded and we got something specific and useful to do to. Certainly that was true for me. After reading Ramsey's book, I am sure that his mood swings were more severe than my own and that mine ceased sooner. Perhaps Moses, Noble, Volckmann, and Blackburn also just took a little longer to abandon sterile recriminations against Washington and to busy themselves making life less agreeable for the Japanese.

Be that as it may, Volckmann had begun to dominate the Moses-Noble organization months before the colonels were captured by the enemy in June 1943. He tightened operating procedures, reorganized northern Luzon, and improved communications among the various guerrilla units there.[46] Then he tried to absorb my command into his by invoking what he called the "understanding" I had reached with Moses and Noble. I simply ignored his blandishments as I had those of his predecessors. Nothing happened.

Why did all these efforts to unify the guerrilla movement fail? To Doyle Decker, who spent most of the war in Lt. Clay Conner's command, the answer was obvious: all the guerrilla leaders were egoists striving to be little kings in the areas we controlled—a view shared, incidentally, by others who had been enlisted men in the prewar U.S. Army.[47] Anderson largely agreed, notably in the case of his rival Ramsey, but he added that he did not think the ambition to command was itself reprehensible.[48]

No doubt mere pride and vanity did figure prominently in the failure to unify, but other considerations seemed to me then and seem now to have been more important. For one thing, many U.S. guerrillas were unwilling to serve under certain others for what seemed to them serious, practical reasons: they knew each other too well and lacked confidence in either the personal character or professional talent of their colleagues.[49] As for me, I never thought the bickering for top billing was of much importance because I considered the whole idea of centralized leadership unrealistic. In 1942–43 individual guerrilla units were still ill organized and scattered all over Luzon, many of them miles away from any others, often over a mountain range or two in the bargain. Communications were so primitive and uncertain that some units did not receive directives from Thorp or Merrill or Ramsey until weeks after they were sent. A good example of one guerrilla's lack of knowledge about others appears in a letter from Anderson to Merrill and "Collier" (Calyer) near the end of 1943. Andy said he was pleased to learn of the existence of their organization and would be glad to establish a cooperative relationship. He added that he would appreciate any information they might be able to send him about Ralph McGuire.[50] He was unaware that McGuire had been killed nearly a year before.

In any case, all of us guerrillas together were never strong enough to pursue any concerted action against the Japanese, and every leader and every area had problems that differed from every other. Some central authority sending out orders and unsolicited advice would not have improved matters. Interestingly, to me anyway, both Anderson and his executive officer, Col. Jaime Manzano, eventually came around to agree with me about the matter—though it took Andy until 1985 to do so.[51]

Still another reason for the chronic discord among Philippine guerrillas was one that is simply a part of all warfare. Members of any alliance tend to be at least somewhat suspicious of one another. They generally have different strategic aims and often differ about the best tactics. Not least important, the political and military leaders of each nation in a coalition try to dominate their opposite numbers in the governments and armies of their allies. Such mistrust and rivalry is usually even more intense among guerrillas. The Spanish irregulars who fought so fiercely against Napoleon in 1808–13 also squabbled incessantly among themselves. In World War II the guerrillas of Greece, Yugoslavia, France, Italy, and other European countries were divided primarily between Communists and non-Communists, and since these factions had diametrically opposed objectives, serious cooperation was impossible.[52] Soviet guerrillas were an exception, but they were so closely controlled by the high command of the Red Army that they were virtually a part of it rather than guerrillas in the usual sense. American and Filipino guerrillas came into a similar relationship with the U.S. Army only in the spring of 1945.

All this confusion within and among guerrilla bands had reached a state of fabulous complexity by 1944, when various Philippine leaders took a hand. Air ace Jesus Villamor came from Australia to Negros to try to further guerrilla unification. From far-off Saranac Lake, New York, where he lay dying of tuberculosis, President Manuel Quezon sent his personal physician, Dr. Emgidio Cruz, to the Philippines to make clandestine contact with high government officials and as many guerrillas as possible and try to coordinate their activities. From Manila, Manuel Roxas began to weave an intelligence net that was intended to serve all guerrillas. And long afterward, Ferdinand Marcos—by then the embattled president of the Philippines—claimed that he had dedicated himself, albeit unsuccessfully, to the unification of all guerrillas throughout the Islands.[53]

None of these men, Americans or Filipinos (save those who died), ever really gave up until American troops actually landed at Lingayen Gulf in January 1945. In the last half of 1944, while I was trying to arm new units, transmit intelligence to Australia with newly received radios, and distribute largesse from submarines, I constantly receivied "orders" and "suggestions" from Anderson, Volckmann, Merrill, and the agents of several different Filipino guerrilla leaders. Since I had no intention of submitting to any of them, on August 8 I radioed SWPA to request clarification of my status. As I had suspected would be the case, General MacArthur did not reply directly. Perhaps he did not want to take sides openly? Maybe he was not dissatisfied to see us at odds with one another? Perhaps he thought such bickering was simply of no importance? Whatever his motives, thereafter he simply addressed me directly in radio messages, without making reference to anyone else. I considered that fact my answer and assumed what I wished to: that LGAF was an independent command. Actually, my message to SWPA was designed to clear myself if any of my aspiring superiors should try to make trouble for me later. I felt sure, for instance, that Volckmann would have been delighted to have me court-martialed.

My relations with all these self-baptized "commanders" varied greatly from one to another. My dealings with Colonel Merrill and his executive officer, Colonel Calyer, were of little real importance, but since they were more complicated than any others, they give some idea of how chaotic guerrilla relationships and pretensions could become. On February 15, 1943, Calyer reminded the rest of the world that Merrill was the senior American line officer on Luzon and therefore commander in chief of all USAFFE guerrillas there.[54] Twenty-one months later, after repeated complaints about shortages of everything, lack of direction from Australia, and the failure of every known mode of communication to effect regular contact with SWPA headquarters, Merrill confessed that his efforts to unify the maverick guerrilla outfits on Luzon had failed. Of the many roadblocks that had impeded his progress, he said, I was number one.[55] The last was the only point on which members of the Merrill-Calyer organization ever seemed able to agree.[56] In October 1944, Calyer sent identical instructions to Al Hendrickson, who was my area commander in Tarlac, and to Alfred Bruce, who was supposedly Merrill's man there. Bruce and Hendrickson were enjoined to work together under Calyer's direction, the better to resist the Japanese and secure a measure of cooperation with the Huks. They were also instructed to relay the news that Calyer expected me to cooperate in these endeavors.[57]

Not much came of this, for several reasons. I replied to Calyer on November 24, 1944, that my headquarters was now in direct contact with GHQ, SWPA, from which I therefore took my orders. In an effort to soften this unwelcome news, I offered to send him a transmitter (we were then getting them by submarine), some codes, and a representative from SWPA as well.[58] Hendrickson, always a forthright soul, took the position that since he was a member of LGAF, Calyer had no business giving him orders about anything. To complicate matters further, the embattled area Al had long been trying to subdue was claimed simultaneously by his command, the Huks, and Bruce.

Still worse, he and Bruce disliked each other and were in the habit of communicating in brusque one- or-two line orders that bordered on insults. Last, one of Bruce's underlings, "Colonel" Mallari, got into a skirmish with some of Hendrickson's men in a dispute over jurisdictions and promptly complained to Bruce that some of his (Mallari's) men had been wounded. He reported that Hendrickson had called Bruce a thief and a Huk and had added the further insult that Bruce, Merrill, and Calyer did nothing but sleep in the mountains. (The undiplomatic Hendrickson was not far off target with this last gibe. John Boone, the Merrill organization's nearest major guerrilla neighbor, had complained several months before that "Zambales is in turmoil again because of incompetence.")[59] The "Colonel" said his men were so enraged at such calumnies that they wanted to fight it out on the spot.[60]

Bruce was sufficiently angered by Hendrickson's letters and attitude that he complained bitterly to Calyer about Al's ego, his "rudeness" and arrogance, the "thugs" he had for "followers," and his propensity to antagonize everyone from the Huks to "Colonel" Mallari. He thought the only "imaginable" excuse for such conduct was that Al "was just a Dope" who was "seldom found sober."[61]

As if all this was not complicated enough, Clay Conner—who, like Boone, seemed sometimes the vassal of Ramsey, sometimes of Merrill, and often a sovereign in his own right—complained to Merrill on January 22, 1945, two weeks *after* the American landings at Lingayen Gulf, that Pampanga was in chaos because the area was full of brevet colonels who claimed to be answerable to Ramsey rather than Merrill and who therefore refused to take orders from Conner.[62] (The Feudal terminology here is not inappropriate, for the relationships of Luzon guerrilla leaders often did resemble those of the feudal aristocracy in early medieval Europe.) Five months earlier Ramsey had ignored a directive from Merrill to appear for a conference and to bring along in writing whatever authority he possessed for his assumed rank and duties.[63]

Robert Lapham in 1941, a portrait taken in Manila as a Christmas present for his parents. They received it in December, after the war had begun.

A dinner party at the Army-Navy Club in Manila, August 3, 1941, when living was comparatively easy for American servicemen in the Philippines. Except for Lapham (second from right, standing), every man pictured was either killed or captured when the Philippines fell in 1942.

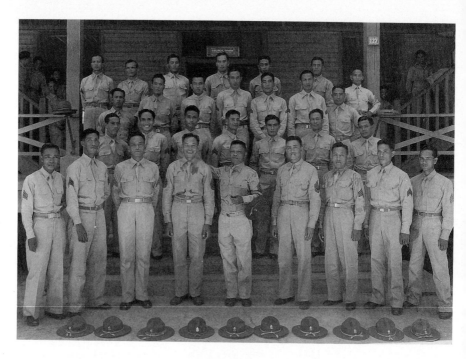

A retirement party for the smiling First Sergeant of Lapham's company shortly before the war. Unfortunately the sergeant's retirement was short-lived; he returned to active duty as soon as the war began.

Lapham and his men on maneuver shortly before the war. On his right is Lieutenant "Shorty" Moore, his company commander throughout the battles on Bataan. Moore was captured but managed to survive the prison camps.

A scene on the Central Plains of Luzon, taken during the dry season. Lapham and his guerrillas operated there and on the surrounding mountains throughout the war.

A typical Philippine town. In some towns a single artesian well was used by the entire population. The two-wheeled, horse-drawn passenger cart shown is a *calesa,* the principal means of transportation before the war.

Above left: Lieutenant C.P. Olay was one of Lapham's faithful bodyguards for most of the war. *Above right:* Sergeant (later Lieutenant) Esteban Lumyeb was one of his original companions when their tiny party left Colonel Thorp near Mt. Pinatubo in 1942. He saved Lapham's life a few months later when he nearly died of malaria and dysentery. *Left:* Captain (later Major) Federico Doliente, whom Lapham called "a tough hombre," was one of his best officers and most enthusiastic fighters. On one occasion he cut off the head of a Filipino mayor who was pro-Japanese. He later became a police chief for the Japanese and an invaluable spy for Lapham.

Above: Antonio (Tony) Hernandez and his men, photographed probably shortly after the unit was demobilized in 1945. Tony (back row, standing second from left) was Doliente's executive officer and succeeded him when he was captured. He was one of Lapham's closest personal friends. To Tony's left is Lieutenant Membrere, tall for a Filipino, who would sometimes lead patrols at night and pretend he was Lapham to confuse enemies. *Below right:* Emilio Hernandez, Tony's brother and the commander of Lapham's squadron in Bulacan.

This photo of Lapham, taken shortly after the Lingayen Gulf landings in 1945, ran in newspapers all over the United States. His hometown paper said he looked like a "Hollywood cowboy." Note how much he had aged in four years.

Lapham discusses Japanese troop movements and defenses and guerrilla locations with General Innis P. Swift after the Lingayen landings. *Below:* Lapham and others worked together after the war to determine which Filipino guerrillas deserved U.S. compensation. Kneeling is Major Jerimia Serafica, one of Lapham's top commanders. Standing, far left, is Captain Tony Estrada, a staff officer, and seated on Lapham's right is Captain D.V. Lucas, former adjutant to Alfonso Arellano. Standing center is Lieutenant Membrere. The rest were officers from Serafica's and other units.

On June 13, 1945, Lapham and other American guerrillas were decorated with the Distinguished Service Cross by General MacArthur in Manila. Shown here after the ceremony are, front row, left to right: Lapham; Manuel Roxas, first postwar president of the Philippines; and Harry McKenzie, Lapham's executive officer. Back row: Ray Hunt, Lapham's area commander in Pangasinan Province; and F.M. Verano, a Filipino writer and the liaison between Hunt and Roxas when Roxas was clandestinely aiding the guerrillas.

The Philippine Legion of Honor medal was presented to Lapham three times—in 1947, when the medal was unavailable, and later at the Philippine embassy in Washington. The third presentation, shown here, was during a business trip by Lapham to the Philippines in 1964. Presenting the medal was Colonel Macario Peralta, Philippine secretary of defense and a former guerrilla leader in the Visayan Islands, assisted by D.V. Lucas, at right.

Then there was the case of Ray Hunt. His claimed jurisdiction (derived from me) overlapped somewhat with Conner's (derived from whom?); yet Ray insists to this day that he never even heard of Conner's existence until many years after the war. (As a matter of fact, I didn't either!) Before long I quit paying much attention to either complaints or demands from Merrill's people. When I received a letter from one of them, I usually answered it, and I recall advising Hendrickson to avoid antagonizing them, but that was normally about the extent of my concern with them.

When Calyer had dispatched his "unified efforts" directives to the four winds, Anderson, predictably, had tried to calm everyone down. His own reply was a series of refusals, but his letter was politeness epitomized. He sprinkled it liberally with "please" and "sorry," repeatedly expressed his "desire" to comply with Calyer's requests and his "regret" that he was unable to do so, and ended by offering to be helpful in any way he could.[64] At the time I didn't know what Anderson had written to Calyer, so I did not take as much care to be conciliatory, but at least I avoided exacerbating matters. I wrote to Merrill expressing gratification that he was in contact with Hendrickson. I offered to send him, as I had offered Calyer, a radio transmitter if he needed one or to recode his messages and relay them to Australia, and I said I would direct Hendrickson to give him some medicine if he wanted any.[65]

By December there were people at SWPA headquarters who had heard enough. Capt. Bartolomeo Cabangbang issued a memo to all unit commanders on Luzon to stop our petty squabbling. It gave a bad impression of all of us, he said, and had in the bargain aroused the combined mirth and contempt of the Japanese. We were ordered to compose our differences and prepare to work together in the great struggle to come. (Maybe it was a fitting denouement to the whole dismal business that I never received a copy of this memo.) Then even the flamboyantly named Captain Cabangbang gave up; five days later another memo from him informed anyone who happened to get it that General MacArthur did not want to establish a unified command on Luzon at this stage of the war after all.[66] Thereafter, SWPA directives were addressed to Anderson, Volckmann, and me en masse, as if it made no difference whether we were together or separate or some subordinated to others. I was convinced that my judgment from the beginning had been vindicated: that the obstacles of nature, the widely differing conditions in various parts of Luzon, and the sharply contrasting characters, personalities, and purposes of guerrilla leaders rendered effective centralized control over Luzon irregulars impossible. When one adds the consideration that as late, as October 1944—three months after we had gotten two-way radios and were sending daily reports—SWPA headquarters was still not sure whether my units, by now comprising many thousands of men, were independent or controlled by Volckmann, it is hardly surprising that MacArthur abandoned his former efforts to impose uniformity on a place so vaguely comprehended.[67] For my own part I seldom gave much thought to this whole rigamarole because it climaxed in December 1944, when we were feverishly engrossed in preparing for the imminent Allied invasion.

On February 21, 1944, Anderson mentioned in a letter to me that he had heard nothing from Ed Ramsey since the preceding November. Two weeks later he circulated an order signed "Bernard L. Anderson, Capt. Infantry, U.S. Army Commanding." It declared Ramsey relieved of his command of the Second Military District and ordered him to report to Anderson's headquarters with the least possible delay. The order also appointed me Ramsey's successor with full powers in all matters in northern Nueva Vizcaya, northern Nueva Ecija, Pangasinan, Tarlac, and northern Tayabas provinces. Ed raised no protest against this action; indeed, he never made trouble of any kind for me. His response to the unification efforts of Merrill and Calyer was also like mine: he either ignored the colonels entirely or pleaded that "conditions" prevented him from acceding to their requests.[68]

Anderson's munificent bequest to me did exacerbate my longstanding difficulties with Russell Volckmann, however. Andy either did not have an accurate map of Luzon or was unaware of generally accepted jurisdictional lines that put the northern portions of Nueva Vizcaya and Tayabas provinces clearly within Volckmann's domain.[69] Otherwise, my relations with Anderson were complicated but in no way unpleasant. Throughout 1944 he wrote me regularly on a broad array of subjects: codes and their uses, proper preparation of maps, thanks for a few things I had done for him, his satisfaction with my intelligence reports, the desirability of sending such reports promptly, the practical advantages of writing in military style, my chances of getting various supplies from him and from Australia, the prospect for promotions, the chance that SWPA might replace him as "commanding officer," the need for care in the selection of an executive officer, his desire that I contact Volckmann about supplies from submarines, his desire that I come to see him thereafter, and much else.[70]

All these communications concerned mundane matters; all were friendly in tone. In my dealings with Anderson he was invariably considerate, often generous. He had, after all, let me keep his officer, Harry McKenzie, and had ceded to me a portion of his domain in southern Nueva Ecija. Yet there was always an easy assumption on his part that he was commander in chief of all Luzon guerrillas and that the rest of us knew this and accepted it without demur.

Russell Volckmann was a different sort—indeed, different from any of the other leaders of irregulars in at least one important way. Most of us feared to keep detailed records of our organizations and activities, for if these were ever seized by the enemy the Japanese would wreak a bloody vengeance on us all: guerrillas, the civilians who had aided us, and their families. But Volckmann, holed up in the high, steep mountains of the far north, was less likely to be successfully raided by Japanese patrols than those of us in the lowlands farther south. Whether from this consideration, or from the force of military habit, or from sheer egoism, he kept detailed records throughout the war and turned them over to commanders of the American forces who led the Lingayen landings in January 1945. In this way his activities as a guerrilla leader were the first to become known to military authorities, news reporters, and historians, with the not surprising result that his contribution to the eventual Allied reconquest of Luzon has been exaggerated in written history. Volckmann did organize and train a large body of guerrillas in the north during the war, and these units did give an excellent account of themselves just before the Lingayen landings and afterward—but no more than did my forces or those of several other guerrilla leaders. It was just that he kept records while we, more careful, did not, and that most history is composed from written records.

In 1944 Volckmann returned to his old ambition to incorporate my organization into his, a design he had dropped for a time after the deaths of Moses and Noble. By the fall of 1944 he had what were, by his own definition, five regiments of well-trained guerrillas. Perhaps that incited him to try again. I assumed at the time and still think that his motive was empire building pure and simple, but it is possible that he had other reasons for acting as he did.[71] One thing for sure: he had some peculiar ideas. For instance, he once issued what seemed to me a supremely silly order to kill all dogs for miles around so the Japanese would get no warning of guerrilla patrols. Since the dogs, true neutrals in war, warned us of Japanese patrols quite as much as the reverse, that order did not strengthen my faith in Volckmann's wisdom.

Renewed trouble with him followed the announcement I sent out on April 6, 1944, that at Anderson's request I had assumed command of the Second Military District, and that all organizations in it would henceforth be responsible to LGAF headquarters. More than four months passed; then a strange letter came from Volckmann. Part of it was matter-of-fact. He thanked me for sending him some supplies, asked me to send him sulfa if I had any, proposed to establish a regular system of runners between his headquarters and mine to facilitate communications, offered to send me three men to help unload the submarines expected soon on the east coast, and asked that supplies intended for him be addressed in a manner that he hoped would prevent looting en route. But then the letter went on to complain that I was intruding into his territory, a matter he hoped would be straightened out after his report on it reached Australia. Meanwhile, he would be guided by the last orders he had received from Moses and Noble, and he hoped that I had received a previous letter of his to this effect.[72]

Three weeks later (now *five* months after my announcement that I had assumed command of the Second Military District), I received a letter saying that "this damn order has caused me too much trouble" and charging that I had exceeded my authority because northern Nueva Vizcaya had never been in the Second Military District.[73] That was unquestionably true; I had laid claim to it, tongue in cheek, only because Anderson had told me it was within my domain and because I knew that doing so would irritate Volckmann. I never really intended to operate in that rough and mountainous area, because I preferred life on the plains. But now Volckmann had risen to the bait. He informed me that though he disliked quarreling between units, if I continued to let my guerrillas kill his officers and men, he would move in a whole battalion and straighten things out.[74] I responded that I would be happy to cooperate fully with his command, but my own orders came directly from SWPA, and I would continue to act as I thought best until I received orders from there to change my tack. I informed him that my Pangasinan area commander, Ray Hunt, had assured me that Lt. Tom Chengay and his men had *not* attacked Volckmann's followers. I added that these troops were well disciplined and accustomed to acting within orders. Finally, I assured him that I would remind all LGAF troops afresh to be sure to avoid attacks on his men.[75] Volckmann then threatened to have me court-martialed, and appealed to SWPA to have me placed under his command. Presumably he wanted formal authorization for having already listed Harry McKenzie and me among "officers under his command."[76] He added that my pretensions had been hampering his intelligence work, delaying his reports, and producing armed conflicts between his followers and mine. SWPA ignored him, and so did I.

Next, he tried to pry my area commanders away from me. In November 1944 he sent runners to Hendrickson's headquarters with orders to bring back a roster of Al's troops. Al's cantankerousness had often made trouble for LGAF, but this time it stood us in good stead; he flatly refused to comply.[77] Volckmann then threatened to have Ray Hunt court-martialed if Ray and his units did not leave me and join his command. I told Ray to ignore this threat and assured him that Volckmann could not court-martial a guerrilla for desertion, since a guerrilla is a volunteer, or for disobeying orders that Volckmann had no authority to give in the first place. I followed up with a letter to Hendrickson, advising him that he need not succumb to threats from Volckmann, heed unsolicited advice from Merrill, or pay attention to an officer named Cruz from Marking's guerrillas who had proffered him both orders and advice. I reminded him that we were all members of LGAF, an independent outfit, answerable only to SWPA.[78]

It is necessary to retain perspective about all this intramural acrimony. My troubles with Volckmann were persistent and irritating, but they were only paper exchanges, never anything like as serious as my hostile relations with the Japanese or the Huks. (Oddly, Volckmann never mentions them in his book, *We Remained.*) Most American operators, like Volckmann and me, barked a lot and exchanged many paper admonitions and warnings but seldom really fought one another.

The nature of the squabbles had changed since 1942 too. Early in the war, disputes within and between guerrilla groups had been mainly over what our duties were and what our policies should be, much complicated by rivalry for access to food and arms, all exacerbated by personal grudges. By 1944 we were quarreling mostly over jurisdiction: who should rule whom.

It was the Filipinos whose feuds were truly bloody. For instance, early in 1944 Ed Ramsey had to make a trip through the south Luzon jungle, an area supposedly controlled by his nominal subordinates. If civilized relationships had existed among them, he could have traversed the district in two days. His satraps, however, were as quarrelsome as they were savage, with the result that Ed spent a week being passed cautiously from one gang to another while they pursued their *real* interests: ambushing, kidnapping, torturing, and murdering one another.[79]

Of all the real and alleged Philippine guerrilla leaders with whom I had any dealings, the one about whom it has always been most difficult for me to make definitive judgments is Ferdinand Marcos, who long after the war became a much criticized president of the Philippines. The worshipful writer of a "campaign biography" of Marcos in 1964 depicted him as an intrepid war hero who had received more military decorations than any other Filipino in history and whose brilliant wartime career reached its climax in his persistent efforts to unite all Filipino guerrillas.[80] After Marcos's downfall in 1987, other books began to appear claiming that Marcos the War Hero was a fraud, that he had received most of his decorations years after the war or even after he had become president, that he did not do and could not have done most of the deeds attributed to him.[81]

I cannot say positively which view of Marcos is true. I did not have much to do with him during the war, somewhat more afterward. I have read both the campaign biography and his critics' allegations. It seems to me that the critics have the stronger case, that much of Marcos's wartime heroism was imaginary or at least exaggerated; nevertheless, the whole question has been grievously muddied by postwar American and Philippine politics. Moreover, so many fantasies about politics in other parts of the world are cherished by so many Americans and the irresponsibility of much of the media is such that it seems to me the whole question needs to be dissected and considered piece by piece.

First of all, during the war Marcos had no discernible guerrilla following anywhere in LGAF territory. I don't know what he had elsewhere, but I suspect not much. Ray Hunt points out that Marcos would not likely have been willing to join Volckmann's guerrillas as an individual in 1945 if, as claimed, he commanded 8,200 of his own guerrillas in his Ang Mag Maharlika organization. Ray thinks it was only a "paper" organization.[82] Some of Ray's own guerrillas actually arrested Marcos in October 1944 for trying to raise money in Pangasinan, ostensibly to build an airfield so the Roxas family could be flown to America. Marcos probably would have been jailed for this until the end of the war had not Roxas, whom Ray and I knew to be a secret friend of us guerrillas, vouched for him.[83] Whatever his deeds, intentions, efforts, or ambitions, Marcos did not affect me in any significant way during the war.

Ferdinand Marcos's father, by extreme contrast, was unquestionably a collaborator with the Japanese, for which bad judgment he paid a ghastly price. In April 1945 he was executed by Filipino guerrillas in a particularly horrible way. In parts of Europe before the

French Revolution (1789–99) those who had committed spectacular or especially abominable crimes were sometimes punished by having their arms and legs tied to four horses, which were then driven off in four different directions.[84] For Marcos's father, carabao were used instead of horses, and pieces of the victim were then hung in a tree. The savagery of this execution reflected more than just distaste for collaborators. Many Filipinos are passionate enthusiasts for revenge on their enemies. Many years earlier a rival Filipino politician, Julio Nalundasun, had defeated and humiliated the elder Marcos. Ferdinand—then a young law student—had killed Nalundasun in reprisal. Several of the guerrillas who carried out the gory execution of Marcos senior, in turn, were friends and relatives of Nalundasun. They were commanded by an American officer whose superior was Colonel Russell Volckmann.[85] But the whole loathsome business concerned only Marcos's father, not Ferdinand.

I went back to the Philippines on business in 1964 and returned again with my wife for a visit in 1986. We were treated splendidly on both occasions and were accorded a long and friendly conversation with President Marcos in 1986. At a time when U.S. journalists were writing about how dangerous it was to live in the Islands and predicting imminent revolution there, my wife and I walked unaccompanied all over Manila and traveled widely in central and northern Luzon visiting old friends and acquaintances from World War II days. We were never harmed or threatened by anyone and saw no evidence of anything unusual. In fact, it seemed to me that conditions in the Philippines had improved somewhat since the 1940s, despite the fact that the population had tripled in four decades. The journalists who wrote so much about how "unsafe" it was in the Philippines wrote much less about how truly unsafe it was for anyone to walk about in sections of dozens of American cities in those same years. They also neglected to mention that Marcos had campaigned throughout the Islands accompanied by only a handful of troops or bodyguards during the same years that American presidents were taking far more elaborate precautions to ensure their safety even on routine trips.

As a people, we Americans and our leaders often know little about the rest of the world and remember only what we wish to about our own land. Though Filipinos esteem education highly and have a far larger educated class per capita than almost any other developing country, the Philippine Republic is still a Third World nation in many of its political attitudes and practices. Democracy is not firmly rooted in much of the world, be it Asia, Africa, Latin

America, or most of eastern Europe. It thrives mainly in northwestern Europe, North America above the Rio Grande, and in the old British dominions.

In those "democratic" regions the most impressive family fortunes have been made in shipping, lumbering, mining, smuggling, the fur trade, banking, publishing, manufacture, railroads, real estate, stock market manipulation, or some other species of private enterprise (often with much covert aid from allies in government). Many Continental European fortunes were derived from overseas colonial empires. But most Third World fortunes have been made in politics: from taking bribes and from routinely using an official position to enrich one's family and friends. In most parts of the world little notice is taken of such practices; they are just the perquisites of high office, the way government has always been carried on. Rulers in such places often invest much of their politically acquired wealth in foreign countries or put it into Swiss bank accounts so if the evil day comes when they are turned out of office (but not lynched), they can rush abroad and spend the rest of their lives in some quieter part of the world where they have thoughtfully secreted some of their assets.

As long as such rulers do not grow unduly strong or threatening, as long as they refrain from undermining American interests and occasionally make themselves useful to Washington, we ordinarily limit ourselves to periodic tut-tuts about their unconcern for democracy. If they make trouble for us, though, or if their political complexion offends the Best People in Washington, Hollywood, academia or among U.S. television performers, we begin to hear a great deal about what thieves and tyrants these foreign rulers are and how imperative it is that they be replaced in their homelands by true friends of democracy. Soon they are overturned but their replacements are usually incompetent and, unhappily, still have *their* fortunes to make. Within a short time there is a new horde of grafters at the public trough, and life goes on as before.

So it has seemed to me in the Philippines. Ferdinand Marcos was certainly not a tower of virtue but neither was he a unique scoundrel or an unusual Third World ruler. He was only moderately honest or moral, but who can gaze at the American houses of Congress or a dozen U.S. administrations in the twentieth century and say that the ethical eminence of our rulers has been a continuing source of inspiration to us all? (And we, remember, are one of the *better* governed nations.) Ferdinand Marcos stole rather more than many rulers, and the extravagant Imelda, with her thousands of pair of shoes, made an ideal target for the satire of those sturdy exemplars of ascetic living, U.S. journalists and politicians. Ferdinand Marcos certainly exaggerated his wartime service to his homeland, but he did not evade such service. He did not bring about the spiritual reformation of his people or make the Philippines dramatically prosperous, but neither did he harm his native land or its people in the ways so many other rulers have done in so many lands in our bloody century. Most of the basic problems of the Philippines are nonpolitical anyway, overpopulation being foremost. War hero or not, Marcos has been castigated more than he deserved by many whose moral grandeur was not obviously superior to his own. Corazon Aquino, his successor as president, was certainly a more attractive and ethically inspiring person, but, individuality aside, her accession was merely the passing of power from one rich, politically active Filipino family to another. The Aquino fortune was built on sugar; that of Marcos more directly on politics.[86]

— 8 —
Troubles with the Huks

Of all the differences I had with outlaws, other guerrilla bands, and power-seeking fellow American irregulars, none were as persistently vexatious as those with a native Philippine guerrilla organization, the Hukbalahaps, or Huks. The Huk movement had ancient antecedents. The Spaniards who arrived in the sixteenth century and various native Philippine families gradually turned much of the fertile central plain of Luzon into great estates—primarily sugar and rice plantations worked by peasant sharecroppers. Many of the latter fell hopelessly into debt to their landlords, and peasant unrest was endemic for generations. Some of it seemed occupational, some primarily cultural; for instance, peasant uprisings almost always took place in areas where the Pampango language prevailed.

Philippine rebellions against Spain in 1896 and America afterward, by contrast, were essentially nationalist rather than rural-agrarian and developed primarily in and around Manila, where Tagalog is the predominant language. Before World War II, peasant revolutionary sentiment made little headway in areas inhabited by Illocanos or Tagalogs; it was strongest in the sugar-producing areas of Pampanga and Tarlac provinces, where many peasants worked in sugar mills, rather than in Pangasinan, Nueva Ecija, and much of Bulacan, where most farm families had a few acres of their own riceland.

By the 1930s much of this rural discontent, especially in the sugar mills of Pampanga, was channeled into a peasant-labor movement perhaps most accurately termed Christian socialist. It was led at first by Pedro Abad Santos. Don Perico, as he was called, was the extraordinarily knowledgeable son of an intellectual family. Generous, undogmatic, resembling Gandhi in some ways, he had a few hundred admiring followers when he was succeeded in 1938 by a young peasant named Luis Taruc.[1] Though Taruc had a romantic, even dreamy, streak in his complex makeup,[2] he was an energetic and capable organizer and public speaker. The movement employed strikes as a tactical tool but was not particularly violent. Most of its demands were for a return to "the good old days"—a partly real, partly mythical time when landlords had extended interest-free loans to peasants and had advanced them rice when family supplies ran low. The complainers also wanted broader distribution of the land to those who cultivated it, and greater honesty and generosity from landlords, police, and government soldiers. Almost none of these uneducated farmers were true Communists in the sense of possessing any knowledge of Marxist "science." Few of them had even heard of Karl Marx.

But there also grew up in the Philippines, as in other lands around the globe, a native Communist Party. Its numbers were small and its leaders were educated urbanites, primarily members of the Lava family from Manila. As is typical of Marxist intellectuals, these leaders knew little about agriculture and cared less. Their ultimate objective was the usual Communist one: to proceed by any and all means to communize the whole earth, starting with their own homeland. They planned to base their movement on labor unions, rather than "reactionary" peasants, and to develop "revolutionary consciousness" among the people.[3] Nevertheless, throughout the 1930s Communists infiltrated peasant organizations and claimed credit for rural unrest provoked by others. They tried to polarize Philippine politics by urging peasants simply to seize the lands of their overlords, and clamored for immediate independence from the United States.

In 1935, when Stalin imposed the Popular Front tactic on Communists everywhere, Philippine Marxists dutifully began to pose as fearless fighters against fascism. They were sufficiently persuasive that the Commonwealth of the Philippines freed some of their jailed leaders in 1938.[4] At about the same time they began to get considerable ideological encouragement and tactical advice from Chinese Communists.[5] These new comrades persuaded them to negotiate an alliance, then a union, with the Socialists under Abad Santos and Taruc. Nominally, the two groups formed a Popular Front, but in fact the Communists seized control of what their partners had built and dominated the combined movement thereafter, even though Taruc remained as "front man."

Thus a movement that had originated in peasant socialist idealism had changed its character profoundly. By the time World War II began, its leaders had developed or accepted the orthodox Marxist strategy of waging war and revolution at the same time. They would ally nominally with any groups who supported war against a foreign enemy, but at the same time they would use every opportunity to discredit and destroy all the social, economic, occupational, and ideological groups who opposed them in their own country. If successful, the war would end with the foreign enemy defeated, their domestic rivals first duped and then routed, and their country turned Communist with themselves as its rulers.

Luis Taruc was a relatively unsophisticated man and a believing Christian. Whether he ever became a "real" Communist in the sense of wholeheartedly believing Marxist metaphysics is uncertain. At first he knew little about the real designs of intellectual Marxists; he always seemed to dislike Marxist dogmatism; and he frequently thought tactics demanded by Party leaders were unwise. Long after World War II he rejected Marxism, but at the time he was confident that no harm would come from allying with Communists against the common Japanese enemy.[6] Of course he had plenty of company in his naiveté. Shoals of what a sharp-tongued observer once called the "progressive unintelligentsia" of the Western world believed for decades after 1917 that Communists were only "reformers" like themselves, albeit more vocal and violent ones, and that honest cooperation with them in pursuit of common worthy objectives was possible. I cannot claim that I was well versed in Marxist doctrine, purposes, and strategy in 1942. Indeed, my first impression of the Huks was favorable: they seemed serious, determined, and ready to fight the Japanese. Thinking back, I am not sure I knew then that they *were* Communists. With further contacts, however, my suspicion of them grew, then settled into fixed animosity after they tried to murder my executive officer.[7]

It was during the spring of 1942 that Taruc's socialists and the real Communists, along with various lesser groups professing to be anti-fascist, held a series of meetings from which emerged a new organization, or at least a new name; Hukbo ng Bayan Labon sa Hapon (Peoples' Army to Fight the Japanese), Hukbalahap for short; or, shorter still, Huk. At about the same time, Colonel Thorp had sent out word that he was accepting recruits for irregular warfare and that such men would be officially recognized as USAFFE guerrillas. A number of Americans and Filipinos soon came to Camp Sanchez to enlist. As related earlier, I led several Huks up to Thorp's camp for dinner and a conference but took no part in the discussion there, and I never talked to Thorp about it afterward. All I recalled of the incident was that the visitors were a tough-looking bunch. Though it was obvious later that there had been sharp disagreements at this meeting, it appears that some kind of arrangement—most likely a misunderstanding—was reached. Thorp seems to have conferred some quasi-official authority on the Huks,[8] which they at once misused to seize weapons from civilians and to assure farmers that they were now operating with the approval of General MacArthur.[9]

Thorp wanted still closer relations with the Huks, so on July 7, 1942, he sent Anderson, Barker, and others to coordinate plans with Taruc and some of his associates. Seemingly, each side had much to gain if a genuine agreement could be reached. The Huks had already won some credit among local Filipinos by making several small raids and one spectacular attack on the Japanese. On March 14, 1942, even before Bataan fell, a Huk named Felipa Culala but known to her followers as Dayang-Dayang had set an ambush near San Miguel in which some thirty to forty Japanese soldiers and sixty-eight Philippine Constabularymen were killed by Huks, who then salvaged thirty-eight rifles. This success had sent peasant morale soaring and given a big boost to Huk recruitment.[10] Such credit could easily be translated into food and supplies for USAFFE forces. Moreover, at that time the Huks were both more numerous and better organized than any USAFFE units, and they were well acquainted with the countryside. What our side could offer was training by professional military men, official recognition of the Huks by the U.S. Army, and eventual pay for their services by the American government. The Huks could reciprocate by making all USAFFE trainers colonels in the Huk army.

But differences proved more basic than hope of mutual advantage. Thorp was convinced that the only worthy objective of military action was victory. To ally with the Huks because they were fellow enemies of the Japanese seemed to him mere good sense, but he wanted no part of commanding an armed political party. He also believed that guerrillas should pursue a long range plan of destroying Japanese installations, communications, and roads, whereas the Huks wanted to curry favor with civilians by undertaking minor raids and patrols that could not have any important influence on the outcome of the war. Given these fundamental disagreements, the best the conferees could manage was a paper promise to "cooperate" and to share equipment and supplies, while allowing the Huks "independent action" on "organizational and political matters."[11] It has been contended that the Huks lost by their refusal to give way, since a pact would have allowed them to pose, simultaneously and convincingly, as friends of Filipinos, friends of the United States, and patriots defending their homeland against the Nipponese invaders. In practice, though, it mattered little, since from the start the Huks violated even the flimsy paper agreement.

The Americans at large in central and north Luzon in 1942 were sharply divided about what stance we should adopt toward the Huks. Blackburn and Volckmann, who both had a low opinion of Thorp, thought it typically stupid of him to act arrogant and deny the Huks political cooperation.[12] One can only reply that both those men were too isolated to have serious contact with real Huks and that subsequent events bore out the soundness of Thorp's growing suspicion of Huk purposes. At the time, I thought Thorp's primary mistake was something quite nonpolitical: his insistence upon staying in the vicinity of Mount Pinatubo, where fairly low, rolling mountains—unlike the high, wild crags of the ranges farther north—made for a weak defensive position.

Col. Gyles Merrill persistently favored making deals with the Huks because he admired their pugnacity. In 1942 he insisted that it should be possible to reach some accord with them.[13] For more than two years he tried to keep in touch with Taruc. Eventually he made his own agreement with the Huks. Predictably, no true cooperation resulted.[14] Blair Robinett, an American escapee who kept in regular contact with Merrill but stayed with the Huks throughout the war, had a generally favorable opinion of them which he never entirely abandoned.[15] Joe Barker, in his lamentably short career as a guerrilla leader, became aware of their general unreliability but still thought they might be brought into USAFFE if handled skillfully.[16] By far the most well disposed toward the Huks, though, was William J. Gardner, a half-Apache regular army noncom—now a lieutenant—much admired for his bravery if not for his political judgment. He got on well with all Filipinos and regarded it as mere common sense for Huks and USAFFE forces alike to ignore politics, forget old feuds and differences, unite their forces, and fight the Japanese together.[17] He even urged Merrill to *order* all USAFFE units to do so.[18]

Others among Merrill's officers who were more politically knowledgeable than Gardner mistrusted the Huks from the start. Capt. George E. Crane described them in the summer of 1942 as 5,000 well-armed true Communists who recognized no authority but their own, fought the police, and terrorized civilians to get whatever they wanted; he predicted that USAFFE guerrillas would have trouble with them.[19] James Boyd regarded Thorp's early efforts to cooperate with them as doomed to failure because of the unbridgeable differences between the two groups.[20] Neither Anderson nor Ramsey had any illusions that the Huks were idealistic reformers rather than real Communists; and neither expected anything to come of negotiating with them.[21] One of Anderson's aides wrote that he had given up such efforts as early as July 1942 because it was evident to him that the Huk leaders could not control their own field troops.[22] An unnamed observer summed up a lot in the remark that more ECLGA men were killed in action by Huks than by any other enemies, even the Japanese.[23]

In 1942 Clay Conner admired the Huks because, he said, they had both rifles and flamboyant leaders, were well organized, had an efficient intelligence system, and actually fought the Japanese. Yet he soon began to notice that he was almost always raided by the Japanese within a day or two of Huk contact. Then he saw Huks go into small barrios and take guns away from USAFFE guerrillas there. Finally, when he was saved from a Huk ambush only by the loyalty and quick wits of some of his Negrito followers, the last of his illusions about these smart, brave, "progressive," anti-Fascist warriors evaporated.[24]

It is difficult to describe the Huks fairly, because most generalizations about them can be countered with other contrary generalizations. Many Filipinos who have written favorably about them have been too compromised by their own association with the Huks or too beholden to them for political support to be truthful. Many Western scholars, English-speaking ones especially, try to fit the Huks into some conventional ideological category, an effort which, numerous Filipino writers allege, distorts the spirit of the Huk movement.[25] William Pomeroy, an American Communist, described the Huk army of World War II as one in which equality existed between officers and men because they were all comrades and democrats who were fighting not for pay or self-aggrandizement but for freedom and a just social order. No one coerced or humiliated others; but rather, those who criticized their fellows did so in friendly fashion to help them improve. Their organization loved the people, treated them fairly and justly in all matters, helped them with their work, paid them for whatever was taken from them, and punished the landlords and traitors who oppressed them. It cleansed the area of ideological foes, organized mass schools to teach peasants useful things for war and peace, and cooperated heartily with other organizations who resisted the Japanese. As a consequence the Filipino people loved, respected, and supported Hukbalahaps.[26]

If there is a National Guard in Heaven it might merit some description like this, but even Luis Taruc acknowledged that the longer the war lasted, the farther his followers fell below such advertised ideals.[27] The vaunted idealism of the Huks existed mainly in the imaginations of those Western "progressives" who see a reincarnated George Washington whenever some bloodstained bandit comes out of a jungle, rifle in hand, and starts talking about "freedom" and "social justice." Yet Pomeroy's idyllic picture of the Huk movement was not entirely false. Some of its leaders were real zealots, and some of their followers were truly inspired by the Marxist ideal, but most ordinary Filipinos who became Huks did so for reasons that had little to do with Marxist metaphysics. Many joined because they sought revenge against the Japanese who had killed or mistreated members of their families, or because it seemed safer to be in some irregular military force than outside, or simply because they wanted to eat regularly.[28] More than a few were ordinary criminals who became Huks mostly to loot. Others were like Carlos Nocum, who joined in order to fight the Japanese but who disliked Marxist dogmatism and discipline so much that he and his men switched over to my LGAF forces in 1942.[29] Still another was Capt. Angelo Jimenez. He grew disenchanted with the Huks, met secretly with me, and in May 1944 joined LGAF with all his men and assumed command of one of our squadrons. (Interestingly, after the war his squadron was given credit for past service clear back to the date when its members were originally inducted by Col. Thorp. To my knowledge, this was the only instance when this was done).

The Huks had a good background for guerrilla activity because Communism is essentially conspiratorial, and the spiritual sons of Marx and Lenin are taught not to be scrupulous or to forswear violence Also, their organizational methods were ingenious and effective. Most Huks carried identification cards ostensibly issued by the Japanese but actually forged. Leaders were always known by imaginative aliases, usually the names of figures from history such as Vespucci or Marco Polo. They raised large numbers of passive guerrillas and civilian supporters by creating a Barrio United Defense Corps in every village they controlled. Members were compelled to swear to assist Huk guerrillas in any way possible, regardless of risk to themselves, and especially to supply the guerrillas with money, food, shelter, equipment, and young male recruits. These newcomers had to sign a sworn statement that they hated the Japanese, a paper that their superior officers could then allow to fall into the hands of the Japanese if the conscripts ever made any trouble. More active guerrillas were secured by sending recruiters into areas where they knew everyone and could thus pick loyal men and keep out spies or unreliable persons.[30] The Huks numbered their squadrons much as we did and attached to each one a "political adviser" whose business it was to keep the men in line ideologically and to convert civilians to Communism.[31]

On the march, Huk units would often adopt an interesting ploy. Instead of bunching together for (presumably) greater safety, the men would string out over half a mile or more. This had two advantages: it made the unit seem much larger than it really was, and in case of a Japanese ambush only a few men would be killed or captured, while the majority disappeared into the bush. Unlike regular troops, who hate to abandon their buddies and who are taught not to do so, no guerrilla expects help from another if the latter can save his life by fleeing.

Since they waged war primarily for political rather than military purposes, the Huks were never a serious military threat to the Japanese. In fact their most effective combat squadron was not Filipino at all but composed of Chinese Communist veterans of campaigns in mainland China in the 1930s.[32] The Huks' real forte was propaganda warfare, whereby they posed to the Filipinos as the most ardent of nationalists. One of their favorite ploys was to stage numerous small raids, partly to "blood" their own troops, partly to demonstrate to Filipinos their zeal to strike blows at the enemy.[33] By "enemy," they meant all USAFFE forces quite as much as they did Japanese. Huk functionaries and pamphleteers regularly denounced USAFFE as an infamous aggregation of imposters and robbers who oppressed the poor to benefit the rich and who sought to make Filipinos slaves of America while adopting a "superior" attitude toward honest patriots like themselves.[34] Our propagandists replied with broadsides accusing the Huks of an amazing array of vices and crimes, and warning that we would not even consider negotiating with them until they promised to reform—in advance, in detail, and in writing.[35] They riposted with lengthy disquisitions on "social justice" and their hatred of "collaborators," whom they usually identified with landlords. Sometimes they tried to curry favor with local people by gifts of food or arms.[36] Some Americans were receptive to their palaver about "social justice"; others were not but, like Lt. William "Chief" Gardner, were still reluctant to think ill of anyone who would fight the Japanese.[37]

In my experience with them, the Huks were shrewd, formidable, and above all, treacherous adversaries. They pretended to seek friendly cooperation with anyone who would help them fight the foreign invaders and then denounced anyone who disagreed with them as a puppet of those invaders. They extolled Philippine nationalism and then strove to deliver the archipelago, bound hand and foot, to Moscow. They posed as champions of the Filipino people and then kidnapped, looted, tortured, and murdered any who would not support Huk designs. They bought arms if they had money but stole them if they did not or if the owners refused to sell. They called other guerrillas to conferences and then ambushed or cheated those who came. When the others ceased to come, the Huks invaded their spheres of influence and fought battles against them. My forces spent at least as much time watching, fending off, resisting, and occasionally fighting Huks as we did Japanese.[38] All parties on Luzon bore some responsibility for the endemic squabbling that went on, but the unrest there owed more to the Huks than to any others.[39] From their persistent hostility toward us the main gainers were the Japanese; the main losers were the civilian population and the resistance movement overall.

My first encounter with Huks set the tone for most of those that followed. Early in the war a small Huk unit and a small unit of my own met, talked in friendly fashion, ate supper together, and all went to bed. When my men awoke the next morning the Huks were gone, and so were our guns and supplies. Our first dealings that drew blood grew out of their favorite tactic of inviting other guerrillas to conferences. In February 1943 my executive officer, Harry McKenzie, received such an invitation to try to negotiate some kind of working agreement with the hosts. En route to the appointed meeting place he was ambushed and shot in the chest.

Harry survived only because of an improbable string of lucky breaks. First, the bullet missed his vital organs. Second, both his wife, Mary, and his adjutant, Manuel Bahia, happened to be with him. Though the rest of our men fled into the jungle, Mary and Manuel stayed with Harry. All three were taken prisoner by the Huks. Third, for no reason that I ever discovered, the Japanese decided to raid the Huk camp. In the ensuing confusion Mary and Manuel managed to get Harry out of sight and then to effect the escape into the forest in the middle of the night. There they happened to run into some twenty or thirty of our men who were moving southward and had already gotten close to the site of the ambush, a few miles south of Muñoz. Next day they got Harry to a doctor, and he lived. Meanwhile I hastily assembled five or six hundred guerrillas from the squadrons of some of my best operatives—Doliente, Serafica, Nocum, and Joson—and tried to find the Huks, but they had melted into the hills and barrios.

Not surprisingly, USAFFE personnel soon refused to accept invitations to such meetings, so the Huks had to resort to unvarnished force to expel rivals from territories they coveted. McKenzie had one more narrow escape. He and a Filipino were caught inside a house when a gun fight broke out between one of our units and a Huk detachment, but the pair managed to slip away unhurt.

A typical fight with the Huks developed once in 1944 up in the Sierra Madre when they ambushed one of our patrols that was protecting Filipino *cargadores* carrying supplies sent to us from Australia. A gun battle erupted, and the Huks stole some of the supplies. Another engagement accidentally developed into a melee with tragicomic features. Some of Lt. Juan Pajota's men got into a fight with some Huks. A few Japanese nearby heard all the shooting and concluded that some of their men must be in trouble. Soon a three-cornered battle developed in which everyone shot at everyone else. Eventually all parties realized what was happening, whereupon all three sides beat a hasty retreat.

Most of the time we sought merely to prevent Huk expansion. SWPA, after all, wanted guerrillas to gather intelligence that might be of great value months or years in the future, not pick fights with rival guerrilla groups or the Japanese. Moreover, early in the war the Huks secured such a firm hold on southern Tarlac and the southern half of Nueva Ecija that we had little hope of dislodging them. Their efforts to expand northward, however, did produce repeated encounters—not resembling Waterloo or Gettysburg exactly, but serious enough. In one of these, which the LGAF-USAFFE area liaison officer called "the battle of San Juan," 4,000 rounds were allegedly fired by the Huks at our guerrilla unit, while our boys, anxious to save precious ammunition, responded with a mere 500 rounds. Although the Huks won that battle, one warrior on our side directed automatic rifle fire so skillfully that our forces were able to withdraw with only a single casualty. Another hero of the day was Capt. Al Hendrickson who, in the words of our liaison officer, "with his three men also help calm under circumstances," an achievement that enabled that officer himself to execute an orderly retreat. The scale of this confrontation can be judged by its aftermath: the victorious Huks ransacked the barrio, carried away a raincoat worth 100 dollars in Philippine Commonwealth money, and stole 105 dollars of the same currency from a former judge.[40] However minor the skirmish, though, it was typical of the bad time the Huks persistently gave Hendrickson in southern Tarlac province.

One memorable set-to did involve some 650 of our men, though most of them arrived too late to do any fighting, and we had to content ourselves with chasing the Huks away. Occasionally we captured a few. Sometimes we would get back at them by attacking some Japanese installation in a locale where we knew the civilian population supported the Huks. Then the wrath of the Nipponese would fall on these people rather than on Filipinos who supported us. I have been asked if they ever deliberately attempted to assassinate me. I don't know. There was a price on the head of every guerrilla leader, but if the Huks endeavored to seek me out individually I never learned of it. So persistent were they in their determination to vex us, however, that only two months before the American landings that began the reconquest of Luzon, I ordered the movement of most LGAF squadrons southward to counter an expected invasion of our territory by a large body of Huks.[41]

How complicated matters could become in central Luzon is indicated by our many-sided relationship with the Japanese, the Huks, and the Philippine Constabulary. The PC had existed before the war but was completely reorganized by the Japanese occupation force. They wanted it to be not merely a Philippine national police force but something of an auxiliary army as well, one they could use against guerrillas and also one day against American invaders. They calculated that the Constabulary could absorb casualties that would otherwise be Japanese, and that its presence fighting alongside Japanese troops against Americans would allow the Nipponese to appear as friends of Filipinos, helping them defend their homeland against white imperialist exploiters.

The key weakness of this whole scheme was something the Japanese knew but could not admit, even to themselves: their Constabulary was untrustworthy. Many of the Filipinos who volunteered to serve in it were veterans of the Bataan campaign, where they had gained considerable military experience. They had since been retrained by their Japanese mentors and, supposedly, properly immunized against a recurrence of their previous pro-Americanism. But who could be sure what sentiments lurked in their hearts? In fact, many of them were still hostile to their conquerors; others simply needed a job to feed their families but felt no special loyalty to their new employers. In any case, a majority of Filipino civilians regarded with suspicion a uniformed national police force whose ties with the cruel invaders seemed so obvious.

This situation crystallized in December 1943 when we had a conference with Colonel Cruz, the Constabulary's inspector for Central Luzon, and Col. Godofredo Monsod, senior Constabulary inspector in Nueva Ecija. We reached a number of understandings. If civilians were treated well by Constabulary men, we would reciprocate. If the PC did not send patrols into areas we dominated, or if such patrols were sent but never discovered anything, we would not ambush PC patrols. Surreptitious cordiality blossomed rapidly thereafter. Some of our men began to wear PC uniforms, to live and work beside real Constabulary men and routinely gather information of every sort. PC men either gave us or told us where to find arms, ammunition, food, medical supplies, and other useful commodities. If they had to arrest guerrillas to please their nominal Nipponese masters, they usually found some pretext to release them eventually. If a PC patrol ventured into the mountains to search for us, it often returned much depleted. Survivors would say they had fought a battle with guerrillas and had suffered heavy casualties. The truth usually was that the missing men had defected to the LGAF and kept their guns.

Of course the Japanese eventually learned of these subterfuges, in considerable measure because Colonels Cruz and Monsod were too bold about their collaboration. Eventually they and several other ranking PC officers were arrested and executed. Monsod's successor, Maj. Alfonso Arellano, continued the "cooperation" but was much more circumspect about it. The particular way he and I usually met was indicative of his careful nature. If he wanted to talk to me, which was not often, I would get word to be at a certain deserted spot along a certain road at a certain time. He would arrive in his staff car and pick me up, and we would repair to a convenient barrio or simply drive around for a while until our business had been transacted. Then we would laugh together at the Japanese and part.

On several occasions we discussed just when and under what conditions it would be most advantageous for Major Arellano and his followers to defect to our side. Perhaps fortunately, the enemy decided for us. In the middle of 1944, increasingly suspicious of the PC, the Japanese abruptly disarmed all its members. Arellano deserted at once and became one of my regional commanders. Most other PC men did not follow his example until December 1944, when an American invasion was clearly not far off, but during the preceding year so many of them had found so many ways to help us that they might as well have been in the LGAF. One particular case illustrates the situation well.

In 1946 some Huks and their sympathizers pressed charges of treason against Major Arellano in a Philippine court. They alleged that as an officer in the Constabulary, a Japanese puppet organization, he had fought against the Huks, patriots who had heroically resisted the enemy invaders. Arellano, understandably frightened, asked me to testify on his behalf. I submitted an affidavit describing in some detail how he had used his position in the Constabulary ever since December 1943 to work closely with me in furthering the activities and objectives of the resistance movement. I added that he had done so loyally and ably until the end of the war.[42]

For all our mutual hostility, we and the Huks had many of the same problems and often tried to deal with them in similar ways. If we were too weak to undertake real battles with the Japanese, so were they. Despite all their bellicose talk they spent more time collecting intelligence than fighting, as we did. Most of our men were guerrillas only at night and became farmers at daybreak. So did theirs. We did not begin to get any material aid from Australia until the middle of 1944; they, unlike their Marxist brethren in Europe and Indonesia, never got any outside help at all beyond a couple of Chinese squadrons and a military training school their Chinese comrades had set up for them near Mount Arayat shortly before the war began. The Chinese Communists, after all, were inundated with their own problems.

Overall, the Huks were extremely troublesome for us and near the end of the war may even have made a deal with the Japanese for arms to use against us.[43] Yet ultimately, they were unsuccessful. Why? Pomeroy, relentlessly applying Marxist "scientific analysis," said the reason was that the Huk movement succumbed to "infantile leftism": that is, they let hopes obscure "objective revolutionary conditions," and therefore the "struggle for national liberation" did not mature sufficiently to succeed in the wartime Philippines [44]

Taruc and Kerkvliet found other serious shortcomings; in their view the Huks picked too many fights with enemies and consequently suffered heavier losses than they could reasonably bear. I am skeptical. The Huks did engage in numerous skirmishes with the Japanese, but neither they nor we ever had enough ammunition for large-scale sustained combat. Yet at the end of the war the Huks were in a relatively strong position militarily. They had acquired a quantity of arms and ammunition in the last months of the war, whether surreptitiously from the Japanese or more openly from people in the U.S. Army who knew little about Communism and to whom one bunch of Filipino guerrillas looked much like another. Too many of our people were willing, even anxious, to give arms to anyone who seemed to want to fight the Japanese. Ray Hunt relates with extreme disgust that early in 1945 he was ordered by high-ranking officers in the U.S Sixth Army to deliver munitions to the Huks, despite his repeated protests that they were Communists.[45] In any case, I certainly did not have the impression that they had been bled of their strength by too much fighting and dying earlier in the war.

Kerkvliet and Taruc acknowledge that the Huks had harmed themselves grievously in other ways as well, and in my opinion it was these factors that were crucial. Many, including Taruc himself, resented harsh Communist discipline. Too many "enemies" had been kidnapped and executed. Habitual lying and deceit, though not formal sins in the Marxist church, had severely undermined the spirit of comradeship that existed among the Huks early in the war. Leaders had grown selfish, used faithful followers to exalt themselves, and often acted impulsively. Supplies had never been sufficient, and too many recruits had not taken training seriously. The movement had produced too many thieves who had stolen too much food and "liberated" too many carabao from hapless peasants.[46] Too many "crazies" had seized too many Filipino women and committed too many other crimes that ordinary people find hard to forgive or forget. In this connection Doyle Decker relates one of those anecdotes that indicate more than their tellers intend. He says he heard a tale during the war that a Huk leader had once arrested Ed Ramsey for making improper advances to Filipino women. This was "the laugh of the year," Decker comments, adding that the Huk kingpin should also have arrested himself, all his own men, and half the male population of the Islands.[47] Overall, the Huks continued too long to fight USAFFE rivals when we were obviously growing in strength and public credit.

Not the least self-destructive of the Huks' faults was their incurable quarrelsomeness. Disagreements over strategy and tactics occur in all political movements, and some leaders always want to boss others: witness our own incessant bickering, which has already been chronicled exhaustively. But Marxist revolutionary movements are especially prone to dissension because Marxism is so complex and elaborate an ideology that never ending disputes over doctrine complicate the usual arguments about methods and the struggles for power. Finally, all Philippine politics is intensely personal and riddled with factionalism. The Huks were thoroughly imbued with all these traditions of dissent, which, collectively, severely curtailed their movement's popularity and influence.[48]

— 9 —
Communications
with Australia

Early in the war one of the most vexatious problems for all guerrilla groups was that we had no regular, dependable means of communicating with one another, much less with SWPA Headquarters in Australia. Only occasionally did some message get through. In 1942 Guillermo Nakar, a captain in the Philippine army who had refused to surrender when Corregidor fell and who had held on to a battalion of infantry in northern Luzon, managed to acquire a radio transmitter from Capt. Everett Warner before Warner surrendered to the Japanese. With it he sent a few weak radio messages to MacArthur while the general was still on Corregidor, conveying a little information about conditions where he was. Soon the enemy captured and executed him. Many months afterward a radio message reached Australia from Capt. Ralph B. Praeger, a cavalry officer who, like Nakar, had refused to surrender and had fled to the Cagayan Valley in far northern Luzon. Along the way he had salvaged a transmitter from a mine in Kapugao and used it to send considerable information about his alleged 5,000 guerrilla followers and his undeniable need for arms and ammunition.[1] Soon Colonels Moses and Noble borrowed Praeger's transmitter to convey similar messages to SWPA headquarters: our followers are many and our potential is great, but we need supplies, arms, ammunition, and a dependable transmitter of our own. Unfortunately, like Nakar, Praeger was captured in August 1943, and the feeble linkage with SWPA was again broken.

Australia had better luck with the guerrillas farther south. Radio communication was established, precariously, with Macario Peralta on Panay in November 1942; with Wendell Fertig on Mindanao in January 1943; and with others on Cebu and south Negros in February. General MacArthur was much encouraged by these developments. In December 1942 he dispatched Capt. Jesus Villamor to the Visayan Islands by submarine with orders to work his way northward into Luzon. Along the way he was to establish escape routes to get Americans and Filipinos from the islands to Australia, train people in gathering and conveying intelligence, organize resistance to the Japanese, and distribute propaganda. He toiled eleven months at this delicate and precarious task.[2] Soon after Villamor's departure Col. Charles M. Smith and Chick Parsons, both well known to Filipinos, were sent by submarine to Mindanao and the Visayas with similar instructions and radio transmitters which they distributed to various guerilla units.

In June 1943 Gen. Courtney Whitney, who was in Australia, was put in overall charge of communications and the organization, supply, and coordination of guerrilla activities all over the Philippines. He realized at once that we would need considerable technical aid from outside if we were to realize our full potential. He handpicked several hundred Filipino officers and men and sent them to Camps Cook and Beale in California to be trained in sabotage, radio operation and repair, meteorology, distributing propaganda, combatting Japanese propaganda, and above all, gathering intelligence. When their instruction was completed, these men were smuggled back into the Philippines to help us.[3] Emphasis was also laid on preparing guerrillas in the interior to strike at the Japanese from the rear whenever American landings might take place in the Islands. It was all designed to tighten the bonds between guerrillas and Australia and to ready everyone for eventual reinvasion of the Philippines. These men were soon reinforced by some 600 selected U.S. volunteers who were trained in Australia in the same pursuits as well as in coast watching, plane watching, making booby traps, and handling artillery.[4] They were then assigned throughout the Philippines.

By late 1943 even such an out-of-the-way operative as Maj. Parker Calvert, commander of Volckmann's first district, had gotten a transmitter into working order.[5] Off to the south it was Anderson's good fortune to have with him some Philippine Scouts who were capable radio technicians. He sent a couple of them to Manila, where they got jobs with the Japanese and managed to steal enough parts to make a transmitter for Anderson, who operated it with a diesel engine that would run on coconut oil.[6] Andy was so overjoyed at his good fortune that he deluged Australia with messages, which at once created problems. One was that the Japanese intercepted so many that Andy had to move his transmitter after every orgy of broadcasting. Another was that there had been no prior arrangement about signals between Australia and any guerrilla band that lacked an official transmitter; hence swpa headquarters was dubious about the authenticity of so many rapid-fire communications. So they sent Andy a list of a hundred personal questions such as "What was your mother's maiden name?" Only when he had answered all these correctly were they reassured that he really was who he claimed to be.[7] Then they put him on a schedule.

My own communications problems were more basic. I did not have two-way radio contact with anyone until the spring of 1944. I had to rely on the stable of runners I had developed in 1942 to keep me in contact with nearby organizations, with Manila, and with islands to the south. From them I gradually learned that southern guerrilla organizations were more advanced than most of ours on Luzon, that a growing number were in regular radio contact with MacArthur, and that some were receiving supplies from Australia by submarine. I sent off information and requests for aid, hoping that the submarines that landed supplies on Mindanao and the Visayas would eventually try to contact us. The only logical place was somewhere along the east coast near the town of Baler. This was rough country, thinly populated, and across the Sierra Madre from us, but it did have several bays and coves that looked like good landing spots. Even better, it was not strongly garrisoned by the enemy. Our Squadron 103, led by Capt. Abdon Aquino, already dominated the area around Carranglan and Pantabangan in Nueva Ecija as well as Baler itself. Here we assigned men to the monotonous task of watching the coast day after day to look for American or Japanese ships and submarines or just to pick up scraps of information.

Both couriers and radios had serious drawbacks. With the courier system, nobody could ever be sure that a message sent would really arrive. It was seldom that swpa sent any specific reply, and even if one did come it was always months later and thus likely to be irrelevant. How often we imagined that many of our troubles could be alleviated if only we had a transceiver. In fact, however, radio problems, were quite as vexatious and even more numerous than those with runners. To start with, the best U.S. transceivers weighed a ton. No man or single animal was strong enough to carry one through mountains, swamps, and jungles to its destination. Even lighter (and less reliable) ones had to be carried by horses and carabao, who often bumped and jiggled their cargos so much that they wouldn't work at journey's end. It was not the least of Courtney Whitney's contributions to Allied victory that he eventually found some transceivers in England small enough to be carried by one man. He at once ordered dozens of them, then hundreds.[8] But lesser troubles abounded as well. Codes and operating signals were often misunderstood, generators wouldn't work, batteries ran down, a radio would send but not receive (or vice versa), nearby iron deposits or inconveniently located mountains ruined transmission, the operator's watch would not work so he didn't know when it was the assigned time to transmit, essential spare parts were missing, and nobody nearby ever knew how to fix anything. In isolated locales it might take six weeks to get news of trouble out to somebody who could do something about it and get that person back to the site of the problem. By then, of course, the overall situation would have changed.[9] To be sure, vaunted Yankee ingenuity (and Filipino too) sometimes proved equal to coping with these vexations—but *only* sometimes.

In August 1943 Volckmann and Anderson, working independently, managed to put together largely homemade radio units with which they could sometimes communicate with each other.[10] Macario Peralta's transmission outfit on Panay was so weak that he was able to render it usable only by setting men to work in relays pedaling furiously on a bicycle for three hours in order to store enough electricity to transmit for fifteen minutes.[11] More typical was an experience of Donald Blackburn in the summer of 1943. He had gotten a water wheel and generator from a place where Americans had once lived in the mountains of northern Luzon. He dammed a nearby stream and charged a battery he happened to possess, only to have the radio break down, following which his dam broke and washed everything downstream.[12] Ed Ramsey still found the courier system so unsatisfactory that he risked his life in an effort to get to the island of Mindoro, where he expected to get a radio from a Major Phillips. When he eventually did get there, he learned that Phillips had been killed by the Japanese and his radio destroyed. All he brought back from his trip was a particularly grisly memory. He had spent a night as the guest of "General Ernie," the evil chieftain of a gang of bandits who masqueraded as guerrillas. When Ramsey arrived, these gentry were engaged in torturing three prisoners. "General Ernie" asked that he and his followers be sworn in as guerrillas under Ramsey's command. Being in no position to object, Ed obliged his host. Not to be outdone in hospitality, his new vassal then cut the throats of the prisoners so their cries would not deprive Ed of needed sleep.[13]

We were all eager to secure radio transmitters for another reason too. In 1943 Captain Villamor reported to Australia that the guerrillas of Luzon were divided, ill trained, badly in need of medical supplies, poor in maintaining secrecy in intelligence work, and susceptible to Japanese propaganda. He urged that we be accorded immediate recognition by SWPA to boost our morale and reduce rivalries and that we be sent arms, ammunition, radios, medical supplies, and money.[14] A year later Panlilio lamented that many civilians simply could no longer stand up under the pressures to which they were subjected. They were nearing starvation as the Japanese took more and more of their rice. Many grumbled that they were wasting their lives, that the invaders would never be driven out, that Washington did not really care what happened to Filipinos, that their sufferings were—as Japanese propaganda insisted—the fault of the guerrillas, and that even if they wanted to fight the enemy they had no appropriate weapons.[15]

I heard all this at the time and must admit that such complaints had substance, yet it seemed to me that differences in morale varied more between city and country than from one time during the war to another. I believe both Villamor and Panlilio exaggerated. For one thing, Villamor grew increasingly morose and bitter as the war lengthened and the sufferings of his fellow Filipinos increased visibly. He also gradually convinced himself that his homeland's misfortunes were the fault of the Americans. His memoirs, published a generation after the war, have a strongly anti-American flavor. Perhaps he and Panlilio did describe accurately the food shortage in Manila and environs, but where I was, in Luzon's "rice basket," there was enough for everyone to eat. Moreover, there are always counter-currents in human affairs. If some Filipinos concluded that their salvation lay in collaboration with their conquerors, many others were increasingly convinced that the general thrust of war news and the steady growth of guerrilla organizations and numbers indicated ever more strongly that the Allies would win eventually; therefore, one should be pro-American and patient. Which group was more numerous? Which tendency was stronger? I think the latter, though of course there were no public opinion polls then. Still, the tenuousness of the situation and the notorious volatility of public moods did make one anxious to secure more guns, more supplies, and a specific promise of a future invasion. Even a radio that worked would help some.

A big break in our fortunes came in May 1944 when our coastwatcher program began to pay dividends. One day the watchers spotted a sailboat with several men aboard at Dibut Bay, a few miles south of Baler on the Tayabas coast. Its skipper was Capt. Robert V. Ball. He said he had been sent from Samar (one of the Visayan Islands) by Col. Charles Smith to contact Luzon guerrillas, to bring me a transmitter, and to stay with LGAF to operate it.

Ball was an imaginative fellow who did not mind straying from the path of military orthodoxy if he thought it necessary to attract attention. When the war began, he was an air force radio operator at Del Monte Field on Mindanao. He was taken prisoner when the base surrendered but soon escaped and joined a band of guerrillas. From bits of this and that scrounged from the air base he managed to construct a workable radio and transmitter and tried to establish radio contact with Australia, but nobody would answer his messages. In desperation he invented a regular broadcast called "Hot Poop from the Hot Yanks in the Hot Philippines." He hoped somebody would hear it and reply, if only out of curiosity. As noted earlier, SWPA headquarters managed to establish radio contact with some guerrillas in the southern Islands in 1942, but they did not respond to Ball for weeks because they found both his approach and his messages puzzling and suspected a Japanese trick of some kind. In 1942 Mindanao was a primitive place, thinly populated save in occasional coastal towns. Before long, American submarines were able to slip into isolated harbors occasionally to bring news and supplies to guerrillas there and to bring a few men back to Australia with them. Eventually SWPA became convinced that Ball was not a Japanese imposter. After a time he was evacuated via submarine to Australia, where he was instructed to try to establish contact with other guerrillas farther north and was sent off to Samar. It was from there that he had ventured to the east coast of Luzon, as described above.

One of Capt. Aquino's subordinates, Lt. Alipio, set up a small camp for Ball, secured food for him, and provided him with both guards and runners. One runner was immediately sent to Aquino and another, a Lieutenant Bernabe, to me. Bernabe was a good choice to guarantee quick access and to impress me with the importance of the mission, since he was the officer in charge of our coast watchers and he and I were already acquainted.

I was in the middle of a meeting with McKenzie and several squadron commanders when Bernabe suddenly peered into our room in conspiratorial fashion, then sidled up to me and said he had an important message that he must tell me privately. I shooed out all the other officers except McKenzie, but it was an empty gesture. Filipinos not only love gossip and hate to keep secrets; they are also near clairvoyant at putting together rumors and unusual conduct to guess what is in the wind.

Bernabe had a good story to tell, and he did not diminish it. He said an American named Ball had landed in a small boat from a submarine, bringing with him not only a radio transmitter but large quantities of canned meat, coffee, American cigarettes, and other delicacies that made our mouths water. He even had a little book of matches on which the words "I Shall Return" appeared over General MacArthur's signature; he said Ball had given it to him. As it turned out, Ball did have a radio for us, but only a few cigarettes and a couple of cans of food. His transportation had also been rather less grandiose than advertised: he had come from Samar in a sailboat—a major reason his provisions were scanty. Ball himself had been entirely truthful throughout. He had told people on shore repeatedly that he had not come by submarine but they just nodded and exchanged knowing winks. I would bet that even now, half a century later, a few people around Baler would still insist that he came in by submarine or even that they "saw" him get off the sub.[16]

Lieutenant Bernabe had arrived at our meeting late in the afternoon. We hastily adjourned for supper and caught a few hours of sleep, planning to set out for Baler about midnight so we could cross the San José road before daylight. Everybody was eager to embark on what optimists were sure would be a splendid adventure. Only with difficulty did I manage to limit our party to about ten of McKenzie's headquarters staff and no more than fifteen of my current "traveling squad."

Getting to Baler meant seventy or eighty miles of hard hiking over a mountain range. We almost didn't make it. The most direct route passed between the towns of Bongabon and Rizal, territory where we knew some of the local population were friendly to the Huks, some to the Japanese, and only a few to us. Nonetheless, I felt confident that if we kept moving and did not look for trouble, we could make it through without mishap. We crossed the main road at daybreak, as planned, went perhaps half a mile farther, and stopped for breakfast. A civilian guide went off to a nearby barrio to procure food. He was gone longer than I thought he should have been, but presently he returned with a large pot of rice, which we soon devoured. I was nervous and suspicious. Why had the guide taken so long to get food? Where were the curious civilians who usually showed up to gawk and question us? Maybe it was a premonition; anyway, I decided quite suddenly that we should move on. After my earlier effort to form a unit of horse cavalry had proved impractical, we had gotten rid of most of our horses, but we had kept a few in case it was necessary to get somewhere quickly, to ease the transport of someone sick or injured, or just for myself and a few others to ride in rough country now and then. Now four of us who had horses saddled them and started off; the rest of our party followed on foot. We hadn't been on the road ten minutes when we spotted a large party of Japanese, maybe three hundred yards in front to our left, simultaneously running toward us and deploying for battle. Soon they dropped into a nearby irrigation ditch and opened fire. One of their first shots killed my favorite horse, which immediately drove me into a frustrated rage. Here I was about to make my first contact with the outside world in two years and these slant-eyed villains were not only trying to stop me but to kill me in the bargain. I cannot recall ever being more incensed.

Practical considerations abruptly and no doubt providentially interrupted my fury. There were only about two dozen of us, while there appeared to be at least 150 Japanese dedicated to our immediate destruction. It was no time for heroism; our only hope was to get out of there. So we began to shoot and withdraw, hoping eventually to lose our foes. We managed to do so about two in the afternoon by hiding in some tall cogan grass. For hours Japanese patrols passed back and forth, often frighteningly close by.

This was one of the most anguished days I can recall for another reason as well—thirst. We rarely carried canteens on our travels, since there was always water in barrios, and streams are plentiful all over Luzon. On this day I took my last drink about 10:00 A.M., and I did not get another until late that night. Going twelve to fourteen hours without water under the burning sun of a Philippine summer is an experience like no other.

We scattered and hid separately during that terrible afternoon. When darkness fell and we managed at last to find one another again, I divided our slim forces. McKenzie, two others, and I formed one squad. The other men I sent back the way we had come. They were to draw enemy fire away from my group and, in the long run, warn other units of what had happened. Our luck was good, and both squads escaped. I now decided to press on toward Baler Bay by a somewhat different route. We managed to evade numerous enemy patrols and slip into a barrio at the foot of the mountains where some of our men had friends. There we got some food, water, and rest. Next morning we took the primitive road from Bongabon to Baler and followed it most of the way to Ball's camp, forced-marching much of the time. We reached him less than a week after first learning of his existence. It surely should have been one of the most memorable events of my life, but at the time I felt let down because I had believed Bernabe's extravagant tale about a submarine full of munitions, food, and other luxuries. It would be three months before that miracle materialized.

Nonetheless, Bob Ball and I hit it off from the first and soon became good friends. He was normally quiet and easygoing but had a lively sense of humor. As a radio operator he was incredibly skilled;

I have never seen anyone else send and receive Morse Code as rapidly. Right off he used his radio to send accumulated intelligence reports directly to Australia.

Since Ball had arrived in just a small sailboat, he had only a very limited cargo of either food or radio equipment. Nonetheless, during the summer of 1944 other sailboats began to land elsewhere along the east coast of Luzon bearing some equipment, and more such material was being packed through jungles northward from submarines that had landed in islands farther south. Anderson, for example, got both a transmitter and other supplies in this way in June. He at once urged me to try to contact Volckmann and let him know that supplies were coming and that he too should soon have radio equipment. I agreed, then checked with SWPA for permission. My old companion Esteban Lumyeb, who had left Camp Sanchez with then-Sergeant Short and me two years before, now took one of Ball's radios and an operator and delivered them to Volckmann. By July 1, 1944, I finally got a transmitter all my own that enabled me for the first time in the whole war to contact SWPA headquarters directly. After some weeks of the trials, errors, and tribulations that seemed inseparable from radios, Volckmann, Anderson, and I were communicating with each other routinely and were linked to SWPA as well.

The coast watchers, who had already done invaluable work, were much cheered by these successes and redoubled their efforts. Operatives on various Visayan Islands began to extend their radio networks and to integrate them more fully. General MacArthur cautioned all of us anew that our primary business was still collecting intelligence, but he was obviously buoyed up in spirit by Ball's voyage and its aftermath. To raise our morale and taunt the Japanese he took to radioing orders "To my commanders in the Philippines."[17] Even in remote and tempestuous Tarlac the ebullient Capt. Cris Hipolito recorded that events were tumbling over one another so fast that "I have to employ every available typist to tackle the deluge of reports coming in every day."[18]

With the arrival of the radios there came also some arms, ammunition, chocolate candy, toothpaste, razors, needles, cigarettes, and American magazines. In August such commodities came only in a trickle, but with the landing of the first submarine in Dibut Bay about September 1 they began to arrive in floods.

Even the midsummer driblets caused spirits to soar on every side. The long-expected and hoped-for "aid" was finally appearing. Surely liberation would soon be forthcoming! There is no better way to indicate the feelings of our men in the LGAF command than to cite still another quotation from our champion composer of memorable prose, Cris Hipolito: "Imagine our excitement at the sight of those medicines, cigarettes, and brand new bullets. With only a few packs of cigarettes reaching us due to the risk it entailed bringing those all the way from Tayabas, the boys did not want to smoke them at first. They seemed satisfied just smelling them. And there were not a few who kissed Gen. MacArthur's picture in one of those 'I Shall Return' tube-like packs, with tears flowing profusely from their eyes."[19]

Panlilio records that Marking's guerrillas were just as overjoyed as mine when these invaluable supplies and culinary delicacies began to arrive, though she adds that it was disheartening to hear again from MacArthur that we should just collect information instead of attacking the Japanese. She was also profoundly disappointed to learn a short time later that Anderson had burned most of the U.S. magazines and propaganda he had received.[20] Her feeling was certainly easy to understand, but Andy had his reasons. Typically cautious, and fearful of bringing harm to the Filipinos who supported him, he knew that any Filipino caught by the Japanese with such material in his possession might be tortured and murdered. Maybe I was more callous than Anderson or maybe he and I just judged "imponderables" in a different way; whichever, my response was like Panlilio's: we should circulate these materials and try to maximize their impact as propaganda.

One thing the whole endeavor demonstrated, at least to me, was MacArthur's astuteness. Because he was habitually embroiled in the dismal conflicts of American politics his ideological enemies have done their best to destroy his reputation by depicting him as a bumbling egomaniac. Like all of us he had deficiencies of character, but nobody matched him for understanding the psychology of Oriental peoples and devising strategies for dealing with them. He also understood that a major aspect of leadership is looking and acting like a leader, especially when one is leading ordinary, uncomplicated people. To put his picture and "I Shall Return" on packets of cigarettes, candy, and the like was not mere self-inflation. The message had a real impact on Filipinos. It told them that he had not forgotten or forsaken them, and so helped buoy their morale in difficult times. It also told the Japanese defiantly that they would never defeat him, that he was coming to get them; that the "Rising Sun" would soon be setting.

Another of MacArthur's typical acts of calculated defiance of the enemy was to create a "guerrilla postal service." He had special stamps printed in Australia and smuggled into the Philippines by submarine. I never saw any of these, but many other guerrillas took to putting them on their mail. Manila post office employees routinely processed such mail. If questioned about it they would reply blandly that they hadn't noticed the stamps.[21]

I have always thought that MacArthur's strategy of hopping from base to base and island to island, being patient and keeping casualties down, was much superior to that of the U.S. Navy, which consisted of pounding straight across the Pacific, storming one island after another on the way to Japan itself. MacArthur's employment of a nice blend of material aid and psychological reassurance was likewise the tactic best suited to the situation in the Philippines in the summer of 1944.

Ever since landing at Baler in late May, Ball and I had spoken about the possibility of a submarine landing in that vicinity sometime in the future, but the matter had not passed beyond mere conversation because of the problems involved in getting radios to Anderson and Volckmann and then getting all the transmitters and receivers in working order. It was only in July that I began to consider the subject systematically with Australia. My Radio Log Book has half a dozen entries between July 17 and July 28, 1944, discussing the pros and cons of several possible landing places. Eventually we decided on Dibut Bay. It was only five miles from Baler, which housed the nearest Japanese garrison, but it was an exceedingly tough five miles across the rough, steep, heavily forested end of a mountain range that jutted out into the ocean between the bay and the town so that one could not see either from the other. From Baler it would be a three- or four-hour hike of the most arduous sort over this jungle-clad mountain end to reach our camp on the beach. Dibut Bay itself was deep, narrow, and sheltered by mountains—no small advantage to any submarine captain, well aware that no craft is more vulnerable to naval artillery than a submarine caught on the surface or in shallow water.

Though I did not know it at the time, this fact of naval life had been demonstrated dramatically on March 2, 1944, by the very submarine, *Narwhal*, that we were to meet. On that date the sub, with Capts. Clyde Childress and Ernest McClish on board, had tried to land supplies near the mouth of the Augusan River on the north coast of Mindanao. The water was too rough at the usual site, so the commander nosed his craft as far as he dared into the mouth of the river. This created one of those classic foul-ups that plague all military operations: in this case a fearfully difficult unloading because the cargo slated for this site was buried beneath other stuff that would have been unloaded elsewhere first had it not been for the rough water. Murphy's Law operated in the Philippines quite as remorselessly as in other parts of the world: abruptly a Japanese ship appeared and dropped depth charges that almost sank the *Narwhal*.[22]

With this harrowing experience still fresh in his memory, the skipper of the *Narwhal* wanted explicit plans made well in advance that would enable him to get in and out of Dibut Bay with no time or motion wasted. He also insisted that Anderson and I, the actual guerrilla leaders, should be on hand to supervise the whole operation and take possession of the cargo, which would be split between us. I stayed around Baler for several weeks but put the time to good use. We built rafts to transfer our goods from the submarine to shore, developed and practiced a signal system, and made preparations to transport our treasures-to-come back to our home bases. We didn't get very fat that summer. The soil around Baler is mediocre at best, so the local inhabitants grow barely enough to feed themselves. Fortunately, Lieutenant Aquino's Squadron 103 was able to supply us with some rice and vegetables,[23] and a local tribe of Negritos brought us fresh meat and fish periodically.

The *Narwhal* was to arrive August 31, 1944. The night before, I borrowed a few hours from Uncle Sam and for the first time in three years wrote a letter to my parents. Like some others, I found this a surprisingly difficult task.[24] Maybe it was because I'd been separated from loved ones for so long and had led a life with which other family members would be totally unfamiliar. Perhaps I felt that whatever I might say about what I had been doing or feeling would seem totally alien to my correspondents, or would be misunderstood, or would cause them to worry needlessly. I do recall that it seemed both irrelevant and trivial to try to write about something "back home" with which I was no longer familiar and which, in fact, no longer interested me. My state of mind puzzled me, then and now.

The letter itself caused considerable commotion when it reached its destination. I had given it to the submarine captain and assumed that somebody would eventually mail it to my folks for me. But, as a jaundiced enlisted man (probably in George Washington's army), observed long ago, the War Department exists to do your thinking for you. People there intercepted the letter and forwarded it to my parents along with a letter of their own, a procedure that took several weeks.

When my mother saw a letter from the War Department in the daily mail, she was afraid to open it because the last my parents had heard about me had come in a similarly "official" notice back in April 1942 that I was missing in action. Now, thoroughly agitated, she phoned my father at his office. He told her to open the letter; she did so and immediately exclaimed that it was from me. My father said he would be right home, but before leaving he told everyone in his office about it, and all these people at once called *their* families. Within a few minutes the word was spreading all over town.

When my father got home my mother was industriously (and uncharacteristically) mowing the lawn, so excited that she felt she had to do *something* while waiting for him. Only then did both of them read my letter carefully—and only then did they notice that the envelope also contained a message from the War Department. It cautioned them to say nothing about my letter lest this endanger the lives of others, the national interests of the United States, and, no doubt, current management of the universe. So they had to rush to the phone at once, call everyone at Dad's office, and tell all those people that they should tell everyone *they* had phoned to keep everything secret. By then, of course, it was like putting toothpaste back in the tube. Somehow the Allies won the war anyway.

The day the submarine was to arrive we carefully checked all the recognition signals that would precede contact. We made sure our reflecting panels were spaced properly, and I got well out into the bay in a small boat so the submarine crew could see me plainly before committing themselves irrevocably to landing. All day we watched fruitlessly for our long-awaited visitor. Then, early in the evening, the sub suddenly rose right out of the sea like a gigantic whale— between me and the shore! I was simultaneously thrilled and dumbfounded. The thing looked as big as a battleship.

Before dark we were unloading at full speed. The *Narwhal* was in very close to shore in the deep bay. We quickly ran a line from it to shore and tied the end around a big tree. Then we put into the water the large bamboo rafts we had built, tied one end of a rope to each of them and the other end to the ship-to-shore line. Thus a raft could be loaded quickly aboard the submarine, reeled in by men on shore and unloaded, retied to the main line, and reeled back to the sub.

As soon as this procedure was going smoothly, the *Narwhal*'s captain invited me aboard to enjoy a feast of ham sandwiches and coffee. The crowded little ward room where I ate seemed as luxurious as a fabled New York nightclub. Days later I found that part of our cargo was a delicious new kind of army chow called K rations. I didn't know that most GIs called their contents dog biscuits and other colorful, often vulgar, names. To me, after so many months of a guerrilla diet, even the Spam tasted like prime T-bone steak.[25]

It took about four hours to unload a splendid assortment of 1,000 weapons, ammunition, food, medical supplies, radios, newspapers, magazines, cigarettes, and sundries onto the beach. Then the crew quickly checked their craft for stowaways, put me back in my little sailboat, and slipped beneath the waves as swiftly and silently as they had come. I felt suddenly lonesome and homesick, but the melancholy reverie did not last long, for right at my feet the beach was piled high with dozens of crates, boxes, and bags. I still remember the thought that struck me sharply: "What in hell am I going to do with all this stuff?"

Occasionally, bizarre items would turn up in such shipments. Once a crate labeled Thompson submachine guns proved to be full of old U.S. cavalry sabers. Filipino guerrillas distributed them anyway, with the result that the Japanese were soon complaining of attacks on their outposts by Filipino "terrorists" wielding long curved swords.[26] The most interesting items in this particular shipment were several 1.5-cubic-foot tin boxes, soldered shut, which contained about $1,000,000 in counterfeit Japanese currency, all printed in 1943. This paper fortune was to help me meet my varied needs.

The different ways in which we responded to this opportunity are more interesting to me now than they were at the time. First off, I was offered $50,000 in genuine Philippine pesos in addition to the bogus enemy money, but because Chick Parsons told me I would have to account for it, I declined. I was also offered some real American money, but not wanting to be accountable for that either, I turned it down as well. After all, I hadn't handled any real money for more than two years, and LGAF had gotten along fine without it, so why complicate my life? By contrast, Parsons gave Anderson $50,000 in American money on September 1, 1944, and, for whatever reason, said he did *not* have to account for it. Andy, who was both honest and careful with money, did order all his subordinates to account for whatever portions of the sum they were given. Only one did not. Alejo Santos was not a man who trusted others; he wanted total control of everything relating to those guerrillas he had brought with him into Anderson's organization, and $20,000 disappeared under his control.[27] It was more interesting, to me anyway, that Anderson actually burned up some of the money (as he did the magazines), fearing that if the Japanese caught any Filipinos with such new currency, they would know at once that the bearers had been supplied by Americans.[28] War not only burns up money in a metaphorical sense; sometimes it does so literally as well.[29]

Unloading had gone smoothly, and now there was nothing to do but settle down to the arduous job of actually moving and distributing our goods. We had built some barracks and warehouses in coconut groves a short way back from the beach to store our supplies briefly and to hide them from air observation by the Japanese. This particular shipment comprised about thirty tons, and we were to get another twenty tons about a month later on the submarine *Nautilus*. Together this would comprise our share of the 1,627 tons sent out to all Philippine guerrillas in the whole war. (Some 600 tons of the total went to Mindanao, much the closest and easiest place to land supplies.) My portion was to be divided among all the larger LGAF units. Each of them was to send men to Dibut Bay to get their share and carry it away. Several camps had been arranged about a day's march apart along the trails. The original plan was for my men to carry one LGAF unit's load a day's march from the beach. There some fifty men from the receiving unit, who had hiked in, would be waiting to take their portion the rest of the way back to a base camp in the lowlands over the mountains, where Harry McKenzie would preside over the final apportionment. Then another unit's men would hike in, and the process would be repeated.

Although carrying heavy loads on one's back is not delightful anywhere, we did not anticipate that transport would be a major problem. There were steep mountains nearby but also considerable open plateau and low rolling hills. Jungle existed only here and there, and the area was crisscrossed by many animal and Negrito trails. But things did not go according to expectations. Men laden with forty- to fifty-pound packs soon found the trek through the mountains harder than any of us had expected. Within a couple of days our men were worn out. I got tired just getting myself through.

Thus we had to send for units from the lowlands to come all the way up into the mountains to lug away their own shares of the supplies. This increased the risk of discovery, because it meant that many more people knew the location of our base camp. But luck was with us, and we were never raided. A group of packers would arrive one day, prepare their loads, and leave the next. On their way they would pass the next unit coming up. Back at LGAF headquarters our men sorted supplies, issued weapons and ammunition, and set up loads for still other companies of packers to carry back to their individual units. Eventually we got radios, arms, and supplies to their intended destinations. The *Nautilus* landing and subsequent distribution of goods took place early in October. It brought another 1,000 assorted submachine guns, carbines, BARs, grenades, rocket launchers, .50-caliber machine guns, .45-caliber pistols, plus enough medicines that we were even able to smuggle some into Cabanatuan prison late in the year,[30] and enough dynamite to "blow Bataan off the map," as the loquacious Leon Beck put it.[31]

The whole operation was not easy—and certainly not fast. I still have a copy of a letter I wrote to Al Hendrickson off in Tarlac, dated November 13, 1944. I thanked him for sending men to help unload and transport supplies from the submarines and promised to send him his share as soon as I could. Even more telling about the lack of speed was an exchange of letters late in December, less than two weeks before the Lingayen Gulf landings began, between Colonel Merrill up in the Zambales Mountains and Captain Cabangbang down near Manila. Merrill grumbled about still not having a reliable radio; Cabangbang emphasized how difficult and uncertain it was to get anything over the Sierra Madre but promised to send a good radio as soon as he could.[32] For myself, two aspects of the whole operation were extremely gratifying. First, some of the commodities we got from the subs were gradually divided among all my troops. Second, I got out of the mountain wilds at last and returned to what had come to seem like civilization near Umingan.

The most memorable aspects of the whole operation had nothing to do with the hard work of packing. Many of our men had purposely arrived at Dibut Bay unarmed, expecting to get new weapons from the submarine. We did indeed issue new arms to all hands, followed by an instant training course in their care and handling. The reasons for this were practical. If we happened to be ambushed by Japanese or Huks while the guns were inside the packs, most of us would be dead before we could extract, load, and fire the new arms. If the men were allowed to carry the guns before being taught how to use them, the result would be the same. What followed, however, was unforeseen, at least by me. As soon as our men considered that they were safely away from the beach, they unlimbered their new guns and began to blaze away at anything in sight with all the enthusiasm of kids at an ice cream–eating contest. Had I not known the trail, I would have had no trouble following it merely by looking for trees with bullet holes and chunks of bark shot off. I must admit that I couldn't entirely resist the spirit of the thing either. I fired a few shots with my new carbine just to see how that unfamiliar weapon worked.

A far more moving experience came after we had crossed the mountains and were hiking through an area of rolling plains around Lake Pantabangan near the eastern border of Nueva Ecija. We heard a rumbling noise that rapidly grew louder and soon realized that it must be coming from airplane motors, but it sounded more powerful and ominous than the noise made by familiar Japanese planes. Suddenly wave after wave of big American aircraft came into full view; simultaneously beautiful yet menacing in aspect. Emotion engulfed us totally at a sight more exhilarating even than the appearance of the submarine. All of us dropped our packs and began to leap for joy, shouting, laughing, cheering, crying, and waving our hats.[33] All I could think of was that at last some of the targets we had so longed to destroy would be bombed, that after all the hardships and disappointments and narrow escapes it had all been worthwhile, that now we were going to win the war for sure. Even now, half a century later, I cannot recreate in my mind the feelings I had then without shedding tears.

The arrival of submarines and the sight of our planes gave the morale of all of us a shot of adrenalin. A guerrilla movement must have some strong faith to survive, be it love of freedom, a yearning for national independence, or a passion to impose an ideology on others. But much else is essential to keep it going: arms, ammunition, a good communications system, capable leadership, planning, discipline, and direction.[34] Not least important is an intangible: outside encouragement. The longer the war lasted, the more every guerrilla leader yearned for recognition from SWPA headquarters. To receive supplies was incontrovertible evidence at last that he had not been forgotten, that General MacArthur knew who he was and appreciated his activities. His prestige, influence, and self-assurance soared thereafter. I have never forgotten the letter of appreciation and instruction that the *Narwhal* brought me from MacArthur.

I carried it around to show people for many weeks afterward.

It was clear that major developments were in the wind: there would soon be bridges and Japanese installations to blast and communication lines to destroy. This impression was strengthened by the appearance of more American planes and then air raids. Pilots engaged in the raids were much encouraged when Anderson's men managed to rescue some seventy of them who had crash-landed in the eastern mountains or offshore.[35]

In my units we grew positively euphoric when SWPA radioed us to select sites for air drops so that they could supplement what they had sent us by submarine. We did so, and kept men by them to watch for drops, but no drops ever came. Probably the planes were wanted elsewhere, or SWPA decided we already had all the materiel we really needed.

Of course, it was evident that if submarines could bring cargo in, they could also haul men out. Captain Wilbur Lage, a classmate of mine at the University of Iowa, Lt. Charles L. Naylor, and Sgts. Wilbur Jellison and Rudy Bolstead departed with the *Narwhal,* and Lieutenant Kerrey would have gone too had he not drowned tragically in a rough sea on his way to the point of embarkation. I and some others could also have left, since we had been in a combat zone for nearly three years, but we felt obliged to stay with our troops and see the war through to the end.

The number of my squadrons had grown steadily, if slowly, throughout 1943 and early 1944. As new weapons became available in the fall of 1944 and our men began to strain at the leash to use them on *somebody,* I began to form new, reserve squadrons at a more rapid rate. I even added a Chinese unit of seventy men, following a request from the secretary of a Chinese military organization in Manila.[36] The new troops were sent west to Tarlac, usually the most troubled of my provinces.

On January 4, 1945, the day the first news came that an invasion was imminent, I activated all seventy of our squadrons. A similar process had been going on throughout the Philippines. By the turn of 1945 some thirty-six of the forty-eight provinces in the Islands were controlled by guerrillas rather than by the Japanese.[37] I must have been caught up in the spirit of those last few months more than I realized at the time, for on October 6, 1944, I wrote again to my parents. The letter included the truculent assertion, "I have never surrendered to the damned Japs and I never will."[38]

— 10 —
Preparing
for the Invasion

In the last few months of 1944, as it grew increasingly evident that an American invasion was not far off, the Japanese began to think more of defending themselves and less of fighting guerrillas. U.S. planes flew over much of Luzon to bomb, strafe, and merely observe, all to the vast delight of ourselves and Filipino civilians. Enemy air defenses seemed unaccountably weak, and few Japanese planes responded aggressively to American attacks, news that we and other guerrillas hastily conveyed to SWPA.[1] In mountainous areas, by contrast, whether down around Manila, off to the west, or in the highlands to the north of my headquarters enemy actions of some types intensified. Nipponese troops were observed streaming into the hills carrying supplies, laying down telephone lines, and preparing defensive positions. It would gradually become clear to us that "the Tiger of Malaya," Gen. Tomoyuki Yamashita, was changing his defensive strategy for Luzon. No longer did he plan to fight a major battle on the plains north of Manila. Now he intended to stand with his back to the mountains so guerrilla bands such as mine could not stab him in the rear when he faced the expected American frontal assault.[2]

Around Manila, though not in LGAF territory, the Japanese began to pick up more Filipinos suspected of aiding guerrillas, to be interrogated under torture and then murdered.[3] Off in the Zambales Mountains west of Tarlac City the Nips undertook a series of raids designed to destroy the guerrillas commanded by Hipolito, but the redoubtable Captain Cris, supported by Al Hendrickson, managed to employ a delaying action against the enemy and to entrench his own men in the Zambales foothills, after which the Japanese left them alone.[4]

In some areas, notably down around Manila but not where I was, guerrilla sabotage destroyed so many means of Japanese transport, even to farmers' carts and carabao, that the enemy turned on defenseless Filipinos and forced men, women, and children alike to haul Japanese supplies on their backs many miles up into the mountains. In murderous despair they often beat, starved, raped, and murdered these hapless *cargadores* and other civilians who were merely in the way.[5] It was a gruesome foretaste of what desperate Japanese troops would do on a much larger scale in Manila itself.

Other developments, apart from these Japanese actions, would have indicated to a sharp-eyed observer that important events were not far off. Though José Laurel, president of the Japanese-sponsored Philippine Republic, was widely regarded as a collaborator, he was actually in an almost impossible position. He had to make the pressures of war as light as possible on his countrymen and simultaneously avoid offending their occupiers and oppressors. When it became apparent that an American invasion impended and that a sweeping Allied victory thereafter was a distinct possibility, the position of the harried Laurel descended from extremely difficult to hopeless. In desperation (and perhaps confusion as well) he drew up a statement that included the ludicrous declaration "My loyalty to America can be removed only by cutting my head off." Copies were hurriedly dispatched to various guerrilla units, at least one of which (not mine) had tried to assassinate him back in June 1943. In April 1945, Laurel would flee to Formosa and from there to Japan. Meanwhile, everyone intensified preparations for the long-hoped-for open war against the Japanese.

It has been alleged that when American troops landed on Leyte in October 1944 the pent-up hatreds and anxieties of Filipinos burst forth in open guerrilla warfare all over the Philippines. Factually, that is a gross exaggeration, but as a description of guerrilla *attitudes* it is accurate. Gathering intelligence was still the most important of our activities, and I had to remind our LGAF agents repeatedly not to abandon this work either before or after the Allied landings, merely because they might prefer to shoot at Japanese troops.[6]

Most of the time, being "at war" means sitting around waiting for something to happen. Actual combat, of course, is dramatically different. For the individual soldier it is a melange of danger, noise, excitement, anxiety, filth, stench, blood, and sheer terror. For ardent spirits, true "natural soldiers" (a small minority anywhere), this milieu is attractive. Gen. George Patton called it life's highest experience. For those who have some strong personal or ideological commitment, battle with hope of victory is what they focus on, and they yearn to get at it. For many others, bored by long inactivity, it is at least a change, something meaningful to do.

All this was much in evidence in the fall of 1944. The first trickle of the long-awaited "reinforcements"—a small but steady flow of arms, radios, and supplies—stimulated enthusiasm to put this new equipment to immediate use against the foe. Then came the Leyte landings in October and the virtually unopposed American air activity over Luzon. Training in ambushes, night operations, and sabotage was intensified. Sharp little skirmishes with the enemy took place more frequently. If I inquired why a certain one had occurred, I could predict the reply virtually word for word: "We were just out scouting, sir, as you said, when we accidentally ran into this Jap patrol . . ." I knew, and my men must have known I knew, that more likely they had set an ambush and had lain in wait for an hour or two for the Japanese patrol to fall into it "accidentally."[7] This sort of thing happened so frequently all over LGAF territory that the Japanese steadily moved their garrisons out of small places and concentrated them in larger towns.[8]

"Official" combat took place much less frequently than did these "accidental" skirmishes. In the last months of the war I kept a formal record of encounters with enemies, either ordered by me or reported by my various area, sector, and squadron commanders. In the five weeks between November 29, 1944, and January 4, 1945, when we received notification from SWPA that American landings in Luzon were imminent, my men were involved in only six authorized engagements or battles forced on us. Three of these were against the Huks: once they ambushed us, and twice they attacked us openly. Our forces suffered about sixty-five casualties in these encounters, the enemy perhaps ninety. On one occasion we intercepted some Japanese patrols and inflicted about twenty casualties; on another, 300 enemy troops caught some of our men in an ambush and killed about twenty. In the last of the six incidents, January 4, 1945, we derailed a train loaded with Japanese troops.[9]

Of all the supplies sent to us by submarine, what appealed most to me and positively elated my men were the arms and ammunition. That does not diminish the fact that the radio transmitters were far more vital. The value of plentiful and accurate intelligence in war simply cannot be overrated. Professional soldiers and military writers like to believe that wars are won by bravery and brains, in that order, and certainly those two qualities are obvious assets in most human activities. Nonetheless, the outcome of many battles, even whole wars, has been due to what spies discovered or to what counterintelligence experts deduced from the raw information available to them. The brilliant cryptanalyst William Friedman broke the Japanese code before Pearl Harbor, and the information derived thereafter about Japanese dispositions and plans proved invaluable to U.S. forces throughout the whole war, in Europe as well as in the Pacific. Information relayed to Australia by radio from coast watchers contributed much to Allied success in the Solomons campaigns of 1943–44, American landings on Leyte in October 1944, and landings on Mindoro a few weeks later. Japanese messages intercepted by decoders in a tunnel under a hill near Monkey Point on Corregidor early in 1942 helped the United States win the battle of Midway.[10]

Though neither I nor other guerrillas were aware at the time of these intelligence achievements or of their immeasurable value, it was obvious to us that General MacArthur was intensely preoccupied with the subject. Occasionally, a particular communication from the supreme commander, perhaps couched in the stately language he could employ so skillfully when he chose, impressed the matter indelibly on my memory. In the personal letter delivered to me by the captain of the *Narwhal*, for example, the general thanked me and the people of the Philippines for our "splendid service to the Allied cause," stressed the vital importance of accurate intelligence to aid our common endeavors, urged me to convey to SWPA everything I could possibly discover, promised to send supplies and expert operators to help me develop my communication system, and ended by asking me to tell the Filipino people wherever I could that their day of liberation was not far off.[11] I still have the letter, and I have never forgotten the impression it made on me.

Before the submarines began to arrive in late summer of 1944, the supply of intelligence from Luzon had lagged behind the quantity of information flowing into Australia from Mindanao and the Visayas. As soon as we got our new transmitters, we did our best to catch up. This was not always easy, for even when the equipment worked properly radio transmission and reception were replete with quirks and oddities. Variations in the weather or atmospheric conditions could affect it strangely, and transmission across the equator to Australia was always unpredictable. Sometimes my signal could not be heard there, or was blotted out by static. By contrast, exchanging information with California, even though it was five or six times as far away, was so much easier that we often sent our intelligence reports to an army station in San Francisco for relay to SWPA headquarters. Another nuisance was the need to move our stations frequently because the Japanese could locate them by triangulation. This problem did lessen gradually, for once we knew a transmitter was coming we could build many station sites for it in advance. The transmitters became steadily smaller too. By the end of 1944 most of them were about the size of big old-time radios. Those brought in by submarine could be carried by one man in a backpack made for that purpose and shifted quickly as necessary.

Some radio complications were more subtle, however. On my trip back to the lowlands after unloading the first submarine, I stopped in Pantabangan to visit a Chinese sawmill owner with whom I had become acquainted. The first time I met him, I was impressed mostly by his daughter, a creature of such extraordinary beauty that she might have become a source of temptation to someone of less lofty moral stature than I. He also had a gold statue of Buddha which had been entrusted to him by Chinese friends in Manila for safekeeping from the Japanese. When he came to live at his mill in Pantabangan in 1942, he built a little shrine for the statue. Japanese troops had no reason to go near this sawmill but once in a while a patrol went there nonetheless. On one such occasion they found the Buddha, but instead of stealing it the soldiers seemed awestruck. They solemnly paid prayerful reverence to it and treated the Chinese mill owner with respect thereafter.

This time when I stopped to renew acquaintance, my host inquired whether there was any question I would like him to ask the Buddha. I told him that I was uncertain whether the site I had selected for my radio station was a good one. He replied that such a question could properly be referred to Buddha and brought out two intricately carved stones, flat on one side and rounded on the other so that with the flat sides together they formed an ovoid object. Holding them, he said some prayers, then dropped the stones, took note of the pattern they formed on the ground, and warned me that I had not chosen a good place. With typical Occidental self-assurance I ignored Buddha's counsel and set up my station as planned. Unhappily, even though it was on fairly high ground and in moderately open territory, we could not get any messages in or out; we had to move farther into the hills to the site my Chinese friend had told me the Buddha recommended. The only "scientific" reason my compatriots and I could figure out was that the first site must have been on top of a mineral deposit. As for Buddha, he may have lived long before radios were invented but he knew where they should be sited nevertheless.

During the autumn and early winter of 1944, SWPA was relentless with its orders, urging, and reminders to be indefatigable in collecting every conceivable sort of information about whatever might facilitate or hinder an invasion. The information itself was specified in excruciating detail.[12] I recall particularly a letter from MacArthur on November 25 directing us to tell Filipinos that he expected loyal responses from all of them and warning that any who aided the Japanese would be hunted down promptly and charged with treason.[13] This was supplemented by specific instructions to survey the whole area we controlled, make every possible advance preparation for combat, and plan in detail an extensive program of sabotage to be put into effect when orders came from Australia. This was backed up four days later by a top secret radio message ordering us to be prepared to undertake a full-scale offensive against the Japanese and maintain it for four days without outside help. The supreme commander concluded by promising to send us another radio, some dynamite, and demolition specialists and urging us to stay alert, reassure civilians, and await further orders. On December 2 and again on the December 18 we received even more detailed instructions about these matters from Captain Cabangbang, who had set up transceivers in the Bulacan Military Area the month before and was now relaying and supplementing SWPA's orders and wishes to us.[14]

I am proud to say that all my area, district, and squadron commanders, their men, and friendly Filipino civilians worked, observed, and reported zealously for months to enable us to supply abundant information to SWPA, about all the subjects raised with us and a good many others. It would require a hundred pages just to list all the information they eventually turned in to me, but a summary may indicate the scope of their activities and diligence. At various times we reported 2,000 and 3,000 Japanese troops accompanied by 200 Philippine Constabulary men and 2,000 drums of gasoline at various places on Luzon; 3,000 enemy troops at Urdaneta with four small tanks; 10,000 Japanese in the hills south of Paladpad; 15,000 more along the National Highway; 4,000 more near a certain barrio; 500 in one place, 800 in another, and 15,000 in a third along Dingalan Bay; a division and a half along the Zambales coast, three more divisions in Pampanga, and 1,500 PC nearby, though perhaps half of these were really pro-American; 3,000 ground troops aboard fourteen transports off Port San Fernando, and 200 Nip engineers at Manoag; fifty Japanese guarding the supply depot at Damortis in the railway warehouse north of the station, plus 100 who guarded an ammunition dump at Batac barrio school; 400 infantrymen at Rosario, 900 troops and one mountain gun at Binalonan, 5,000 troops and some guns in a nearby convent, and 2,000 more at Inbac.[15]

We were happy to report that many of the Japanese troops we were seeing near the end of 1944 looked ragged, haggard, weary, and weak. We often heard that they were jittery from U.S. air raids and were tiring of the war, especially its short rations. Bayonet practice seemed about the only activity that aroused their zeal as much as ever. There had been no observable improvement in any of their war machines, ground or air; they were visibly short of aluminum; their iron was of poor quality; and pilot training was down to three months before combat.[16]

In August, watchers often noted that enemy troops were moving from remote areas to locations along major highways, and that a cavalry unit with 400 Japanese and 300 American horses had arrived near Lingayen Gulf. Two or three months later many troops began to stream out of Manila and points south into Pangasinan and places farther north. Trainloads of civilians from Davao and Manila often came with them. Sometimes the trains would stop to pick up soldiers who had been increasingly reduced to riding in animal-drawn carts or simply hiking and carrying their supplies with them.[17] Our observers also took note of the kinds and numbers of these vehicles and what cargo they carried. Some watchers made careful distinctions between machine guns and antiaircraft guns, noticed the difference between full and empty gasoline drums, and even discovered that there was a Japanese mechanic on one load. A particularly sharp-eyed lookout reported that no less a dignitary than General Yamashita himself, surrounded by a convoy of tanks and motorcycles, had passed through Talavera in Nueva Ecija province at 1:00 P.M., January 3, 1945, headed north.[18]

We reported to SWPA where the Japanese were siting their heavy artillery: on mountain tops around San Clemente, along the National Highway, along Dingalan Bay, on the Bataan coast near Mariveles, all along the Lingayen coast from Dagupan to San Fabian, even as precisely as 400 meters from a church steeple in a certain town.[19] We noted that the enemy had mined the Jones and Ayala bridges, and had placed two big guns to guard a bridge at Bitailak near Dingalan Bay.[20] Our observers recorded that enemy troops were digging trenches or had commandeered Chinese, Manchurian, and Filipino civilians to dig them from San Antonio to San Narciso, from San Clemente to Lingayen, between Makalad and Malabode on both sides of the Mangatarem River. They were also improving port facilities at Damortis in La Union province; putting barbed wire entanglements along the Rosario-Damortis road; mining the beaches at Baler Bay; fortifying the Batangas coast, Olongapo, and portions of the Lingayen coast; and were widening the road from Bongabon to Bitulac.[21] We were able to inform Australia that the Japanese had installed radar equipment in Dagupan, Lingayen, Damortis, and Lupao; were using Balen Hill at prewar Camp Dau as a hospital,[22] and were moving British and American internees from Santo Tomas prison in Manila to points unknown.[23]

We were particularly vigilant to report as much and as precisely as possible what was taking place at and around Japanese airfields: that there were camouflaged planes at Nichols Field near Manila; that Mariveles Field at the tip of Bataan had been improved; that Carmen Field seemed to have been abandoned; that the San Marcelino airstrip in Zambales province had been improved, ackack guns installed there, and some hangers built under trees to hide the planes; that planes were camouflaged east of the streetcar tracks and northwest of a bombed building on the north side of the landing strip at Pateros; that the Stotsenberg parade ground was being reserved for fighter planes; that an emergency field and twelve camouflaged fighter planes were located nearby; that at Clark Field the Japanese flew planes only at night and hid them during the day; and that Iba Field was used only by observation planes, but that there were twenty-five Japanese fighter planes at other fields nearby.[24]

Our reports of the locations of Japanese supplies were even more precise; large stores of plywood in the Santa Clara Lumber Mill; 400 drums of gasoline and four empty tanks with a capacity of 50,000 gallons at Aguilar; forty tanks hidden alongside the road by a barrio school building; food supply dumps two kilometers northwest of the same barrio; gasoline dumps under bamboo groves near Pateros, along the road to Pasig 500 yards west of the bridge and close to a gas station that had been machine-gunned; 500 drums of gasoline under bamboo groves 500 meters south of the Tarlac municipal hall near a private hospital; other gasoline in another bamboo thicket along the Zambales coast; the precise location of dynamite in the side of a certain hill and of alcohol and sugar supplies at Manoag.[25] A recurring theme in dozens of such reports was that commodities were stored in schools, convents, churches, bamboo groves, or thickets of large trees where the Japanese seemed to think the goods would be concealed or the Allies would not expect them to be hidden.[26]

We also discovered and reported where Japanese troops were housed: in the homes of civilians; in cogon grass huts along the edges of jungle in such-and-such places; in a large house close to the Tarlac-Pura-Guimba road, its roof fixed to keep off the rain; in a certain Pampanga sugar mill; in a roomy schoolhouse; in several places near Baler, where the enemy had also dug many foxholes and set up a radio station 400 meters north of a bridge; and in a list of specified buildings in Manoag.[27] We added details about how well or badly Nipponese troops seemed to be armed;[28] the news that torpedo launching devices had been seen in the Lingayen area;[29] figures on Japanese alcohol and sugar production;[30] even the news that a certain Philippine manufacturer was turning out large amounts of castor oil.[31]

We reported in detail the results of Allied bombing raids: a hanger damaged at Clark Field; near Manila, gasoline dumps missed on the south side of a bridge over the Pasig and Pateros river junction; 75 percent of the Japanese in Bamban killed by U.S. bombing and strafing; at Lingayen Field three planes destroyed on the ground, three cadre buildings partly burned, and a supply building wrecked. Especially gratifying were the results of major raids on Manila on September 21–22: 2,000–3,000 Japanese casualties, 90 percent of Japanese military installations hit, and some forty to sixty ships, mostly inter-island boats, sunk in Manila harbor.[32]

We did not neglect to repeat our own needs: outboard motors to speed the unloading of submarines; arms and supplies of many sorts but especially ammunition; even any mail that might have accumulated for Hunt, Hendrickson, or others long out of contact with the outside world.[33]

Finally, we did not forget SWPA's repeated requests for more information about the Huks. We forwarded the names of eight or ten of their leaders and the towns in which they were currently staying. We emphasized that they were loyal to neither Japan nor America because they were true Communists who would try to seize power at the end of the war; that they probably had more troops in reserve; and that when they were not actively making trouble for us, they devoted much effort to plundering civilians.[34]

Overall, our LGAF intelligence network could only be called excellent, as SWPA headquarters officially acknowledged. I do not say this to boast, since the hard work and risks of careful watching, recording, questioning, listening, and frequenting often dangerous places was done by others, both guerrillas and civilians. The exact detail of many of the reports still impresses me when I reread them half a century later.

Typical pages from my Radio Log Book, which recorded chiefly messages sent to and received from MacArthur's headquarters in Australia between mid-summer 1944 and spring 1945. It illustrates what careful observers many Filipinos were.

At the turn of the New Year we finally got the message for which we had waited so long: "Beginning at dark on Fourth January proceed to destroy targets assigned by this Headquarters under plan of sabotage communicated to you by message of Two Nine November . . . " At once we got on the radio and sent the news to all our units, while runners who had been waiting impatiently around LGAF headquarters for days took off like Paul Revere to confirm it in person. Everybody was wild with excitement. We would fight at last! Few of my men even tried to sleep more than a few minutes at a time for the next few days. At just that time the Japanese were severely handicapped by a shortage of supply vehicles, made worse for them by shortages of fuel and lubricants and still worse by Allied land- and carrier-based air attacks. My guerrilla bands sought to multiply their miseries. We blasted bridges, cut communication lines, knocked holes in highways, ambushed truck convoys, and attacked enemy garrisons. What especially delighted my men was sabotaging the railway system, above all, derailing Japanese trains. Once they managed to send one sailing off the track as it rounded a curve between Muñoz and Guimba, dumping all the troops aboard into rice paddies alongside the track. For the saboteurs it was the high point of the whole war. Between January 4 when the preliminary Lingayen bombardment started and January 9 when the landing began, the Japanese Fourteenth Area Army could move only a trickle of essential supplies to its defensive positions.[35]

During the frantic four days between reception of SWPA's order to go to war and the actual Lingayen landings, the pandemonium that prevailed around LGAF headquarters seems to have been duplicated in our field units. Our orders from Australia were to be prepared to operate on our own for four days, suggesting that the landings would come no later than January 8 or 9, so I ordered our units to go all out. Before the first night was over, practically every one of our squadrons managed to get into at least one or two fights with the Japanese.

Soon our scouts reported that the enemy was planning a major raid on our current headquarters: Japanese would come toward us from four different directions. Meanwhile our radios, always prone to conk out at the slightest provocation, had grown so temperamental with heavy usage that I was afraid to move the station lest we lose contact with the rest of the world. Instead, I called in a few of my men nearby and prepared to try to hold out against the impending attack. As it turned out, the Japanese had not planned to hit on January 6 or 7, as our informants had feared, but on the tenth. Luckily for us, other guerrilla units hit them first, and the Lingayen landings began on January 9 so they called off the surprise party they had prepared for us. The whole episode ended in a half-comical though grim sort of way. One night we got an order to designate a spot where we would like to receive supplies by air drop. I specified our headquarters. A night or two later we heard a plane circling nearby and naturally assumed that it was an American craft getting ready to drop the promised supplies. Then it flew right over us, and we heard something falling through the air. Suddenly there were a couple of explosions maybe a hundred yards away—too loud for mere falling crates, but we thought perhaps the pilot had dropped something that would make more noise just to help us locate the containers. Our men searched but found nothing. Next morning we looked again. There were two bomb craters.

I was never more proud of my LGAF guerrillas than in those days preceding the Lingayen landings. At night they launched attacks on Japanese garrisons and installations. In the daytime, virtually without sleep, they combed the countryside to pick off the numerous Japanese stragglers who often seemed hardly to know what had so suddenly hit them. One terrible engagement convinced me, if I ever needed convincing, of what brave soldiers Filipinos can be if properly trained and aroused. When patrols got word that a company of Japanese had entered a barrio nearby and were looting and killing the inhabitants, my men rushed off to the place. After several hours of sniping just outside the barrio, the enemy was beginning to give ground when a large force of other Japanese who had heard all the shooting came up to reinforce their brethren. Worse yet, still more Japanese soon came marching down a main road nearby. All of them combined to attack my contingent from every direction. With no chance to escape, they fought till darkness—and almost to the absolute end: only six out of sixty-five lived to slip away in the night. How many Japanese died we never knew, because nobody bothered to count their corpses. Certainly there were many, for they had outnumbered our men greatly and had seemed as glad as we were to break off the murderous action. When night came we were able to recover the bodies of our men for burial next day.

I have described this battle of virtual annihilation many times in public and private, and I am often asked, "What sort of people are the Filipinos? Are they all as good fighters as this? Or good at all?" It is impossible to answer briefly or precisely. It is like asking what sort of people Americans are. Some Filipinos are brave; some are not. Many are fine people; some are scoundrels. And so on. Most of them I found to be generous and hospitable, nearly all intensely personal in their feelings and loyalties. If you are having a hard time and they like you, most of them will help you all they can. If you have more than they do, quite a few will try to even things up by taking what they can. As soldiers they are more excitable and less steady than Americans, probably from inadequate training, but no less loyal to their country or, especially, to individual leaders. If they have confidence in a leader they will follow him anywhere and bitterly resent any effort to take him away or to shift them to someone else's command. The great majority of my men were unreservedly loyal; they would take orders from nobody but me or my representatives and would not even recognize guerrilla leaders from any organization other than the LGAF.

Most civilians were like the guerrillas. They hid us and fed us, knowing that they were thereby risking their lives. They saw their homes burned and their crops and animals destroyed because the Japanese knew or suspected that they were aiding us. Those captured by the Japanese were subjected to the most frightful pain, often followed by death. Of course, one can never base policy on assumptions that particular individuals can endure torture to any given degree, but surprisingly few revealed anything of note. Once I lay sick in hiding, with about ten men, less than a quarter-mile from a certain barrio. Some enemy troops seized the mayor and tried to make him tell them where I was. They beat him with clubs and fists, then held his head under water, brought him up, revived him, questioned him anew, and dunked him again until he finally drowned. One of my own men was hung for five hours by his wrists, which were tied behind his back, all to try to make him admit that he was a guerrilla. He absolutely refused and was finally released. When I questioned him later about the experience he said, "Oh, it wasn't so bad. After the first hour my arms became numb and didn't hurt as much."

Some, of course, were vastly different. To be pro-Japanese did not necessarily make a person a rascal, for honest differences of opinion exist during wars as well as in peacetime. The most contemptible Filipinos, in my estimate, outside of occasional sadists and psychopaths, were those who betrayed their own people to the Japanese in return for money and position for themselves. Such a person once turned in one of my captains. My man readily admitted to his captors that he was an officer, adding that as such he would never betray his men. For several days they beat him, stabbed him with bayonets, and inflicted on him atrocious indignities better left to the imagination. Then they took him to a cemetery and told him he had one last chance to talk. When he refused, they executed him. He was a small man, even for a Filipino, and the Japanese officer who had overseen the whole abominable proceeding was sufficiently moved by the incredible bravery he had witnessed to pay the victim one of the few compliments I have ever heard come from a Japanese. He said, "Little man, little talk."

A few Filipinos—some of them referred to earlier—were monsters of cruelty. Ed Ramsey notes that late in the war, if one of his units captured a Japanese or a Filipino collaborator, the usual procedure was to interrogate the man as long as seemed fruitful, then kill him. He acknowledges that most of his men hated this task, but

one fifteen-year-old boy not only did it routinely but seemed positively to relish it. He became an expert in jabbing a bayonet behind
the victim's left collarbone directly into his heart, thus killing him
instantly. The rest of Ramsey's men held the boy in superstitious
horror. They refused to sleep in the same hut with him and claimed
that in the dark his eyes would glow like red coals. Ed admits that
his own feelings toward this inhuman creature did not differ much
from those of his men.[36] Of course, criminal lunatics exist among all
peoples, and this psychopath was no more typical of Filipinos than
he would have been of Americans. Luckily, I never had anyone like
him in my command.

— 11 —
The Landings

During the summer of 1944, when high political and military authorities were debating whether to land in the Philippines or bypass them and land on Formosa, Douglas MacArthur argued vehemently that it would be politically disastrous to ignore an opportunity to liberate the homeland of our Filipino allies. He also contended that hundreds of thousands of Filipinos would immediately extend every aid to an American invasion force and that guerrillas in the islands would augment U.S. combat strength, advantages that would not exist on Formosa. His judgment was soon vindicated.

Less certain was the judgment of Sergio Osmena, Quezon's successor as president of the Philippines, who landed with MacArthur on Leyte in October. One of his first acts on his home soil was to incorporate officially into the Philippine army all the guerrilla forces recognized by MacArthur. The general had intended such recognition to be accorded only to guerrillas who had some military background, not to civilians who had become guerrillas during the war, but Osmena failed to make this distinction clear. As a result, phony guerrilla outfits sprang up like mushrooms after a rain.

On January 8, 1945, the day before the Lingayen landings began, LGAF headquarters received a radiogram from SWPA placing all our forces under operational control of the U.S. Sixth Army (though we were not formally absorbed into it). Over the next few days Anderson, Volckmann, and I met the Sixth Army's commanding general, Walter Krueger, on shore and had the transfer confirmed for our respective forces.

The actual landings on January 9 took place in LGAF territory. They were not difficult, though complications ensued soon afterward. A month before the invasion General Krueger knew that landing conditions on the eastern Lingayen shore, where the Japanese had landed three years before, were easier than on the southern shore. But he also knew from information gathered by Ray Hunt's guerrillas and passed on by me to SWPA that the eastern shore was heavily defended and the south shore only weakly. Volckmann's guerrillas had added, reassuringly, that General Yamashita intended to mass his troops in the mountains several miles inland and would not strongly contest landings anywhere along the beaches. Furthermore, U.S. carrier strikes around Manila had led the Japanese to expect landings there, so they had not moved as many troops to the north as they might otherwise have done.[1] Even so, as often happens in amphibious operations, there was much confusion among U.S. forces getting ashore.[2]

As soon as I knew the landings were actually in progress, I gathered about fifteen men and set off for the Lingayen coast some forty miles to the west. The most satisfying part of the journey was to see American planes overhead.[3] We also saw a few stray enemy soldiers along the way, though most of the Japanese were strongly dug in at positions they expected to defend indefinitely. I wanted to capture the stragglers, but my men killed them whenever they caught any. We tried to hail a U.S. Jeep careening down a road, but the driver ignored us. The driver of a second Jeep was less urgently preoccupied and gave me a ride to his unit headquarters; from there I was promptly taken to see Gen. Innis P. Swift, who questioned me at length about Japanese numbers, arms, habits, plans, and related subjects. Afterward I was sent up to First Corps headquarters at Dagupan. Nobody there gave me any specific orders other than the usual instructions to collect intelligence and provide regular troops with guides who were familiar with the immediate locale.

A newspaper reporter then interviewed me and took my picture. Years later Andy Warhol, who made a living persuading people that he was an artist-philosopher, spoke confidently of a future in which each person would be a celebrity for fifteen minutes. He suffered from a cramped imagination: my picture and interview made me a newspaper celebrity all over the States for an entire day. My hometown paper commented that in my garrison hat, long sideburns, native clothes, and Japanese-style shoes with the toes cut out, I looked like a "Hollywood-style cowboy."[4]

Actually, the first person from LGAF to make contact with U.S. regulars was Lt. Tom Chengay, Ray Hunt's tough little Igorot commander of Squadron 221. Tom's troops were promptly fed, clothed, and armed and soon sent into action. Tom was utterly amazed, as I was a few days afterward, to see the thousands of troops supplemented by incredible quantities of U.S. weapons, supplies, and food that were unloaded from an armada of transports and stacked in veritable mountains on shore. Prominent amid this flood of materiel were innumerable tanks—and what tanks! They were not the puny "tin cans" of 1941–42, armed with what now seemed like popguns, but thickly armored steel monsters bearing cannons that three years before had existed only in the field artillery. The spectacle not only bore no relationship to the Filipino world to which I had grown accustomed during the preceding three years; it did not resemble anything I had ever seen in the prewar United States either.[5] There is no question in my mind that the Allies won World War II by sheer numbers, amounts, quantities: more men, more guns, more money, more industry, more ships, more planes, more food. The joke that used to go around in U.S. war plants, "if we run out of bullets we'll shoot dollars at them," camouflaged a fundamental truth about the whole war, European and Pacific. More immediately, it was incontestable that the phantom "reinforcements" awaited so impatiently ever since January 1942 had arrived at last—with a vengeance.

As for intelligence, I was able to give our American officers much information about terrain, local Filipinos, my own officers, and not least about the scale of fighting to be expected. For weeks beforehand we had singled out every Japanese installation of any importance, designated an LGAF unit to attack it, and had the men rehearse what they would do when the Great Day came. Not surprisingly, they had been extremely active in the days leading up to January 9. They had been involved in forty-eight different official engagements—"official" meaning authorized by me or some other LGAF officer; nobody had any idea how many unrecorded freelance enterprises had been undertaken by two or three or a dozen guerrillas. During those days LGAF units had staged fourteen assaults on garrisons or outposts, thirteen ambushes of Japanese trucks or cars, and five attacks on enemy patrols; they had derailed three trains, ambushed two convoys, otherwise badgered our foes eleven times, and even found time to fight one small battle with the Huks. We had killed at least 675 of the enemy at very light cost to ourselves.[6]

Of all the intelligence LGAF had been able to provide SWPA, the most important was secured by Juan Utleg, Ray Hunt's G-2, about Japanese installations around Lingayen Gulf. Also highly useful was the extensive information Al Hendrickson had collected about the location of enemy airfields, ammunition dumps, and supply depots in Tarlac. All such news had been forwarded to my headquarters to be collated with what other LGAF personnel were gathering elsewhere, then sent to Gen. MacArthur's headquarters. This procedure was followed partly to reduce duplication and partly because the transmitters we had received via submarine varied considerably in strength. Those possessed by Hendrickson, Hunt, and other LGAF commanders enabled them to communicate among themselves and with me, but only my own was strong enough to reach Australia.

Even so, the flood of intelligence that poured into SWPA nearly swamped that organization, since all the other guerrilla units on Luzon were active too. Moreover, SWPA was getting additional information from radio intercepts, captured documents, and the interrogation of enemy prisoners. In an effort to correlate all of it and separate the wheat from the chaff, General Willoughby appointed Maj. Steve Mellnick to head the Philippine section of G-2. One of his first acts was to compose a printed guide indicating what types of information were most wanted, and send it to guerrilla units.

Such efforts soon yielded great dividends.[7] For one thing, intelligence gathered by guerrillas who had had at least a bit of training in what they were doing tended to be more accurate than what was derived from ordinary Filipino civilians, many of whom would say "yes" to anything suggested from a mere desire to please the questioner.[8] Learning from us and other guerrillas that Japanese strength on Luzon was much greater than he had supposed, MacArthur increased the strength of his invasion force repeatedly until eventually more American troops were committed to the conquest of Luzon than to the invasions of either North Africa or Italy.[9] We had also prepared many detailed maps of towns and even of buildings where the enemy had stored supplies, enabling U.S. bombers to avoid the destruction of much valuable materiel.[10] Finally, the Japanese soon realized how much we knew about everything they possessed and had planned. The discovery did not elevate their morale.[11]

After gathering intelligence before the landings, there were many services we could perform for the U.S. regular army once it was ashore. The thousands of us all over Luzon were now in the "real" army and could fight alongside our fellows in a regular campaign to free the Philippines. We were at once set to patrolling, guarding ammunition and supply dumps, watching bridges and rear area installations, acting as scouts and guides, and clearing civilians out of the way of troops. Not least, we could help sort out real guerrillas from the hordes of frauds who invariably showed up as soon as U.S. troops came into an area, identifying themselves as heroes who had been valiantly combatting the common enemy for the last six months to three years.[12] Worse, for years afterward they pressed claims on the U.S. government for back pay and other compensation.

Within a few days after the landings, guerrillas from every point of the compass, elated by the opportunity to strike open blows at the enemy, were seizing or occupying everything in sight. When U.S. regulars landed twenty-five miles north of Bataan along the Philippine west coast, they encountered not Japanese but a small boat-load of Colonel Merrill's guerrillas, who had already chased all the enemy out of the area. When other Americans from the Cyclone Division rushed inland from southern Bataan to seize the San Marcelino airstrip, they found that future Philippine president Ramon Magsaysay's guerrillas had grabbed it three days earlier.[13] LGAF units seized Aguilar and Urbiztondo along the Agno River, and Malasiqui north of it.[14] Al Hendrickson's troops took part in several days of hard fighting around Tarlac City and Clark Field.[15]

Altogether, in the month from January 10 to February 10, LGAF forces initiated or took part in sixty-one "official" actions. We ambushed, attacked, or merely encountered twenty-five Japanese patrols or other bodies of troops in the open field; attacked eight garrisons; ambushed eight individual enemy trucks, three convoys, two Makapili, and one Japanese officer; raided the Cabanatuan prison camp (see below) and followed with three mop-up raids; took part in the siege of Muñoz; raided a Japanese bivouac area; attacked three enemy snipers and three others plundering civilians; attacked one foeman who was trying to ambush us, another moving supplies, another threshing rice, and a pilot who had been forced down; and sabotaged a bridge for good measure. In all these actions we estimated that we killed about 1,500 of the enemy at a loss of 157 of our own men.[16]

Generally speaking, General Yamashita's decision to make his stand in near-roadless jungle-covered mountains and to undertake only nominal resistance down on the plains was sound. It minimized the effectiveness of U.S. air power, tanks, and heavy ground weapons. It did, however, have a crucial weakness: it was favorable to guerrilla operations, and all the guerrillas were on our side. Abruptly, the nature of our war effort changed. Instead of trying to hide from the Japanese, we searched for them everywhere in the mountains and on the plains. If they evaded us in one locale, they had to face other guerrillas somewhere else, not to speak of several million civilians thirsting for vengeance. Few of the enemy survived.

The most spectacular and, to me, the most satisfying LGAF operation in these hectic days was our collaboration with the Sixth Rangers of the U.S. Army to liberate 513 Allied prisoners of war from Cabanatuan prison camp, January 28–31. The plight of the prisoners there had been on my mind for many months. Most of them were men who had survived the Bataan Death March or had been taken there after the fall of Corregidor. How many had passed through the gates of Cabanatuan altogether or how many were still alive there, nobody knew for sure. Wild rumors had circulated around USAFFE headquarters in Australia since early 1944 that 250 American soldiers had been beaten to death by their captors on the first day of their imprisonment, that thousands had died since, that many hundreds had been shipped to Japan on slave ships, that uncounted hundreds had been worked to death in the camp, that heaps of dead were routinely buried in common graves, that as many as 3,000 men were still alive there, though perhaps barely, since some of them were said to have lost as much as 100 pounds.[17]

I was not the only one to have pondered the possibility of liberating these prisoners; it had been much on the mind of Maj. Bernard Anderson too. Throughout 1944 we urged SWPA to let us try to rescue the POWs. We wanted especially to make the attempt in late October or early November when we thought the Japanese would be preoccupied with resisting the Leyte landings, but all we could ever get was assurance that when landings began on Luzon, rescuing the prisoners would be given top priority. That never satisfied us, because we feared that once the Japanese thought such an invasion imminent, they would kill all the prisoners. These forebodings were well founded, it might be added, for we discovered after the war that had U.S. troops actually invaded the Japanese home islands, the enemy would have begun their defense by executing all their American POWs.

Capt. Juan Pajota, one of my most imaginative and energetic officers, was as concerned about the whole matter as I was. We often discussed every imaginable aspect of a rescue operation, particularly once unmistakable signs appeared that Japanese control of the camp was loosening. Battle-hardened camp guards had been replaced by young boys fresh from Japan who were much less cruel than their predecessors. Nipponese officers had also grown more civil. Discipline and vigilance had slackened sufficiently by the fall of 1944 that smuggling was taking place routinely. Then one night some of the stronger prisoners slipped through a fence, killed a brahma steer, cooked the meat, and had a feast for the first time in nearly three years—while Japanese guards watched but did nothing. They seemed confident that the Makapili would warn them if danger arose. Unfortunately for them, by late 1944 most of the Makapili had been killed by guerrillas or townspeople, and those remaining were too afraid to reveal anything.[18]

It must be emphasized that the refusal of SWPA to let us go ahead was not due to stupidity at MacArthur's headquarters or to indifference to the fate of the imprisoned men. There were sound reasons for holding back. We could almost certainly have attacked Cabanatuan successfully and gotten the prisoners out. But what then? Whether there were 3,000 or the "more than 500" that I estimated late in 1944, most of them would be weak, sick, and likely dispirited in the bargain. Even had they been willing to join our LGAF forces, they would have been not an asset but a heavy burden. Theoretically, we might have marched them over the Sierra Madre to the sea, but hard realities were against it; most of them would have had to be carried. SWPA knew all this, and at bottom I did too, but I found it hard to think clearly when I was so emotionally committed to their rescue. Captains Pajota and Eduardo Joson assured me enthusiastically that they could find enough Filipino civilians to carry all the men, but even I was not optimistic enough to credit that. And if we did somehow manage to get all the men to the coast, the U.S. Navy could not promise a successful evacuation: seaplanes could not carry enough men and would soon have been detected; twenty or thirty submarines might have sufficed but the navy did not have that many at hand and did not dare risk all they did have in a venture of this sort. Maybe one or two subs could have run a shuttle to a ship miles offshore, but that would have been time consuming and likely to be detected.[19]

When the Lingayen landings took place and thousands of U.S. troops swarmed ashore, however, the prospect of rescuing the prisoners at once seemed brighter. I raised the question again, this time with General Krueger. He assigned his G-2, Col. Horton White, and White's assistant, Maj. Frank Rowale, to consider the whole venture and make appropriate plans. They soon consulted Lt. Col. Henry Mucci, who eventually led the actual raid, and me, since I had extensive personal knowledge of the whole area. Mucci was "all business" from the first. A former West Point football player, he was a physical culture enthusiast. When he had assumed command of a pack mule outfit, he was determined to turn it into a body of "Rangers." What that would mean to those in the unit was made clear to them the first day they arrived in New Guinea in 1944. As soon as they landed, Mucci ran, not walked, straight up a hill to report in to the commanding officer.[20]

Now, on Luzon, in mid-January 1945 he was leading over a hundred U.S. Rangers plus two Alamo Scout teams. The Alamo Scouts were an elite outfit composed mainly of men who had grown restless from inaction and so had volunteered for duty where they hoped to find adventure and excitement. They and the Rangers had already successfully pulled off two small raids. Now, one of the first things Mucci did was to require each of his men to take a blood oath that he would die rather than allow any harm to come to the prisoners. Then, no doubt acting on Krueger's orders, he forbade me to go along on the raid because, he said, my life was too valuable to risk.[21] I suppose I should have been flattered, but I really did not have a strong reaction of any kind. I knew Cabanatuan was guarded only lightly and that there were no Japanese between it and us. To surprise its garrison and liberate the inmates, it seemed to me, would be little more than a large-scale patrol operation in which it would not matter whether I went along or not. Afterward, I was surprised that the press made such an extravaganza of it. Anyway, I was able to contribute two excellent officers, Joson and Pajota, and some four hundred men to the venture. I immediately sent a note to Pajota, who was in a barrio near Cabanatuan, to bring me fifty land mines that had been delivered to us by submarine for a special mission, and then hidden.

Colonel Mucci and his chief aide, Capt. Bob Prince, left the "fine tuning" of the plans to their subordinates, each of whom was to consult with me and then work out just what he and his men should do during the raid. Once Mucci and Prince had reviewed the whole composite and made a few final changes, everything was set. Lt. Bill Nellist, an uncomplicated man with a high sense of duty, led the Alamo Scouts. With a few of my guerrillas as guides they did an outstanding job of reconnoitering the whole area before the actual attack.[22] Mucci was uneasy about whether guerrillas, accustomed to hit-and-run attacks, could endure what he expected to be a prolonged direct fight against a strong enemy.[23] I was not. Filipino officers, like those in any army, vary greatly in quality, but those I had assigned Mucci were neither Philippine army neophytes nor political appointees but two of my own seasoned guerrilla volunteers. I had a lot of faith in Eduardo Joson and especially in Juan Pajota, who had already displayed competence before he ever joined LGAF.[24] Then, after joining, he was the one who had suggested Dibut Bay as a good landing place for a submarine along the Tayabas coast, and it had proved ideal. I was confident that he and his men would come through.

When Mucci's host started off on the four- or five-hour hike from my headquarters (now in Guimba) to the Cabanatuan camp, it consisted of 122 Rangers and 250–300 LGAF guerrillas. Near the town of Cabanatuan about 150 unarmed Filipinos were added. These people did not fight or even accompany the troops; instead, they made ready a lot of carabao carts to carry off any prisoners who might be unable to walk. To the disgust of all of us, Captain Joson had to leave twenty of his men in a barrio to guard the rest against being stabbed in the back by Huks while they were fighting the Japanese. Relations with the Huks had sunk to a new low when they saw the end of the war coming; they were resentful that LGAF officers had U.S. commissions while their own officers did not.[25]

For anyone who judges his prospects by omens, on this occasion they were mixed. As the raiders were making their way through tall grass, several big birds suddenly fell dead from the sky; nobody ever knew why. Soon after that, while the whole contingent was going through a barrio as quietly as possibly to avoid alerting anyone, a large contingent of good-looking young girls appeared abruptly and began to sing the American and Philippine national anthems—and that proved to be a mere prelude to a big feast. Obviously numerous ordinary Filipinos had learned or sensed that a major enterprise of some sort was impending, though there was no indication then or later that anyone told the Japanese anything about it.[26]

Omens or no, the raid went off almost perfectly. Pajota's and Joson's guerrillas put up roadblocks on each side of the camp to intercept any Japanese troops that might try to interfere. The attack itself came after dark and completely surprised the Nips. New P-61 Black Widow planes, as deadly as their name and equipped with radar that enabled their pilots to see in the dark, blasted enemy vehicles and equipment. They were seconded ably by Rangers who shot up a lot of Japanese trucks with bazookas.[27] So far as could be determined, there had been about 75 Japanese on duty in the stockade and perhaps 150 others who had entered the camp that day to rest. All were killed.[28] On our side the casualties were extremely light. By our count immediately afterward, the doctor who accompanied the Rangers and one Ranger were killed, one prisoner died of a heart attack, seven other Americans were wounded, and twelve Filipinos were wounded. All the wounded recovered, and 513 prisoners were rescued. Recounts later raised our death toll to around twenty-five.[29]

In several ways the foremost hero in the operation was Capt. Juan Pajota. Before the actual attack he had managed to accumulate more men and four more machine guns than I knew we possessed. Immediately after the rescue Juan retreated in a direction designed to draw pursuers away from the liberated men. Meanwhile, several hundred Japanese in the town of Cabanatuan immediately to the north had been alerted by all the shooting and rushed southward. Pajota ambushed them along a small river and fought a fierce delaying action there for two hours. Incredibly, his unit did not suffer a single casualty, though scores or perhaps hundreds of the enemy were killed. This battle was Pajota's finest hour.

Juan's later life was not without rewards, for he once received a temporary appointment as military governor of Nueva Ecija, the province of which his compatriot Eduardo Joson became governor. Yet his life ended on a sadly ironic note. He had often said that his dearest wish was to become an American citizen someday, and when he was able to come to the United States in December 1976, he at once filed for citizenship—but he died of a heart attack a few days before a decision was to have been made. Thus ended the life of a true hero who richly deserved what he wanted so badly but did not quite get.

Some estimates of the total number of Japanese killed inside the camp during Pajota's ambush and in the Filamerican mop-up in Cabanatuan City afterward run as high as 2,000. My own guess would be that 300–500 is more likely. I don't think anyone knows for sure.[30]

A few of the rescued prisoners were so bewildered by the rush of totally unexpected events that they had not wanted to leave the camp. Others among those I saw afterward were obviously sick or so thin they could hardly walk, but they were not as wretchedly debilitated as I had feared;[31] most people gradually become acclimated to almost anything short of death itself. But to say this does not diminish the invaluable support we got from civilians. They helped carry many POWs out of the camp bodily, hauled them away in carts, got them medical treatment, and hid them from Japanese recapture. Had these people been pro-Japanese rather than pro-American, the whole rescue would have been impossible.[32]

Though the Cabanatuan raid was an overwhelming success in every miliary sense, it ended on a sour note. The Huks, increasingly fearful that the United States would ignore their equivocal contributions to what began to look like a general victory over the Japanese, had decided that they must win some battles quickly to impress the Americans. That required more weapons, which they could acquire only by taking them away from other guerrillas or from the Japanese. They had tried both, renewing pressure on the Nipponese in the fall of 1944[33] and intensifying their harassment of guerrillas as well. Now, they tried to prevent the victors of Cabanatuan from moving through a village they controlled. When Captain Prince responded by threatening to call down artillery (which he did not have) on them, they backed off.

The first time I met General Krueger I warned him, as well as other high U.S. military and civilian officials, that the Huks were dangerous and treacherous and should be disarmed and disbanded. Three of my ablest officers, Capts. Dioscoro M. de Leon, Juan Pajota, and Carlos Nocum, had written letters seconding my warning.[34] Krueger had replied, in effect, that his business was defeating the Japanese, not making political policy, and that he needed everyone he could find who was willing to fight the enemy. Of course, it is true that professional military people who take an obvious political stance in public are at once reminded—by either those who are always anxious to discredit the military or those who dislike the policy espoused—that it is the business of soldiers to take orders and fight and the business of elected civilian authorities to determine political policy. If the military simply obey orders and the result is something distasteful, then the same people say the soldiers should have placed national, religious, humanitarian, or some other values above mere obedience and urge that they be tried as war criminals or otherwise chastised. As in so many areas of human affairs, you can't beat Monday morning quarterbacking. In this case, subsequent events showed that Krueger could have saved others much trouble if he had listened to those of us who had been combatting Huks for three years. Relations between the Huks and USAFFE guerrillas in 1945 continued to be the same melange of broken promises, violated agreements, admonitions, warnings, threats, and self-justifications as in prior years. Their character is evident from an examination of correspondence that passed among various parties on both sides.[35]

Nevertheless, the Cabanatuan raid had a bright side beyond liberation of the prisoners. A few days afterward I received a letter from General Krueger relaying a message from MacArthur to the effect that the commando raid was "magnificent and reflects extraordinary credit on all concerned." Krueger added, "It is desired that this message from the Commander-in-Chief be conveyed to each member of your command who participated in this operation."[36] Naturally, all of us concerned were pleased to be so recognized and praised.

In retrospect, it's clear that the Cabanatuan raid symbolized more than appeared to be the case at the time. It was soon followed by U.S. raids on Santo Tomas prison in Manila and several other places where American prisoners were held, assaults indicating the lengths to which Americans would go to rescue their fellow citizens and the value we attach to single human lives. The prodigality with which the Japanese spent human lives defending such places, and their employment of kamikaze pilots to undertake suicide attacks on American ships, demonstrated just the opposite: how little value our foes attached to any single human life. It must have strengthened the general American resolve to fight the war through to complete victory no matter the price.

After the Lingayen landings American troops met only light opposition as they pushed southward, yet they moved "with all deliberate speed," taking nine days to advance the first thirty miles. There were several reasons for the leisurely pace. General Krueger's army was grievously encumbered by the weight of its transport, which required bridges capable of supporting thirty-five tons to cross rivers.[37] He ordered the air force not to bomb bridges in front of him, but along the west coast of Luzon the guerrillas had done their sabotage too well: because they had destroyed all the strong bridges over tidal streams, troops often could not advance at all until repairs were made or fords found.[38] Caution was also induced by the desire to keep down casualties, a consideration that worried Filipinos who wanted U.S. forces to parachute in both men and guns as fast as possible so both they and guerrillas could begin killing Japanese before the Japanese killed them.[39] Given these circumstances, it took American forces four weeks to get to Manila, about a hundred miles. The Japanese had taken only twelve days in December 1941.

Immediately after the liberation of prisoners in Cabanatuan, I helped besiege some Japanese west of Muñoz, where they had buried some of their tanks in order to use the cannon as artillery. We had a terrible time literally shooting them out of the ground. Afterward I still remained formally "unassigned," held in reserve, and so not pinned down to any special duty. I took advantage of this condition to use the Jeep I had been given to accompany the First Cavalry Division on its way to Manila. We arrived just after a couple of our LGAF units had helped liberate the inmates of Santo Tomas prison camp there. I spent several hours at Santo Tomas one day looking for some civilians I knew who had been there, but I never found them. I also spent some time with artillery spotters who were guiding the shelling of the post office in Intramuros (the old Spanish section of Manila), where some Japanese were hiding. Manila was destroyed in 1945 not by indiscriminate aerial bombardment but by artillery. In this case the gunners skipped shells along the street and into the doors of the post office until they completely wrecked the place. When it was over, I rounded up some of my men who had accompanied the invading force as scouts on its way southward. We scrounged some transport and all went back north.

— 12 —
The Last Months

The reconquest of the Philippines was different from any other Pacific campaign in that it was the only one in which large, organized guerrilla forces backed by a generally loyal civilian population made an important contribution to the defeat of the Japanese. Not coincidentally, it was also by far the most costly campaign for the Japanese in the whole war. Half the Nipponese troops who died in World War II did so in the Philippines.

Before the Philippine campaigns of 1944–1945 the U.S. Army had never had the opportunity to use guerrillas. When army leaders observed the combined zeal and skill with which our guerrillas battled the enemy in the days immediately preceding and following the Lingayen landings, and in such enterprises as the Cabanatuan raid, they were deeply impressed. Within a few days Sixth Army leaders asked that we organize a regiment to be attached to the Twenty-fifth Infantry Division of the Sixth Army. Consequently, several LGAF squadrons underwent rapid transformation into regular combat troops. This was carried out at Rosales, at a breakneck pace. With 5,000 to 6,000 men who were well trained and tested, and about the same number of relatively untested reserves, I had less than two weeks to establish and staff new headquarters, cut orders, institute a record-keeping system, make reports, teach the new staff how to continue these activities routinely, and create the First Infantry Regiment, which would integrate with the Twenty-fifth Division. Somehow we got it done by January 20: no mean feat. There followed a brief training period, then action alongside regular U.S. Army troops.

Considering the circumstances, the metamorphosis was smooth, yet no such lightning transition could take place without problems of some kind. The immediate one was that while General Krueger was glad to have us, he still thought of guerrillas as aides, to be assigned to peripheral duties. Neither rank-and-file irregulars nor their leaders were content with such a restricted role. They were avid to hunt down and shoot Japanese soldiers, not just guard an ammunition dump somewhere. Russell Volckmann was notorious for interpreting his orders so broadly that he came close to doing as he pleased. Many a subordinate guerrilla commander, inside or outside his organization, did likewise. As early as February many guerrilla units were drawing regular U.S. equipment and supplies, and were liberating towns and villages before American regulars could reach them. Above all, my guerrillas and many others were driving the Japanese troops back and forth relentlessly between the mountains and the plains, and slaughtering them by the thousands.

Regular army officers from the platoon level on up began commandeering guerrilla units, including some of mine, and attaching them to their existing forces. In February alone I received twenty-nine letters of thanks, praise, or commendation from U.S. officers ranging from major generals down to captains. A few praised me personally, more emphasized the quality and helpfulness of the whole LGAF organization, still more singled out various area or squadron commanders for their cooperative spirit and the fine work they and their men had done in collaboration with U.S. regulars. Some requested that various LGAF units be allowed to remain with their own to continue the struggle. It was all extremely gratifying, as was the judgment of a Philippine student of the war some years afterward who asserted that by gathering intelligence and fighting the enemy, LGAF had done more to advance the cause of freedom in central Luzon than any other organization.[1]

Unfortunately, some of the regular officers who praised LGAF men so freely would sometimes simply dismiss guerrillas once they were no longer needed, without making any further provision for them. Then it would be up to the men to make their way back to their former units in any way they could, and up to me somehow to get them all back in their proper places once more. Not until February 17 were Luzon guerrilla units at last formally recognized as a part of United Nations forces. These legalities aside, our men continued to fight as splendidly as ever, now alongside U.S. regulars, in the spring campaigns and northward down the Cagayan Valley during the last six months of the war. By June we had reached our maximum effectiveness. We had 10,000 to 12,000 men actively engaged; we had formed a second LGAF regiment and attached it to the Thirty-second (Red Arrow) Division; we were getting regular air support in combat; and in some places where morale was low among regulars, guerrillas had become the primary assault forces and regulars the de facto support troops.[2]

Fighting throughout the Central Cordillera of Luzon in the spring of 1945 was as ferocious as anywhere in the Pacific during the whole war. It was especially intense along the Villa Verde Trail. This pathway went up, over, and down mountains into the southern end of the Cagayan Valley, the richest agricultural region of northern Luzon. American engineers riding bulldozers under heavy Japanese fire gradually managed to widen it into an eight-to-twelve foot road, often hung on the edges of precipices hundreds of feet high. The Japanese were strongly dug in, in foxholes and in both horizontal and vertical underground tunnels. They were well camouflaged, with their positions carefully sited so they could cover U.S. areas of advance with artillery, mortar, machine-gun, and rifle fire. The hillsides were "steep as a cow's face," as an old rural phrase had it, and covered with razor-sharp kunai grass. Heavy rains produced constant mud slides that compelled frequent rebuilding of the precarious roads and redigging of trenches that had caved in. Hand-to-hand combat was commonplace. The enemy employed sharpshooters, infiltration, ambushes, booby traps, and such tactics as slipping up close enough after dark to throw twenty pounds of dynamite into American lines, followed by a hand grenade to detonate it. Our troops replied with artillery barrages, burning Japanese out of caves with flamethrowers, and burying others alive by sealing their cave openings with bombs and dynamite. So savage was the combat that it took the Thirty-second Division 119 days to advance twenty-five miles along the Villa Verde Trail and finally break Japanese resistance there. Throughout the campaign our guerrillas fought alongside the Red Arrow men. They were led by Capt. Ray Hunt, the liaison man between them and regular U.S. forces.[3]

My own activities that spring combined those of a troubleshooter with those that accrue to a "utility man" in baseball. I worked intermittently at Sixth Army headquarters. I also had a Jeep at my disposal and used it to travel around a good deal, making sure that our First Regiment was properly supplied and treated well. Among other activities I occasionally pinchhit as a spotter for artillery. This was an invaluable service for ground troops because the spotter could fix targets precisely for U.S. gunners. It was also a distinctly thrilling experience, for the spotter plane flew only 150 to 200 feet high and thus made an ideal target for enemy ground fire. Most of the time such fire was sparse, however, because the Japanese feared it would reveal their own positions; only when they were occasionally caught in the open would they blaze away with all they had. Enemy planes never bothered me at all. By then few of them were left.

The quality of guerrilla units in 1945 varied enormously from excellent to worthless. Most of the latter sort were hardly true guer-

rillas at all; some were still, in effect, gangs of bandits and extortion-
ists who pillaged peasants and *talked* about fighting the enemy.
What their civilian victims and true guerrillas thought of them had
been demonstrated in straightforward Oriental fashion on Leyte:
when American patrols disarmed some of these buccaneers, they
were immediately seized by local civilians and hung upside down
with their heads atop ant hills.[4] At the other end of the spectrum,
Volckmann and his 18,000 guerrillas received much official praise,
which they deserved, though my LGAF men and other guerrilla
groups were equally deserving. As noted earlier, the high reputation
of both Volckmann and his private army owed much to his skill in
public relations.[5]

The extent to which history is colored by those who write it
can be illustrated by posing a hypothetical question: suppose the
only extant account of the deeds of Volckmann had been written by
Ernesto Rodriguez Jr., author of *The Bad Guerillas of Northern
Luzon?* Rodriguez acknowledges that most of Volckmann's troops
fought well in 1945, but he also contends that many of them were
scum of the earth who committed numberless terrible crimes for
which they were never punished. He charges that they abused civilians more shamefully than any other resistance group in the whole
archipelago, names various leaders as monsters in human form, and
describes their atrocities vividly. He admits that Volckmann may
not have known what some of his subordinates were doing (though
the same plea by General Masaharu Homma did not prevent Americans from executing that Japanese officer as a war criminal), but
criticizes him sharply for either not knowing or for failing to rein in
his lieutenants.[6]

How much Volckmann knew of the deeds of some of his underlings and whether or not he took proper preventive measures I have
no way of knowing. Subordinates often did things on their own that
they knew their superiors would not have approved, and crimes and
atrocities were commonplace all over the Philippines throughout the
war. All I can say for certain is that one of the main reasons I visited
my units regularly was to keep cognizant of what was going on, a
state of affairs officially recognized by an army Guerrilla Affairs
Division investigation which credited LGAF with being the best-
disciplined guerrilla organization on Luzon. Of course, certain LGAF
individuals occasionally did shameful things, but my men never engaged in wholesale criminality of any sort.

Overall, guerrillas performed better than expected. Whether as
regulars or support troops, they saved thousands of American lives.

Marking's units broke through Japanese defenses at a critical juncture in a battle for Ipo Dam and thereby saved Manila's water supply. Other irregulars extensively sabotaged Japanese efforts in southern Luzon. Volckmann's units conquered most of the northern Luzon coast. They and my own LGAF forces fought alongside U.S. regulars all over central and north Luzon. My men were especially prominent in the push toward La Union province, along the Villa Verde Trail, in the savage struggle for Balete Pass, in the Cauco Valley, protecting Highway 5, and aiding the regulars to withstand "banzai" attacks by the Japanese.[7]

No less valuable was the support accorded Filamerican forces by the mass of Filipino civilians. Thousands of them—railway workers, truck drivers, engineers, clerks, government officials, guides, carriers of everything—pitched in to help us in every way they could. Nor should the remnants of the Philippine Scouts be forgotten. As soon as they heard that American troops were landing again, most of those tough Scouts who had survived Bataan or Corregidor rushed to "report for duty" once more and get a chance to fight their oppressors again.[8] The longer the war lasted, the more I came around to the state of mind Edwin Ramsey says gripped him as well, regarding the Philippines as something like a second home and feeling that the battle of the people for liberation from their conquerors was my fight as well as theirs.

The contributions of guerrillas were especially important in the spring of 1945 because many units in the Sixth Army suffered from serious morale problems. It was not that the men lacked bravery, for there were many daily acts of heroism; it was, rather, that most soldiers of any nationality simply wear out after a time. Some revive and fight with zeal after a period of rest and recreation. Others seem to have just so many campaigns and battles in their nervous systems and become permanently "burned out" once their limits are reached. The Red Arrow Division had the most trouble, so its situation is perhaps most instructive. Its members had been involved in hard jungle fighting for three years all over the south Pacific. Thirty percent of its troops had been overseas since early 1942 and had been through three, four, or five major campaigns before invading the Philippines. After two months of fierce combat in the mountains of Leyte, they were sent to northern Luzon 25 percent under strength and after only two or three weeks rest. Combat losses were especially heavy among officers and noncoms in the first two or three months after the Lingayen landings, a good indication that morale was not high among the rank and file. Replacement officers and noncoms were of indifferent quality at best.

Because General Yamashita had at least twice as many troops on Luzon as U.S. intelligence had supposed, American infantrymen had to be kept on the front line almost continuously, whereas normally they would have been rotated to rear areas for rest and recuperation. With the war rapidly winding down in Europe, more and more men began to think about their own chances of being rotated home. Bogged down in mountains heavily defended by Japanese along the Villa Verde Trail, they complained that their replacements were slow to arrive. Moreover, infantrymen always see the worst side of any locale they happen to occupy: in the tropics not pith helmets, broad verandas, cool drinks, and lissome girls clad in sarongs but swamp water flavored with chlorine, hot steel helmets, insects dead and alive, dust, malaria, dengue fever, dysentery, jungle rot, steaming, filthy foxholes, and everywhere an oppressive stench.[9]

The beleaguered Japanese found the ubiquitous filth especially depressing. One remarked that with no toilets either in the barrios or on mountain roads in northern Luzon, human waste was scattered everywhere, both outdoors and in what was left of buildings. Anywhere one looked there were decomposing human bodies covered with flies and emanating a paralyzing stink. In barrios the manure contributed by pigs and geese compounded the fetid mess. Nobody washed his hands or changed clothes for weeks at a time, lice were everywhere, and diseases multiplied predictably.[10] This was the environment Leon Beck had in mind when he observed, "You will never get a war movie authentic until you put smell into it."[11] (I must add here that wherever I was, the pigs, chickens, dogs, birds, and associated creatures scavenged for one another with fair efficiency and the human inhabitants of barrios swept up offal and rubbish regularly. Thus, the barrios I saw were much cleaner than those the Japanese say they encounted in the wilds of northern Luzon.)

In these grim circumstances the alternation of stifling hot days and cold, wet nights in the mountains added pneumonia to the list of standard tropical diseases. Small wonder that combat fatigue and psychological casualties multiplied.[12] The pressure got to some of us guerrillas, too, in various ways. Throughout most of the war Al Hendrickson had been in Tarlac, an especially tough and dangerous place because it was a center of the Huk movement. He had borne up well under the strain, all things considered. Then, about Christmas time in 1944, Al broke his ankle when his horse fell on him while wading a river. A month later, only half recuperated from this mishap, he was caught in an enemy ambush. A machine gunner missed him by inches, but he broke his ankle again leaping into a bomb crater. Within a minute a GI, providentially nearby, killed a Japanese soldier who was about to impale Al on his bayonet. Al now had to go to a hospital to have his rebroken ankle set. The whole experience seemed to bring him close to the breaking point. Never one to pass up a drink, he began to drink too much. Given the constant pressure he had endured and his worsened physical disability, it seemed to me both unfair to him and risky to his troops to leave him in command of men destined for battles to the death with the Japanese. I recommended that he be sent back to the States.

Ed Ramsey, underweight and overstrained throughout the war, felt himself growing steadily weaker in the spring of 1945, at a time when he was seriously overworked trying simultaneously to train and equip guerrillas and to integrate thousands of them into the U.S. Sixth Army. Then he was struck with appendicitis. The Filipino doctor who removed his appendix gave him a lot of pills thereafter to keep him going at his work, even though both he and the doctor knew that what he needed was a complete rest. The combined mental and physical pressures proved more than he could stand. He suffered two nervous breakdowns in May 1945.[13]

In my own way, I too gave out in the spring of 1945. One night walking back in the dark to where I was then staying, I fell into a hole and broke my shoulder. A young, inexperienced army doctor set the break and encased me in a cast in which my arm was strapped across my chest. It was the wrong kind of cast entirely, though perhaps I should have been grateful that at least he did not imprison the wrong *arm* in his creation. Fortunately for me, he was soon transferred. His replacement, seeing at once that the cast was unsuitable, cut it off and discovered that what had originally been a simple break had been made a good deal worse by the misplaced efforts of his predecessor: muscle pressure and the cast had pulled the break apart. He had to operate, reset the bone, and make me a new cast that held my arm straight outward from shoulder to elbow, then at a right angle from elbow to hand, horizontal to the ground, with my hand pointing forward. I stayed in the field hospital only a few days, but that was ample time to meditate on the difference between my present plight and my rapid recovery from malaria and dysentery nearly three years before after treatment by a Filipino witch doctor.

I was able to move in and out of the hospital freely, and I still had my Jeep and a driver, so I remained in overall command of LGAF and tried to look after things while riding around with my arm extended rather like the yardarm of an old sailing ship. But it soon became obvious even to me that our outfit needed a leader in good health and capable of rapid motion, so I resigned my command to Harry McKenzie, who soon thereafter passed it on to Maj. Alfonso Arellano.

The appointment of Arellano as CO was not popular with many of our men. He had formerly been a district commander of the Philippine Constabulary, and only a few of our top squadron commanders knew that he had been working closely with us from the time of his appointment until his open defection to our side late in the war. Thus, to most of the men Arellano looked like a long-time collaborator who had changed sides when he saw that the Allies were going to win. In actuality he was an able and experienced officer. The first Filipino graduate of the U.S. Army Artillery Center and School at Fort Sill, Oklahoma, he became chief of staff of the Philippine army after the war.

Meanwhile, however, my accumulating misfortunes had gotten me down somewhat. I still have a letter I wrote to my sister on March 25, 1945. In it I noted that I felt tired, discouraged, homesick, uncertain about my future, and half ashamed of all the publicity I had been getting back home, because it seemed to me then to be undeserved.

Japanese morale too frayed around the edges as the war wound down, though the zeal with which many enemy troops still resisted would seem to belie that statement. American infantrymen complained bitterly that the enemy fought with irrational fervor. Even when forced into some hopeless position they refused to surrender, and it took long, miserable days, weeks, or months to root them laboriously out of caves with explosives or flamethrowers that had to be carried twenty miles on the backs of GIs. Everywhere the murderous ingenuity of Nipponese soldiers seemed undiminished. They crawled into unexpected places, dug holes where it seemed impossible to break ground, dressed in U.S. uniforms or women's clothing to penetrate American lines, let trucks go down roads unmolested so they could be ambushed from behind, faced foxholes or snipers "the wrong way" so Americans could pass unharmed and then be shot in the back, mined foxholes, left sandal tracks in the mud or abandoned cooking fires to lead us into ambushes, and fired single shots just to keep our troops awake at night.[14] (Interestingly, our guerillas sometimes adapted more readily to "total" war of this sort than did Sixth Army or Eighth Army regulars.) In such fierce engagements as the battle for Salacsac Pass in the northern mountains (March–April 1945) Japanese soldiers still fought like wild beasts even though many of them had lost an eye or an arm to grenades that exploded too soon or were thrown a couple of seconds too late. Those severely wounded were allowed to die, given poison so they could commit suicide, or taken to hospitals that resembled slaughterhouses. The less seriously wounded were often sent, half-healed, back to the front to fight again.[15]

Such combined ingenuity and savagery on the part of the Japanese and the corresponding USAFFE tendency to "take no prisoners" derived from several sources. Notoriously, wars are waged with the fewest restraints when each side regards the other as naturally inferior, less than completely human. To kill enemies wholesale then becomes not murder of people like oneself but the mere extermination of vermin. By the latter stages of World War II each side had suffered so much at the hands of the other that sheer yearning for revenge had blotted out most civilized instincts. Many Japanese soldiers also fought on desperately for the same reason that General Yamashita hung on so tenaciously in the Luzon mountains: they believed they were winning precious time for their countrymen to fortify the home islands and prepare better for the coming American invasion. The American disinclination to take prisoners owed much to bloody experience: Japanese sailors who survived a sinking ship would carry grenades with them to kill anyone attempting a rescue; soldiers would play dead or wounded and then shoot medics who tried to help. Variations on these themes were endless.[16]

Even so, all human beings have their limits. By early summer many Japanese were clearly near the end. To start with, the army available to Yamashita for the defense of Luzon had been gravely weakened by the transfer of many of its best men to the earlier struggle for Leyte. Most of the remaining units had only recently been formed from the remnants of shattered divisions, men rescued from sinking ships, and survivors of wounds and diseases. Yamashita's army had less than a quarter as many vehicles as its American opponents. Fuel and lubricants were so short that many a Japanese truck ran on distilled pine root oil. Munitions were inadequate, and Luzon's whole transportation system had been wrecked by American bombing and guerrilla sabotage. The surviving officers were second rate; communications and construction equipment were in short supply; and medical goods were scanty. Worst of all, food was inadequate and growing scarcer by the day. The soldier's regular rice ration of three pounds per day had been cut to one pound or less in November 1944, cut again to a mere half-pound in some units in January, again to a few spoonfuls in the spring. The results were predictable. By June 1945 starvation and tropical diseases were taking ten times as many men as combat. It was Bataan in reverse, with Japanese victims this time. Enemy prisoners secured in the last few months of the war were often wounded, starved, and suffering so badly from beriberi that they could no longer fight, retreat, or even commit suicide.[17]

To say that one individual is typical of thousands is always precarious, doubly so in the case of Tetsuro Ogawa who was Japanese but not a soldier at all; he was a civilian teacher attached to an army unit on Luzon. Moreover, he was clearly a thoughtful, intellectual person, different in psychology from most ordinary Japanese infantrymen. Yet what still stuck in his memory twenty-seven years after the war must have made some impressions on other Japanese in the mountains of northern Luzon in the spring of 1945. Ogawa was clearly dispirited, weary of filth and stench and a starvation diet of fried catfish washed down with ethyl alcohol made from sugar cane and used impartially for drinking and for automotive fuel.[18] He was fed up with army propaganda about phantom victories and "advances to previously prepared positions" every time some new Pacific island was lost. Among themselves he and his friends cursed Tojo and general headquarters for waging the war at all, for botching the job, for deceiving the people, and for ruling like despots—though he acknowledges that they did not criticize themselves for having loyally supported such a regime when the war was going well, or regret the rapid growth of Japanese power in the early stages. [19]

But now he listened to friends who told him not to try to go back to Japan, for he would likely be killed by American planes or submarines en route; better to stay in the Philippines, use his wits to survive, forget the notion that surrender was dishonorable, take his chances that the Americans would spare those who surrendered, and then try to make Japan a better country after the war was over. He admits that he was impressed and that he passed the advice on to others. Then, right at the end of the war, when he did surrender, he was amazed that a guerrilla captain treated him and other Japanese humanely, even giving them food and cigarettes. Those he had been taught to despise as ignorant barbarians had acted civilized, while he and his countrymen, who had been told that they represented righteousness, had degraded themselves: "It was indeed a complete defeat."[20] Another thoughtful Japanese put the same feelings into somewhat different words: "We can find very little with which to comfort ourselves and find too many things over which we feel only shame and regret."[21]

Sadly, the worst erosion of morale in the latter stages of the war took place among the Filipinos, and not just among soldiers. The travail of those Filipino civilians who were well educated, sensitive, and intelligent consisted primarily of wrestling with private demons. Yay Panlilio wrote to Carlos Romulo, for whom she had once worked on a Manila newspaper, that the war had wrenched her soul, had exposed her to every possible emotion, and had been by far the stiffest test of the human character she had ever endured.[22] Romulo said that when he entered the wreckage of Manila and learned what the Japanese had done he wanted to hunt through the ruins and cut the throat of the first Japanese he saw. When he found his mother soon after and discovered that enemy soldiers had tortured her so mercilessly that she could no longer walk, his immediate impulse was to gloat aloud over every Japanese killed anywhere. He adds that he could not quite bring himself to kill, however, for two oddly different reasons: he had seen so much blood and suffering that his own lust for vengeance, however justified, had been dulled; and, as a Christian and a Rotarian[!], he was ashamed of such feelings. But his old passion surged anew when Generals Homma and Yamashita were tried for war crimes. As the charges against them and their troops were specified, he got "a glimpse into the depths of depravity that can lurk in human souls that it is almost worth a man's reason to see."[23]

For ordinary Filipino civilians the accumulated pressures of war lay less in the realm of philosophy than in the vivid, hellish experiences and fears of everyday life. Most Americans have no real comprehension of what the Filipino people endured in World War II. We lost fewer than 500,000 killed out of our population of 150 million: a million Filipinos died, 6 percent of their 17 million people, or losses proportionately eighteen times as grievous as ours. Other millions were brutalized on a scale exceeded only among the Jews and several peoples of east-central Europe. The United States suffered no physical destruction at all, but in the summer of 1945 Philippine schools, transport, hospitals, sanitary facilities, housing, newspapers, banks, universities, hotels, libraries, government offices and records all lay in ruins: burned, smashed, shot up, scattered, or in hopeless disrepair. Manila was more thoroughly sacked than any major city in the world save Warsaw or—those special cases—Hiroshima and Nagasaki. Industrial production had regressed to its 1897 level.

No single incident can ever truly typify such a debacle, but one in the spring of 1945 has stuck in my memory. I was returning from inspecting troops when a woman ran out of a house to flag down my

Jeep. She told me, semihysterically, that five children had been torn up appallingly by the explosion they had unwittingly set off while playing with a hand grenade. My driver and I loaded two of them into the Jeep, and had a passing truck pick up the other three, and got them all to a field hospital, whose personnel were overworked treating wounded soldiers and so not happy to see their case load supplemented by civilians. Nonetheless the hapless kids, wracked with pain and bewilderment, did get their wounds disinfected and bound up.

Notoriously, the sufferings of war are not confined to deaths and personal injuries. As prices rose dramatically throughout the conflict, wages and salaries never kept pace, so city people in particular gradually grew more and more hungry. Along with ordinary government officials, most of whom were moderately honest in normal times, they now had to live by graft and theft. The price controls and rationing imposed by the government were universally evaded. People planted vegetables in empty lots and even along sidewalks, but most of what matured was stolen either by the Japanese or other Filipinos. Japanese invasion currency became totally worthless in the months just before the American landings, leaving the country without legal tender and reducing most transactions to barter. People who had luxury goods were compelled to surrender them for food, not in routine trades but by grim haggling that left mutual animosity in its wake. All sorts of food "substitutes," edible and inedible, appeared. Many a dog, cat, or worse made its final appearance in this world on a restaurant menu under some designation such as "beef," "chicken," or merely "fricassee." The writer of a letter to the editor of the *Manila Tribune* complained that so many cats were becoming restaurant fare that the city was threatened with a plague of rats.[24] Others speculated that dogs might become extinct as they had in Paris for a time during the Great French Revolution.[25]

In the desperate scramble to stay alive ordinary civic organization broke down. By late 1944 people were publicly starving to death, stinking corpses lay unburied in the streets for days amid piles of garbage and rubbish, and eggs cost an incredible $8.00 apiece. Clothing and other necessities became as scarce as food. Those injured and taken to hospitals were expected to bring their own medicine and bandages. Theft, smuggling, black marketeering, bribery, price gouging, embezzlement, hijacking, and "protection" selling seemed universal. More different kinds of vice flourished than in ancient Sodom and Gomorrah. Graves were robbed to get the clothing and gold teeth of the corpses. Kidnapping and murder multiplied amid a din of denunciations of "collaborators," though more often than not the motives of the criminals were financial or personal. In the last months of the war Filipino stevedores systematically looted American ships at temporary piers as well as supply dumps and depots inland. The streets of Manila teemed with hawkers of every imaginable product that could be stolen. Hordes of Filipino girls flocked to American troops to undertake joint assaults on several of the Ten Commandments.

Most odious of all were the "parasites" and "peso patriots," swine who had been pro-Japanese early in the war but turned pro-American when it became obvious the Allies would win, scoundrels who had done nothing more strenuous than wait for MacArthur to come and save them but who now strutted about waving pistols, seizing food, bellowing at "civilians," and telling everybody what fierce guerrilla fighters they had always been, all the while trying to exchange their worthless Japanese currency for U.S. dollars. One American guerrilla observed glumly that the whores in Manila had contributed more to the Allied cause than these "sunshine patriots" because the whores had at least put thousands of Japanese soldiers in hospitals with venereal diseases.[26]

All these conditions were worse in Manila than elsewhere, but in the war's latter stages they were spreading into smaller cities and towns as well. To many Filipino writers this sad spectacle has long seemed clear evidence of national demoralization. As one put it, World War II was the darkest interlude in 500 years of Philippine history, "a period of general decadence, when time seemed to have moved backwards, and when civilization seemed to have retrogressed from modern to barbaric times, especially where Japanese soldiery was concerned." He added that the Japanese had taught Filipinos to relegate women to the lowest stratum in society, as in Japan itself, and had given lessons in lying, empty promises, treachery, and thievery "from some of which some Filipinos have not fully recovered to this day."[27]

I think the critics are too hard on their countrymen. The Philippines were certainly in shambles in the summer of 1945, but these are conditions that usually exist where heavy fighting has raged. It must also be emphasized once more that the most destructive fighting took place in cities, Manila above all; and that newspapermen especially, but other writers too, tend to concentrate on events and conditions in big cities, rather than see what prevails in the hinterlands. Ordinary farmers and villagers out in the countryside where I was did not seem any more "demoralized" than they had ever been or than other people might have been in similar circumstances. Perhaps the most grimly ironic aspect of the whole situation was that in the immediate aftermath of all this desolation the U.S. government thrust independence onto the Filipinos and said, in effect, "Go fend for yourselves."

Ought we to be surprised that all parties, Americans, Japanese, and Filipinos, were visibly cracking under the strain of war by 1945? No. Crises of every sort notoriously bring out both the best and the worst in humanity. When communities are hit by earthquakes, tornados, hurricanes, volcanic eruptions, fires, or floods, many people struggle bravely to help their neighbors, feed them, and get them back on their feet once more, but extra police and the National Guard also have to be summoned to keep in line the packs of scoundrels who hasten forth to steal everything in sight and commit personal crimes against the unfortunate people whose lives have already been sorely disrupted. It is the same with disasters that are directly or indirectly of man's own making: train and ship wrecks, plane crashes, street riots, and, above all, war. Mountain climbers risk their lives to struggle to the site of a high-altitude plane crash but sometimes have a hard time beating the ghouls who rush to rob the dead or dying passengers.

War is the supreme tester of the relative strength of the varied components in humanity's dual nature. The most selfless and heroic deeds are mingled inextricably with the basest conduct of which our species is capable. Usually it is when discipline breaks down, when ordinary order backed by force is absent, that the vilest conduct becomes most evident and prevalent. How thin is the crust of civilization, so slowly and carefully constructed; how easily is it ripped apart by the barely stifled primitive impulses within us all and by the frank barbarism of many who are normally restrained mostly by the threat of punishment.

— 13 —
The Japanese War Effort

Whether wars are waged by regular troops, by guerrillas, or both, their outcome always depends heavily on the strength, shrewdness, and efforts of the enemy. Every war is preceded by unsuccessful diplomacy on the part of one or more of its participants; otherwise, it would not take place. In all wars, errors—often grievous—are made by both sides on both strategic and tactical levels. In combat, shortcomings in prewar preparations are exposed relentlessly. Different parties correct their mistakes at different rates and to different degrees: some never correct them. Many an American soldier in World War II wondered, "What must the other armies be like if we're winning the war?" Behind the jest lurked a grim truth, for indeed wars are often more truly lost than won. We guerrillas in the Philippines survived only partly by our own wits and efforts. We also owed a lot to the follies and the fumbling of our adversaries.

In both world wars the Allies "won" because we had more of everything and because our enemies committed more grievous errors than we did. On the grand strategic level the policies of the government of Wilhelmian Germany (1888–1918) set a standard for ineptitude that has rarely been approached. They frightened Germany's neighbors so profoundly that England and France, inveterate enemies for 900 years, became allies and remained so through both world wars. Germany also drove Czarist Russia into the arms of Britain and France, even though Russia had long been the rival of Great Britain from Constantinople across Asia to the Pacific, and even though France and England were the major bulwarks against the sort of political and social reaction typified by Romanoff Russia. German policy even succeeded in driving neutral and isolationist America into the grand alliance against the Central Powers, thus assuring Germany's eventual defeat. This bungling remained unmatched until the 1930s, when Britain, France, America, and lesser democratic states grasped desperately at every excuse to avoid confronting Germany and Italy until a second global war became the only alternative to Nazi domination of Europe.

Russia, Britain, France, and the United States fought for different national objectives in World War I. British politicians bickered with British generals; French and Russian politicians and generals did likewise; then they all squabbled with their opposite numbers in other countries about preeminence and strategy. Finally, they turned their contentiousness on the Americans, who had become their main hope of eventual victory. High-ranking German authorities dictated to their Austrian allies, then disputed among themselves about whether to make their primary effort against Russia in the east or the British and French in the West.

France was caught unprepared to face the German blitzkrieg in World War II *seven months* after its awesome striking power had been displayed on the plains of Poland. National morale collapsed, the French army was routed in a month, and France's British allies took a perverse pride in escaping the same fate by an eyelash at Dunkirk. Josef Stalin, celebrated in Communist propaganda as the world's foremost authority on all serious subjects, employed third-rate Soviet troops ineffectually against Finland in the "winter war" of 1939–40. He thereby confirmed the widespread misapprehension abroad that the Russian army would be as inept in a new war as it had been in 1914–1917. The action was virtually an invitation to Germany to invade the Soviet Union. Stalin then ignored more than ninety warnings that Nazi Germany did plan to attack. When the German onslaught finally began, hundreds of Russian planes were caught on the ground, and Stalin suffered a nervous breakdown. Yet the USSR came away on the winning side in the war. How? One of the most obvious reasons was that Hitler's excursion into the Balkans in the spring of 1941 delayed the invasion of Russia by six weeks and enabled "General Winter" to come to the aid of the battered and bloodied Soviets a crucial six weeks sooner. Another was that German refusal to treat the Ukrainians in a civilized fashion turned these potential friends into enemies and led them, in despair, to defend Russia rather than aid its German invaders.

Italian antiaircraftmen began their war in North Africa by shooting down their own war minister, and their comrades fought ineptly thereafter. Allied bombing in western Europe in the first year and a half of the war cost more in men, money, and equipment than the damage done to the enemy. Even though American cryptanalysts had cracked the Japanese diplomatic code, much of our Pacific fleet was utterly surprised and destroyed at Pearl Harbor, and most of our Far Eastern air force was caught on the ground and destroyed on Philippine airfields eleven hours later—a pair of disasters for which the most generous explanation is gross incompetence from the White House down through the U.S. intelligence services to those who actually had to dodge the first bombs. Little was learned from the bloody experience either, for we were repeatedly caught by surprise after World War II in Korea, Cuba, Vietnam, and elsewhere.[1]

The British surrendered Singapore when they still had ample ammunition and plenty of well-fed men to use it. During the war itself the U.S. Navy was frequently at odds with General MacArthur about strategy, priorities, the allocation of supplies, and other vital matters. MacArthur disliked and distrusted President Roosevelt, who would have relieved the general of his command had he not feared political repercussions. British generals were convinced that Prime Minister Winston Churchill did not comprehend war any better than the politicians and generals in Washington whom they privately derided. Hitler could never decide to concentrate German brains and resources on jet plane research, or V-1 and V-2 rockets, or atomic research, or submarine production, and so failed to secure the supremacy in any of these areas, one of which alone might have brought him victory. Neither British nor American political leaders would take Gen. Charles De Gaulle seriously, though he personified that portion of France still willing to fight. And anyone who has gotten this far in this book is painfully aware of how incessant was the rivalry and squabbling among both American and Filipino guerrillas throughout World War II.

At the tactical level the British sank one of their own ships while tracking the German battleship *Bismarck*. When British and American troops waded ashore in Sicily in 1943, transport planes and gliders flew overhead to undertake a mass parachute drop to support them, but the air forces of the two allies had neglected to consult beforehand with their respective naval comrades; as a result, many of them were shot down by Allied antiaircraft fire.[2] In the Pacific our submarines sank Japanese ships carrying U.S. prisoners of war to Japan, our ships torpedoed each other, and U.S. planes bombed their own troops more than once.[3] When the Americans staged an amphibious landing on foggy Kiska in the Aleutians on August 15, 1943, all the Japanese had long since departed, but this did not prevent the confused invaders from inflicting a number of casualties on one another.[4]

The Germans, though widely regarded as the ablest practitioners of war in the twentieth century, were little better at times. Luftwaffe pilots were so poorly trained for support of naval operations that early in World War II they sank two of their own destroyers.

The German navy was so badly prepared for amphibious operations that its forces were mauled by Polish troops when they undertook landings around Danzig at the outset of the German attack on Poland in early September 1939.[5] In December 1942, when German troops were dying of cold, hunger, shortage of supplies,and Russian bullets around Stalingrad, what did the Luftwaffe drop for them? Food? Ammunition? Winter clothing? No, only innumerable cellophane covers for grenades, four tons of marjoram, and a couple of million contraceptives. So it has gone throughout history, ancient, medieval, and modern.

So why devote a separate chapter to the blunders and follies of the Japanese government and military establishment in the conduct of World War II? The reason is that the Nipponese outdid their opponents in this sphere. The spectacular Japanese successes in the first months of the war seemed to belie the misgivings of Adm. Isoroku Yamamoto, the planner of Pearl Harbor,[6] but they were misleading. The triumphs were due to the unpreparedness of their enemies; surprise, the greatest advantage in war, anytime, anywhere; and brilliant advance planning that soon proved untypical. For a brief period these victories disguised the fundamental folly in the prewar diplomacy of the Japanese, the chaos at the center of their government, the savagery of their many domestic rivalries, and the brainlessness with which they treated the many East Asian peoples they conquered.

The most basic weakness of Japan as a nation between the World Wars was that it had become Westernized ("modernized") in many obvious and superficial ways but underneath remained largely patriarchal, even feudal, its people theoretically subservient in all things to a "divine" emperor. Ordinary citizens were told they were the emperor's children and persuaded that life's highest ideal was to die for him. This had all sorts of pernicious consequences. Narrowminded military people ordered wanton assaults that had no chance of success and merely wasted the lives of brave men. This foolishness, once rooted, led inexorably to the kamikaze attacks of the last months of the war.

Years before, in 1931, the conquest of Manchuria, which was set up by an assassination, proved all too typical of the spirit of prewar Japanese policy. It seemed a splendid success then, gained at the expense of nothing more lethal than disapproving words in democratic states and paper condemnations in Geneva. But the domestic aftermath of the "triumph" was ruinous. Army leaders began to exploit Manchuria for themselves, to espouse an openly luxuriant, decadent style of life, to increase their malign influence in Japanese politics, to adopt a superiority complex toward other Orientals, and to view with indulgence the crimes committed by their troops. Both the military and the bureaucrats wasted, dissipated, stole, and fought among themselves for the spoils of politics and war. Armies have never been renowned for their moral stature, but this one raped so many women that it was said half-seriously that there was not a virgin left in China. Such conduct undermined army discipline and burned hatred of Japan into the souls of scores of millions of Chinese.

When other nations observe such conduct but only complain and do not act, those temporarily on top of the world easily wallow in arrogance. Japanese businessmen reaped huge profits from military orders, education grew increasingly militaristic, the Greater East Asia Co-Prosperity Sphere was extolled by nationalist orators, and the European dictators Hitler and Mussolini became widely admired. Tokyo seemed unaware that Japan was steadily fomenting resentment, mistrust, detestation, and fear among all its neighbors and rivals. Most civilians, ignorant of foreign affairs generally, unaware of the atrocities of their army in China, and prone to believe whatever their government told them, grew uncritically enthusiastic about the general drift of Japanese policy. This was especially true of young "idealists," famous then as now for their "pure" hearts and modest knowledge. The whole nation grew intoxicated by "success."

The optimistic notion that "times make the man" is belied by the history of wartime Japan. No nation more sorely needed great leaders then, but what did Japan get? The Zaibatsu business combine, avid for profits; bureaucrats concerned mainly with their personal careers; Baron Matsuoka, the nation's foremost diplomat, a showoff and hypocritical blowhard; Fumimaro Konoye, a premier of considerable ability but scant courage; and Hideki Tojo, a "hard" man with a good memory but no statesmanlike qualities. These people and the lesser figures who surrounded them were never able either to persuade or to compel the army, navy, and bureaucracy to cooperate rather than quarrel. They bungled the draft so badly that highly skilled technicians who crafted crucial components for weapons were drawn into the army as common soldiers and their skills lost to the war effort.[7] They left so few farmers on the land that city people were short of food and became undernourished. Black marketeering flourished, and rural-urban hostility grew.[8] Inflation raged uncontrolled, and no effective preparation was made to deal with heavy American bombing of Japanese cities or its aftermath. There were not even plans to disperse the various departments of the government in 1945.[9] Little wonder that a U.S. official after the war remarked that during the first months of 1942 he had marveled at Japan's successes and wondered how the U.S. could ever reverse them, but once the conflict had ended he wondered how Japan had been able to undertake it at all.[10] A young Japanese naval officer, who had been ordered to become a kamikaze pilot but was saved when the war ended abruptly, put it more bluntly. He said he would not have minded dying for Japan, but he hated the thought of dying a "dog's death" for the nation's rotten rulers. He wished he could have died attacking generals and ministers.[11]

Of all the ruinous vices to which Japanese ruling circles were addicted, the most spectacular was poisonous feuding between the army and navy. It was not mere "interservice rivalry": the two branches of Japan's armed services frankly regarded each other as enemies. "Horse dung" was what Adm. Soemu Toyoda, commander in chief of the combined fleet, called his army counterparts, adding that he would rather have his daughter marry a beggar than an army man.[12] Japan may have presented a totalitarian exterior but she was actually engaged in three different wars at the same time: the war against the Allies, the war between her own army and navy, and constant political infighting.[13] Some bluntly blame the whole Pacific War on the Japanese navy. They claim the war was fought essentially over whether the army or the navy should get the bigger chunk of the nation's military budget. The army wanted a strategy that would lead to the eventual penetration and seizure of much of Siberia, but the Navy needed the fuel and raw materials of the Dutch East Indies and so followed a southern strategy of seizing it, dragging the army unwillingly along. This strategy aroused the intense suspicion and hostility of the United States. In Washington, meanwhile, Admiral Kichisaburo Nomura—perhaps the worst ambassador in Japanese history—systematically misrepresented everything that came from Tokyo. The war, and disaster, followed apace.[14]

Saburo Sakai, Japan's greatest air hero, an ace who shot down sixty-four Allied planes in World War II, relates with disgust how the war began for him. On December 8, 1941, he and other navy pilots were flying south from Formosa to Clark Field in the Philippines when they spotted far below a formation of nine bombers flying towards them. Assuming at once that these must be American planes sent north to attack Formosa, he and eight other pilots dropped out of formation and dived on the intruders, only to discover that they were Japanese army planes out on a routine training flight. On day one of the most risky war Japan had ever undertaken, the army had simply disdained to let the navy know what it was doing.[15]

The same spirit persisted throughout the war. In prison after Japan's defeat ex-Premier Tojo complained that both services had often refused to consult him about the most important strategic decisions. The navy had declined to inform him what day Pearl Harbor was to be attacked or even how much time might remain for diplomatic maneuver.[16] Neither service told him the truth about the battle of Midway until a month after the event.[17] Neither service would ever accept a unified command in a battle zone. As a result many important battles in the Pacific (Guadacanal, Bougainville, Saipan) were lost in large measure because the army refused to support the navy properly.[18] Early in 1942 the army, piqued at having lost a jurisdictional battle to the navy, left the latter without air cover during its attack on Singapore (though in that instance victory came anyway).[19] Navy intrigue did much to bring down the Tojo government in July 1944, but since the navy did not want to acknowledge this in public, it allowed General Kuniaki Koiso to become premier but then forced Admiral Mitsumasa Yonai into the cabinet to prevent the army from dominating the new government.[20]

Contention over available raw materials and shares of military production was so intense that each service had its own key factories from which it could derive all of the output instead of having to divide it. On one occasion the army intensified its campaign in Burma merely to keep the navy from getting more than half of overall current war production.[21] The oil that was absolutely essential for the prosecution of the war was split about evenly between the two services only because the army controlled about 85 percent of Japan's oil resources, while the navy controlled 85 percent of the tankers.[22] The navy established its own motor corps for land transport; the army had its own submarines; and each service had a separate system of weather stations (and the civilian government a third).

Interservice hostility extended to incredibly petty matters. One service demanded a right-hand thread screw and the other a left-hand thread for identical purposes.[23] In the very last months of the war the army and navy quarreled over the right to scrounge for copper in the debris of bombed-out Tokyo; eventually the smoking ruins of Japan's capital had to be divided between them for scavenging.[24] Little wonder that a top-level strategic conference in Tokyo on October 19, 1944, began with a furious argument between army and navy representatives and ended in raging disagreement. The navy wanted to commit its entire force to an effort to destroy Adm. William Halsey's Third and Adm. Thomas Kinkaid's Seventh U.S. Fleets, after which they expected to crush MacArthur's invasion force on Leyte. The generals objected heatedly; they claimed that chances of success were slim and that the whole Japanese navy could be lost, leaving even the home islands defenseless. The admirals declared that it was now or never for a supreme test of strength with the U.S. Navy. They got their way and the generals left cursing. In the battle of Leyte Gulf that followed soon after, most of the Japanese fleet was destroyed, just as the generals had feared.

Of course, interservice rivalries, inflated egos, and maneuvering for both personal and postwar service advantage were deplorably common in the American services as well as the Japanese. General MacArthur, Adm. Ernest J. King, Gen. George Kenney, and shoals of lesser brass wrangled repeatedly about who had the right to command here or bomb there. Wretched rivalries and intrigues among army, navy, and marine factions,[25] even between rival code-breaking groups in the Navy,[26] seriously hampered American naval operations, especially amphibious operations, in the Pacific throughout the war. It eventually required a debate before President Roosevelt himself to decide whether or not to bypass the Philippines before invading Japan.[27] Even so, no American officers ever pursued interservice feuds with the suicidal zeal of their Japanese counterparts.[28]

In itself, competition between the armed services of a nation is not necessarily harmful. Why did rivalry between the Japanese army and navy descend to self-destructive lunacy? A major reason was that the two services were inspired by and infused with different traditions. The army tried to perpetuate the code of the medieval samurai warrior, whereas the navy, which had come into existence only in the last half of the nineteenth century, had been deliberately modeled on the navies of the Western Powers, notably Britain. In fact, a Western tour was part of a Japanese naval officer's formal training. Consequently, the navy had a much more "modern" outlook and even a Western code of honor. While this by no means displaced the traditional Japanese code, to which the navy also clung incongruously, the army viewed it with profound suspicion and doubted that the navy was still truly "Japanese" in spirit and loyalty.[29]

Innumerable Japanese bureaucrats were as inept or irresponsible in their own ways as the military chiefs. Individuals intent on making personal careers became rivals of all their peers. They were also rivals of the military people and often hostile to them but never made any serious effort to close ranks and impose some united national policy on the warring services. Instead, they joined in the early scramble for the spoils of war and rivaled the generals and admirals in war profiteering and luxurious living.[30] Young people especially were appalled by these odious parliamentary politicians and venal bureaucrats. A few became Communists, but most, out of respect for the royal family, became extremists of the right rather than the left: fanatical nationalists whose naiveté was promptly exploited by the professional military to strengthen the latter's domination of all Japanese life.[31]

Never in the whole history of Japan, which supposedly stretches back through the mists of time to 660 B.C., was its society so muddled or ruling circles so inept as in the years 1922–45. This was painfully evident when the time came for Tokyo to administer the vast territories and 150,000,000 new subjects so suddenly acquired in the initial conquests of December 1941 and early 1942. No advance plans had been made to train and supply the teachers, technicians, overseers, officials, or even propagandists essential for a smooth transition. Just as the economy of Japan itself was never mobilized efficiently, so needed resources in conquered territories were never exploited systematically but simply seized when some crisis impended.

This slapdash and ultimately catastrophic performance contrasts sharply with the shrewdness displayed by the Japanese long before World War II and in the half-century since 1945. In the decades after their islands were opened to the West in the mid-nineteenth century, scores of Japanese missions and bodies of experts had studied the legal, educational, industrial, scientific, naval, and other practices of leading foreign nations and adopted for themselves whatever principles and usages seemed either innately superior or best suited for their own people. For this they were often criticized by foreigners as mere imitators devoid of originality or inventiveness. Such a patronizing attitude was absurd. Is it not a mark of intelligence to adopt for oneself the highest achievements and most advanced techniques of others?

The same spirit was evident again after World War II. Once the wartime blunderers were driven from office, old social strictures loosened, the Japanese government modernized, and the armed forces reduced to a domestic police force, the Japanese people again displayed the industriousness, skills, and intelligent approach to practical problems that had characterized them from 1870 to 1920. Government and industry began to work together closely to wage what amounted to undeclared economic warfare against the rest of the world in general and the United States in particular. Economic development was planned carefully, and hundreds of teams of government officials, executives, engineers, and technicians once more scoured the offices, factories, and laboratories of the developed world to observe and learn the most advanced scientific, technical, industrial, and organizational procedures. Tokyo provided diplomatic support, tariff protection, subsidies to strategic industries, and a bewildering array of formal and informal regulations, restrictions, and sharp practices that had the overall effect of maximizing Japanese exports and keeping foreign goods out. Japan's competitors, especially the United States, remained wedded to traditional free-trade conceptions that perceive commerce as mutually beneficial and refused to recognize Japanese practices as essentially economic warfare. Consequently, within a few decades the Japanese, though defeated militarily in World War II, have been able to build the world's most modern industrial complex. As has often been the case in modern wars, a generation or two after the event it is hard to tell who won.

But back in 1941–42 this evolution lay in the future. At that time, to use American football terminology, after a brilliant opening series of plays moved the ball rapidly to midfield, the Japanese offense degenerated into a succession of fumbles. In conquered lands native labor was exploited without mercy, native nationalist movements were handled maladroitly, and red tape produced a glut of some essential product in one place while a chronic shortage existed somewhere else.

Military planners seldom coldly calculated their chances of attaining a certain objective at a certain cost, or attempted to determine whether it might be more profitable in the long run to placate an enemy rather than fight. Instead they plunged into war heedlessly, depending on national elan and expansive talk about Oriental brotherhood to produce victory. In the same spirit, they seemed to think the whole complex business of managing an empire efficiently would come to pass naturally. In fact, it proved quite beyond the capacity of Japanese administration.[32]

Some observers have insisted that the Nipponese were more intelligent and skillful administrators than this description indicates, that they were particularly adept at persuading Filipinos to give them information, which they then used effectively to hunt down guerrillas in 1943 and 1944.[33] I am not convinced. When you compel "cooperation" by torture and terrorism; when, even then, you get only some of the guerrillas you seek, while the rest live on to kill tens of thousands of your troops; when they are enthusiastically aided in this endeavor by those whom you have induced to "cooperate" but who still hate you fiercely, "efficient administration" hardly seems the most accurate description of your efforts.

A crucial factor in Japan's eventual defeat was lack of the raw materials essential to wage modern war. Japan is a poor country in food, oil, iron, coal, other mineral wealth, and forestry products. Aluminum was essential to make the bodies of planes; copper was a vital ingredient in electrical goods; rubber was essential for tires and much else; oil in vast quantities was necessary to fuel land, sea, and air vehicles; tungsten was vital to harden steel; and such minerals as molybdenum, cobalt, nickel, and mica should have been secured in large quantities with regular replacement assured. Yet in December 1941 all these and other commodities were in short supply, and no plans had been made to stockpile even minimum quantities or to establish dependable access to the food surpluses of southeast Asia. No leaders of the army, navy, or civilian bureaucracy seemed able to see any needs beyond their own in the immediate future. Nobody appeared to have any idea what the *nation* might need in six months or two years, or how it could be acquired, beyond the mere hope that everything necessary could be secured by rapid conquest of southeastern Asia and the western Pacific. Typical of top-level muddle in this sector was the handling of molybdenum, copper, and tungsten. Government edicts set the prices of these metals so low that anyone who had any immediately hoarded it or tried to sell it on the black market. At legal prices production levels could not be met. The problem was never solved.[34]

Another shortage never dealt with satisfactorily by Japan, fortunately for the success of us guerrillas, was manpower. In the first months of the war the Japanese conquered so many places that there were too few troops to govern, police, and defend them all. Many educated, knowledgeable Japanese were astounded at the audacity of their leaders in presuming to challenge, simultaneously, two of the most powerful political entities on earth, the United States and the British Empire. A few such as Admiral Yamamoto had warned that America was intrinsically far stronger than Japan and thus bound to win a long war. Japan's only military hope, he thought, was to make extensive conquests quickly, fortify them strongly, then settle down to a long struggle of attrition and hope that the Americans in particular would tire of the bloodshed and eventually accept the new status quo.[35]

To revert again to a sports metaphor, Japan no longer played to win; it played not to lose. As any athlete knows from hard experience, the vast psychological difference between the two often translates into a practical difference as well: those who play merely not to lose surrender the initiative and in fact then frequently *do* lose. As our enemies settled down to hold what they had seized, the U.S.

war machine shifted rapidly into successively higher gears. By 1943 Allied forces were attacking all over the western Pacific.

It was the same with guerrillas. In 1942 we could only hide out, try to avoid capture, and begin to organize. But since our foes, distracted by too many commitments, failed to crush us, we were able to gain strength and confidence and eventually to play an important role in crushing *them*. As the war lengthened, Japanese troops on garrison duty in the Philippines dwindled in number and (usually) in quality. It appeared to me that save for an occasional spasmodic effort to capture or punish some guerrilla leader for troubling them unduly, the enemy used the Philippines mostly as a staging area; a place to train and condition their green troops by having them chase us through the mountains, jungles, and rice paddies. After some practice at this their men would be shipped elsewhere for active combat. Thus Japanese strength in the Philippines varied with the rise and fall of their war needs in general but was always considerably below what was required to control the Islands firmly. Except in a few cities, enemy troops were moved about regularly from one locality to another. By contrast, we usually stayed in one vicinity for longer periods, soon came to know individual Filipino civilians much better than did our foes, and could make our weight felt more readily and consistently. Statistics indicate the result overall. In the 1940s there were about 1,000 municipalities in the whole of the Philippines. By the time of the Leyte landings in the fall of 1944, fewer than 200 of them had Japanese garrisons; the other 800 were openly or secretly controlled by guerrillas. Even the 200 Nipponese garrisons controlled only the centers of the towns, and only then when they were physically present.[36]

By the fall of 1944 there were 126 radio stations and twenty-seven weather stations reporting regularly to SWPA, backed by 182,000 organized and increasingly armed guerrillas. Nearly every irregular leader of any consequence in the Islands had agents in Manila collecting and exchanging information. All this would have been wildly impossible had the enemy ever been able to station large numbers of good troops permanently in the Philippines. To put the matter in more human terms, how ironic it became that even though the Japanese were the occupiers and nominal masters of the Philippines, a Nipponese pilot who bailed out anywhere over the Islands was killed, whereas an American pilot was rescued either by civilians or by guerrillas.[37]

Aside from Admiral Yamamoto, the Japanese high command seemed blind to the consideration that war is political as well as military—indeed, that without specific political, economic, or ideological goals, war makes no sense at all. At the peak of Japan's successes it never seemed to occur to Tokyo to propose some concessions and offer a negotiated peace to either Britain or the United States, or to try to split them apart when Britain was engrossed in the European war against Germany. Top military people simply wanted to fight on to total victory without regard for anything else and appeared to have no doubt that such victory was possible. Even when defeat had become virtually certain, they never tried such an elementary ploy as attempting to placate their enemy in hope of getting easier peace terms. Their only program was complete victory followed by imposition of the Greater East Asia Co-Prosperity Sphere, a scheme whose fraudulence had by then become painfully evident.

I have always wondered what would have happened had the great mass of Japanese, leaders and led, not grown swell-headed with their early successes but remained content to seize merely the French and Dutch possessions in the Far East. The United States in 1940 was sunk in isolationism, suffused with "America First" sentiment, emotionally hostile to "colonialism," and filled with resentment of Europeans who had reneged on their debts from World War I and seemed as unregenerate and warlike as ever. Would we have gone to war with Japan to help the French and Dutch recover their lost colonies? I doubt it strongly. Would we even have gone to war to help the British regain Singapore and Malaya had Japan left American possessions alone? Again, I doubt it. How many Americans had resolved aloud or silently never again to "pull British chestnuts out of the fire"? We easily forget that Congress renewed the draft law by only one vote in the summer of 1941, nearly two years after the German conquest of Poland, fifteen months after the fall of France, many weeks after the German invasion of the Soviet Union. It is undeniable that Japanese attacks on Hawaii and the Philippines were planned brilliantly and executed with skill, but they were madness on the strategic level, for the surest way to unite U.S. internationalists and isolationists, appeasers and interventionists, Democrats and Republicans was to invade U.S. territory and shock us into enraged action.

Of course, it is understandable that a Japanese imperialist viewing the world from Tokyo in mid-1941 might have concluded that centuries would pass before prospects for Japanese expansion would again be so favorable. The European great powers had either been defeated by or were at war with Germany, except Italy—which like Japan, was allied with the Third Reich. America was neutral, internally divided, and militarily unprepared. Meanwhile the whole Orient lay unguarded. But governments ought to be more cautious than dreamers or enthusiasts for particular causes. Had the Japanese government been more careful about whom it antagonized, more restrained in its ambitions, willing to pursue those ambitions more slowly and with some obeisance to international shibboleths, Tokyo might today be the capital of a vast multinational empire spread all over the western Pacific and eastern Asia. Many students of international affairs have marveled at the ruinous impatience of both Germany and Japan in the twentieth century. Had both produced governments of sufficient sagacity to stay out of wars, the skill and industry of their peoples would long since have enabled them to establish their economic domination of Europe and eastern Asia respectively.

Perhaps foremost of all Japan's follies was the failure to recognize the inherent weakness of its own economy, compared with that of either Britain or the United States, much less of the two combined. It was bad enough that the whole Japanese war machine was hopelessly dependent on overseas raw materials; worse, before the war most of these had had to be transported over long sea routes in American ships because the Japanese merchant marine alone was inadequate for the task. When the battle of Midway in 1942 decimated the Japanese navy and the battle of Leyte Gulf in 1944 destroyed most of the remainder, Nippon's merchant marine was deprived of any serious protection against American surface ships, submarines, or planes. And despite highly skilled scientists and technicians, Japan could never standardize its industrial production because most machine tools had been imported variously from the United States, Britain, Germany, France, Belgium, and a dozen other places and were therefore not standardized among themselves. Soon American coal and steel production was thirteen times that of Japan, our plane production four times as great, small arms and ammunition output twenty times greater.[38]

Along with the enormous increase in American production came comparable improvement in quality. In December 1941 Japan had more trained pilots, and those were veterans of the fighting in China who were usually more skilled than their inexperienced American counterparts. The best Japanese fighter plane, the famous Zero, was king of the Far Eastern skies. But by 1945 it was Japanese pilots who were green, because the air aces of the early war had not been retired to train successors but kept fighting until most of them were killed. Hundreds had been shot down at Midway in June 1942,

the Philippine Sea in June 1944, Leyte Gulf in October 1944, and numerous lesser engagements. Their American opposite numbers had
become not only superior but vastly more numerous. Now it was
American P-38s, Grummans, and Hellcats that were supreme in the
air. In the last few months of the war Japanese engineers devised superior new craft, but like the jet planes of their German allies in
Europe they were too few and too late to make any difference. It was
the same with ships, tanks, and all other war machines.[39]

Perhaps the most striking disparity was in submarines. Because
America had called for the abolition of submarines at the farcical
disarmament conferences of the interwar years, the Japanese concluded that we regarded them as unchivalrous and inhumane weapons and would not use them much in a future war. Tokyo should
have read the early sixteenth-century Florentine political sage Ma-
chiavelli, who advised the Prince never to wage war on republics, for
once normally peaceful people become thoroughly aroused they hate
their enemies to the death and will employ any means to destroy
them. Japan had expected to enjoy a permanent advantage in under-
sea combat but soon found itself hopelessly outnumbered in U-boats
as well as ten years behind the United States in radar and sonar research and therefore unable to cope with our submarines even on a
one to one basis. The general destruction of both its surface and
underseas fleets soon followed. The few Japanese subs left were reduced to hauling particularly valuable freight, to the dismay of their
crews, who had been trained to fight.[40] To sum up: American superiority in modern science and industrial capacity became overwhelming. For the rulers of Japan to expect to overcome it by invoking the
fanatical courage of their soldiers, supplemented by a miracle of unspecified character, was absurd.[41]

Throughout the war we battled the enemy in propaganda contests
quite as much as with guns and bullets. The conflicts varied markedly in form, technique, and effectiveness, but as in military conquests, time favored us. Early on, the Japanese undoubtedly got the
better of us. Considerable American propaganda came via shortwave
from San Francisco, but not many Filipinos had radios in the early
1940s, so few could listen. Moreover, the messages tended to be long-
winded and saturated with benevolent generalities.[42] Early in the war,
too, much U.S. propaganda had to be concocted by guerrillas like me,
who lacked training in this sphere and whose efforts, consequently,
were often amateurish. Japanese propaganda, by contrast, was initially persuasive, especially since Japan seemed to be winning.

Yet that hoary old adage is as true as ever, "The proof of the pudding is in the eating." Nipponese efforts suffered from weaknesses that eventually proved fatal. The most elementary one was that many Japanese radio announcers had not been properly trained to speak other languages and so habitually mispronounced words or fell into malapropisms—all to the derisive amusement of foreign listeners. Much enemy propaganda was also crude and lacking in insight. For instance, Tokyo never tried to fan the fires of discontent among American troops who believed that both General MacArthur and political leaders in Washington had willfully deserted them.

When the war began, the greatest propaganda opportunity our enemies possessed was to talk about "Asia for the Asians" and call for the cooperation of all Oriental peoples in building the Greater East Asia Co-Prosperity Sphere, a scheme initially attractive to peoples who had long borne the social arrogance, economic exploitation, and political dominance of Europeans and Americans. The language of the plan, even resembling that of the Atlantic Charter composed by Winston Churchill and Franklin Roosevelt, stressed the common Oriental heritage of the Japanese and their new subjects. Its authors decried Western culture as selfish, decadent, materialistic, vicious, and exploitative. To combat this combined plague and threat Tokyo called for all Asians to cease quarreling among themselves and rally behind Japanese leadership in expelling corrupt Caucasians from Asia. Afterward, all the new friends might settle in brotherhood and prosperity to savor the delights of what Nipponese propaganda called "spiritual rejuvenation."[43] To implement this glittering program the conquerors threw out pro-American and pro-European leaders in countries they subdued, took local children to Japan to be educated, set up puppet "republics," sent in Japanese as governors and "advisers," and began to provide "markets" for the products of the places they had overrun.

Unhappily for its designers, this grand plan never worked well. Unquestionably, the most basic reason was that Filipinos, Indonesians, Malays, and others wanted not an Asia led by Japan but independence and freedom to run their own affairs as they chose.[44] To the conquered Orientals the most appealing single feature of the plan was its racism. It was most successful in Burma, where Japanese control was light, and least successful in the Philippines, where Japan was never able to fulfill any of its promises. That inability was, in fact, a major failing of the plan almost everywhere. As already noted, the Japanese administrative apparatus was unequal to the task of governing a huge, alien empire.

Nipponese administrators usually ruled through local native subordinates, just as the French, British, and Dutch had done. The principal difference was that the Japanese were far more coarse, greedy, and cruel overlords than the white predecessors whom their propaganda so industriously reviled.[45] They manipulated native currencies in ways that amounted to ill-disguised plunder, created artificial food shortages that compelled people to do the will of the conquerors in order to survive, forced native businessmen into commercial arrangements that milked them for the benefit of their Japanese "partners," manipulated prices to destroy native wealth and influence, and threw local economies into disarray by continuing abroad the wretched feuding and maneuvering among army, navy, and bureaucracy that so inhibited the war effort in Japan itself. For good measure they closed schools, shut off public utilities, curtailed transport, closed theaters, and banned radios. Finally, they tried to bully the native population into learning the Japanese language. Everywhere they answered complaints or resistance with insults and brutality.

A particularly self-defeating practice of the Japanese was to tell blatant lies. All governments prevaricate brazenly during wars for what seem to them (and sometimes are) compelling reasons. Even I "improved" the truth on occasion, but the Japanese did this more flagrantly than others. British and American war news was usually basically truthful and often contained details that made checking its accuracy possible. The higher component of vague generalizations in Japanese war news caused it to carry less conviction, and much of it was outright fiction. To start with, the army and navy each had its own organization to listen to foreign news broadcasts. When composing war propaganda they ignored each other. They also ignored inconvenient facts, grossly tortured other facts, and even regularly invented "factoids" in their anxiety to outdo each other. Incredibly, they even invented entire battles on occasion, notably a "second air battle of Bougainville." Japanese soldiers were sometimes compelled to fight battles or entire campaigns in order to furnish propaganda in support of some predetermined position taken by leaders. Both battles and the lives of valiant men were lost in this way. To save face, military authorities would then announce that the action had been of no importance. It is not hard to imagine the effect on the morale of men who had seen their comrades thus sacrificed to salve the vanity of some leader or of a certain branch of the service.

Barefaced fabrication was especially harmful to the Japanese in the Philippines, for scores of thousands, even millions, of Filipinos often knew the truth. The invaders, would, for example, publicly pretend that nearly all Filipinos had welcomed them as saviors and that therefore virtually no public support existed for a few tiny handfuls of guerrillas. Then they would blandly announce that their forces had "annihilated" large numbers of guerrillas. After having starved, shot, and beaten to death tens of thousands of Filipino troops on Bataan and Corregidor, they unveiled a monument at Camp O'Donnell in memory of Filipino prisoners of war who had died of "disease" despite the heroic efforts of Nipponese doctors and nurses to save them. They allowed José Laurel, president of their own puppet Philippine Republic, to announce that his regime regarded guerrillas as patriots rather than bandits and to offer them amnesty if they surrendered. Then they undercut their own man by executing some of those who did give up.[46] I was able to take advantage of this blunder in a way helpful to LGAF. When a few of my men surrendered after the amnesty was declared (They were never reinducted into LGAF), I at once balanced them off by ordering others to surrender, pretend to be pro-Japanese, and perhaps get jobs in Japanese agencies where they could collect intelligence for us.

Generally, it did not take most Filipinos long to become complete cynics when their ears were assailed by a litany of fine words about friendship, cooperation, or better days to come. They would laugh in private, make disparaging comments to friends, vie in the invention of sarcastic innuendo, and speak grimly of the Japanese gifts to them of barbarity, black markets, and the "Greater East Asia Co-Poverty Sphere".[47] When they dared, newsboys would sometimes shout, "Read all about it! Turn this around and you'll have the truth."[48]

With experience, we gradually developed greater expertise in combatting Japanese propaganda. General MacArthur frequently broadcast greetings and inspirational messages to both guerrillas and Filipino civilians, stressing that we should not abandon hope but should defy the Japanese and thereby cause them to lose face. Various guerrillas and brave Filipino civilians as well published clandestine newspapers from time to time to rebut Japanese claims and promises. Now and then I typed, duplicated, and distributed warnings to pro-Japanese townspeople, issued what I hoped would be "inspirational" addresses to civilians in many towns during temporary absences of enemy military units, and published war news recently received by radio.

Sometimes our efforts had an entertaining side. The Japanese spent much time and effort, often in the company of some of their reluctant and uncomfortable puppet officials, trying to persuade Filipinos that the Americans could never return, that people should therefore abandon resistance in favor of cooperation, and that good jobs and general prosperity would soon follow. Wherever it became apparent that these efforts were having some influence, we would organize groups of our own, rather like the so-called "truth squads" that American political parties employ to follow their opponents during presidential campaigns to undo the "lies" of the opposition. The favorite themes of our "truth squads" were that the Nipponese were stupid, cruel, hypocritical liars who could never be trusted; that American landings and subsequent victories in places as far apart as New Guinea and the Aleutians showed that U.S. forces were invincible when they were on their home soil or were strongly based; and that it was no safer to cooperate with the Japanese than to resist them, since their deeds showed plainly that they would kill Filipinos of any sort, for whatever reason, any time they felt like it. Our main objective was to ridicule the Japanese and show our disdain for them. Most of our Filipino audiences clearly enjoyed these performances and would laugh heartily if one of our "truth tellers" hurled an especially apt gibe at our foes. We almost always got a better reception from crowds than had our Nipponese predecessors.

In the interest of accuracy I must admit that we stretched the truth sometimes. We tried to keep a radio receiver operating up in the hills so we could hear at least some of the broadcasts regularly directed at the Philippines from San Francisco. Runners would then carry down to my headquarters whatever news had been picked up. Other runners brought us news from other guerrilla groups and from Manila. So, overall, we had a fairly accurate idea of how the war was going. Whether in private conversations in houses, talking to people in the street, or presiding over an appearance of a truth squad," however, I sometimes ornamented Allied successes or implied that a victory gained in Guadalcanal or some other distant place was a likely prelude to other American landings much closer. If listeners pressed me for greater precision, I could retreat into some such convenient observation as that an invasion was unlikely until the end of the rainy season several months hence. Strict truth is undeniably admirable, but it is also true that people live on hope. In war the first essential is to win; hence, the second essential must be to give one's supporters some reason to hope, especially if their homeland is occupied by an oppressive enemy.

It is always difficult for people anywhere to appreciate or even accurately estimate the psychology of those of a different race, nationality, religion, or culture. Americans are notoriously insensitive in this area. The Germans are famed for misreading the psychology of other Europeans. Occidentals have long spoken half lightly, half seriously of "inscrutable" Orientals. But the Japanese of the 1940s had no peers when it came to misunderstanding other peoples, eastern or western, or in gratuitously arousing their resentment and hatred. It was not merely that they exploited without mercy those they had conquered, or that they delighted in humiliating Western people in the presence of Orientals. Rather, it was that—flushed with victory and filled with racial arrogance—the Nipponese also ignored local laws and customs, lorded it over their new subjects, slapped their faces, made them bow to Japanese common soldiers, committed sacrileges in Buddhist temples, tore the caps off Moslems, worked hundreds of thousands of Koreans to death, forced nearly as many girls and women (especially Koreans) into prostitution for the "comfort" of their soldiers, raped at random, stole food, seized the best houses, boats, and cars of the vanquished, and caroused in public while the natives starved. It often seemed that they were determined to prove the truth of everything derogatory that Allied propagandists said about them.

Worst of all was their inhuman cruelty, some of which derived from their military training. The Japanese army endured the toughest regimen in the world. Any soldier had virtual life-and-death power over any other of a lower rank. Physical beating was the usual way of enforcing discipline. Basic training was so unrelentingly savage and sordid that many recruits committed suicide rather than see it through to the end.[49] In battle the wounded were often told to commit suicide or were left to die untended.[50] Soldiers were expected to fight to the death rather than undergo the "disgrace" of surrender to save their lives. In China before 1941 Japanese officers often beheaded civilians with their swords to "toughen" themselves for battle, or compelled others to do so for the same reason. Medical experiments were performed on Chinese victims; germ warfare research involved infecting live people; and poison gas was used periodically—all to acquire knowledge that might be useful in future wars. Okinawans, who were regarded as inferiors by Japanese farther north, were murdered by the thousands as spies or driven to mass suicide when U.S. forces invaded in 1945.[51]

The Allies in general, and we guerrillas in particular, profited immensely from such stupid and swinish conduct. Early in the war most Filipinos were frightened and cooperated cautiously with their conquerors, or at least made no trouble for them. A policy of calculated generosity and kindness then might have paid huge dividends for Japan. But when it became clear that the newcomers intended merely to plunder them, Filipino civilians began to support guerrilla bands like my own.[52] The invaders then resorted to the universally hated practice of enforcing collective responsibility. All who were associated with, supportive of, or merely near anyone suspected of thwarting Japanese designs were to be punished. This meant sadistic brutality, to which Filipinos replied in kind.[53] More often the Japanese seemed just brutal and vulgar; they were loud, noisy, unkempt, and avid to insult or maltreat people. Nothing tied the Filipino people to us guerrillas more securely than the combination of blindness, arrogance, and general villainy of the invaders. It gave us a chance to grow and gain support rather than being wiped out early in the war.

Most of the time, though, it seemed to me that our most effective propaganda was just to be there. When ordinary people could see us walk around openly in barrios and towns, when both they and town officials could talk freely to us and the Japanese seemed unable to do anything about it, and when they saw the numbers of guerrillas grow steadily, it was obvious that we had not forgotten them, clear that we still believed in and planned for an American return. It gave them reason to hope that their patience and suffering would one day be rewarded.

It must not be forgotten either that most Orientals are more impressed by obvious material success or by displays of power than by the mere attractiveness of ideas. Once civilians knew that we still had powerful friends in the outside world, backers who kept track of us and tried to help us by sending supplies and equipment, especially new guns, our presence at once became more persuasive. Our status soared visibly in the last half of 1944 when we began to get all sorts of commodities by submarine from Australia, much of it bearing McArthur's message "I shall return."

I never ceased to be impressed by how much prestige any sane, reasonably competent American still had with Filipino peasants merely by being an American. Though it must sound like bragging, it is factually true that ordinary people regarded me as a hero. They would boast that they had met me or had even just seen me. At the ancient age of twenty-five I was often referred to by my men as "the Old Man." Such adulation could easily turn the head of a saint. A saint I was not, and neither were the other guerrilla leaders who were in my position, but I do think such deference made most of us aware of how valuable we could be if we merely stayed alive and on the job.

The Japanese war effort was also seriously impaired by a number of military decisions that proved to be mistaken. Perhaps the most fundamental was uncritical adherence to the time-honored British tradition of seeking out and attempting to destroy the enemy's battle fleet rather than merchant shipping. Of course, there is much to be said in favor of such a strategy. Historically, it served Britain well in many wars. But all principles and practices are conditioned by circumstances and, in war, by technological changes. German submarine attacks on British merchant shipping came close to knocking Britain out of World War I in the spring of 1917; only the organization of convoys and the adoption of a specifically antisubmarine naval strategy had saved the British. Yet in World War II Japanese admirals ignored that lesson and concentrated on trying to destroy British and American battleships, while Allied submarines gradually sank virtually the whole Japanese merchant fleet. No development could have been more ruinous for a nation compelled to secure most of its war materials overseas. Only in March 1945 did the Japanese finally resort to convoys of as many as twenty merchant ships, and by then it was too late, for the United States had so many submarines that they could be used en masse as "wolf packs." Destruction of Nipponese shipping proceeded unabated. One reason for the extreme lateness of the effort to defend the vital Japanese merchantmen or to attack American merchant shipping seems inexpressibly trivial in retrospect: medals were awarded for sinking enemy war vessels but not for sinking merchant ships.

The navy was used badly in another way too. From service pride, a mere desire to hang on to anything that had been conquered, the navy scattered men and resources all over largely useless island outposts from the Aleutians to the remote south Pacific. Yet with every passing month the Japanese capacity to defend any one place sank closer to zero. It was a strategic blunder comparable in importance to the one Tokyo had made at the very beginning of the war: there had been no need for Japan to conquer and occupy Bataan and Corregidor, because there was no way for U.S. forces to relieve either place. Tokyo could have allowed U.S. and Filipino troops there to "wither on the vine," just as Douglas MacArthur would do with isolated bodies of Japanese troops in many places two or three years later. Instead, they wasted tens of thousands of men, much war materiel, and invaluable time in subduing these bastions, during which the Allies greatly strengthened their own position in Australia.

The chaotic Japanese command structure also made its contribution to defeat in 1944–45. First, it hampered the defense of Leyte.[54]

Then the imperial general headquarters wanted simply to write off Luzon as indefensible, but General Yamashita disagreed. He realized that his forces were under strength, underfed, underequipped, ill organized, indifferently led, short of everything, and able to fight only on defense; nonetheless he believed that an initial retreat into the mountains would allow him to prolong the battle for Luzon sufficiently to enable Tokyo to prepare the Japanese home islands more thoroughly against an anticipated American invasion. This judgment was generally sound, as was Yamashita's desire to abandon Manila. Some of his subordinates disagreed violently with the latter decision, however, and insisted upon defending the city for reasons of mere prestige. They were backed in this by Admiral Sanji Iwabachi, who ultimately disobeyed orders and occupied the city with 17,000 sailors and marines. These men were allowed to run amok, disgracing whatever good name Japan still had among nations by raping and killing some 80,000 Filipino civilians and getting themselves killed in the process. Meanwhile, Yamashita himself blundered by allowing many thousands of Japanese civilians to leave Manila and go into the mountains with his troops. Perhaps he feared that the Filipinos would massacre them—though he could have surrendered them to the Americans. Their presence sorely complicated all his problems of feeding, transport, and defense, just as a similar horde of Filipino civilians had worsened all the problems of the Allied defenders of Bataan three years earlier.[55]

By the spring of 1945 the melancholy result of all these sins of omission and commission was sorely evident. The proud Japanese navy, once invincible, was now nearly invisible, its carrier and submarine strength almost gone. What little was left of the merchant marine was tied up in port, subject to persistent American air and submarine attacks even when docked. Both the army and the navy had lost their conventional air support, for the Japanese air force was being rapidly "transformed into a sacrificial army of guided missiles."[56] Its heralded kamikaze system, far from being a source of strength, was a confession of how weak Japan had become. Many of the suicide pilots were not volunteers but draftees or men who had succumbed to pressure. Kamikaze attacks were a desperate expedient resorted to because acute fuel shortages had made it impossible to train conventional pilots,[57] while relentless U.S. bombing of Japanese factories had reduced plane manufacture to the production of a few inferior craft riveted together by teenage girls. No Japanese fighter plane could now fly high enough (30,000 feet) to challenge a B-29 bomber; no Japanese antiaircraft gun could shoot that high. The air war had come to resemble "a sparrow being relentlessly pursued by a flock of ferocious hawks."[58]

Once more it must be pointed out that Japan had no monopoly on obtuseness. For many months after the war began, American submarine torpedos sometimes exploded before they reached their targets, hit the target but did not explode, dived underneath a target ship, or ran in circles and came back to sink the submarines that fired them. Yet dunderheads in the U.S. Navy Bureau of Ordnance obstinately refused to acknowledge repeated reports of such failures, much less investigate them. They claimed that anything that went wrong was due not to deficiencies in the torpedos but to human error by the submarine crews. Nobody knows how many U.S. submariners died needlessly as a result, or how many Japanese ships should have been sunk that were not, or how much the war might have been shortened had the torpedos functioned properly.[59]

The crucial consideration for both sides, of course, was not who was more fatuous but that the vastly greater resources of the Allies enabled them to endure their mistakes and still push on to victory. Japan could not afford such luxuries. So we guerrillas survived—by our own wits, efforts, and persistence, to be sure, but also because of the manifold misjudgments and follies of our foes.

The seventeenth-century Swedish statesman Axel Oxenstierna once summed up a good deal about public affairs at all times: "If men only knew how badly they are ruled."

— 14 —
Ruminations

Just how valuable were the Luzon guerrillas in World War II? Did we contribute as much to Allied victory as any of our veteran counterparts in General MacArthur's army?[1] Without us, would it have taken twice as many regular troops to defeat Yamashita's forces?[2] I believe the U.S. Army would still have beaten the Japanese on Luzon had we irregulars never existed; nevertheless, we did help the Allied cause significantly. We performed auxiliary services, fought alongside regular U.S. troops to inflict ruinous casualties on the enemy, suffered heavy losses in return, and by our activity saved many American lives and much materiel.[3]

Was it all worth what it cost the Filipino people in lives lost, blood shed, pain suffered, and assets destroyed? One cannot say dogmatically, for to compare the value of a specific number of human lives with the pride or shame of a whole people is like trying to compare pineapples with alligators. Ray Hunt, my old Pangasinan area commander and long-time friend, thinks the Filipino people would have been better off if no guerrilla movement had ever arisen in their homeland.[4] I cannot agree. Nations have lives and memories just as persons do. These collective memories endure for centuries, and the deeds and sacrifices of even a few individuals can sometimes glorify (or blacken) a whole people irrevocably. Protected by the Atlantic and Pacific oceans, we Americans have never been invaded and overrun; hence, we have never had to weigh the intangible value of what often seems like hopeless resistance against the tangible loss of life it entails. For all the guerrillas' faults and crimes, their deeds and example in World War II will long seem one of the brighter pages in Philippine history.

One of the knottiest problems I have ever had to deal with grew directly out of the war: the effort to determine which Filipinos who claimed to have been guerrillas deserved back pay or other compensation for their services. I returned to the Philippines early in 1947 as a consultant to the Guerrilla Affairs Section of the U.S. Army.

Along with Harry McKenzie, a third American officer, and a number of Filipino officers, I spent five months reconstructing rosters and records of those who had served in LGAF units in Nueva Ecija, Pangasinan, Tarlac, and Nueva Vizcaya provinces. Two Filipino officers who had served LGAF well during the war proved especially valuable: Manuel Bahia, who had been McKenzie's adjutant, and Manuel's assistant, Antonio Estrada. Both were fluent in English, able administrators, and eager to do a good job. Manuel had already become a captain in the Philippine army, and Antonio was to make a long career in the U.S. Veterans Administration.

The obstacles that faced us concerning guerrillas all over the Philippines were many and daunting. To start with, there never has been in international law a clear, agreed-upon definition of what separates regular troops from guerrillas and guerillas from bandits. Even when sovereign governments have said they agreed on the matter, their actions have often belied their assertions.

A letter from Al Hendrickson dated January 19, 1949, a year and a half after my task was supposedly completed, indicates some of the difficulties involved. Al wrote that the rosters of some of his men had been lost or destroyed during battles, as had a number of documents he would normally have signed but did not because he was in a hospital for a time in the spring of 1945. Because of this, he said, Criscenzio Hipolito, who was not merely a bargain basement Shakespeare but an able and devoted guerrilla captain as well, had not been properly recognized for his wartime efforts.

Al was probably mistaken about Cris, since his name is listed among the guerrillas, as is his rank (captain), but there were many who could not be found. Some had been in units subsequently recognized by the U.S. Army, but others who were equally authentic and deserving had not. Some had been killed in the fighting, or at the end of the war had quietly gone home to their families, leaving no forwarding address; others had served under assumed names or had simply disappeared. The surviving wives or families of most of those killed had legitimate claims to back pay, but often nobody knew where to find such families. Finally, to qualify for recognition and back pay a guerrilla was required to have been continuously active from his enlistment until liberation. This disqualified many who had been active for a time but then had dropped out. Sorting out the legitimate from the spurious claims in this morass was always difficult and often impossible.

The main thing we could be sure of was that probably three-quarters of the claims were phony. But which? Many cases were equivocal. For instance, what about Filipinos who had done manual labor that was useful to guerrillas but no fighting? Should they now be compensated? Writing two years after the war, Capt. George Philip said emphatically no; they should have been willing to do that much for their country without expecting to be paid.[5] Three years earlier, during the war, Major Anderson had asked SWPA headquarters for guidance on this specific issue. He had "hired" many civilians to work for his command. They had not been given titles, nor had he promised them pay. They had said they wanted to serve their country, after which many of them had done the work of commissioned officers and done it well.[6] Should they now be paid? And what about those who provided food? Harry McKenzie submitted an affidavit to the Philippine government in 1946, pointing out that civilians had often been given receipts for food collected from them and had been assured that the U.S. government would pay them when the war was over.[7] A year later I had issued a formal statement that no more than 1,000 special agents had ever been authorized to collect food and supplies for LGAF, and that we had hired very few civilians to do anything else for us at any time—no matter how many might put in claims now.[8]

Genuine guerrillas usually despised latecomers, and with good reason, but some of the laggard volunteers had long been sympathizers or quiet supporters who would have joined openly had they been in places where joining was possible. Others would not abandon their families, or they were sick, or they were simply not quite brave enough. But how many and which? Some had surrendered to the Japanese and become collaborators, then had betrayed their new masters, and now claimed that a genuine change of heart had preceded their attempt to change sides. How many such claims were valid, and which? Others had been genuine guerrillas but had seemed more concerned to enrich themselves than anything else. Some wild, unruly bandit types, unpopular because of their brigandage, had often made the best fighters alongside regular U.S. troops, whereas law-abiding, God-fearing Filipinos were undoubtedly more admirable morally but often less brave. Should the United States regard "results" as paramount and compensate the outlaw types, or avoid setting the bad precedent of paying in dubious cases? Many people seemed to think that if they had ever done anything, no matter how trivial, they deserved to be compensated.[9] How about the non-commissioned officers in the prewar Philippine army who had served as guerrillas mostly because they thought it would lead to postwar military promotions or establish a base from which they could launch a political career? It would have required a legion of combined geniuses and saints to make their way through this jungle of claims and do justice to everyone, even without the further consideration that the very nature of underground warfare makes it impossible to determine who contributed the most.

Then there were the real "chromium-plated, 24-karat, all-Filipino frauds," as an American advertising flack might have put it: the collaborators who claimed guerrilla service to try to cover their tracks; the thousands who had paid someone to put their names on lists of guerrillas; those who had invented paper organizations that existed only for the express purpose of taking bribes from enrollees; others who had enrolled their own friends and relatives on guerrilla rosters; and windbags whose sole topics of conversation were how unselfishly they had sacrificed and how much they had suffered.[10]

Those of us assigned to the task of bringing some accuracy, order, and justice out of this swamp of fraud and confusion have been accused of showing more interest in playing golf and consorting with local women than attempting to clean this Augean stable.[11] Perhaps this criticism was justified at the very beginning of the process, for some of the officers I worked with mentioned that their predecessors had been taken in by phony guerrillas at the outset. If so, the lesson had been learned well. Our group was skeptical of any but well-founded claims, cautious in their approach to their duties, and competent overall. Of more than a million claims filed for the entire country, those of about 260,000 Philippine veterans and guerrillas were accepted as genuine. On July 25, 1947, the U.S. government authorized back payment for them.[12]

Unfortunately, that was not the whole story. Everybody knew that some of the accepted claims were spurious and that the claims of maybe 100,000 Filipinos who had undeniably been soldiers or guerrillas of some sort—most of them in USAFFE or all-Filipino guerrilla squadrons—had been rejected.[13] This state of affairs was difficult to justify to anyone whose claim had been turned down. Interestingly, those Filipinos who served in the U.S. regular armed forces were allowed, if they wished, to become U.S. citizens without having to go through standard immigration procedures. Civilians, by contrast, even those recognized as legitimate guerrillas, were not immediately accepted. U.S. military authorities have always maintained, in public at least, that all Filipinos were treated fairly. This is surely less than the truth, though I would add that those of us who wrestled with this intractable problem did about as well as we, or probably anyone else, could have. Certainly Capt.

John O. Keider of Guerrilla Affairs Headquarters did an outstanding job overseeing the whole investigation and preparing the overall recommendations. For my part, I was interviewed extensively and asked many questions about the activities of units other than my own, but I spent most of my time trying to straighten out the records of LGAF men.

After having painted this dismal picture of the difficulties facing investigators all over the Islands, it will seem incongruous to assert now that I believe most of my own men were treated justly. Whether we had fewer problems than other organizations of irregulars, adopted a more systematic approach, or were just luckier, I cannot say for sure—probably all three. My approach to the task was to prepare an official roster for each squadron, showing the date of enlistment of each man, the rank he had attained, and any other pertinent information we might have about him. By getting articles in local newspapers, making personal visits over the whole LGAF area, and relying on word of mouth, I was eventually able to contact almost all our squadron commanders and other key officers. Most of them had saved some old records, and from these we labored to reconstruct their rosters. Most of them remembered a good deal beyond their paper records, and we were able to locate many of their men who knew something about their fellow guerrillas. We had separate rosters for men killed in action and usually had little trouble finding their families, since there was generally at least one man in each unit who knew all the others and who thus had a good idea how to find their widows. These efforts were supplemented by going through official SWPA records, which contained many LGAF orders, appointments, reports, correspondence, and other documents. Eventually, we recognized seventy-nine LGAF squadrons comprising 809 officers and 13,382 men as of May 31, 1945 (an impressive growth from a mere twenty-one-man squadron on May 31, 1942). We had suffered 813 recognized casualties.

Uldarico Baclagon, himself a colonel in the Philippine army and the author of *The Philippine Resistance Movement against Japan*, studied these "Reconstituted Rosters of Troops" on which so many of us had toiled. He concluded that there had been about 239,000 guerrillas in the wartime Philippines; that the largest band had been that of Col. Wendell Fertig on Mindanao with 33,000 men; the largest on Luzon, Volckmann's USFIP-NL with 22,000; next largest, Ramsey's 13,000–14,000; then my LGAF, followed by Marking's 12,000 and Anderson's 7,000. I have always suspected but cannot prove that Volckmann's true strength was at least 5,000 below his

claimed figures. During 1944 he had listed me as one of his subordinate officers and part of his organization: thus I think he may have
added many of my men to his own when claiming his total. Of
course, many of my officers and men *were* absorbed into his organization in the summer of 1945 after I had returned home.[14]

In my LGAF units anyway, I think the U.S. Army was generous
in recognition of guerrilla service and in awarding back pay. I had
told my men from the start that they were fighting for their country
and could not be assured of compensation. I think they would have
been satisfied with this had not President Osmena then promised
them back pay. Of course, once the promise was made, my men considered that they deserved payment as much as guerrillas elsewhere,
and I had no basis in equity to do other than support those who had
been true guerrillas. What proportion of the men in other organizations were treated fairly, I cannot say for sure.

On the larger question of whether or not the U.S. government
treated the whole Philippine people justly and honorably at war's
end and after, I have serious reservations. Manuel Quezon once said,
"No nation is worth anything unless it has learned how to suffer and
how to die."[15] Tomas Confesor, a prewar governor of Iloilo and a resistance leader on Panay during the war, once penned a letter to the
governor of Panay expressing the same thought. Because of its
author's exceptional eloquence, his manifesto became famous and
was widely distributed.[16] In their struggles against both Spain and
the United States, 1896–1901, Filipinos had demonstrated that they
did indeed know how to fight and die. They did so again against
Japan, 1941–45.

In the mutual effort of Filipinos and Americans to mount and
maintain guerrilla resistance to the Japanese during the war, a small
number of Americans contributed disproportionately to the leadership of our common endeavor, and we all risked our necks together,
but the bulk of the suffering and dying was borne by Filipinos.
Moreover, without the material aid and support their civilians gave
us, we could not have survived at all. There were schoolteachers
who risked their lives to defy the conquerors by displaying the
American flag in their classrooms. There were guerrillas who offered
to buy U.S. war bonds with the trifling sums of money they sometimes acquired.[17] When Allied victory was gained at last, the Filipinos were the only colonial people in Asia who called it
"liberation" rather than "reoccupation." If there was ever an ally of
America whom we ought to have treated with generosity after the
war, it was the Philippines.

One way to have been generous to ordinary people would have been to offer them a choice of commonwealth status or independence. Of course, given the ardent nationalism rampant in our century and the promise our government had made years before that independence would be granted in 1946, the educated, articulate, well-to-do Filipinos who collectively regard themselves as the "natural" ruling class in the islands would have screamed "betrayal." Nonetheless, I am convinced that in a fair and open plebiscite overseen by neutral observers, with all adult Filipinos eligible to vote and the votes counted by an impartial foreign mission, there would have been a majority in favor of retention of formal connections with the United States.

But that would have prevented many of the "patriots" clamoring for independence from securing high offices, high salaries, expense accounts, chauffeured limousines, prestige at home and abroad, and enhanced business opportunities for themselves and their families and friends, so no doubt cries for "independence" would have grown louder. Still, Western governments should occasionally think of the best interests of *ordinary* people in colonial areas, not just the agitation of "idealists" who long to become ministers, ambassadors, heads of government bureaus, and entrepreneurs with state contracts.[18]

If one tries to estimate generosity in monetary terms, it is hard to say whether we were generous or, if not, whose fault that was. A writer for a trade paper published for export executives describes as "extremely generous" the surplus military property and funds provided to help rebuild the shattered infrastructure of the Islands. He estimates that these payments, when added to "foreign exchange items," were worth more than $3 billion between 1946–50.[19] Ferdinand Marcos's "court biographer" says that the United States tried to restore the bankrupt Philippine government by giving it $100,000,000 worth of war surplus but that President Osmena's cohorts stole most of it.[20] Beth Day sets the value at $200,000,000 and charges that at least 80 percent of it was either stolen outright or soon secured by grafters, a dismal business that established an enduring pattern of corruption.[21]

Filipinos had long been grateful to America for bringing them democracy, education, and lesser benefits. In 1945 the feeling was widespread among them that they had repaid this debt by remaining loyal and shedding their blood lavishly, despite American failure to protect them adequately with more ships, planes, and men before and during the war. Once the war was over, they considered that the

United States had an obligation to restore the shattered homeland of those who had fought and died alongside Americans on Bataan and Corregidor, and to compel their now defeated Japanese oppressors to pay them generous war reparations. But what happened? There seemed to be plenty of money to shower on assorted Europeans: for instance, Yugoslavia received a hundred times as much UNRRA (United Nations Relief and Rehabilitation Administration) aid as the Philippines.[22] Money was also available to rebuild Japan as an Oriental bastion against Communism, and to pour into sinkholes of corruption in India to bolster "democracy" there. Yet the U.S. Congress was niggardly in giving, or even lending, investment capital to the Philippines. Moreover, it authorized smaller payments to Philippine veterans than to their American counterparts, made Philippine independence contingent on signing trade treaties that allowed American business interests to exploit Philippine markets, and demanded ninety-nine-year leases on military bases. We sent their idol, Gen. Douglas MacArthur, off to rule Japan instead of the Philippines and backed corrupt Philippine political candidates as long as they protected American interests.[23] The consequent disillusionment gave rise to ambivalent feelings. Had all the sacrifices been worth the price? Had the Japanese been right, after all, when they said Filipinos must always be Asians, never Westerners? Maybe Pio Duran, an anti-Western intellectual, had correctly claimed that Filipino support of the United States rather than Japan had made them all "apostates of Orientalism."[24]

Some such as Jesus Villamor, the celebrated Filipino fighter pilot, have charged U.S. inattention to Philippine interests to simple racism. Villamor believed that Courtney Whitney and other MacArthur confidants regarded Filipinos as natural inferiors and that Whitney kept information from MacArthur that would have led the general to give more support to guerrillas. The same attitude, he believed, caused officers like me to regard the war claims of Filipino guerrillas as trivial—an attitude which was emphatically not true of me or, I think, of most of the American officers with whom I worked on that infernally complex problem.[25]

The ideological left, of course, saw American concern for the postwar Philippines as limited to securing maximum opportunity for an unsavory clique of high-ranking U.S. officers, American businessmen, and the old, rich, crypto-fascist and largely collaborationist Philippine ruling class. Consequently, this arguement alleges, the Philippines were the only place where U.S. authorities showed no serious interest in punishing collaborators after the war, and nowhere else in the world was there so much "graft and conniving."[26] I have never thought this thesis convincing. U.S. politicians and big businessmen have never enjoyed a monopoly on corruption. They are not even champions. In 1946 the members of the Philippine Congress voted themselves back pay, and civil servants voted en masse for Roxas when he promised *them* back pay.[27] More to the point, one has only to see the newspapers any day in any Western country to read of financial rascality of every possible variety, in all known professions and jobs, in high society and low, in every part of the world.

It has always seemed to me that the ineptitude displayed by the U.S. government in dealing with the Philippines was due not to malice of any sort but to the irresponsibility, concern for personal and party advantage, and general muddle that characterizes most governments much of the time. President Franklin Roosevelt was renowned for his employment of what Winston Churchill once called "terminological inexactitudes": in this case, benevolent declarations and fulsome promises designed to keep up Filipino morale during the war. Little thought was given to whether these could be implemented after the war and, if so, how and to what degree. By 1941 the president was having second thoughts about the desirability of granting independence to the Philippines in 1946, as promised in 1934. So was the U.S. State Department, but a majority in our Congress would not hear of postponement. Politicians in the Philippines, fearing to be thought insufficiently nationalistic, vociferously seconded their American counterparts. Many Filipino businessman, not dependent on votes, were more hesitant. They favored postponement lest sudden self-rule might damage the economy. But "anti-imperialism" is a sacred cause to all correct-thinking Western people in the twentieth century, so the Philippines became independent on schedule in 1946.

The Japanese flattered José Laurel and made him president of their so-called Philippine Republic but then threw him over when he was no longer useful to them. Our government treated Sergio Osmena much the same way. Osmena met with Roosevelt shortly before FDR's death in the spring of 1945. They agreed that collaborators should be arrested and put on trial and that the United States should do everything possible (an elastic phrase in itself) to reconstruct and rehabilitate the Philippines.[28] Meanwhile, MacArthur, who disliked Roosevelt as much as ever, wanted essentially to restore the status quo antebellum in the Islands. When Harry Truman assumed office, he was less interested in the Philippines than Roosevelt had been and also preoccupied with a problem that seemed far more vital: containing the expansionism of the Soviet Union. The American public, notoriously fickle, notoriously uninformed about the past history of much of the world, and notoriously uninterested in the problems of other peoples until some crisis impends, ceased to pay much attention to Philippine policy. Politicians to whom the world's number one problem is always their own reelection, tend to reflect the fluctuating moods of the voters. Those in Washington who had been most interested in the Islands in the past were Secretary of the Interior Harold Ickes, Senator Millard Tydings, and High Commissioner to the Philippines Paul McNutt—none likely to be enrolled on a roster of history's greatest statesmen. Moreover, they disagreed among themselves, and their interest in the Philippines—like that of much of the public—waned rapidly after the war.

American policy toward the Islands at war's end, then, was not coherent in conception and lacked continuity in application either at that time or for decades afterward. The British call this sort of thing "muddling through" and sometimes take a perverse pride in how much of it they have been able to endure over the centuries and still survive. Through much of the twentieth century we have floundered in their footsteps.

At war's end, general chaos—material, moral, or psychological—was at least as evident in the Philippines as anywhere in prostrate Europe. What should be done with, or to, the many Filipinos who had collaborated with the enemy during the war? They had done so in many different ways, often under varying degrees of duress. A knottier question still was whether resistance had been more truly beneficial to the Filipino people than collaboration. Interested parties could, and did, make plausible cases for each stance, frequently denouncing their adversaries as traitors for good measure. Most guerrillas had been admirable, but too many had been mere outlaws. Some peasants had supported the Huks, but most had not. The Huks had fought the Japanese periodically but had also fought and tried to thwart USAFFE guerrillas—which could only aid the Japanese. Many landlords and prominent politicians had been collaborators, but many others had not. President Quezon's heir apparent, Sergio Osmena, had stayed out of the country during most of the war. His chief rival, Manuel Roxas, had remained in the Philippines and had followed a contorted course whose ultimate goal historians still debate. Though many of his supporters were under indictment for treason, eventually all of them were amnestied. Meanwhile, old and new politicians scrambled for power as they had always done, and politics seemed as venal as ever.

Because Japanese garrisons had been concentrated in cities and towns, rural Filipinos had had wartime experiences of enemy occupation quite different from those of their urban cousins. Farmers and dwellers in barrios had often suffered much at the hands of Japanese patrols looking for guerrillas, but they had usually had enough to eat. Urbanites had often lacked food—had even starved to death—because of inadequate transport or, more commonly, because peasants were reluctant to sell food for Japanese invasion currency. Educated or introspective Filipinos often seemed more uncertain than ever whether they were a Spanish-American outpost of Western civilization standing at the portals of Asia or true Orientals who were Westerners only in their own overactive imaginations. In 1945 the Filipinos were an unsettled people, whether contemplating historical legacy, current problems, or a proper future course.[29]

Some of their dilemmas were unique; some common to our whole age. Among the latter was the question "What constitutes treason in the twentieth century?" In Europe's *ancien régime* the matter was quite simple: it was disloyalty to a ruler to whom one owed loyalty or homage. In the nineteenth and twentieth centuries when nationalism has become the true religion of much of humanity, treason has come to mean almost anything harmful to the "nation" or its "people." But a particular government, or even a certain form of government is obviously not identical to "people" or "nation," so does disloyalty to a given *government* make one a traitor to all his countrymen? Is it not possible that to rid a nation of a particularly inept or oppressive regime might really be the highest sort of patriotism? Governments in wartime, whether democratic or authoritarian, view any kind of opposition to their policies as at least marginally treasonous. They even look with suspicion on support that is only tepid.

To whom or what *should* civilized persons owe primary loyalty: religious beliefs, the nation-state to which one belongs, its political leader of the moment, some international ideology of the right or left, humanitarian ideals (always an imprecise conception), or merely family and friends? For most Asians, concern for family is paramount; next, they value the traditions of their race or people above other loyalties. Does the choice depend on whether persons are religious or not? On the *kind* of government under which they live? On the policies of that government? Must soldiers follow orders, no matter what, or are they obliged to heed moral principles instead? But *whose* moral principles, since there has never been any unanimity about what they are? Is mere opposition to government policy treason if it is not accompanied by overt action? Is collaboration with the enemy treason when the collaborators are motivated by a desire to lighten the burdens of war and enemy occupation for their own people? But would not every collaborator plead this when the war was over? How can one accurately judge another's state of mind, in any case?[30]

To the U.S. government, disloyalty always meant opposition to American objectives or efforts. Thus, though the Huks sometimes fought the Japanese, they refused to cooperate with the American effort to do so; therefore, they were considered disloyal and were not accorded U.S. recognition or benefits at the end of the war. The regular Philippine ruling class also regarded them as disloyal because the Huks wanted to change Philippine society in essentials. Any serious non-Communist government would have taken a similarly dim view of the Huks because the primary loyalty of their leaders was to the official ideology of the USSR.

Particularly vexatious to thoughtful Filipinos was the matter of loyalty oaths. President Manuel Quezon, undergoing treatment for tuberculosis in Saranac Lake, New York, during the war, insisted that Filipinos must swear allegiance to his government-in-exile, but the Japanese demanded an oath of loyalty to their puppet Philippine Republic headed by José Laurel. A man who had served in the American army or its Philippine auxiliaries had had to pledge allegiance to the United States, but if he subsequently took any kind of public employment to support his family during the war, he had to swear to uphold the Japanese occupation regime. If a Filipino farmer aided the Huks, he would be treated as an enemy by USAFFE guerrillas; if he aided American or pro-American guerrilla groups, the Huks might pursue him to the death; and support for either Huks or USAFFE forces was regarded by the Japanese as tantamount to treason. Innumerable Filipinos were compelled by circumstances or blunt threats to swear allegiance to a whole series of such "authorities" during the war. By 1945, could conscientious individuals regard any oath as binding? What should their own government, or American authorities, think of them for having changed front several times under coercion? Had perhaps the cynics been right all along that the only important thing in war is to end on the winning side?

If there was one category of "collaborators" who did not deserve to be blamed seriously, it was the ordinary Filipino officials who occupied public offices at the time of the Japanese conquest.

What were they to do? If they emulated Chief Justice José Abad Santos and flatly refused to serve their new masters, they might well be executed, as he was, and replaced by somebody less heroic. How much more sensible it seemed to stay at their posts, perform their duties routinely, support their families, and try to live "normally." Of course some of them used their positions and influence for their own benefit,[31] but more tried to protect Filipino interests as well as they could,[32] and few seemed to have been much influenced by Japanese efforts to indoctrinate them. Many emulated those members of the Philippine Constabulary who went through the motions of collaborating with the Japanese while aiding guerrillas on the sly and waiting for the day when they could change sides openly. Afterward, who could ever be sure which of them had been true patriots and which mere opportunists?

Americans are celebrated for taking highly "moral" views of political problems, a stance that comes easily to people whose country has never been conquered and occupied and so have never had to make the practical adjustments that fate entails. Hence, to us the very word "collaboration" smacks of cowardice and moral degeneracy, even applied to those who were only mildly cooperative with their conquerors. But if those we have vanquished cooperate with *us*, as most Filipinos eventually did after 1898 and as the Japanese did after 1945, we do not think of them as "collaborators" at all but as sensible persons who appreciate our virtues and worthy intentions and will doubtless become good democrats someday. We easily forget, too, that during World War II three of the world's great powers, the United States, Japan, and the Soviet Union, were struggling for control of the Philippines. This posed a problem of extraordinary difficulty for the Japanese-dominated Philippine Republic. We should retain at least some respect for the skill with which Filipino "collaborationist" politicians made their way through it and emerged both independent and non-Communist.[33]

History does not record disasters that timely action forestalled, but there are some that probably would have occurred had there been no Filipino collaborators in World War II. First of all, the Japanese would have had to rule the country directly; or rely on genuinely pro-Japanese figures such as Benigno Ramos, Gen. Artemio Ricarte (the only Filipino officer who never surrendered to Americans after 1898), Prof. Maximo Kalaw, president of the Philippine–Japan Association, and Pio Duran; or resort to mere opportunists—who were generally incompetent in politics. Either direct Japanese rule or that of rascals on the make would have been far harsher than the regimen of the "collaborators." Sergio Osmena reminded both Roosevelt and Truman that the leaders left behind in the Philippines in 1942 could not all simply take to the hills; some had to stay behind to protect and comfort their people as well as they could. Those who had done so, he thought, should be judged primarily by their motives. Were they influenced by fear of the Japanese? A desire for self-enrichment? Hope of defending Philippine interests? A wish to keep up the spirits of ordinary people or to give clandestine aid to guerrillas?[34]

Both Quezon and MacArthur had recognized the dilemma. Before leaving for Corregidor early in 1942 Quezon had even instructed several leading politicians to play varying roles during the war to help see their people through it, and then to forgive one another when all was over.[35] This tactic was in fact widely adopted in eastern Asia and Indonesia. A few politicians would lead independence movements, a few would be pro-Japanese, others would be pro-French or pro-Dutch or pro-British, with the understanding that winners would forgive losers at war's end. Of course there were many who accused one another of collaboration out of personal hatred or political rivalry; others who succumbed only under severe pressure; some who pretended to collaborate in order to double-cross the Japanese;[36] and still others who merely looked bad because anybody who was in any way associated with such cruel oppressors was bound to seem hateful.

The wartime careers of two major Philippine politicians, Manuel Roxas and José Laurel, illustrate most of the problems of those who stayed behind to slip and shift between the Japanese and those who, at least verbally, demanded opposition to them. Laurel was an intelligent, systematic, and scholarly man who had studied both Japanese and Western civilizations extensively and viewed both with cool detachment. The Japanese made him president of their puppet republic in October 1943. His main objective, he said, had been to do his duty, and that duty had been to spare the Filipino people as many hardships as possible. Since his actions in office generally bore out this plea, there is no reason to doubt his sincerity unless one simply regards all wealthy Filipinos as fascists and pro-Japanese rascals.[37]

As nominal president Laurel kept in touch with guerrillas and tried to eliminate bandits from among them. Because he was shy and indecisive, he caved in to Japanese pressure regularly; but because he was also sly and clever, he usually managed to thwart them in some way in the process. When he had to write a constitution for his "republic," it emerged more like the American constitution than anything Japanese. For example, it contained a provision that only the Assembly could declare war; this he hoped, would make it difficult for the Japanese to force the Philippines to go to war. When his masters did compel him to undertake hostilities, he did not say that he had "declared" war against Britain and the United States, but only that a "state of war" existed between them and the Philippine Republic. Then he managed to be so troubled by illnesses and other pressing problems that he never got around to conscripting soldiers to fight in it.

He did eventually pledge all material aid to Japan in this "war" but could hardly make any major contribution, since the Japanese had already stolen everything they wanted in the Philippines. He tried to moderate the sufferings of Filipinos in Japanese prisons, and he besought Generals Tojo and Homma to treat his people more gently. After the war he pleaded that he had observed the canons of international law as well as he could in exceedingly difficult circumstances and that he had always played for time in what he feared would be a long war. Most of his countrymen must have believed him, since they subsequently voted him into the national senate and have routinely numbered him among their presidents.[38]

Manuel Roxas was an even more controversial figure. His enemies depict him as a consummate "slicker" who cultivated the friendship of MacArthur before the war, ingratiated himself with the Japanese during the war, kept in contact with both American and Filipino guerrillas throughout, hid out for several weeks when the American invasion of Luzon began, then slipped into Sixth Army Headquarters and said he was "reporting for duty." Finally, he used his closeness to MacArthur to get a clean bill of political health and a military promotion that provided the base from which he made himself president of the Philippines in 1948. He had cheated all those with whom he had dealt, even the Japanese, and had never given any real help to any guerrillas.[39]

His supporters scoff at these charges. General Willoughby, MacArthur's chief of intelligence—who was in a position to know a great deal about Roxas and his activities—and his deputy, Col. Allison Ind, insist that Roxas could hardly have been a collaborator: when President Quezon sent Dr. Emgidio Cruz all the way from America to the Philippines in 1943 to seek out and question prominent Filipinos. Cruz gave more attention to Roxas than anyone else and from him got a report on all the others to take back to Quezon.[40] Willoughby and Ind reject the suggestion that Roxas was a turncoat.

They assert that he feigned illness for two years[41] to avoid being made president of the Philippine Republic by the Japanese, then caved in and became an "adviser" to Laurel in order to establish cover as a collaborator. From both Laurel and the Japanese he collected valuable information that he relayed to both guerrillas in the field and SWPA Headquarters.[42] Ray Hunt, my area commander in Pangasinan, concurs; he had a number of contacts with Roxas and got much information from him.[43] A majority of the Philippine people must have thought Roxas, like Laurel, did as well as he could in hard circumstances and must have disbelieved the charges of his enemies, for they elected him president of the newly independent Philippines in 1948.

More significant, some have alleged, is what might have happened had only a few things been different. From the safety of Washington, 10,000 miles away, Franklin Roosevelt urged Filipinos to be brave and criticized their officials who were temporizing with the Japanese. Quezon, Carlos Romulo, and lesser Filipino figures likewise wrote and talked a great deal about the virtues of "freedom."[44] Yet those who adopted such a public stance had themselves thought more than a little about the possibility of pursuing other courses. After the war U.S. counterintelligence examined the files of the Japanese Foreign Office and discovered that Quezon had carried on secret talks with Tokyo "just in case."[45] On Corregidor, perhaps with the encouragement of MacArthur, Quezon had sent a letter to Roosevelt complaining bitterly that Washington had betrayed the Philippines and threatening to go back to Manila to die, if necessary, at the head of his people. It was only with great difficulty that the cooler Osmena talked him out of it.[46]

Clark Lee, an American journalist who was all over the Pacific Theater from 1941–1945, thought that if MacArthur had not gotten Quezon, Osmena, and Romulo out of the Philippines and to the United States early in the war, they would soon have concluded that their national destinies lay with Japan rather than America and would have become collaborators. He also believed that Roxas and many others would have gone over to the Japanese had the 1944 Leyte invasion been repulsed.[47]

I have always regarded hypotheses of this sort with skepticism. Roxas and others like him might well have gone over to the Japanese had we lost the war, but I don't think they would ever have done so merely if the Leyte invasion had been repelled. As for most ordinary Filipino people, they hated the Japanese occupation forces because of their habitual brutality, and would have continued to hate them whether Quezon was in Saranac Lake, Manila, or Antarctica. Even in the highly unlikely event that most Filipinos had become pro-Japanese, what would have been the likeliest result? On the highest strategic level Roosevelt would have sided with the U.S. Navy rather than with MacArthur, and the Philippines would have been by-passed instead of invaded. But American resources would have been just as overwhelming, the atomic bombs would still have been available, and the outcome of the war would have been the same—except for people like me. It is hard to imagine how the other Americans and I could have survived in the Philippines.

The most eloquent defense of those accused of collaboration was delivered soon after the end of the war by Claro M. Recto, who had been Laurel's foreign minister. Recto started from the premise that only those who had stayed in the Philippines and had experienced the dangers and problems of wartime life along with the people they served were qualified to judge the behavior of those now accused of collaboration, because only they knew all that had had to be done to placate a ruthless enemy. He added that whereas the main concern of Americans was always to win the war, a goal beside which the sufferings of the Filipino people were incidental, no Philippine public official could look at the matter with that objectivity. He pointed out that Filipinos had remained loyal to America even though any government's moral right to a people's allegiance depends on its ability to protect them. The Hague Convention, general international usage, decisions of the U.S. Supreme Court, and U.S. Basic Rules of Land Warfare all enjoined people in occupied countries to obey their conquerors if they expected to be treated as non-combatants. Yet he and other Filipino authorities who had asked Filipinos to act thus were now called traitors by the American government—even though Washington had already excused its own General Wainwright and others who had been compelled to make pro-Japanese statements, on the ground that they were victims of American unpreparedness. How many Americans, he asked, would have collaborated if the Japanese had landed in California after Pearl Harbor instead of in the Philippines? How would such people now be regarded by Washington? Philippine leaders who had stayed behind to defend their people and share their travail, at whatever cost to their own reputations, were more truly patriots, he concluded, than those who had fled abroad to safety and ease.[48]

Of course, Recto's self-justification is embarrassingly reminiscent of that offered by the Vichy regime and its supporters in France to excuse their collaboration with Germany. Yet the real question is, what was the alternative? Suppose the mass of Filipinos had simply defied the invaders and dared them to do their worst. What would have happened? Most likely one of two things: either the Japanese would have killed or enslaved most of the people of the Philippines, or Philippine society would have been polarized. On one side would have been hard-core collaborators backed by the Japanese army, and on the other the Huks and their supporters. All-out war for domination of the Islands would have followed. This was what the Huks wanted. It would have ripped the fabric of Philippine society to shreds at a frightful cost in human lives. It would have been a national disaster comparable to that of the religious wars (1560–98) for France, the Thirty Years War (1618–48) for Germany, or the combined wars, revolutions, famine, disease, and starvation endured by post-czarist Russia (1917–22).

As for the ordinary Filipino, was his proper course of action to throw caution (and likely the lives of his family) to the winds and fight the invaders, or was it more sensible to swallow one's pride for the sake of family and try to mollify all the contending parties as well as one could? Every public authority claimed to be acting "for the good of the people," but good in what sense, and when? The Japanese said that what the Americans meant by "Philippine independence" was continued American domination, but the Japanese domination being endured right then was much harsher than American had ever been. So what should the ordinary Filipino fight for— even hope for? Were the leaders of any of these governments or guerrilla bands really trustworthy? To put things at their lowest, how could one guess who would triumph ultimately? Only interior illumination could show the ordinary Filipino his proper duty. As for a Filipino leader, the only way he could have satisfied all his countrymen, right and left, and all the wartime and postwar moralists in America and other foreign countries, would have been to fight the Japanese and lose his life in the process.

To sum up: José Abad Santos did refuse to cooperate with the Japanese and was executed.[49] Laurel collaborated to some degree and said he did it to save the Filipino people from a worse fate. Roxas pretended to collaborate with the Japanese while giving aid to both MacArthur and the guerrillas, but his own ultimate intentions are still debated. General Artemio Ricarte was openly pro-Japanese all his life. Emilio Aguinaldo switched a couple of times, ending on the Japanese side. Ferdinand Marcos claimed to be a wartime hero, but most of his great deeds appear to have been invented years after the war. All but one of these men have been both praised as heroes and excoriated as traitors, collaborators, cowards, liars, double dealers, and opportunists. The only one of them praised by everybody is Abad Santos, the man who defied the enemy and was promptly killed for it. Should the Filipinos, then, have become a nation of martyrs?

In 1948 President Manuel Roxas brought the whole dismal business to an official conclusion by proclaiming amnesty for all who had been accused of wartime collaboration. Of course, he was criticized bitterly by those who had hoped to see their ideological or personal enemies punished, and it is true that taking this step can hardly be represented as a deed of pure justice. Nevertheless, it did clear the air and remove a potent source of contention from Philippine public life; thus it deserved to be called a "wise and statesmanlike action."[50] In politics the choice is rarely between a "good" and a "bad" policy; more often it is among several courses of action all of which are distasteful but some of which are worse than others.

— 15 —
Epilogue

Shortly before Japan's surrender, control of all guerrilla outfits on Luzon was placed under a Luzon Area Command headed by Col. James W. Davis. After the surrender all my old squadrons were released one by one from their attachment to the U.S. Army and sent to Philippine army camps to be disbanded. Many LGAF officers and men were eventually absorbed into USAFIP-NL, Volckmann's old organization.

In a personal sense the high point of the summer came for me on June 13, 1945, when Harry McKenzie, Ray Hunt, and I, among others, were awarded the Distinguished Service Cross by General MacArthur at Malacaning Palace, the headquarters of the Philippine government. The ceremony lasted perhaps fifteen minutes. The main thing I remember about it was that MacArthur had a commanding presence and a compelling manner of speech.

Two years later, when I returned to the Philippines to help establish some equitable system of back pay for wartime guerrillas, I was awarded the Philippine Legion of Honor, probably at the suggestion of Major Arellano. Because the medal had just been created but had not yet been minted, it was actually presented to me some time afterward by Carlos Romulo, then Philippine ambassador to the United States, at a special ceremony in Washington. Much later, in January 1962 when I returned to the Philippines on business, various old Filipino friends decided that presentation of the medal in an embassy fifteen years before was insufficient. Arellano, then Philippine army chief of staff, arranged a meeting with former guerrilla chieftain Macario Peralta, now secretary of defense. The upshot was that I was presented the medal again, this time by Peralta, after a full-scale dress parade in my honor at Camp Murphy. It probably established a record of some sort: three presentations of the same award.

Jocularity aside, I felt deeply honored. The Legion of Honor is the highest Philippine decoration that can be given to a foreigner, and I was the third person to receive it, after President Franklin Roosevelt and General Douglas MacArthur. To be put in such company by those among whom I had lived during the war was profoundly moving. Many years later President Ferdinand Marcos presented me with the Philippine Distinguished Service Medal. Both the American army and the Philippine government were generous in their acknowledgment of my services.

At the end of the war I felt something like Rip van Winkle. In January 1942 the U.S. government was incapable of getting a single shipload of men or planes across the Pacific to support our beleaguered forces on Bataan. In January 1945, Lingayen Gulf was covered with hundreds of ships of every sort and size. For months after the war my predominant emotion remained mild bewilderment.

I welcomed the opportunity to come home in July. Even though I had grown to like most Filipinos, there is nothing like being reunited with one's own people after a long absence. Yet I was half-frightened to come back too. My wartime experiences were still so vivid and seemed to so dwarf in importance everything that had happened to me before the war that I found I remembered less of my prewar life than most people. I was also aware that I had changed a great deal since 1941. I had been the premier figure among a lot of people for a long time, a one-man court of law with virtual life-and-death powers over my domain, and I was emotionally reluctant to step down. Now that I was no longer a guerrilla commander, that job seemed to me more important than ever. Could I really exchange it for a lifetime of humdrum civilian employment? Could I ever "fit in" again? I hesitated to put myself to the test. So I did what was momentarily the easiest thing: I stayed in the army. But this was no solution either, for even though I missed the authority I had enjoyed, down deeper I wanted to forget the war. Unlike many other veterans, I have never been much interested in reunions or, until recently, talking or even thinking about my wartime experiences.

My first postwar assignment was to Washington as a staff officer. Looking back, I think I did a good job there. Certainly I gained much valuable experience in drawing up plans and writing concise proposals and reports, all of which stood me in good stead when I eventually went back to the business world. Yet I was in constant turmoil. Decades later the troubles that veterans of the Vietnam War have had in readjusting to civilian life have received much publicity. The difficulties themselves are genuine, but much of the publicity has been produced by persons who have seemed concerned mainly to create the impression that *only* Vietnam vets have suffered from severe physical or psychological problems. That is decidedly untrue. Many survivors of any serious war wrestle with such difficulties. In my case, sometimes I had nightmares about episodes from the war. Periodic attacks of malaria, even dysentery, returned. I had to go back to the hospital to be treated for these maladies and also for worms, and to undertake rehabilitation of my arm, which had still not entirely healed. As a guerrilla I had drunk freely many times with Filipinos when entering villages or at fiestas, but I had always been careful to keep my head clear and my conduct decorous. Now I took to drinking too much. Some basic change had to come.

Nine months after the war I left the army. Two separate developments then brought me around: I got married, and I got back my prewar job. Some ancient sage once said that nothing restores and motivates a man like the love and attention of a good woman. He knew what he was talking about. My wife, Scharlott Junge, helped immeasurably to make the routine of everyday life interesting and attractive once more and to transform me into a reasonably normal civilian. At about the same time I returned to the Burroughs Corporation. There I spent the rest of my working life, eventually retiring as vice-president in charge of industrial relations. It was the second of three good careers I have enjoyed: military, business, and for quite a few years now a busy and fulfilling retirement. Overall, life has treated me well.

Notes

ABBREVIATIONS

BMA Bulacan Military Area (district north of Manila dominated by Bernard Anderson's organization)
(Clanin) Materials copied from the National Archives by Douglas Clanin and given to Robert Lapham
CO Commanding Officer
ECLGA East Central Luzon Guerrilla Army (Edwin Ramsey's organization)
GHQ General Headquarters
LGAF Luzon Guerrilla Armed Forces (Robert Lapham's organization)
PC Philippine Constabulary (national police force)
PHILRYCOM U.S. Army Philippine-Ryuku Islands Command
PMD Philippine Military District (Gyles Merrill's organization; see USPIF)
(Pyle) Materials housed in the Ernie Pyle Museum in Dana, Ind.
RAG Records of the Adjutant General's Office (in National Archives)
SWPA Southwest Pacific Area (wherever General MacArthur and his staff happened to have their operational headquarters at any given time; in Australia during much of the war)
USAFFE United States Armed Forces, Far East (the theater of war commanded by General MacArthur)
USAFIP-NL United States Armed Forces in the Philippines, Northern Luzon (Russell Volckmann's organization)
USPIF United States Philippine Islands Forces (another name for Gyles Merrill's organization; see PMD)

FOR COMPLETE REFERENCES, SEE THE BIBLIOGRAPHY.

1. THE PHILIPPINES, 1941

1. These puerilities are discussed in Lichauco, *Dear Mother Putnam*, pp. 6–7; and Friend, *Between Two Empires*, pp. 192–95.
2. Mellnick, *Philippine Diary*, p. 23.
3. E.g., Long, *MacArthur as Military Commander*, pp. 57–61.

244

4. Capt. Gary James Anloff, on duty in the Philippines in 1941, wrote angrily forty-five years later that nothing was ever done properly or on time in the prewar Philippines; with ineptitude so general and red tape so pervasive, he declared, it was no surprise to him that U.S. forces were everywhere caught unaware and our planes destroyed on the ground on Dec. 8, 1941 (Anloff to Wayne Sanford, Dec. 12 and 22, 1985; Jan. 3, April 3 and 5, 1986, Guerrillas, vol. A–B, Anloff sec.).

Lt. William A. Gardner, of Col. Gyles Merrill's guerrilla band in Zambales province, shared Anloff's convictions. He said that in 1940–41 Gen. Douglas MacArthur was the only high-ranking officer who took seriously the need to build Philippine defenses rapidly, and that American top brass and Filipino politicians were about equally responsible for sending to Bataan a Philippine army "poorly officered, meagerly equipped, and only partially trained" (Wayne Sanford, ed., "William J. Gardner's Story," Guerrillas, vol. C–G, Gardner sec.).

5. See Chapter 4.

6. McGee, *Rice and Salt*, p. 2.

7. Mellnick, *Philippine Diary*, pp. 12–13.

8. Ramsey and Rivele, *Ramsey's War*, pp. 30ff.

9. Beck and Matthews, "Die Free." Beck, who was in the Thirty-first Infantry (the only U.S. outfit that had been entirely abroad since 1916), says nothing else in his unit was any more ready for war than the mortars.

10. Olson, *Anywhere, Anytime*, p. 69.

11. McGee, *Rice and Salt*, p. 27.

12. This was one of many keen observations made by the sharp-witted guerrilla Alfred Bruce, who added, "We sent China condolences and Japan scrap iron"—and soon discovered how sadistic the Japanese could be (Guerrillas, vol. A–B, Bruce sec.)

13. Long, *MacArthur as Military Commander*, p. 67.

14. I am not alone in this. Lt. Samuel Grashio, a pilot in the Twenty-first Pursuit Squadron, says he cannot remember where he stayed in Manila in Dec. 1941, or even whom he associated with in that chaotic period. On Christmas Eve he and a fellow pilot, Leo Golden, got on a boat in Manila harbor merely to go *somewhere*; they had no idea where. Next morning they awakened at Mariveles, at the southern tip of the Bataan peninsula (Grashio and Norling, *Return to Freedom*, p. 10).

15. Ramsey says he once caught a sentry asleep at his post and sent the errant man back to headquarters (where he might well have been executed), only to have the luckless soldier killed by a Japanese bomb on the way (Ramsey and Rivele, *Ramsey's War*, pp. 48–49).

16. Mellnick, *Philippine Diary*, p. 44.

17. E.g., Ramsey and Rivele, *Ramsey's War*, pp. 60–61, 70–71, 76–77. It was true that a large convoy had left Hawaii early in December 1941, bound for Manila. But the war began when it was three days out of port so the convoy was diverted to Australia. For whatever reason the beleaguered troops in the Islands were never told about this, so many continued for months to believe that our "reinforcements" must surely arrive soon. Olson, *Anywhere, Anytime*, p. 25.

18. See Chapter 13 for an extended discussion of this aspect of the Pacific War.

2. FLIGHT FROM BATAAN

1. E.g., Baclagon, *Philippine Resistance Movement*, pp. 93–94.
2. MacArthur, *Reminiscences*, p. 202.
3. Some claim that such units were being formed in Manila in Dec. 1941 even before the city fell. See Agoncillo and Alfonso, *Short History of the Filipino People*, p. 475.
4. Vernon Fassoth, personal communication to B.N. On the origins of the Fassoth camp, see Chapter 4.
5. Dissette and Adamson (*Guerrilla Submarines*, p. 12) think this whole scheme was probably suggested to MacArthur by Chick Parsons, who was later active in establishing submarine contacts between Philippine guerrillas and MacArthur's headquarters in Australia.
6. Most of the information about this endeavor comes from Gen. Charles A. Willoughby, whom MacArthur charged with coordinating the activities of such people and making them an effective intelligence-gathering group. See Willoughby, *Guerrilla Resistance Movement*, pp. 112–13; and Willoughby and Chamberlain, *MacArthur*, pp. 57–61.
7. Hernandez, *Not by the Sword*, pp. 44–51, recounts many such tales and the widespread popular faith in them.
8. Hartendorp, *Japanese Occupation*, 1:301.
9. Whitney, *MacArthur*, pp. 55–57; James, *Years of MacArthur*, 2:150.
10. Sanford, "Col. Claude A. Thorp," pp. 1, 5, 7. Herminia ("Minang") Dizon, Thorp's longtime Filipina personal secretary, says he told her soon after Jan. 7, when they were still in Bagac, that he had submitted to MacArthur the idea of organizing guerrilla units (Dizon, "Complete Data").
11. Various sources include Capt. Charles Cushing, Capt. Louis Bell, Wilbur Lage, Earl Baxter, Rudy Bolstead, and other enlisted men remembered only by their last names: Oliver, Magot, Smith, Sanders, and Wagner. No two of these rosters are the same. Minang and I once agreed on the membership of our party except that she said Cushing was with us, whereas I cannot remember him. Now, more than half a century after the event, probably nobody recalls the list exactly.
12. For Sladky's version, see Sanford, "Col. Claude A. Thorp" pp. 9, 11.
13. Dizon, "Complete Data."
14. Sgt. Alfred Bruce, who became one of the most active members of the Merrill-Calyer guerrilla organization in Zambales province, seems to have been the only person involved in the ambush to notice specifically that a Japanese colonel was killed at the outset (Bruce to Wayne Sanford, Nov. 5, 1984, Guerrilla Additions, Bruce sec.).
15. Ibid.
16. Pamintuan to King, May 16, 1941 (Lapham Papers).
17. Thorp to Pamintuan, March 31, 1942 (Lapham Papers); as Thorp's adjutant, I signed the letter.
18. Pamintuan to Commanding General PHILRYCOM, May 5, 1947 (copy to R.L.); affidavits from Fred Sladky, Nov. 28, 1945, and Herminia Dizon, April 1, 1946 (Lapham Papers).
19. Affidavit by Serafin Buyson (mayor of Balacor), Aug. 7, 1946 (Lapham Papers).
20. Sometimes commands were bestowed on unlikely persons: Soliman was deaf and dumb, but he was given command of a unit of guerrillas by

Clay Conner in Feb. 1945. He was killed by other Filipinos later that summer.

21. Sanford, "Col. Claude A. Thorp," p. 14.

22. E.g., Baclagon, *Philippine Resistance Movement*, p. 194; and Manzano, "History of the USAFFE Luzon Guerrilla Army Forces," pp. 9–11.

23. James Boyd to Wayne Sanford (*Guerrilla Additions*).

24. Anderson Folders, 1:72–73.

25. John E. Duffy, undated account (Thorp Collection).

26. Minang calls her mentor and lover "a great man, a hero, and a martyr" (Dizon, "Complete Data"). It was hardly an impartial estimate.

27. Ibid.

3. AN INDEPENDENT GUERRILLA

1. Some wag once said of Columbus that when he left he didn't know where he was going, when he arrived he didn't know where he was, and when he got home he didn't know where he had been—but that he managed to do it all on borrowed money. I had left Bataan with one dollar bill in my pocket. I still had it.

2. At least one American officer, Lt. Col. Russell D. Barros, shared this view. He said in 1945 that he had found it difficult to organize a guerrilla band in the spring of 1942 because the Sakdals (pro-Japanese Filipinos) were still numerous and active then, and most ordinary Filipinos did not want even to be seen close to an American for fear of possible Japanese retribution (Barros, "Extended Sojourn"). It is true that there were many Filipino fence-sitters early in the war, but the attitude Barros describes was not typical of most people where I was.

3. Anderson Folders, 1:69–70 (1985); and "Answers to Questions" (1951), 3:n.p.

4. Santos, "Guerrilla Activities in Luzon," pp. 1–2.

5. A statement attributed to Frank Gyovai about a certain American colonel (Guerrilla Additions, Frank A. Loyd sec.).

6. Santos, "Guerrilla Activities in Luzon," pp. 1–2.

7. The higher estimates for the total number of Americans at large on Luzon are around 400 (Conner, "We Fought Fear," p. 70).

8. Ramsey and Rivele, *Ramsey's War*, pp. 95–100.

9. In the 1990s it may seem overdrawn to harp on the subject of American escapees who railed at their government and expressed real hatred for MacArthur and other high-ranking officers who had "let them down" by leaving the Philippines for Australia, but the feeling was intense and widespread in 1942; see, e.g., "Extended Sojourn."

10. This was the opinion of an unnamed captain in USAFFE forces in Nueva Ecija, expressed in a letter to "Capt. McQuire (?)", Oct. 12, 1943 (SWPA II). Alfred Bruce concurred ("Fassoth Camp," Guerrillas, vol. A–B). Hartendorp (*Japanese Occupation*, 2:336) says informers were so numerous even in the Santo Tomas prison camp in Manila that inmates there were told by camp authorities not to discuss the war.

11. Monaghan (*Under the Red Sun*, pp. 147–48) describes vividly the disagreeable features of Philippine mountains. Millard Hileman and Bill Main, who both escaped after the fall of Bataan, had the same disagreement over mountains versus plains. Main, a loner by nature, preferred the presumed

greater safety of a mountain hideout, even if food was scarce; Hileman
wanted to live and travel on the plains, danger or no, because he craved both
plentiful food and human company (Hileman and Fridlund, *1051*, pp. 40–69).
12. Volckmann, *We Remained*, p. 105.

4. GETTING ORGANIZED

1. Vernon Fassoth, personal communication to B.N.
2. "A Report on Thorp's Early Formation of Guerrilla Units," Guerrilla
Subsistence File, RAG, Box 256, says that Barker "finally persuaded" Thorp
to organize and assume command of guerrilla units. The report is signed by
"Victor L." and an illegible surname that might be "Shidaker" or possibly
"Shumaker." Minang, then closely associated with Thorp, describes his
change of heart as entirely voluntary (Dizon, "Complete Data," pp. 3, 6).
Though certainty about somebody else's intentions is always problematical,
my guess is that Minang is correct and that Thorp inspired Barker. One
reason for thinking this is that Thorp tried repeatedly to make common
cause with the Huks.
3. See the details later in this chapter.
4. Manzano ("History of the USAFFE Luzon Guerrilla Army Forces," pp.
7–12) lambastes Colonel Thorp and most of his associates as irresponsible
and incompetent. The only exceptions, in his view, were Praeger and Barker;
the latter he credits with persuading a reluctant Thorp to push the formation of guerrilla organizations on Luzon.
5. Alfred Bruce, Nov. 5, 1984 (Guerrilla Additions).
6. Monaghan (*Under the Red Sun*, pp. 149–50) says Jack died in the
mountains, of pneumonia. This is a good example of how not merely inter-
pretations of events but the facts themselves are frequently uncertain in
wartime.
7. Sanford, "Mosquitoes Don't Bite," p. 11.
8. Beck regarded Merrill with obvious affection and thought "the old
man," despite his frailties, was an able officer. Merrill's principal frailty was
love of liquor. Beck says Merrill once told him that as commandant at Fort
Bliss, Texas, he had used his empty tequila bottles to form a border along
the driveway and sidewalks and around all the flowerbeds approaching post
headquarters. Beck acknowledges that during the war he and Merrill consumed considerable Philippine firewater together in their Zambales mountain hideout (notes by Leon Beck about Col. Gyles Merrill, March 1 and 27,
1984, Guerrilla Additions).
9. There is a good description of these tangled transactions in Sanford,
"Mosquitoes Don't Bite," pp. 8, 10–11; and Sanford, "Organization of Guerrilla Warfare," p. 10.
10. Beck and Matthews, "Die Free," pp. 24–25; Manzano, "History of the
USAFFE Guerrilla Armed Forces," p. 28.
11. Ramsey and Rivele, *Ramsey's War*, pp. 127, 135–36.
12. Guerrillas, vol. A–B, Bruce sec. Bruce also pointedly chided Merrill
for having too many officers in proportion to enlisted men in his command,
with the result that everyone in the outfit was unduly rank conscious (Bruce
to Colonel Mallari, Nov. 11, 1944, SWPA II, Mallari sec.).
13. Johnson (*Raid on Cabanatuan*, pp. 15–16) describes Pajota's ambush

of the Japanese. A year and a half later Pajota would play a major role in the rescue of over 500 Allied prisoners of war from Cabanatuan, an action for which he was never adequately recognized or rewarded (see Chapter 11).

14. Hunt and Norling, *Behind Japanese Lines*, p. 78.

15. Beck and Matthews, "Die Free."

16. Hileman says a friendly Filipino doctor offered to brew some *dita* tea for him, but he does not say whether he drank it (Hileman and Paul Fridlund, *1051*, pp. 80–88). Conner ("We Fought Fear," p. 72) said he tried some of the stuff and recovered from an attack of malaria in a couple of days but was warned afterward by an educated Filipino who possessed some medical knowledge that while *dita* did not appear to harm Negritos, it often caused others to become deaf, dumb, or blind.

Robert Mailheau, who was closely associated with Conner for much of the war, tells a markedly different version of this episode. He says the alleged *dita* was really boiled cinchona bark and that several in their group drank it with no bad effects, but that for a time Conner feigned blindness from it, probably in order to evade the household chores he disliked. (Robert Mailheau to Wayne Sanford, April 5, 1984, Guerrilla Additions, Conner sec.).

17. Ramsey and Rivele, *Ramsey's War*, pp. 138–39.

18. Ibid., pp. 102–4.

19. Anderson Folders, 1:162–63.

20. Pierce Wade to Wayne Sanford, n.d., (Guerrilla Additions).

21. Hileman and Fridlund, *1051*, pp. 173–74.

22. Volckmann, *We Remained*, p. 118; Harkins, *Blackburn's Headhunters*, pp. 166–68, 172.

23. Hileman and Fridlund, *1051*, p. 181.

24. Doyle Decker to Wayne Sanford, March 26, 1984 (Guerrilla Additions).

25. Hileman and Fridlund, *1051*, p. 181.

26. Dizon, "Complete Data," pp. 3–4.

27. Ibid., p. 4. Sanford ("Col. Claude A. Thorp," p. 15) thinks Thorp expected an American invasion of Luzon soon. With hindsight, it is obvious that such a notion was wildly fanciful, but all sorts of fantastic hopes circulated in the imaginations of isolated Americans in 1942, and Thorp may have succumbed to such wishful thinking, though Minang's supposition seems more likely. See Chapter 8.

28. William H. Brooks to Mrs. Thorp, Sept. 12, 1946 (Thorp Collection).

29. Col. Virgil Ney's keen analysis of all aspects of guerrilla warfare points out (*Notes on Guerrilla War*, p. 128) what is too easily forgotten, that one of the most effective ways to win supporters, recruit informers, and influence useful people has always been simplicity itself: bribe them, preferably in untraceable gold or other precious metals. To much of humanity such temptation has always been irresistible.

30. Alfred Bruce to U.S. Authorities in the Case of Col. Claude A. Thorp (Guerrillas, vol. A–B). See also Dizon, "Complete Data," p. 4; Sanford, "Col. Claude A. Thorp," p. 15.

31. In an interview forty years afterward Bruce said this had been the fate of a certain "Filipino spy". The context implies strongly that he meant Laxamana. (April 24, 1984, Guerrilla Additions).

32. Dizon, "Complete Data," pp. 4–5.
33. See Castillo and Castillo, *Saga of José P. Laurel*, p. 158.
34. Hunt and Norling, *Behind Japanese Lines*, pp. 98–100, 157–58, 181.

5. GROWING PAINS

1. Lapham to Charles Cushing, Sept. 21, 1942; Lapham to Barker, Oct. 1, 1942 (Lapham Papers).
2. Hunt and Norling, *Behind Japanese Lines*, pp. 130–31.
3. Duque, "Palaruan," pp. 44–45.
4. See Chapter 7.
5. Harkins, *Blackburn's Headhunters*, pp. 143–44, 157–58; Willoughby, *Guerrilla Resistance Movement*, p. 418; Hartendorp, *Japanese Occupation*, 2:303.
6. Harkins, *Blackburn's Headhunters*, p. 90.
7. Moses and Noble to Cushing, undated but late in 1942 (Lapham Papers).
8. As recounted above.
9. Willoughby, *Guerrilla Resistance Movement*, p. 418. It should be emphasized that Australia did not always have accurate information in such cases.
10. Albert Hendrickson, personal communication to B.N. Cushing had refused to leave his guns behind with Hendrickson.
11. Harkins, *Blackburn's Headhunters*, p. 154.
12. Ibid., pp. 152, 158, 175.
13. Hileman and Fridlund, *1051*, pp. 193–99. Interestingly, Hileman added that many times he had been impressed by the courage, wisdom, and kindness not merely of Filipinas—such as the girlfriend he was never able to find after the war—but of other Oriental women as well. He mentions a female Japanese crane operator who was careful not to hurt prisoners with her machine when they worked on the docks in a seaport in Japan, and a Japanese secretary who spoke kindly to him there and gave him oranges regularly (pp. 192, 198–99, 290, 309–10, 319). He was also amazed at how much Japanese authorities on Luzon knew about Americans like him, an indication of how many Filipino informers there must have been everywhere in the archipelago.
14. Thorp Collection.
15. Ramsey and Rivele, *Ramsey's War*, pp. 152, 162–63.
16. Mona Snyder to Robert Lapham, Sept. 9, 1942 (Lapham Papers).
17. Ramsey and Rivele, *Ramsey's War*, pp. 166, 169–73.
18. Ibid., pp. 175–90, 201.
19. Hunt and Norling, *Behind Japanese Lines*, pp. 98–101, 180–1.
20. Ibid., p. 99.
21. Ramsey and Rivele, *Ramsey's War*, p. 161.
22. Lapham to Wayne Sanford, May 10, 1989 (Guerrillas, vol. H–M, Lapham sec.).
23. See Chapters 8 and 10.
24. Ramsey and Rivele, *Ramsey's War*, pp. 165–66, 174–75, 222–23.
25. This is Hendrickson's version as told to B.N. in 1984 and 1986. A summary of this and Hendrickson's early adventures appears in Hunt and

Norling, *Behind Japanese Lines*, pp. 85–88.

26. Lapham, "History of the LGAF," p. 5.

27. Hipolito, "Report," pp. 3–6. Internal evidence indicates that this undated history was composed in 1945 or 1946. One copy was sent to PHILRYCOM and another to me (R.L.).

28. Ibid., p. 5.

29. Ibid., pp. 5–7.

30. Albert Hendrickson, personal communication to B.N. Al did not heap praise on "Capt. Cris" for his literary prowess, but he did say that Hipolito was done an injustice when he was paid only for the time he spent with U.S. invasion forces and nothing for all his valuable services as a guerrilla.

31. An account of Ramsey's activities and tribulations in and around Manila in 1943–44 is in Ramsey and Rivele, *Ramsey's War*, pp. 175–221.

32. There are a dozen conflicting accounts of the mode of these executions. Probably only the Japanese executioners themselves know for sure how the prisoners were dispatched.

33. In 1950 I had to make a formal deposition to the Veterans Administration attesting to Tom Chengay's good character, abilities, and loyalty as a guerrilla to counter the effort by these wartime thieves to gain revenge against him: Robert Lapham, Sworn Deposition before John A. Duschang, Field Examiner for the Veterans Administration, June 14, 1950 (Lapham Papers). A briefer account of these transactions is in McDougald, *Marcos File*, p. 74.

34. For two other and quite different stories about the demise of Enoch French, see Hunt and Norling, *Behind Japanese Lines*, pp. 113, 235 n. 6. The whole episode is still another demonstration of how little real knowledge we had of the activities of other guerrillas at any distance, and how often we had to rely on rumors and native tales as our basis for action. It also illustrates once more the difficulty of writing accurately about Philippine guerrilla activities when there is so much disagreement among sources.

35. Albert Hendrickson, personal communication to B.N.

36. Hipolito, "Report," p. 9.

37. Ibid., pp. 7, 9: with his usual hyperbole, Cris Hipolito labeled Ray an "outstanding" and "beloved" "chieftain."

38. Panlilio, *Crucible*, p. 172.

39. Reported in Reedsburg, Wis., newspaper, June 20, 1945 (Guerrillas, vol. A–B); also Mojica, *Terry's Hunters*, p. 107.

40. Mojica, *Terry's Hunters*, p. 425.

6. Guerrilla Life

1. Willoughly, *Guerrilla Resistance Movement*, p. 149. For a careful consideration of the legal nuances of a guerrilla's position in modern war, see two interesting, and quite different, articles in the *American Journal of International Law*: Trainin, "Questions of Guerrilla Warfare in the Laws of War," 40 (1946), 534–62; and Nurick and Barrett, "The Legality of Guerrilla Forces under the Laws of War," 40 (1946), 563–83.

2. Lear, *Japanese Occupation*, pp. 185–86, describes this practice on Leyte.

3. Hernandez, *Not by the Sword*, pp. 192–208.

4. A good survey of this point of view and the whole subject of guerrilla warfare is Laqueur, *Guerrilla*, esp. pp. 15–18, 29, 42, 51–56, 69, 84–85, 95–98, 112, 131, 162–63.

5. Volckmann, *We Remained*, pp. 125–26. See also Chapter 8 for our troubles with the Huks about this matter.

6. Harkins, *Blackburn's Headhunters*, p. 159.

7. Agoncillo and Alfonso, *Short History of the Filipino People*, pp. 466–67.

8. Chick Parsons put the gist of the matter thus, "I am definitely a guerrilla. I see no sense in risking annihilation in open combat when you can fight, kill, and run—and, later, fight again" (quoted in Ingham, *Rendezvous by Submarine*, p. 97).

9. For a fuller discussion of Filipino collaborators, "fence-sitters," and "patriots" and their motives, see Chapter 14.

10. Willoughby, *Guerrilla Resistance Movement*, p. 363. This view was shared by many others of quite varied political orientation. Cf. Lichauco, *Dear Mother Putnam*, pp. 136–37, 189; Molina, *The Philippines and the United States*, p. 100; Laurel, *War Memoirs*, p. 30.

11. The nuances of this knotty problem are discussed with concern for both principle and hard reality in Ney, *Notes on Guerrilla War*, esp. pp. 14–16, 28–29, 38, 127–30, 214.

12. Lear, *Japanese Occupation*, p. 105.

13. Lear (ibid., p. 96) notes that on Leyte, Antonio Cinco, Col. Ruperto Kangleon's judge advocate, would order the bodies of enemy agents or collaborators to be minced, but their faces left recognizable, then floated downstream or abandoned in the public squares of barrios as lessons to civilians. I would not call this civilized.

14. President Harry Truman put the same thought more succinctly: "If you can't stand the heat, stay out of the kitchen."

15. See Chapter 8.

16. See Wolfert, *American Guerrilla*, pp. 222–24; and Volckmann, *We Remained*, pp. 28, 34, 128, for examples of such entrepreneurship.

17. In LGAF I required that American IOUs, signed by squadron commanders, must be at least offered for all food purchased (Lapham to Capt. Feliciano Nobres, Aug. 4, 1942, Lapham Papers). Invasion currency was even less valuable than the brief description here indicates, since the Japanese would periodically call up outstanding paper money and replace it with new unnumbered notes, rendering the "old money" worthless and obsolete. Many Filipinos liked to keep Japanese notes as souvenirs, however, especially if I would autograph them.

18. The problems of feeding and supply discussed here existed in all guerrilla groups. Similar concerns on Leyte are described exhaustively in Lear, *Japanese Occupation*, pp. 111–62.

19. Ingham, *Rendezvous by Submarine*, p. 153.

20. Baclagon, *Philippine Resistance Movement*, pp. 127–30.

21. Memoranda from Volckmann to Lapham, Oct. 29 and 30; Nov. 1, 1942 (Lapham Papers).

22. Panlilio, *Crucible*, p. 110.

23. Johnson, *Raid on Cabanatuan*, pp. 146, 148.

24. Panlilio, *Crucible*, p. 302.

25. Arnold, *Rock and a Fortress*, pp. 192, 209–10, 216.

26. Carlos's son Philip II (1556–98), by contrast, was the first "modern" king of Spain. The great Escorial Palace he built on a mountainside near Madrid was a combination church, monastery, office, personal residence, and true center of the Spanish government, for Philip ruled his many peoples and possessions for decades while seldom stirring from it.

27. As in most countries, the inhabitants of the Philippines had long before learned to concoct alcoholic beverages from an interesting array of substances. *Miding*, the most popular local drink, is made from the buds of the nipa palm.

28. Down on Mindanao, Lt. Col. Ernest McClish, who was sometimes criticized for his alleged lack of seriousness, got on remarkably well with Filipino civilians and established advantageous relations with them by being affable and approachable and taking part enthusiastically in their fiestas. Considerable personal acrimony existed among the officers under Col. Wendell Fertig (overall commander of the Mindanao guerrillas), but there is no evidence that McClish's freewheeling attitude did any damage or that he failed to keep matters in proper perspective (Clyde Childress, personal communication to B.N.). Though I knew nothing about McClish then, he and I obviously had a similar attitude toward Filipinos.

29. Representative directives (among many) are MacArthur to Macario Peralta, June 17, 1943, and MacArthur to Gyles Merrill, Dec. 30, 1944, both in SWPA I. Another such "directive" was delivered in person by Chick Parsons, MacArthur's liaison man. In Jan. 1943 guerrillas led by Clyde Childress and Ernest McClish, the chief lieutenants of Wendell Fertig in Mindanao, attacked the town of Butuan at the mouth of the Augusan River and fought the Japanese there for nine days. They succeeded in seizing three boats useful for navigation on that river before being driven into the jungle by Nipponese reinforcements. A month or two later Parsons showed up from Australia via submarine and reminded McClish and Childress sharply that it was far more important to gather information, set up coast-watcher stations, and keep the civilian population well disposed to Americans than to waste scarce ammunition fighting mini-battles with the Japanese.

30. Sanderson, *Behind Enemy Lines*, p. 213.

31. Lear, *Japanese Occupation*, pp. 84–86.

32. Ramsey and Rivele, *Ramsey's War*, p. 148.

33. Mojica, *Terry's Hunters*, pp. 62–64, 102–3, 169, 178, 252–53, 264–65, 280–335, 365–67.

34. Ingham, *Rendezvous by Submarine*, pp. 107–8.

35. Hileman and Fridlund, *1051*, pp. 77, 180.

36. RAG, Guerrilla Activities File.

37. Alfred Bruce, "The Death of Elias Arquiles" (Guerrillas, vol. A–B, Bruce sec.).

38. Doyle Decker's diary, pp. 8–9 Guerrilla Additions, Decker sec.). Decker once ate some generic "chicken" given to him by Negritos. He said that it had a peculiar taste and he awoke the next morning with a bad case of diarrhea (p. 12).

39. Hileman and Fridlund, *1051*, pp. 103ff., 182.

40. Conner, "We Fought Fear," pp. 80–87. Of course, Conner had personal reasons for esteeming Negritos too, as recounted later in this chapter.

41. Ibid., 81.

42. Mellnick, *Philippine Diary*, p. 251.

43. See Chapter 8.

44. Ibid.

45. Harkins, *Blackburn's Headhunters*, pp. 43–44; Castillo and Castillo, *Saga of José P. Laurel*, p. 93; Lachica, *The Huks*, pp. 70–71.

46. Santos, "Guerrilla Activities in Luzon," pp. 2–4.

47. Brines, *Until They Eat Stones*, pp. 73–75. Aquino was the father-in-law of Corazon Aquino, the American-educated and -sponsored president of the Philippines 1986–92.

48. Ricarte, *Memoirs*, pp. xxiii, xxv.

49. Breuer, *Retaking the Philippines*, p. 15.

50. Steinberg, *Philippine Collaborators*, p. 58.

51. Baclagon, *Philippine Resistance Movement*, p. 200; McDougald, *Marcos File*, p. 86.

52. Doyle Decker to Wayne Sanford, April 4, 1984 (Guerrilla Additions, Decker sec.).

53. Robert Mailheau to Wayne Sanford, Feb. 21 and Jan. 25, 1984 (Guerrilla Additions, Conner sec.).

54. Conner to his parents, Aug. 1 and Nov. 1, 1943 (Guerrilla Additions, Conner sec., pp. 4–5. He said he had read the Bible, and "the lessons I learned were far greater than a four year college education." He was also sure that God had helped him survive malaria. Cf. Alfred Bruce, Nov. 5, 1984 (Guerrilla Additions).

55. Robert Mailheau to Wayne Sanford, Jan. 25, 1984 (Guerrilla Additions, Mailheau sec.).

56. Conner, letters to unnamed parties, Nov. 1, 1943, and Sept. 9, 1945, Guerrilla Additions, Conner sec.; Doyle Decker to Douglas Clanin, May 9, 1985, ibid.

57. Mailheau to Sanford, Feb. 21, 1984 (Guerrilla Additions, Conner sec.); Decker to Sanford, Jan. 28, 1985 (Guerrilla Additions, Decker sec.).

58. Doyle Decker, undated letter probably written to Sanford in 1984 or 1985 (Guerilla Additions, Decker sec.).

59. Mailheau to Wayne Sanford, Feb. 21, 1984 (Guerrilla Additions, Conner sec.). Decker says he once "heard" that right after the war Conner wrote a fictional version of his wartime adventures, including this bizarre marriage, but threw it in the ocean on his way back to the States (Decker to Douglas Clanin, May 9, 1985, Guerrilla Additions, Decker sec.).

7. CHRONIC DISCORD

1. Even the moderate guerrillas often pressed hard on the Filipinos who supported them. Peter Calyer and Gyles Merrill, the two highest-ranking guerrillas-to-be, were in no way tyrannical men, yet nearby Filipinos in the Zambales Mountains habitually referred to them as "Col. Corn" and "Col. Kamote [*camote*]" because of the regularity with which they demanded those foods (Hileman and Fridlund, *1051*, p. 176).

2. Leon Beck, "First Days of Freedom," following "Death March" (Guerrillas, vol. A–B). This appears to be either part of an interview with Wayne Sanford or a response to a questionnaire submitted by Sanford in 1985. Col. Peter Calyer had intervened on this occasion to remind the others that Beck too was an American soldier and to persuade them all to wait until he was strong enough to travel again. Understandably, Beck had a high opinion of Calyer thereafter.

3. Hileman and Fridlund, *1051*, pp. 22–23.

4. Alfred Bruce to U.S. Authorities, Comments on Occupied Philippines III (Guerrillas, vol. A–B, Bruce sec.).

5. Doyle Decker says his first priority was always to save himself, and that this was true of all the other Americans too, if they would be honest about it (Decker to Douglas Clanin, June 11, 1985, Guerrilla Additions, Decker sec.).

6. Leon Beck to Wayne Sanford, probably a telephone conversation (Guerrillas, vol. A–B, Beck sec.). For the problems of trying to create an effective guerrilla force from the remnants of a defeated army and masses of angry and frightened civilians, see Valeriano and Bohannan, *Counter-Guerrilla Operations*, pp. 17–20, 49.

7. Harkins, *Blackburn's Headhunters*, pp. 112–30.

8. Ramsey and Rivele, *Ramsey's War*, pp. 145, 154.

9. Hunt and Norling, *Behind Japanese Lines*, pp. 170, 178, 209–10.

10. Leon Beck to Wayne Sanford, Feb. 12, 1984 (Guerrilla Additions, George E. Crane sec.).

11. Sanford, "Mosquitoes Don't Bite," pp. 8, 10.

12. Hileman and Fridlund, *1051*, pp. 92–129, 137, 144, 162–74.

13. Harkins, *Blackburn's Headhunters*, pp. 96–100, 109.

14. See Chapter 4.

15. Several letters and reports in Guerrillas (vol. A–B, Bruce sec.). refer to trouble of this kind. Ramsey says he and Barker took vows of celibacy for the duration for this very reason (Ramsey and Rivele, *Ramsey's War*, p. 125). If so, he did not keep his; see Chapter 5.

16. Harkins bestowed this sobriquet on an American officer in northern Luzon early in the war (see Chapter 5). Agoncillo (*Fateful Years*, p. 654) refers similarly to the same person.

17. Spence, *For Every Tear a Victory*, p. 190.

18. Ibid., p. 190. Spence does not name the officer but says he was eventually court-martialed and that Ferdinand Marcos, future president of the Philippines, acted as prosecutor (p. 195).

19. Agoncillo, *Fateful Years*, pp. 735–37. There is some uncertainty about Fenton's true character; see Hunt and Norling, *Behind Japanese Lines*, pp. 73–74, 231 n. 7, for a brief consideration. Agoncillo devotes chap. 14 of his long book to the careers of other brutes, torturers, and criminals, both American and Filipino. Rodriguez, *Bad Guerrillas*, deals exclusively with this dismal subject and the consequent animosity.

20. Many books are filled with frightful examples of such cruelties. For an overview, see Agoncillo, *Fateful Years*, pp. 683, 699, 701–09.

21. These instances are related by Donald Blackburn; see Harkins, *Blackburn's Headhunters*, pp. 235, 272.

22. Hileman and Fridlund, *1051*, p. 180.

23. Interview with ex-Ranger Marvin W. Kinder by Wayne Sanford, July 10, 1984, Recollections of the Raid, pp. 14–5.

24. Robert Lapham to Capt. Joseph L. Barker, Oct. 1, 1942 (Lapham Papers).

25. Beck and Matthews, "Die Free," p. 24.

26. Beck to Wayne Sanford, Feb. 11, 1984, (Guerrillas, vol. A–B).

27. Volckmann, We Remained, p. 150.

28. Harkins, Blackburn's Headhunters, p. 70.

29. Hileman and Fridlund, 1051, pp. 170–77. Others then with Hileman responded in the same way; cf. pp. 174, 177.

30. Anderson Folders, 1:101–3, 222–23.

31. Mojica, Terry's Hunters, pp. 273–80; Agoncillo, Fateful Years, 2:686–700, 764–78.

32. Barros, "Extended Sojourn," p. 8.

33. Agoncillo, Fateful Years, 2:761.

34. Ibid., 2:656; Arnold, Rock and a Fortress, pp. 17–39; cf. Chapter 9.

35. Sutherland, Guerrilla Resistance Movements, intro. and pp. 9–11. General Sutherland (March 31, 1945, also signed by Gen. Charles Willoughby) says this work is a collection of monographs published previously by the Philippine subsection of SWPA. Twenty-seven years later Willoughby published a reference work of sorts with almost the same title but with considerably updated information. Sutherland's book indicates that SWPA knew about the turmoil on Luzon only in a general way. He thought there might be 300,000 guerrillas there if reports from various groups could be believed; he had only the vaguest notion of what was going on in the Zambales Mountains area; and he was not sure when Ralph McGuire had "died" (he had been murdered nearly two years before.)

36. Cannon, Leyte, pp. 15–17.

37. Grashio and Norling, Return to Freedom, pp. 133–34.

38. Clyde Childress, personal communication to B.N.

39. See Chapter 4.

40. Breuer, Retaking the Philippines, pp. 14–15.

41. When writing letters or replying to questionnaires forty years afterward, other guerrillas who knew Ramsey often employed far less flattering adjectives: e.g. Leon Beck (Guerrillas, vol. A–B, Beck sec.); Doyle Decker to Douglas Clanin, June 27, 1985, and Decker to Wayne Sanford, July 13, 1985 (Guerrilla Additions); Santos, "Guerrilla Activities in Luzon," pp. 6–7, 9; Pierce Wade to Sanford, April 18, 1984 (Guerrillas, vol. N–Z, Wade sec.); Frank Bernacki to Doyle Decker, Aug. 1, 1985 (Guerrillas, vol. A–B, Bernacki sec.).

42. Sanford, "Organization of Guerrilla Warfare," pp. 9–10.

43. Ramsey and Rivele, Ramsey's War. One is reminded of a remark of Chancellor Otto von Bismarck of Germany (1870–90) on being told that Italy was demanding territorial concessions in Africa: "What? Has she lost another battle?"

44. Santos, deposition before a field representative of the Veterans Administration, Feb. 1, 1951 (Anderson's Guerrillas, RAG Box 249); Santos, "Guerrilla Activities in Luzon," pp. 5–9.

45. Santos ("Guerrilla Activities in Luzon," p. 9) says he finally advised Boone to ignore all three of them, since they seemed unable to resolve their own quarrels.

46. Volckmann, *We Remained*, p. 122; Harkins, *Blackburn's Headhunters*, p. 105.

47. Doyle Decker to Douglas Clanin, March 26, 1985 (Guerrilla Additions, Decker sec.); Robert Mailheau to Wayne Sanford, Jan. 25, 1984 (Guerrilla Additions, Mailheau sec.); Leon Beck to Sanford, n.d. [probably 1984] (Guerrilla Additions, Beck sec.).

48. Anderson Folders, 1:50–52.

49. Documents in the Pyle Museum are replete with many American guerrillas' unflattering opinions of many others, both from the war years and in interviews and questionnaires of the 1980s. Representative instances among scores (all from Guerrilla Additions) are Doyle Decker to Clanin, March 3, 1985, about Blair Robinett; Decker to Sanford, Oct. 9, 1984, about Frank Gyovai; Albert Hendrickson to Sanford, May 14, 1984, about Conner, Merrill, and Calyer; Gyovai, n.d., about Robert Mailheau; Mailheau, n.d., about Joseph Donahey; Leon Beck to Sanford, Feb. 28 and March 21, 1984, and April 1985, about Ramsey, Robinett, Edward Fisher, and Daniel Cahill; Beck and James Boyd, April 1985, about John Boone. Cf. also Beck about Volckmann, April 1984 (Guerrillas, vol. A–B); Gerald Wade to Sanford, March 20, 1984, about Volckmann (Guerrillas, vol. N–Z).

50. Anderson to Merrill, Nov. 29, 1943, (SWPA II, miscellaneous correspondence sec.).

51. Manzano expressed agreement with me in his "History of the USAFFE Luzon Guerrilla Armed Forces" p. 25, written not long after the war; cf. Anderson Folders, 1:48.

52. In Yugoslavia the animosity between Draja Mikhailovich's Chetniks and Marshal Tito's Communist Partisans was legendary. The latter became official heroes on the Allied side because the Russian, British, and American governments ultimately decided to support them. The Partisans' principal interest was that however the main war turned out, Yugoslavia should be Communist at the end of it; to the Chetniks, preventing that development took precedence. In France and Italy it is estimated that in the last days of the war and the first weeks of "peace," perhaps 100,000 people in each country were murdered in the fighting between Communists and non-Communists, intensified by punishment of "collaborators" and "class enemies" and spiced by innumerable acts of private vengeance. Who could have expected general guerrilla "cooperation" where hatreds of such intensity were so widespread? The situation in the Philippines was equally complex.

53. Arnold, *Rock and a Fortress*, pp. 200–201. See below in this chapter for a fuller discussion of Marcos's activities, real and alleged.

54. Peter D. Calyer, Feb. 15, 1943 (Guerrillas, vol. C–G, Calyer sec.).

55. Merrill to MacArthur, Aug. 8, 1943, and Nov. 6, 1944, (SWPA I); Merrill to MacArthur through C.O. Iloilo Forces, n.d. [probably spring 1944] (SWPA I); Merrill to Capt. Cabangbang, Dec. 23, 1944, (SWPA I, COPI sec. det); Merrill to MacArthur, Nov. 22, 1944 (SWPA I).

56. E.g., Calyer to 2nd Lt(!) Lapham, Oct. 21, 1944 (SWPA II); Lt. William Gardner to Capt. Albert Hendrickson, Nov. 26, 1944 (Guerrillas, vol. H–M); two letters from Lt. A.A. Arengo of Old Broncho Unit to Merrill, Nov. 30, 1944 (SWPA II).

57. Calyer to Bruce, to Hendrickson, and to Lapham, Oct. 21, 1944 (SWPA II).

58. Lapham to Calyer, Nov. 24, 1944 (SWPA II, Hendrickson sec.).

59. John Boone to Ramsey, March 9, 1944, ECLGA, Bataan Military District File, p. 45, RAG, Box 246. Boone's own official position was cloudy. He appeared at times to be affiliated with Ramsey, at times with Merrill, at other times as independent as I was.

60. Hendrickson to Bruce, Sept. 26 and Oct. 5, 1944 (SWPA II); Calyer to Hendrickson, Oct. 21, 1944, and Hendrickson to Calyer, Dec. 31, 1944 (SWPA II, Hendrickson sec.); William Gardner to Hendrickson, Nov. 6, 1944 (Guerrillas, vol. H–M); Col. Eliseo V. Mallari to Bruce, Jan. 16, 1945 (SWPA II); Bruce to Mallari, Oct. 20, 1944, and Nov. 21, 1944 (SWPA II, Mallari sec.).

61. E.g., Bruce to Calyer, Oct. 16, 1944, and Jan. 26, 1945 (SWPA II); unsigned to "Pedro," Nov. 12, 1944 (SWPA II, Gardner sec.).

62. Conner to Merrill, Jan. 21, 1945 (SWPA I, Conner sec.).

63. Merrill to Ramsey, Aug. 29, 1944 (Guerrillas, vol. N–Z).

64. Anderson to Calyer, Nov. 3, 1944 (SWPA II, Anderson sec.).

65. Lapham to Merrill, Nov. 21, 1944 (SWPA II, miscellaneous correspondence sec.).

66. C.B. Cabangbang, Memo to all Unit Commanders, USPIF in the Field, Dec. 3 and 12, 1944 (SWPA I, Cabangbang sec.).

67. Sutherland, *Guerrilla Resistance Movements*, p. 44. On the same page is Volckmann's remark that "contact with this group [Lapham's] has not been very satisfactory."

68. Calyer to Ramsey and Ramsey to Calyer, ending Sept. 1944 (SWPA II, Ramsey sec.).

69. Which made further difficulty; see below.

70. All these letters are in my possession (Lapham Papers).

71. Cf. Hunt and Norling, *Behind Japanese Lines*, pp. 163–64 for a consideration of other possible motives.

72. Volckmann to Lapham, Aug. 21, 1944 (Lapham Papers).

73. See above.

74. Volckmann to Lapham, Sept. 11, 1944 (Lapham Papers).

75. Lapham to Volckmann, Sept. 28, 1944 (Lapham Papers).

76. Volckmann to Commanding General SWPA, Aug. 21, 1944 (Guerrillas, vol. N–Z, Volckmann sec.).

77. Hendrickson, interview with Douglas Clanin, Oct. 15, 1984 (Guerrilla Additions).

78. Lapham to Hunt, Oct. 31, 1944 (Hunt Papers); Lapham to Hendrickson, and Lapham to Bruce, Nov. 13, 1944 (Guerrillas, vol. H–M, Lapham sec.).

79. Ramsey and Rivele, *Ramsey's War*, pp. 213–21. See also Chapter 9.

80. Spence, *For Every Tear a Victory*, esp. p. 170.

81. See, e.g., McDougald, *Marcos File*, esp. pp. 1–107; and Seagrave, *Marcos Dynasty*, esp. pp. 80–81, 86, 89, 132–33.

82. Ray Hunt, personal communication to B.N. and R.L.

83. When Ray issued the order for Marcos's arrest, Oct. 9, 1944, Marcos did not have a "reputation" of any sort. To Ray, he was just another barefoot Filipino who had come into his camp from the jungle. There was no reason whatever to think that he would one day become president of the Philippines.

84. A famous case of this sort was that of Robert Damiens, who in 1757 tried to assassinate the worthless French king, Louis XV.

85. Seagrave, *Marcos Dynasty*, pp. 46–47, 97, 110.

86. I might add that Bernard Anderson, who lived many more years than I did in the Islands and was therefore better acquainted with the nuances of Philippine public life, did not think Marcos was an untypical Filipino politician or that his homeland suffered in any unusual way from his long tenure in office (Anderson Folders, 1:213).

8. Trouble with the Huks

1. Lachica, *The Huks*, pp. 27–45, 62, 66ff., 82–88.
2. Ibid., pp. 22–23.
3. There is a good comparison of the two major strains of the Huk movement in Kerkvliet, *Huk Rebellion*, esp. pp. 39, 49–51, 227–30, 255–60. Kerkvliet is well disposed toward the agrarian socialists among the Huks and passably friendly to the doctrinaire Marxists. Seemingly, none of the Filipino Communist leaders of the 1930s appreciated the realism of Mao Tse-tung's strategy of basing the movement among peasants rather than industrial workers in rural Asian states (Lachica, *The Huks*, p. 100).
4. Taylor, *Philippines and the United States*, pp. 92–96. Taylor is more critical than Kerkvliet of Philippine Marxists and their designs.
5. Campbell, *Guerrillas*, p. 124; Pomeroy, *Guerrilla Warfare and Marxism*, p. 35.
6. The evolution of Taruc's thought was spread over twenty-five years, many of them spent in prison. He chronicles it in *He Who Rides the Tiger*, a book written in 1967 with the assistance of Douglas Hyde, an Irish ex-Communist. Many years before, Taruc had published *Born of the People*, a tract full of doctrinaire Marxism which he later said had been inserted by José Lava, general secretary of the Philippine Communist Party. More likely, it derived from an American Communist, William Pomeroy; cf. Pomeroy, *Guerrilla Warfare and Marxism*, p. 23.
7. My first encounter is described below.
8. Ramsey has a simpler explanation: he thinks Taruc forged the signatures of Thorp and Barker and his own to an "agreement" (Ramsey and Rivele, *Ramsey's War*, p. 115).
9. Unsigned, "*Hukbo Organization Plan*," Feb. 21, 1945 GRLA-28, RAG, Box 257 (Clanin).
10. Lachica, *The Huks*, p. 107. Dayang-Dayang was later purged by other Huk leaders in one of their interminable intramural quarrels over doctrine and tactics. A Filipino writer says the reason was that she openly sought to enrich herself by plunder (Agoncillo, *Fateful Years*, 2:668, 672). MacArthur's chief of staff claimed that she was secretly in contact with USAFFE guerrillas and was betrayed by her own men to her Huk superiors (Sutherland, *Guerrilla Resistance Movements*, p. 14).
11. Hernando J. Abaya, *Betrayal*, p. 216. See also Conner, "We Fought Fear," pp. 73–74, 78; Sanford, "Anderson's Guerrillas," p. 7.
12. Harkins, *Blackburn's Headhunters*, pp. 78–80.
13. Memo from Merrill to Capt. Bell, Sept. 17, 1942 (Guerrillas, vol. H–M, Merrill sec.).
14. Copy of Merrill-Huk agreement, Dec. 1, 1944 (Guerrillas, vol. H–M, Merrill sec.). See also Abaya, *Betrayal*, pp. 216–17, 219; Lachica, *The Huks*, p. 113.

15. Wayne Sanford, "Organization of Guerrilla Warfare," p. 7.

16. Capt. Joseph R. Barker to parties unknown (top half of the letter is gone) and undated, though internal evidence suggests late summer 1942 (SWPA I); Barker to Merrill, Sept. 19, 1942 (Guerrillas, vol. A–B, Barker sec.).

17. E.g., Gardner to John Boone, April 7 and 13, 1944 (Guerrillas, vol. A–B, Boone sec.); Gardner to Col. Peter Calyer, April 27, 1944 (Guerrillas, vol. C–G, Gardner sec.); Gardner to Colonel Wright, May 24, 1944 (Guerrillas, vol. C–G, Calyer sec.); Sanford, "His Friends Call Him 'Chief,'" pp. 3–9.

18. Gardner to Merrill, March 26 and May 25, 1944 (SWPA, II, Gardner sec.).

19. Crane to General Brougher, Aug. 23, 1942 (Guerrillas, vol. C–G, Crane sec.).

20. James Boyd (Guerrilla Additions).

21. Anderson Folders, 1: 41; Ramsey to Sanford, April 30, 1985 (Guerrillas, vol. N–Z, Ramsey sec.).

22. Maj. Bert Pettit to Anderson, Jan. 28, 1948 (Guerrillas, vol. N–Z, Pettit sec.).

23. "The ECLGA: Origins and Organization (1942–1945)," n.d. (Guerrillas, vol. N–Z, Ramsey sec.).

24. Conner, "We Fought Fear," pp. 80, 86.

25. Lachica, *The Huks*, pp. 2–10, 35–38, 110.

26. Pomeroy, *Guerrilla Warfare and Marxism*, pp. 229–37; and to a lesser degree, Agoncillo, *Fateful Years*, 2:671, 676–78; Abaya, *Betrayal*, pp. 217–23; and Lee, *One Last Look Around*.

27. Taruc, *He Who Rides the Tiger*, pp. 19–31. Kerkvliet (*Huk Rebellion*, pp. 71, 73, 76) presents a rosy interpretation of Huk intentions and deeds overall but also admits that practice sometimes belied principle.

28. Conner, "We Fought Fear," p. 76.

29. With Nocum himself, distaste for the Huks seems to have been permanent. Years later I was told that he had joined the Philippine army after the war and had died fighting the Huks.

30. Conner, who was closely associated with Huk units for a time in 1942, describes this whole system ("We Fought Fear," p. 76).

31. The Red Army followed the same course in the European war. Soviet political commissars were especially hated by the Germans; any who were caught by the Nazis were executed, often after being tortured in an effort to extract information.

32. Baclagon, *Philippine Resistance Movement*, p. 169; Lachica, *The Huks*, p. 109.

33. Taylor, *Philippines and the United States*, pp. 111–12, 121–22.

34. Good examples of this genre are a pamphlet reprinted in SWPA II, Ramsey sec.); and Moises Apostol (from HUK GHQ) to Roy Tuggle, Asst. to Executive Officer of USPIF, Jan. 19, 1945 (Guerrillas, vol. N–Z, Robinett sec.); and Santos, "Guerrilla Activities in Luzon," pp. 9–10.

35. Pedro Viudez, Chief of Staff, BMA Headquarters, to Supreme Authority Hukbalahaps, May 19, 1944, RAG. Cf. also Alejo Santos to USPIF, Ball Division Hdq., Oct. 12, 1944, Anderson's Guerrillas, RAG. Tuggle to Juan de la Cruz, Huk CO, Jan. 13, 1945 (SWPA II, Tuggle sec.). Viudez and Santos both belonged to Anderson's organization.

36. Early in the war Casto Alejandrino, the mayor of Arayat, near Clark Field, gave civilians rice from granaries and arms taken from a small ammunition depot abandoned by retreating American troops (Kerkvliet, *Huk Rebellion*, p. 79).

37. Taylor, *Philippines and the United States*, pp. 111, 118, 123. Prime Minister Winston Churchill of England, a vigorous and outspoken anti-Communist before World War II, found his country allied with the sinister Soviet dictator Josef Stalin during the war. When twitted about his altered stance, he replied that if the devil was fighting Adolf Hitler he (Churchill) would at least make a favorable reference to him in the House of Commons.

38. The experiences of other USAFFE guerrillas were much like my own. One of Anderson's units once fought a three-day battle with the Huks near San Isidro in Nueva Ecija, and on another occasion fell into an "accidental" engagement with them in Bulacan in the course of which 109 Huks were said to have been killed (Lachica, *The Huks*, pp. 109, 112–13).

39. Kerkvliet says that in January 1945 I wrote to Counter-Intelligence Corps that the Huks were a "subversive . . . radical organization" whose "major operations and activities of carnage, revenge, banditry, and hijacking . . . never [have been] equalled in any page of history of the Philippines" (*Huk Rebellion*, p. 115). I no longer have the document in which that opinion allegedly appeared and cannot now recall the exact words I used fifty years ago, but the quotation is an accurate representation of what I thought about Huks at that time.

40. Lt. Johnny L. Storey to Capt. Harry McKenzie, Sept. 19, 1943 (Lapham Papers). Many Filipinos are prone to exaggerate when citing numbers; I would guess that the Huks may have fired 400 rounds in this "battle," and our own men perhaps 50.

41. Lapham to Capt. Ray Hunt, Oct. 31, 1944 (Hunt Papers).

42. Arellano to Lapham, Feb. 8, 1946; Lapham: Affidavit on Arellano's Behalf, 1946 (Lapham Papers).

43. After his surrender to the enemy, Millard Hileman was sent briefly to Old Bilibid prison in Manila. There he found an American who had been captured by the Huks and then, seemingly, simply turned over to the Japanese (Hileman and Fridlund, *1051*, p. 209. By the latter part of 1944, SWPA was receiving reports that the Japanese were giving arms to the Huks as a cheap means to fight USAFFE guerrillas (Sutherland, *Guerrilla Resistance Movements*, p. 13).

44. Pomeroy, *Guerrilla Warfare and Marxism*, pp. 14, 34–35, 45–47. Pomeroy insists that the same factors were responsible for the failure of the Huks to gain power in the Philippines in the 1950s and for the death of Che Guevara in Bolivia in 1967. Jorge Maravilla (in Pomeroy, pp. 239–42) agrees. Cf. also p. 283. Laqueur (Guerrilla, p. 293) notes that Taruc and the Lava brothers lacked the leadership qualities of Mao Tse-tung, and that Ramon Magsaysay was a far abler nationalist leader in the postwar Philippines than Chiang Kai-shek was in China. He ascribes the postwar failures of the Huks to these considerations.

45. Ray Hunt, review of *He Who Rides the Tiger* by Luis Taruc (Hunt Papers).

46. Alfred Bruce, "Comments on the Occupied Philippines," II (Guerrillas, vol. A–B, Bruce sec.). Bruce describes a practice that grew common among the Huks: if they heard that the Japanese were planning to plunder a barrio, they would rush to the place first and eat or carry away everything they could lay their hands on. Of course, this denied the food to the Japanese, but the impression that such conduct made on the victimized peasants is not hard to imagine.

47. Decker to Sanford, March 24, 1985 (Guerrilla Additions, Decker sec.).

48. For varied post-mortems and misgivings, see Taruc, *He Who Rides the Tiger*, pp. 6, 17–22, 34, 50–53, 79, 167–68; and Kerkvliet, *Huk Rebellion*, pp. 216–18, 232–33, 247. Taruc's tempestuous life had tragic overtones, both ideologically and personally. His first wife died of disease; his second was killed in a battle against Philippine government troops. Taruc himself continued to fight the government after 1945 but finally surrendered in the 1950s. He spent years in prison. By 1975 he had swung around 180 degrees to the Catholicism of his youth, had become a leader of Faith Incorporated, and was cooperating with the Marcos government. He had "finally found a peaceful way to help the plight of his farmers and underprivileged" (Johnson, *Raid on Cabanatuan*, p. 275).

9. COMMUNICATIONS WITH AUSTRALIA

1. Sanford ("Supplying the Philippines," p. 1) says Praeger's first contact was established in November 1942; Whitney (*MacArthur*, p. 130) gives Jan. 3, 1943.

2. Cannon, *Leyte*, p. 19.

3. Romulo, *I See the Philippines Rise*, pp. 117–18.

4. Ingham, *Rendezvous By Submarine*, pp. 136–37; Panlilio, *Crucible*, p. 285.

5. Volckmann, *We Remained*, p. 137.

6. Anderson Folders, 1:55–56.

7. Sanford, "Anderson's Guerrillas," p. 7.

8. Whitney, *MacArthur*, p. 91.

9. E.g., see Lapham, Radio Log Book, vol. 3, Sept. 9–23, 1944; Wolfert, *American Guerrilla*, pp. 190, 199, 239–40, 243, 247, 253, 273, 290–91; Harkins, *Blackburn's Headhunters*, pp. 151, 156–63, 170–71; Bernard Anderson to Robert Lapham, June 9, 1943 (Lapham Papers).

10. Johnson, *Hour of Redemption*, p. 116.

11. Romulo, *I See the Philippines Rise*, pp. 38–39.

12. Harkins, *Blackburn's Headhunters*, pp. 170–71.

13. Ramsey and Rivele, *Ramsey's War*, pp. 211–38.

14. Willoughby, *Guerrilla Resistance Movement*, 263–75.

15. Panlilio, *Crucible*, pp. 214–15, 239, 248–49.

16. Like lots of other people, many Filipinos love to make a good story better, or even invent one, to make a desired impression. For instance, in Feb. 1985 I received a letter from Pablo Corderias, who had been one of my bodyguards, vividly recalling that I had once been talking to civilians in a barrio when some Japanese soldiers happened to come by. Luckily, he said, somebody saw them in time, pushed me into a log that had been hollowed out for pounding rice, and hastily covered me with a board that was conveniently

close by. The soldiers then came over and sat down on the board while they talked to some local people. Now I don't say that this couldn't have happened, but I have no recollection of it, and it does strike me as the sort of experience a person would not be likely to forget. Yet not least surprising, a goodly number of other Filipinos have told me this same story about myself. Some even claim to have witnessed it.

17. Various aspects of these developments are discussed by Cannon, *Leyte*, pp. 19–20; Breuer, *Retaking the Philippines*, pp. 21, 35; Volckmann, *We Remained*, p. 157; Willoughby, *Guerrilla Resistance Movement*, pp. 203ff., 450–63; Ind, *Allied Intelligence Bureau*, pp. 224–26; and Anderson to Lapham, July 4 and 27, 1944 (Lapham Papers).

18. Hipolito, "Report," p. 9. Doubtless it was responses like this one that have caused wags to say that if enemies of the United States were serious about destroying us, they would not spend vast sums and effort building nuclear bombs and ICBMs; they would instead burn all our carbon paper and sabotage our typewriters or, in more recent decades, put sand in our computers and copiers.

19. Ibid., p. 9. Cf. Ingham, *Rendezvous by Submarine*, p. 15.

20. Panlilio, *Crucible*, pp. 249–54, 265.

21. Breuer, *Retaking the Philippines*, p. 21.

22. Sanford, "Supplying the Philippines," p. 6.

23. But they didn't stuff us. As early as July I was complaining to Aquino that we wanted to move to a new location because we were out of food (Lapham, Radio Log Book, vol. 1, July 13, 1944).

24. Ray Hunt records that he had to start four times before he could compose a letter to his parents and sisters, whom he had not seen for six years and from whom he had heard nothing for three (Hunt and Norling, *Behind Japanese Lines*, p. 195). Sam Grashio couldn't think of anything to write to the wife he had married shortly before going to the Philippines and who had borne him a child he had never seen (Grashio and Norling, *Return to Freedom*, p. 140).

25. Leon Beck acknowledges that after many months of living on jungle fare, he savored K rations just as I did, though the combat troops he encountered soon after the Lingayen landings thought he was crazy (Beck and Matthews, "Die Free," p. 27).

26. Breuer, *Retaking the Philippines*, p. 20.

27. That Santos was an independent man does not necessarily mean or imply that he was a dishonest one; he may well have spent the money for the purposes intended.

28. Anderson's Guerrillas, Activities File, pp. 6–7, RAG, Box 259; Sanford, "Anderson's Guerrillas."

29. Before Corregidor fell, the Americans burned considerable U.S. currency and sank great numbers of Philippine silver pesos in one of the deepest parts of Manila Bay.

30. Cabanatuan prisoners had already collected money among themselves and established contact with outsiders who were able to smuggle some drugs into the camp and thus save some lives (Keith, *Days of Anguish*, pp. 124, 145). Of course our contributions were a valuable supplement.

31. Quoted in Beck and Matthews, "Die Free." See also Sanford, "Anderson's Guerrillas," p. 9.

32. Cf. Merrill to Cabangbang, and Cabangbang to Merrill, both December 29, 1944. In a communication to John Boone the next day, Cabangbang promised him Merrill's old radio plus the services of a man who knew how to repair radios. SWPA, vol. 1, Cabangbang sec.

33. The unrestrained joy of Luzon guerrillas at their first sight of American planes seems to have been remarkably similar everywhere. Cf. Hunt and Norling, *Behind Japanese Lines*, p. 178; Conner, "We Fought Fear," p. 86; Panlilio, *Crucible*, pp. 258–59; and Hernandez, *Not by the Sword*, pp. 166–70, 201.

34. Chick Parsons stressed this consideration (Ingham, *Rendezvous by Submarines*, p. 20). See also Mojica, *Terry's Hunters*, p. 384; and Ney, *Notes on Guerrilla War*, pp. 30–35.

35. Bernard L. Anderson, Answers to Questions, 1951, in Anderson Folders, vol. 3; and June 20, 1945, Guerrillas, vol. A–B, which gives twenty-seven rescues.

36. Lim Lang Bing to Robert Lapham, Aug. 29, 1944 (Lapham Papers).

37. James, *Years of MacArthur*, 2:508. To maintain proportion: the thirty-six provinces dominated by guerrillas were generally those that had the smallest populations and the weakest Japanese garrisons.

38. Reported in *Quad City Times* (Iowa), April 20, 1975, p. 3D.

10. Preparing for the Invasion

1. Castillo and Castillo, *Saga of José P. Laurel*, p. 274; Hipolito, "Report," p. 10.

2. Ramsey and Rivele, *Ramsey's War*, pp. 285–88. Ramsey says he knew all this because some of his men ambushed a Japanese staff car near Manila and got important papers off the body of a dead officer. I never *knew* anything official or precise about Japanese war plans, but one could surmise a great deal from what our intelligence operatives learned, as well as from everyday observation.

3. Ramsey and Rivele, *Ramsey's War*, pp. 290–91.

4. Hipolito, "Report," p. 10.

5. Mojica, *Terry's Hunters*, pp. 426–27.

6. Archer, *Philippines' Fight for Freedom*, p. 188, asserts that guerrilla warfare actually broke out on all sides. My letters to Capt. Ray Hunt of Nov. 26, 1944, and Jan. 13, 1945 (Hunt Papers), indicate my efforts to control the bellicose desires of LGAF intelligence operatives.

7. Hernandez says the guerrillas around Manila became so intoxicated by the atmosphere of autumn 1944 that they ambushed Japanese with complete disregard for the bloody burdens this laid on the backs of civilians (*Not by the Sword*, pp. 170–71, 174–75, 177–78). My men were better disciplined than that.

8. Baclagon, *Philippine Resistance Movement*, p. 152.

9. Robert Lapham, "Record of Activities," based on reports received as of Feb. 12, 1945 (Lapham Papers).

10. For an excellent brief survey of this subject, see Breuer, *Retaking the Philippines*, pp. 33–44, 100–101, 245.

11. MacArthur to Lapham, Aug. 14, 1944 (Lapham Papers).

12. Lapham, Radio Log Book, vol. 1, Aug. 8, Sept. 26, and Nov. 1, 1944; vol. 4, Nov. 23 and 25, Dec. 3, 6, and 30, 1944, and Jan. 6, 1945, are representative samples.

13. MacArthur to All Filipino and Allied Resistance Leaders in the Field, Nov. 25, 1944 (SWPA I, Cabangbang sec.). I would like to claim I was clairvoyant, for I had sent a similar letter of instruction to Hendrickson a few days earlier, Nov. 13, 1944 (Lapham Papers).

14. Lt. J.H. Manzano, "Brief History of the Bulacan Military Area, p. 4. Anderson Guerrilla Activities File, RAG (Clanin); Cabangbang to all USPIF Intelligence Officers In the Field, Dec. 2 and 18, 1944 (SWPA I, Cabangbang sec.).

15. Lapham, Radio Log Book, vol. 1 (scattered); vol. 2, Nov. 27 and 29, Dec. 2, 1944; vol. 3, Sept. 23 and Oct. 13, 1944.

16. Ibid., vol. 1, Aug. 2, 1944; vol. 2, Oct. 13, Nov. 5 and 9, Dec. 3, 1944; vol. 4, Jan. 8, 1945.

17. Ibid., vol. 1, Aug. 5, 1944; vol. 2, Oct. 13 and Nov. 9, 1944; vol. 3, Oct. 12, 1944.

18. Ibid., vol. 2, Nov. 29, 1944; vol. 3, Sept. 26, 1944; vol. 4, Jan. 3, 1945.

19. Ibid., vol. 1, Aug. 1944; vol. 2, Nov. 12, 27, and 29, 1944; vol. 3, Sept. 23 and 24, Oct. 12, 1944; vol. 4, Jan. 6, 1945.

20. Ibid., vol. 1, Aug. 1944; Book 2, Oct., 1944, Nov. 29, 1944.

21. Ibid., vol. 1, Aug. 1944 (scattered); vol. 2, Nov. 12, 27, 29 and Dec. 3, 1944; vol. 3, Sept. 23 and 24, 1944; vol. 4, Jan. 6, 1945.

22. Ibid., vol. 2, Nov. 28, 1944; vol. 3, Sept. 23, 1944.

23. Ibid., vol. 2, Oct. 1944.

24. Ibid., vol. 1, Aug.–Sept 1944 (scattered); vol. 2, Nov. 5 and 12, 1944; vol. 3, Sept. 23 and Oct. 12, 1944; vol. 4, Jan. 6, 1945.

25. Ibid., vol. 1, Aug.–Sept. 1944 (scattered); vol. 2, Nov. 5, 9, 21, 29 and Dec. 2, 1944; vol. 3, Sept. 23 and 26, 1944; vol. 4, Jan. 2 and 6, 1945.

26. Ibid., vol. 2, Oct. 1944 (scattered), Nov. 9, 13, 27, 28, 1944; vol. 3, Sept. 26 and Oct. 12, 1944.

27. Ibid., vols. 1–2, Aug.–Sept. 1944 (scattered), Nov. 9, 1944; vol. 3, Sept. 23 and 26, 1944; vol. 4, Nov. 20, 1944.

28. Ibid., vol. 3, Oct. 12, 1944.

29. Ibid., vol. 2, Nov. 28, 1944.

30. Ibid., vol. 1, Aug. 1944 (scattered); vol. 2, Nov. 9, 1944.

31. Ibid., vol. 1, Aug. 1944 (scattered).

32. Ibid., vol. 2, Nov. 5, 9, 12, 28, 1944; vol. 3, Oct. 9, 1944.

33. Ibid., vol. 1, Aug.–Sept. 1944 (scattered); vol. 2, Nov. 21, 1944; vol. 4, Nov. 22, 23, 27, 1944, Dec. 1944 (scattered), Jan. 6, 8, 9, 10, 1945.

34. Ibid., vol. 1, Aug.–Oct. 1944 (scattered); vol. 2, Nov. 20, 1944.

35. Lapham, "History of the LGAF," p. 11; Ross-Smith, Triumph in the Philippines, p. 91.

36. Ramsey and Rivele, Ramsey's War, pp. 264–66.

11. The Landings

1. Agoncillo, Fateful Years, 2: 860.

2. Ross-Smith, Triumph in the Philippines, p. 127.

3. Doyle Decker, off in the Zambales Mountains to the west, recorded in his diary (p. 13) that when he and his companions first saw the planes, they began to sing "California Here We Come" (Guerrilla Additions, Decker sec.). Our feelings were comparable.

4. Dean Schedler in *Davenport-Bettendorf* (Iowa) *Times-Democrat*, Jan. 16, 1945 (clipping in Guerrillas, vol. H–M, Lapham sec.).

5. Saburo Sakai, Japan's premier air ace, had the same feeling near the end of the war as he watched the squadrons of new, different, and better U.S. planes appearing every day in the Pacific (Sakai, Caidin, and Saito, *Samurai*, pp. 209, 215–23, 236–39, 245). So did Millard Hileman when he saw the vast array of U.S. supplies pour into Japan at the end of the war there (Hileman and Fridlund, *1051*; pp. 240–49).

6. Lapham, "Record of Activities," (Lapham Papers).

7. Bernard Anderson says MacArthur once told him personally that 90 percent of war is having good intelligence; if you know where the enemy is and what he has, you can figure out how to deal with him. He added that guerrillas had given him the best intelligence he had enjoyed in this war and had thereby saved many American lives (Anderson Folders, I: 208).

8. Cannon, *Leyte*, p. 250.

9. Long, *MacArthur as Military Commander*, p. 162.

10. Whitney, *MacArthur*, pp. 183–84.

11. Romulo, *I See the Philippines Rise*, p. 209.

12. Cannon, *Leyte*, p. 250.

13. Breuer, *Retaking the Philippines*, pp. 127–28.

14. Ross-Smith, *Triumph in the Philippines*, p. 79; see also pp. 164, 168, 180, 212, 220, 252, 310, and 313 for later successes.

15. Hipolito, "Report," p. 11.

16. Lapham, "Record of Activities" (Lapham Papers).

17. Romulo, *I See the Philippines Rise*, p. 212. Carlos Romulo, Mac-Arthur's press officer, was at USAFFE headquarters, where he had heard all these and similar tales.

18. Johnson, *Raid on Cabanatuan*, pp. 66–67; Johnson, *Hour of Redemption*, p. 219; Keith, *Days of Anguish*, pp. 145–52.

19. Johnson, *Raid on Cabanatuan*, pp. 39–42; Johnson, *Hour of Redemption*, pp. 139–40. Guerrillas on Mindanao faced a similar problem. Col. Claro Laureta, a PC officer who commanded a local guerrilla unit near Davao, was sure he could successfully break into the Davao POW camp and give the inmates a chance to escape. But he had only three hundred men and twenty rounds of ammunition for each of their rifles—so little ammunition, in fact, that his unit beheaded spies instead of shooting them. Thus, he and his men would have had no way of either protecting the newly liberated POWs or transporting them through mountains, swamps, and jungle to ships off the coast. See Mellnick, *Philippine Diary*, pp. 241–46; Grashio and Norling, *Return to Freedom*, p. 115. Both Grashio and Mellnick were members of a group of nine Americans and two Filipinos who made a sensational escape from the Davao camp in April 1943.

20. Marvin W. Kinder (a Ranger who took part in the Cabanatuan raid), interviewed by Wayne Sanford, July 10, 1984, p. 8 (Recollections of the Raid).

21. Johnson, *Raid on Cabanatuan*, pp. 29, 33, 72–73, 76–77, 104.

22. Henry Mucci, "Rescue at Cabanatuan" (Recollections of the Raid).
23. Johnson, *Raid on Cabanatuan*, p. 162.
24. See Chapter 4.
25. Johnson, *Raid on Cabanatuan*, pp. 84, 106.
26. Ibid., pp. 112, 134–37, 142.
27. Mucci, "Rescue at Cabanatuan," p. 18 (Recollections of the Raid).
28. Michael J. King "Rangers: Selected Combat Operations in World War II," p. 61 (Recollection of the Raid).
29. In 1946, Romulo (*I See the Philippines Rise*, p. 214) said twenty-one Filipinos died in the raid. A couple of months after the raid Mucci ("Rescue at Cabanatuan," p. 19) said twenty-seven "raiders" were killed. He did not break this down among Rangers, Scouts, and Filipinos (Recollections of the Raid).
30. Johnson, (*Raid on Cabanatuan*, pp. 258, 269) says 1,275 of the enemy were killed and 260 wounded. For Pajota's ambush, see King "Rangers," pp. 63–69 (Recollections of the Raid).
31. One of the Rangers who took part in the raid did note that physically moving the POWs out of the camp posed no serious problems because most of them weighed only a hundred pounds or so. (Marvin W. Kinder interview, p. 31; and King, "Rangers," (Recollections of the Raid).
32. Kinder interview, p. 71 (Recollections of the Raid).
33. Baclagon, *Philippine Resistance Movement*, pp. 167–68.
34. GRLA-28, RAG, Box 257 (Clanin).
35. E.g., José Banal CO of Huk Seventh Military District, to Roy C. Tuggle, Nov. 28, 1944; Tuggle to Col. Gyles Merrill, Jan. 13, 1945; Merrill to Tuggle, Jan. 12, 1945; Tuggle to Juan de la Cruz, Huk CO, Jan. 13, 1945; Tuggle to Merrill, Jan. 18, 1945 (SWPA II, Tuggle sec.). Also agreement signed between Huks and Merrill's representatives, Dec. 1, 1944 (*Guerrillas*, vol. H–M, Merrill sec.); Capt. Alfred Bruce to Col. Peter Calyer, Jan. 17, 1945 (SWPA II, Bruce sec.); Lt. Henry Clay Conner to Merrill, Jan. 14, 1945 (SWPA I, Conner sec.).
36. Col. John B. Cooley (for General Krueger) to Commanding Officer LGAF, Feb. 2, 1945 (Lapham Papers).
37. Long, *MacArthur as Military Commander*, p. 164.
38. Ross-Smith, *Triumph in the Philippines*, p. 334. Two letters of Jan. 28, 1945, from Roy C. Tuggle CO of PMD (SWPA II, Tuggle sec.) make it clear that sabotage had often been much too thorough. He now wanted all local units ordered to *preserve* bridges, find fords across rivers, secure and transport timber to repair bridges, and post guards to prevent their further destruction as well as prevent the Japanese from damaging them or laying mines nearby—all because U.S. forces needed them to move rapidly.
39. Hernandez, *Not by the Sword*, p. 201.

12. THE LAST MONTHS

1. Estrada, "Guerrilla movement in Pangasinan." p. 50.
2. There are extended descriptions of all these developments in Ross-Smith, *Triumph in the Philippines*, pp. 201, 220, 233, 264, 274, 316, 325–27, 334, 351, 422, 454–78, 487, 541–74, 651, 657–58; and a briefer version in James, *Years of MacArthur*, 2: 688–90, 741–46.

3. For more extended accounts by participants, in this bloody campaign, see Hunt and Norling, *Behind Japanese Lines*, pp. 205–9; Carlisle, *Red Arrow Men*; and Blakeley, *32nd Infantry Division*, pp. 220–49.

4. Valtin, *Children of Yesterday*, pp. 142–43.

5. See Chapter 7.

6. Rodriguez, *Bad Guerrillas*, pp. x–xi, 33–48, 57–69, 72–75, 115–32, 140–53, 185.

7. Lt. Col. A. Arellano, CO of Ist Regt. LGAF-USAFFE, to Adjutant General, June 22, 1945, Philippine Archives, Box 246.

8. Olson, *Anywhere, Anytime*, pp. 195, 203.

9. Valtin (*Children of Yesterday*, p. 294) quotes Maj. Gen. W.B. Woodruff's remark about why combat in the Pacific was often more depressing to American soldiers than action in Europe: "In Europe when we advance we really capture something. Out here we just capture another island, important though it may be, that looks much like all the other islands. As one doughboy remarked after we had just cleaned out a small objective—'Well, there's another half million coconuts.'"

10. See Ogawa, *Terraced Hell*, pp. 93, 212, for examples. War has always been notorious for the filth that accompanies it, doubtless the major reason that medical casualties are normally many times as great as battle casualties. So far as we know, the first large-scale, long war in the history of the world in which deaths from fighting exceeded those from disease was World War I (1914–18)—and even that is true only if the global influenza epidemic of the fall and winter of 1918–19 is not counted.

11. Beck and Matthews, "Die Free," p. 28.

12. See Ross-Smith, *Triumph in the Philippines*, pp. 504–7, 532, 652–58, on the morale problems of U.S. troops in the spring of 1945.

13. The tensions Ramsey endured and his responses to them are described throughout Ramsey and Rivele, *Ramsey's War*; his collapse in May is discussed on pp. 326–29. When he got back to the States, Ed weighed ninety-three pounds and was beset with malaria, amoebic dysentery, anemia, and acute malnutrition. He soon suffered another nervous breakdown (p. 333).

14. Valtin gives many examples of such ruses (*Children of Yesterday*, pp. 276–77).

15. Ogawa, *Terraced Hell*, pp. 95–98.

16. Breuer (*Retaking the Philippines*, p. 250) describes some of these tricks. Valtin, *Children of Yesterday*, discusses the broader considerations that contributed so much to the intense brutality of the Pacific war; see, e.g., pp. 1–17, 71, 87, 100, 115, 127, 420, 424–27. Cf. also Ogawa, *Terraced Hell*, p. 99. For Yamashita's strategy, see Chapters 10 and 13.

17. James, *Years of MacArthur*, 2: 681; Potter, *Life and Death of a Japanese General*, pp. 126, 141; Ross-Smith, *Triumph in the Philippines*, pp. 91, 93, 100–101, 174, 232, 334, 421, 554; Rutherfoord, *165 Days*, p. 159.

18. Ogawa, *Terraced Hell*, pp. 91–93, 143, 212.

19. Ibid., pp. 85, 105, 170, 187, 191.

20. Ibid., pp. 37, 54, 160–61, 171, 216.

21. Kodama, *I Was Defeated*, p. 195.

22. Romulo, *I See the Philippines Rise*, p. 176.

23. Ibid., pp. 185, 222–23.

24. Hartendorp, *Japanese Occupation*, 2: 108.

25. Alfred Bruce, Comments on the Occupied Philippines (Guerrillas, vol. A–B, Bruce sec.).

26. Ibid.

27. Mojica, *Terry's Hunters*, pp. 1–2. Others who have sounded the same note are Agoncillo, *Fateful Years*, 2: 545–91, 759, 853, 886; Castillo and Castillo, *Saga of José P. Laurel*, pp. 224–26, 298–99; Lichauco, *Dear Mother Putnam*, pp. 11–12, 80–81, 105, 148–53, 169–70, 192–94. Tomas Confesor, a prewar governor of Iloilo and an inspiring resistance leader during the war, observing the noisy eleventh-hour "guerrilla heroes," grumbled, "Even the Japs in Tokyo are now pro-American" (quoted in Abaya, *Betrayal*, p. 102).

13. The Japanese War Effort

1. Clark, *Man Who Broke Purple*, a biography of the brilliant cryptanalyst William Friedman, describes these and other disasters at some length (pp. 138–201, esp. 168–77).

2. Thaddeus V. Tuleja, "Admiral H. Kent Hewitt," in Howarth, *Men of War*, p. 326.

3. Examples of such blunders are cited in Lee, *One Last Look Around*, pp. 271–76.

4. Decades later muddle had not changed much, but the art of politico-military doubletalk had advanced markedly. Those who died in foul-ups in Vietnam or in the Gulf War of 1991 were said to have succumbed to "friendly fire."

5. Keith W. Bird, "Grand Admiral Erich Raeder," in Howarth, *Men of War*, pp. 53–55.

6. See below for more about Yamamoto.

7. Kato, *Lost War*, pp. 167–68. Kato was a prominent newspaperman before the war and a Westernized liberal, as Japanese went then.

8. Ibid., pp. 170ff.

9. Kodama, *I Was Defeated*, pp. 128, 156, 163. Kodama led a varied life and was active in Japanese politics.

10. Meo, *Japan's Radio War*, p. 10.

11. Kodama, *I Was Defeated*, p. 165.

12. Ibid., pp. 120–22.

13. Meo, *Japan's Radio War*, p. 16; Kato, *Lost War*, p. 99.

14. Cook and Cook, *Japan at War*, pp. 90–95, 456–58.

15. Sakai, Caidin, and Saito, *Samurai*, p. 46; see also pp. 72–74 for similar examples.

16. Stephen Howarth, "Admiral of the Fleet Isoroku Yamamoto," in Howarth, *Men of War*, p. 114.

17. Meo, *Japan's Radio War*, p. 268.

18. Kato, *Lost War*, pp. 106–7.

19. Meo, *Japan's Radio War*, pp. 16–17.

20. Ibid., pp. 16–17; Kato, *Lost War*, p. 111.

21. Kato, *Lost War*, pp. 106–7.

22. Elsbree, *Japan's Role*, p. 43.

23. Meo, *Japan's Radio War*, p. 268.

24. Kodama, *I Was Defeated*, p. 167.

25. Information on this dismal subject is scattered throughout the contributions in Howarth, *Men of War*. It is especially pronounced and detailed in the final chapter, Benis M. Franks, "Lieutenant General Holland M. Smith," pp. 566–85.

26. Robert W. Love Jr., "Fleet Admiral Ernest J. King," in Howarth, *Men of War*, p. 84.

27. Breuer, *Retaking the Philippines*, pp. 259–60.

28. Ibid., p. 44.

29. Howarth, "Admiral," in Howarth, *Men of War*, pp. 111–12.

30. Kodama, *I Was Defeated*, pp. 40, 66–67, 123–27; Cook and Cook, *Japan at War*, pp. 261ff.; Kato, *Lost War*, pp. 128–29, 166; Ogawa, *Terraced Hell*, p. 45.

31. Kodama, *I Was Defeated*, pp. 29–31, 35–37, 42–43, 49–51.

32. This whole subject is described systematically in some detail by Calvocoressi and Wint, *Total War*, pp. 673–710 (esp. 703–5), 721–22, 783–9.

33. Mojica, *Terry's Hunters*, pp. 337–64.

34. Kodama, *I Was Defeated*, p. 130. See also pp. 108, 120, 122 for consideration of similar problems.

35. Cook and Cook, *Japan at War*, pp. 20–21, 77–83; Kato, *Lost War*, pp. 87–88.

36. Kalaw, "Filipino Opposition," p. 345.

37. Alfred Bruce to Col. Mallari, Nov. 6, 1944 (SWPA II, Mallari sec.).

38. Cook and Cook, *Japan at War*, pp. 171–76.

39. Sakai, Caidin, and Saito, *Samurai*, pp. 209, 215–23, 231, 236–39, 245, 275ff.

40. Kato, *Lost War*, p. 164.

41. A Japanese newsman interviewed years after the war called it "stupid" (Cook and Cook, *Japan at War*, p. 479).

42. Brines, *Until They Eat Stones*, pp. 112–14.

43. Hernandez, *Not by the Sword*, pp. 150, 152; Ward, *Asia for the Asiatics*, pp. 56–58.

44. Elsbree, *Japan's Role*, pp. 10, 66, 75.

45. A typical example was a Japanese naval officer with neither previous training nor experience in administration who was sent to supervise an enclave of the East Indies. He began by thinking of himself as a "liberator," but in combined despair and fear of punishment he soon resigned himself to the tyranny and corruption all around him (Cook and Cook, *Japan at War*, pp. 105–11.

46. Hartendorp, *Japanese Occupation*, 1: 485–86, 507–8, 513; 2: 126 n. The double cross was not always one way; some guerrillas would surrender just to rest for a while. One told a woman he had once worked for as a houseboy that he had surrendered four times in order to rest, get a favor from the government, and look for a chance to steal something useful that he could take back to his guerrilla group (2:128).

47. E.g., ibid.; Hernandez, *Not by the Sword*, pp. 102, 129–30; Kato, *Lost War*, p. 145; Elsbree, *Japan's Role*, pp. 66, 75.

48. Hartendorp, *Japanese Occupation*, 1:508.

49. A novel that paints an unforgettable picture of the pre-1941 Japanese army—its spirit and its training and practices—is *Long the Imperial Way* by Hanama Tasaki, who served in it several years during the 1930s.

50. Interestingly, when Japan defeated China in their brief war of 1894, most of the Japanese fatalities were caused by infected wounds and, especially, disease. Tokyo promptly prescribed a more balanced diet and better hygienic practices for its soldiers, cleaned up military hospitals, and sharply upgraded standards of sanitation throughout the military services. Only ten years later, in the Russo-Japanese War of 1904–5, medical casualties fell dramatically. Yet when Japan invaded the Philippines in 1941, it was quite as unprepared for warfare in the tropics as the Allies and promptly suffered the same extensive casualties from malaria, dysentery, dengue fever, and other maladies as did the Americans. So much for the widespread faith that history is the record of human progress.

51. These and other atrocious incidents and practices are described by various aging Japanese who lived through World War II and were interviewed by Haruko and Theodore Cook nearly half a century afterward. See Cook and Cook, *Japan at War*, pp. 40–46, 74–75, 105–113, 145–67, 192–99, 364–66, 432–37, 441–47, 472–77.

52. Ogawa, the Japanese teacher attached to an army unit in the Philippines, said that sometimes when soldiers stole rice from Filipino granaries at night they would leave worthless military scrip as payment. Technically, they had made a purchase; actually it was the act of a "thief leaving his calling card." (*Terraced Hell*, p. 56).

53. On Panay young girls sometimes sold poisoned saki to Japanese soldiers, while guerrillas on one side and Nipponese soldiers on the other killed each other in sickening ways. More than 2,000 islanders perished thus (Cook and Cook, *Japan at War*, p. 429).

54. Falk, *Liberation of the Philippines*, pp. 28–35, 59.

55. Ross Smith, *Triumph in the Philippines*, pp. 90–91; Ogawa, *Terraced Hell*, p. 103.

56. Potter, *Life and Death of a Japanese General*, p. 123.

57. By the summer of 1944 Japanese pilots got, at best, six months of training (U.S. pilots, two years), and their quality had fallen off proportionately. In 1941–42 it had not been unusual for nine dive bombers to score nine hits in practice; by 1944 the average was more like one hit (John Wukovits, "Admiral Raymond A. Spruance," in Howarth, *Men of War*, p. 170).

58. Kodama, *I Was Defeated*, p. 152, and see also pp. 138–39, 149–51; Kato, *Lost War*, p. 194.

59. There is a good brief discussion of this situation in Edward L. Beach, "Admiral Charles Andrew Lockwood," in Howarth, *Men of War*, pp. 414–16.

14. RUMINATIONS

1. This is claimed in Dupuy, *Asian and Axis Resistance Movements*, p. 32.

2. Volckmann, *We Remained*, p. 216. Volckmann believed that Luzon guerrillas inflicted 50,000 casualties on the enemy after January 9, 1945.

3. Agoncillo, *Fateful Years*, 2:776. Agoncillo thinks that had it not been for the guerrillas and the failure of the Japanese to win over the bulk of Filipino civilians, Japan could have inflicted casualties on the Americans in the Islands at something like the Iwo Jima rate until the atomic bombs were dropped. This is a mere opinion, of course, but an informed and certainly a sobering one.

4. Hunt and Norling, *Behind Japanese Lines*, pp. 213–14.

5. Capt. George R. Philip, Cav., to Commanding General PHILRYCOM, Sep. 27, 1947, ROTC *Hunters*, Statements and Records, RAG, Box 258.

6. Anderson to CO of SWPA, Aug. 24, 1944. Anderson's Guerrillas Activities File, RAG, Box 259.

7. Harry McKenzie to Republic of the Philippines, Aug. 3, 1946, RAG.

8. Robert Lapham, formal statement, Sept. 3, 1947, LGAF General Information File, RAG, Box 246.

9. Philip, to PHILRYCOM (see n. 5, above).

10. I have a collection of nine forged letters and documents that relate to a single person. In one, dated April 10, 1942, only a day after Bataan had fallen, Colonel Thorp ostensibly appointed one Victoriano C. Luluquisan a "Commander" in LGAF—though LGAF did not yet exist. Others dated in May and June 1942, allegedly from Thorp and me, commissioned Luluquisan a "Lt. Colonel." This was Thorp's own rank and a higher one than I held at any time during the war.

11. See, e.g., Villamor, *They Never Surrendered*, p. 286.

12. Molina, *Philippines through the Centuries*, 2:383.

13. Johnson, *Hour of Redemption*, p. 354.

14. J.E. Palmer, Adjudication Officer, Guerrilla Activities File, "Recapitulation of Recognized Guerrilla Units by Major Commands," RAG, Box 249. Palmer gives 6,668 officers and men and 435 casualties in Anderson's command, and 22,167 officers and men with 3,861 casualties in USAFIP-NL (Volckmann's command). For other estimates, cf. Baclagon, *Philippine Resistance Movement*, p. 532; and the official army history: Ross-Smith, *Triumph in the Philippines*, pp. 573, 651.

15. Steinberg, "The Ambiguous Legacy," p. 165.

16. The full text of the letter is reprinted in Hartendorp, *Japanese Occupation*, pp. 566–69, and a condensed version in Hunt and Norling, *Behind Japanese Lines*, pp. 135–36.

17. Ingham, *Rendezvous by Submarine*, p. 170.

18. I certainly was not the only American soldier in the Islands who thought most ordinary Filipinos would have liked to stay under the wing of the United States, or believed it would have been to their long-term advantage to do so. Among those who share my view are Ray Hunt (Hunt and Norling, *Behind Japanese Lines*, p. 222), Samuel Grashio (Grashio and Norling, *Return to Freedom*, p. 133), and Doyle Decker (Decker to Sanford, May 2, 1985, Guerrilla Additions, Decker sec.).

19. Capotosto, "The Philippines" p. 3.

20. Spence, *For Every Tear a Victory*, p. 197.

21. Day, *The Philippines*, p. 123.

22. Molina, *Philippines through the Centuries*, p. 377. Six years after the end of World War II, Bernard Anderson was already convinced that we had treated many ex-enemy and occupied countries far better than we had the Philippines (Anderson Folders, vol. 1). I have long agreed with Andy on this point, and have also been convinced that our nation has spent far too much in men and money trying to "contain Communism" and to keep peace all over the globe among people who do not wish to be peaceful.

23. For examples of this general viewpoint, see Friend, *Between Two Empires*, pp. 24–25; Lee, *One Last Look Around*, p. 247; Steinberg, "Ambigu-

ous Legacy," p. 187; Day, *The Philippines*, pp. 112–21, 223–24. Lee (p. 251) even thinks some Filipinos voted for Manuel Roxas for president in 1948 from resentment at what they saw as American failure to honor our obligations to their country. Of course this assumes that Roxas was at heart always a collaborator with the Japanese, a view emphatically rejected by no less than General MacArthur.

24. Quoted in Steinberg, "Ambiguous Legacy," pp. 180–82.

25. Villamor, *They Never Surrendered*, pp. xiii–xv, 226, 264, 272, 284–88. Villamor did have a point though, if one considers the matter more broadly. How many Americans, in uniform or out, still casually regard people of different cultures from distant parts of the world as "slopes" or "gooks"? Right after the war, Millard Hileman, not a notably sensitive man, set off with some friends to visit numerous Filipinos who had befriended them in various ways. There followed ten days of drinking, feasting, and mutual jubilation at seeing one another again. Yet to Hileman's disgust, all this left their assigned driver cold. He was a new American recruit to whom all Filipinos were just "gooks" (Hileman and Fridlund, *1051*, pp. 350–70).

26. The quotation is from Seagrave, *Marcos Dynasty*, pp. 126–27. Abaya, *Betrayal*, explores this standard article of leftist faith. See also Day, *The Philippines*, pp. 112–21.

27. Taylor, *Philippines and the United States*, p. 120.

28. Eyre, *Roosevelt-MacArthur Conflict*, p. 144.

29. For a thoughtful consideration of this web of dilemmas, see Steinberg, "Ambiguous Legacy," pp. 182–84, 189.

30. Two excellent studies of these problems and their numberless nuances are Boveri, *Treason in the Twentieth Century*, and West, *The Meaning of Treason*.

31. Steinberg, "Ambiguous Legacy," p. 184.

32. Lear, *Japanese Occupation*, pp. 234–35.

33. A point emphasized in Taylor, *Philippines and the United States*, pp. 96–97.

34. Lee, *One Last Look Around*, pp. 243, 248–49; Agoncillo, *Fateful Years*, 2:909; Day, *The Philippines*, pp. 108–12. De la Costa, *Readings in Philippine History*, pp. 279–80, reprints a speech on this subject delivered by Osmena on Leyte, Nov. 23, 1944.

35. Molina, *Philippines through the Centuries*, 2:335. Laurel (*War Memoirs*, p. 5) says only one action was forbidden: nobody might swear an oath of loyalty to Japan. See also Lichauco, *Dear Mother Putnam*, p. 19.

36. PC men were, of course, prime examples of such "pretenders."

37. An officer in the Hunters guerrillas thinks the Japanese made a major mistake in establishing the Philippine Republic with Laurel at its head. The Nipponese, he says, were close to breaking guerrilla resistance in 1943—until they allowed the wily Laurel to convince them that they must rule the Philippines more leniently if they expected the new regime to become popular with the people. This gave all the guerrilla groups a chance to make a comeback (Mojica, *Terry's Hunters*, pp. 349ff.).

38. An American who was in the Philippine General Hospital in Manila a few days after the puppet republic was proclaimed said Laurel came in one day to visit a mutual friend, F. Theo Rogers of the *Philippine Free Press*. Though accompanied by several Japanese aides, Laurel bent over

Rogers and said in a low voice, "Don't worry, Theo! It won't be long now" (Hartendorp, 1:653).

An American chaplain who was at large on Luzon throughout the war said that when he was in a hospital in Pampanga for four months in 1942, Laurel knew it but never told the Japanese (Rev. John E. Duffy, National Chaplain of the American Legion, to Henry R. Rodriguez, American Legion, Philippine Department, Manila, Jan. 25, 1953, Guerrillas, vol. C–G, Duffy sec.).

The best biography of Laurel is by Castillo and Castillo, *Saga of José P. Laurel*, which depicts him quite favorably. See also Laurel, *War Memoirs*; and Lichauco, *Dear Mother Putnam*, pp. 99, 112, 182–83.

39. Thorpe, *East Wind, Rain*, pp. 159–61. When Roxas was proclaimed a hero and Laurel, Jorge Vargas, and others who had played equivocal roles during the war were exonerated of charges of collaboration, another Filipino politician remarked, "You see, you can eat your cake and have it too" (p. 161). Abaya pens the same indictment of Roxas, at greater length, in *Betrayal*, pp. 10–11, 21–33, 50–53, 59–76, 84, 89–92. He thinks Roxas and those like him should have been tried by "resistance" judges rather than judges appointed by members of their own social class (pp. 110–15). See also Jules Archer, *Philippines' Fight for Freedom*, p. 194.

40. Ind, *Allied Intelligence Bureau*, p. 153; Willoughby, *Guerrilla Resistance Movement*, pp. 52–61, 390–97; Agoncillo, *Fateful Years*, 2:791–94.

41. A law firm associate from prewar days says the illness was genuine and that Roxas lost fifty pounds in 1942 (Lichauco, *Dear Mother Putnam*, pp. 68, 92, 113–14).

42. Willoughby, *Guerrilla Resistance Movement*, pp. 39, 45, 205–6, 285, 383–87, 394–95. Quezon's biographer says that in February 1942 Quezon thought Roxas was so valuable that he urged MacArthur to make every effort to get him out to Australia. In case Quezon himself and Vice-President Osmena should die during the war (which Quezon did), he wanted Roxas to succeed him as president of the Commonwealth (Goettl, *Eagle of the Philippines*, pp. 181–82, 188, 194).

43. Hunt and Norling, *Behind Japanese Lines*, pp. 148–49; Hunt Papers.

44. Agoncillo and Alfonso, *Short History of the Filipino People*, pp. 464–65, 495. Castillo and Castillo, (*Saga of José P. Laurel*, p. 130) cast the same spear at the eloquent Filipino patriot Tomas Confesor vis-à-vis José Laurel: "He [Confesor] was at large and a free agent. It is one thing talking with fiery vehemence when one is in the hills and another when surrounded by sentries, and with a Damoclean sword hanging over one's head."

45. Thorpe, *East Wind, Rain*, p. 163.

46. Eyre, *Roosevelt-MacArthur Conflict*, pp. 42–43, 55.

47. Lee, *One Last Look Around*, pp. 249–50.

48. Recto delivered this defense in a long speech, the gist of which is noted in Taylor, *Philippines and the United States*, p. 104.

49. Samuel Lipman, a musician and writer about music, offers an interesting analysis of a similar situation in the European war ("Furtwangler and the Nazis," 44–49). Wilhelm Furtwangler, the famous conductor, was uninterested in politics but stayed in Germany and performed throughout the Nazi era. He was often accused, then and afterward, of being pro-Nazi. He replied, like his Filipino counterparts, that those who stayed and resisted were more truly heroes than those who fled into exile and shouted from

abroad. Lipman acknowledges that he is unsure just what to think; that it is difficult to resist anything demanded by a totalitarian regime; that people must often make compromises to live; that it ill becomes persons who live in mild, safe democracies to condemn those whose conduct falls short of the ideal in harsh dictatorships; and that both those who stay behind and those who leave places like Nazi Germany are inevitably compromised to some degree. He concludes mordantly that the only way Furtwangler could have satisfied all his critics would have been to get himself killed resisting the Hitler regime.

50. Taylor, *Philippines and the United States*, p. 110. A major practical consideration bore heavily on the decision too. Because the Japanese had destroyed most of their official records in the last months of the war, tangible evidence was lacking in the cases of many accused collaborators (Archer, *Philippines' Fight for Freedom*, p. 195).

Bibliography

PRIMARY SOURCES AND PERSONAL COLLECTIONS

Much of this book is based on these highly varied materials: orders, directives, correspondence, diaries, histories, newspaper clippings, photocopies of Records of the Adjutant General's Office from the National Archives, replies to questionnaires, tapes of interviews, and more. The majority of these can be found in the archival section of the Ernie Pyle Museum in Dana, Indiana, and are so indicated below (Pyle). Most materials there are not organized chronologically, and few have page numbers. A researcher can extract much information from such a collection, but it is not always easy to cite. Hence, the sources listed here overlap somewhat in order to give the items most frequently cited in the notes their own headings, especially those to be found in the Pyle collections of National Archives photocopies. Several individual files and folders in the Pyle Museum and elsewhere are described in some detail in the hope that having an idea of what to expect will aid any readers who might have occasion to use these materials in their own research.

Anderson Folders (Pyle). These are three large looseleaf folders of assorted materials relating to Maj. Bernard L. Anderson, a prominent Luzon guerrilla leader whose area of dominance abutted that of Robert Lapham. Vol. 1 consists of tapes of interviews with Anderson by Wayne Sanford and Douglas Clanin; vol. 2 is "History of the USAFFE Luzon Guerrilla Army Forces," written mainly by Col. Jaime H. Manzano, Anderson's executive officer; vol. 3 is a collection of miscellaneous documents about Anderson's organization, information about his early life, and statements made by him at various times.

Barros, Russell D. "Extended Sojourn in the Philippine Islands," Aug. 14, 1945. Barros History File, in Records of the Adjutant General's Office, Box 257.

Dizon, Herminia S. "Complete Data Covering the Guerrilla Activities of the Late Col. Claude A. Thorp." 1946. In Thorp File, Records of the Adjutant General's Office, Box 258.

Guerrillas (Pyle). This abrupt designation refers to four volumes of letters to and from, directives to and from, official documents concerning, and freely expressed opinions of many American guerrillas on Luzon. The materials are arranged alphabetically according to the last names of individuals and contained in heavy black notebooks. The volumes are designated merely by letters: the first concerns persons whose last names begin with A or B; the second, C to G; the third, H to M (including much material that relates to Robert Lapham); the fourth, N to Z. All sorts of unlike materials are bunched under the names of individuals, but there are no page numbers and nothing is cross-indexed.

Guerrilla Additions (Pyle). An array of miscellaneous papers, presented alphabetically according to the last names of the American guerrillas involved. It stretches to hundreds of pages (unnumbered) in a huge looseleaf notebook.

Hipolito, Criscenzio M. "Report: Chronological History of Guerrilla Activities of the 2nd Bn. 6th Inf. Regt., LGAF-TMA-PA (formerly the G-2 Units LGAF-USAFFE-TMA)." Undated, probably 1945 or 1946. In Lapham Papers.

Hunt Papers. Letters, directives, and clippings in the possession of Lt. Col. Ray C. Hunt, USAF (Ret.).

Lapham, Robert. "History of the Luzon Guerrilla Armed Forces (LGAF)." A thirteen-page outline history of the guerrilla organization founded, organized, and commanded by Maj. Robert Lapham, 1942–45. The account was written in 1946 but never published. (In Lapham's possession.)

Lapham, Robert. Papers. Correspondence of Maj. Robert Lapham with his mother, sister, and numerous other people in uniform and out; copies of National Archives documents provided by Douglas Clanin; directives (or copies) received from superiors and sent to subordinates during the war; newspaper clippings, and miscellaneous materials. All of it is loose in packages, in no particular order. (In Lapham's possession.)

Lapham, Robert. Radio Log Book, 1944–45. Four volumes of longhand synopses of radio messages sent and received by Major Lapham during the last nine or ten months of the war, the majority to or from MacArthur's headquarters. (In Lapham's possession.)

Manzano, Col. Jaime H., et al. "History of the USAFFE Luzon Guerrilla Army Forces." In Anderson Folders, vol. 2.

Records of the Adjutant General's Office, Philippine Archives Collection, National Archives, Record Group 407 (copies in Pyle).

Box 246. Files of Maj. Edwin Ramsey and subordinates of the East Central Luzon Guerrilla Area; LGAF General Information File. (In Organ II, Pyle).

Box 249. Anderson's Guerrillas; Volckmann's Guerrillas (File 500-22a). (In Organ S, Pyle.)

Box 256. Guerrilla Subsistence File; Southwest Pacific Area notebooks (File 500-3-2). (In Organ II, Pyle.)

Box 257. Barros History File; GRLA-28.

Box 258. Claude Thorp File; Alejo S. Santos File. (In Organ II, Pyle.) Volckmann's History; ROTC Hunters, Statements and Records; Cagayan-Apayao Forces (File 500-22A); Wainwright's Letter of Oct. 26, 1947. (In Organ S, Pyle.)

Box 259. Files of Maj. Bernard Anderson, Maj. Edwin Ramsey, and Col. John Boone and their organizations. (In Organ II, Pyle.) Infantry Rosters; AIM-95; GRLA-9 (with Christopher Bill Reopening Guerrilla Recognition Program). (In Organ S, Pyle.)

Recollections of the Raid on Cabanatuan (Pyle). Among this collection's contents are Wayne Sanford, ed., "Conversations between Claude P.

Daniel and Henry Clay Conner"; Sanford, Interview with Marvin Kinder, CO of 6th Rangers Infantry Battalion, July 10, 1984; Lt. Col. Henry A. Mucci, "Rescue at Cabanatuan," *Infantry Journal* 56 (April 1945): 15–19; Michael J. King, "Rangers: Selected Combat Operations in World War II," 1985, *Combat Studies Institute* (General State College, Fort Leavenworth, Kan.), pp. 55–71.

Santos, Alejo S. "Guerrilla Activities in Luzon, as Related to Col. G. Atkinson," Jan. 20, 1945. In Santos File, Records of the Adjutant General's Office, Box 258 (Clanin).

SWPA I and II (Pyle). Two large notebooks labeled (and cited) "SWPA I" and "SWPA II." (For reasons unknown, the title page of the first says "Vol. 2" but all footnotes cite the outer cover.) The title pages say "Originals of Correspondence Sent Out and Copies of Correspondence Received" and "Origin—Field Headquarters of Various Guerrilla and Army Units SWPA." In Records of the Adjutant General's Office, Box 256, File 500-3-2: "Correspondence Regarding Activities and Guerrilla Forces on Luzon, March, 1943–January, 1945."

Thorp Collection (Pyle). A huge looseleaf notebook filled with letters, clippings, and official papers, all having some connection with Maj. (later Col.) Claude A. Thorp.

SECONDARY SOURCES: BOOKS AND ARTICLES BY ACTIVE
PARTICIPANTS IN THE WAR AND COMMENTATORS AFTERWARD

Abaya, Hernando J. *Betrayal in the Philippines.* New York: A.A. Wyn, 1946.

Agoncillo, Teodoro A. *The Fateful Years: Japan's Adventure in the Philippines.* 2 vols. Quezon City: R.P. Garcia, 1965.

—— and Oscar M. Alfonso. *A Short History of the Filipino People.* Manila: Univ. of the Philippines Press, 1960.

Archer, Jules. *The Philippines' Fight for Freedom.* New York: Macmillan, 1970.

Arnold, Robert H. *A Rock and a Fortress.* Sarasota, Fla.: Blue Horizon Press, 1979.

Baclagon, Uldarico S. *Philippine Campaigns.* Manila: Graphic House, 1952.

——. *The Philippine Resistance Movement against Japan, 10 December 1941 to 14 June 1945.* Manila: Munoz Press, 1966.

Beck, Leon, and Neal Matthews. "Die Free: The Escape of a Bataan Battler." *San Diego Reader,* April 23, 1992, pp. 18–29.

Blakeley, H.W. *The 32nd Infantry Division in World War II.* Madison, Wis.: 32nd Infantry Division History Commission, n.d.

Boveri, Margaret. *Treason in the Twentieth Century.* London: Macdonald, 1961.

Breuer, William B. *Retaking the Philippines.* New York: St. Martin's Press, 1986.

Brines, Russell. *Until They Eat Stones.* New York: Lippincott, 1944.

Buenafe, Michael. *Wartime Philippines.* Manila: Philippine Education Foundation, 1950.

Calvocoressi, Peter, and Guy Wint. *Total War: Causes and Consequences of the Second World War.* New York: Penguin, 1979.

Campbell, Arthur. *Guerrillas.* London: Arthur Books, 1967.

Cannon, M. Hamlin. *Leyte: The Return to the Philippines. The U.S. Army in World War II.* Vol. 2, pt. 5 of *The War in the Pacific.* Washington, D.C.: Department of the Army, 1954.

Capostosto, Albert. "The Philippines: An Overseas Market with Surplus Dollars." *Export Trade and Shipper*, Feb. 9, 1948, pp. 1–4.

Carlisle, John M. *Red Arrow Men: Stories about the 32nd Division on the Villa Verde Trail.* Arnold Powers, 1945.

Castillo, Teofilo del, and José del Castillo. *The Saga of José P. Laurel.* Manila: Associated Authors, 1949.

Clark, Ronald. *The Man Who Broke Purple.* Boston: Little, Brown, 1977.

Conner, Henry Clay "We Fought Fear on Luzon." *True*, Aug. 1946, pp. 69–87.

Cook, Haruko Taya, and Theodore F. Cook, eds. *Japan at War: An Oral History.* New York: New Press, 1992.

Day, Beth. *The Philippines: Shattered Showcase of Democracy in Asia.* New York: Evans, 1974.

de la Costa, H., S.J. *Readings in Philippine History.* Manila: Bookmark, 1965.

Dissette, Edward F., and H.C. Adamson. *Guerrilla Submarines.* New York: Ballantine, 1972.

Dupuy, Trevor N. *Asian and Axis Resistance Movements.* New York: Franklin Watts, 1965.

Duque, Venancio S. "Palaruan: The Unknown Symbol" *Legion's Forum*, Dec. 1947, pp. 17, 44–45.

Elsbree, Willard H. *Japan's Role in Southeast Asian Nationalist Movements, 1940 to 1945.* Cambridge, Mass.: Harvard Univ. Press, 1953.

Estrada, William L. "A Historical Survey of the Guerrilla Movement in Pangasinan, 1942–1945." Master's thesis, Far Eastern Univ., Manila, 1951.

Eyre, James K., Jr. *The Roosevelt-MacArthur Conflict.* Chambersburg, Pa.: Craft Press, 1950.

Falk, Stanley. *Liberation of the Philippines.* New York: Ballantine, 1971.

Feldt, Eric A. *The Coastwatchers.* New York: Oxford Univ. Press, 1946.

Friend, Theodore. *Between Two Empires: The Ordeal of the Philippines, 1929–1946.* New Haven, Conn.: Yale Univ. Press, 1965.

Goettl, Elinor. *Eagle of the Philippines: President Manuel Quezon.* New York: Messner, 1970.

Grashio, Samuel, and Bernard Norling. *Return to Freedom.* Tulsa, Okla.: MCN Press, 1982.

Harkins, Philip. *Blackburn's Headhunters.* New York: Norton, 1955.

Hartendorp, A.V.H. *The Japanese Occupation of the Philippines.* 2 vols. Manila: Bookmark, 1967.

Hernandez, Juan B. *Not by the Sword.* New York: Greenwich, 1959.

Hileman, Millard E., and Paul Fridlund. 1051: *An American POW's Remarkable Journey through World War II.* Walla Walla, Wash.: Words Worth Press, 1992.

Howarth, Stephen, ed. *Men of War: Great Naval Leaders of World War II.* New York: St. Martin's Press, 1993.

Hunt, Ray C., and Bernard Norling. *Behind Japanese Lines.* Lexington: Univ. Press of Kentucky, 1986.

Ind, Allison. *Allied Intelligence Bureau.* New York: McKay, 1958.

Ingham, Trevor. *Rendezvous by Submarine: The Story of Charles Parsons and the Guerrilla Soldiers of the Philippines.* Garden City, N.Y.: Doubleday, 1945.

James, D. Clayton. *The Years of MacArthur, 1941–1945.* 2 vols. Boston: Houghton Mifflen, 1975.

Johnson, Forrest Bryant. *Hour of Redemption: The Ranger Raid on Cabanatuan.* New York: Manor Books, 1978.

———. *Raid on Cabantuan.* Las Vegas: Thousand Autumns Press, 1978.

Kalaw, Maximo M. "Filipino Opposition to the Japanese." *Pacific Affairs* 18 (Dec. 1945): 340–45.

Kato, Masuo. *The Lost War: A Japanese Reporter's True Story.* New York: Knopf, 1946.

Keith, Billy. *Days of Anguish, Days of Hope.* Garden City, N.Y.: Doubleday, 1972.

Kenworthy, Aubrey S. *The Tiger of Malaya: The Story of General Tomoyuki Yamashita.* New York: Exposition Press, 1953.

Kerkvliet, Benedict J. *The Huk Rebellion: A Study of Peasant Revolt in the Philippines.* Berkeley: Univ. of California Press, 1977.

Kodama, Yoshio. *I Was Defeated.* Tokyo: Radio Press, 1959.

Lachica, Eduardo. *The Huks: Philippine Agrarian Society in Revolt.* New York: Praeger, 1971.

Laqueur, Walter. *Guerrilla: A Historical and Critical Study.* Boston: Little, Brown, 1976.

Laurel, José P. *War Memoirs.* Manila: Lyceum Press, 1962.

Lear, Elmer. *The Japanese Occupation of the Philippines, Leyte, 1941–1945.* Ithaca, N.Y.: Cornell Univ. Press, 1961.

Lee, Clark. *One Last Look Around.* New York: Duell, Sloan and Pearce, 1947.

———. *They Called It Pacific.* New York: Viking Press, 1943.

Lichauco, Marcial P. *"Dear Mother Putnam": A Diary of the War in the Philippines.* n.p.: n.d.

Lipman, Samuel. "Furtwangler and the Nazis." *Commentary,* March 1993, pp. 44–49.

Long, Gavin. *MacArthur as Military Commander.* Princeton, N.J.: Van Nostrand, 1969.

MacArthur, Douglas. *Reminiscences.* New York: McGraw-Hill, 1964.

Manchester, William. *American Caesar: Douglas MacArthur, 1880–1964.* Boston: Little, Brown, 1978.

McDougald, Charles C. *The Marcos File.* San Francisco: San Francisco Publishers, 1987.

McGee, John H. *Rice and Salt.* San Antonio, Tex.: Naylor, n.d.

Mellnick, Steve. *Philippine Diary, 1939–1945.* New York: Van Nostrand Reinhold, 1969.

Meo, L. D. *Japan's Radio War on Australia, 1941–1945.* New York: Cambridge Univ. Press, 1968.

Mijares, Primitivo. *The Conjugal Dictatorship of Ferdinand and Imelda Marcos.* San Francisco: Union Square, 1976.

Mojica, Proculo L. *Terry's Hunters.* Manila: Benipayo Press, 1965.

Molina, Antonio M. *The Philippines through the Centuries.* 2 vols. n.p.: U.S.T. Cooperative, 1961.

Monaghan, Forbes J., S.J. *Under the Red Sun.* New York: Declan X. Mc-Mullen, 1946.

Mydans, Carl. "The Rescue at Cabanatuan." *Life,* Feb. 26, 1945, pp. 34–40.

Netzorg, Morton J. *The Philippines in World War II and to Independence (December 8, 1941–July 4, 1946): An Annotated Bibliography.* Ithaca, N.Y.: Cornell Univ. Press, 1977.

Ney, Virgil. *Notes on Guerrilla War: Principles and Practices.* Washington, D.C.: Command, 1951.

Nurick, Lester, and Roger W. Barrett. "Legality of Guerrilla Forces under the Laws of War." *American Journal of International Law* 40 (1946): 563–83.

Ogawa, Tetsuro. *Terraced Hell: A Japanese Memoir of Death and Defeat in Northern Luzon, Philippines.* Rutland, Vt.: Tuttle, 1972.

Olson, John E., with Frank O. Anders. *Anywhere, Anytime: The History of the 57th Infantry.* Privately printed, 1991.

Panlilio, Yay. *The Crucible.* New York: Macmillan, 1950.

Pomeroy, William J., ed. *Guerrilla Warfare and Marxism.* New York: International, 1968.

Porter, Catherine. Review of *The Fall of the Philippines* by Louis Morton. *Pacific Affairs* 18 (Dec. 1954): 375–77.

Potter, John Deane. *The Life and Death of a Japanese General.* New York: New American Library, Signet, 1962.

Quad City Times, April 20, 1975.

Ramsey, Edwin Price, and Stephen J. Rivele. *Lieutenant Ramsey's War.* New York: Knightsbridge, 1990.

Reel, Frank A. *The Case of General Yamashita.* Chicago: Univ. of Chicago Press, 1949.

Ricarte, Artemio. *Memoirs.* Manila: Bureau of Printing, National Heroes Commission, 1963.

Rodriguez, Ernesto R., Jr. *The Bad Guerrillas of Northern Luzon.* Quezon City: J. Burgos Media Services, 1982.

Romulo, Carlos. *I See the Philippines Rise.* Garden City, N.Y.: Doubleday, 1946.

Ross-Smith, Robert. *Triumph in the Philippines: The U.S. Army in World War II.* Vol. 2, pt. 16, of *The War in the Pacific.* Washington, D.C.: Department of the Army, 1963.

Rutherfoord, William de Jarnette. *165 Days: The 25th Division on Luzon.* Privately printed, 1945.

Sakai, Saburo, with Martin Caidin and Fred Sato. *Samurai.* New York: Bantam, 1978.

Sanderson, James D. *Behind Enemy Lines.* New York: Van Nostrand, 1959.

Sanford, Wayne L. "Anderson's Guerrillas." *World War II Chronicle,* March–April 1990, pp. 3, 5, 7, 9.

———. "Col. Claude A. Thorp: The Father of American Guerrilla Warfare." *World War II Chronicle,* March–April 1989, pp. 1–15.

———. "His Friends Called Him `Chief.'" *World War II Chronicle,* Sept.–Oct. 1989, pp. 3–9.

———. "Lapham's Guerrillas." *World War II Chronicle,* July–Aug. 1989, pp. 3–9.

———. "'The Mosquitoes Don't Bite': Serving with Merrill's Guerrillas on Luzon." *World War II Chronicle,* Nov.–Dec. 1989, pp. 4–11.

———. "The Organization of Guerrilla Warfare on Luzon, Philippine Islands, April 1942 to January 1943." *World War II Chronicle*, May–June 1989, pp. 3–10.

———. "Supplying the Philippines." *World War II Chronicle*, April 1992, pp. 1–6.

Santos, Alfonso P. *Philippine-Nippon Tales*. Quezon City: Interline, 1978.

Seagrave, Sterling. *The Marcos Dynasty*. New York: Harper and Row, 1988.

Segura, Manuel F. *Tabunan: The Untold Exploits of the Famed Cebu Guerrillas in World War II*. Cebu City: M.F. Segura, 1975.

Spence, Hartzell. *For Every Tear a Victory: The Story of Ferdinand E. Marcos*. New York: McGraw-Hill, 1964.

Steinberg, David J. *Philippine Collaborators in World War II*. Ann Arbor: Univ. of Michigan Press, 1967.

Steinberg, Joel. "The Ambiguous Legacy: Years at War in the Philippines." *Pacific Affairs* 45 (1972–73): 165–190.

Stewart, Sidney. *Give Us This Day*. New York: Norton, Popular Library, 1947.

Sutherland, Richard K. *Guerrilla Resistance Movements in the Philippines*. General Headquarters Southwest Pacific Area, 1945.

Taruc, Luis. *He Who Rides the Tiger*. New York: Praeger, 1967.

Tasaki, Hanama. *Long the Imperial Way*. Boston: Houghton Mifflin, 1950.

Taylor, George E. *The Philippines and the United States: Problems of Partnership*. New York: Praeger, 1964.

Thorpe, Elliot R. *East Wind, Rain*. Boston: Gambit, 1969.

Toland, John. *But Not in Shame*. New York: Random House, 1961.

———. *The Rising Sun: The Decline and Fall of the Japanese Empire, 1936–1945*. New York: Random House, 1970.

Trainin, P. "Questions of Guerrilla Warfare in the Laws of War." *American Journal of International Law* 40 (1946): 534–62.

Valeriano, Napoleon T., and Charles T.R. Bohannan. *Counter-Guerrilla Operations: The Philippine Experience*. New York: Praeger, 1962.

Valtin, Jan. *Children of Yesterday*. New York: Reader's Press, 1946.

Villamor, Jesus A., as told to Gerald S. Snyder. *They Never Surrendered*. Quezon City: Vera-Reyes, 1982.

Volckmann, Russell. *We Remained*. New York: Norton, 1954.

Ward, Robert S. *Asia for the Asiatics: The Techniques of Japanese Occupation*. Univ. of Chicago Press, 1945.

West, Rebecca. *The Meaning of Treason*. New York: Viking, 1947.

Whitney, Courtney. *MacArthur: His Rendezvous with History*. Westport, Conn.: Greenwood, 1977.

Willoughby, Charles A. *The Guerrilla Resistance Movement in the Philippines*. New York: Vantage Press, 1972.

———, and John Chamberlain. *MacArthur, 1941–1951*. New York: McGraw-Hill, 1954.

Wolfert, Ira. *American Guerrilla in the Philippines*. New York: Simon and Schuster, 1945.

Yap-Diangco, Robert. *The Filipino Guerrilla Tradition*. Manila: MCS Enterprises, 1971.

Index

efforts to unify guerrillas, 115, 117-18;
astuteness, 149-50, 156; "I shall
return," 149, 218; instructions for
American landings, 163; urges
invasion of Philippines, 172; policy for
postwar Philippines, 230; vouches for
Roxas, 236
Magsaysay, Ramon: his guerrillas seize
San Marcelino airstrip, 176
Mailheau, Robert: cures tonsillitis with
iodine, 46; opinion of Conner, 100
Main, Bill, 105; prefers mountains to
plains, 247-48 n 11
Makapili, 99, 176-77
Mallari, Col., 116
"mallet cats": tales about, 47
Manchuria, Camp: establishment of,
32-33; escape from, 44
Manriquez, Maj. Romulo: involved in
sale of contraband, 63-64
Marcos, Ferdinand, 228, 239; efforts to
unify guerrillas, 114, 122; claims to be
war hero, 122, 125; death of father,
122-23, 258 n 84; Lapham's estimate
of, 123-25, 259 n 86; awards Philippine
Distinguished Service Medal to
Lapham, 242
Marcos, Juan, 26; patrol leader, 27,
31-33
Marking (Marcos Augustin), 70-86, 87,
121; animosity towards Hunters,
108-9; joy at receipt of supplies from
submarines, 149; saves Ipo dam, 188
McClish, Capt. Ernest: opinion of
Fertig, 110; submarine landing, 150;
reprimand by Parsons, 253 n 29
McGuire, Ralph, 14; ineptitude, 15;
explosives expert, 16; Thorp's
adjutant, 19; commander of western
Luzon, 36; beheaded by Negritos, 36,
54, 113
McKenzie, Harry, 26, 29, 56, 57, 73, 111,
119-20, 145-47; joins LGAF, 38-39;
wife of, 39-40; dislikes Hendrickson,
68-69; liquor supply, 90; shot by Huks,
134; apportions submarine cargo, 154;
briefly commands LGAF, 191; work on
Filipino claims, 223-24
McNutt, Paul V., 231
Mellnick, Maj. Steve: instructs troops,
4; becomes head of Philippine Section
of G-2, 175; escape from Davao,
266 n 19

Merrill, Col. Gyles, 35, 43, 54, 108,
111-13, 115, 118, 155; organizes group
in Zambales mountains, 37-38,
248 n 8; and Thorp, 37, 110; efforts
to dominate Lapham, 115-17; efforts
to cooperate with Huks, 130; and
landing on north Bataan coast (1945),
176; demands food from Filipinos,
254 n 1
military units, American: First Cavalry
Division, 183; Sixth Army, 172; Sixth
Rangers, 176-80; Eighth Army, 191;
Fourteenth Infantry, 63-64; Twenty-
First Pursuit Squadron, 68; Twenty-
Fifth Infantry Division, 184; Twenty-
Sixth Cavalry, 4, 24; Thirty-First
Infantry, 4; Thirty-Second ("Red
Arrow"), 185-86, 188-89, 268 n 9;
698th Ordnance, 105. See also LGAF
military units, Philippine: Forty-Fifth
Infantry (Scouts), 4; Fifty-Seventh
Infantry, 4
Minang. See Dizon, Herminia
Miranda, Brig. Gen. Blas E., 110
Monsod, Col. Godofredo: collaborates
with LGAF, 136; death, 137
Morgan, Luis: troubles Fertig, 110; lured
to Australia, 110
Moros, 3
Moses, Col. Martin, 54-55, 59, 112-13,
119-20, 140; establishes organization
in northern Luzon, 111
Mucci, Lt. Col. Henry: leads
Cabanatuan raid, 178-79

Nakar, Capt. Guillermo, 63, 109, 140
Nalundasun, Julio, 123
Narwhal (American submarine), 161;
landings off Mindanao, 150-51; Dibut
Bay landing, 151-53; difficulty
transporting cargo from, 154-55; takes
four Americans to Australia, 157
Nautilus (American submarine): Dibut
Bay landing, 154-55
Naylor, Lt. Charles L.: evacuated to
Australia by submarine, 157
Negritos, 2, 45, 49; behead McGuire,
36; lethal arrowheads, 94; reputation,
94-95; ties with Conner, 101-2, 131;
supply food to Lapham's party at Baler,
151
Nellist, Lt. William: in Cabanatuan
raid, 179

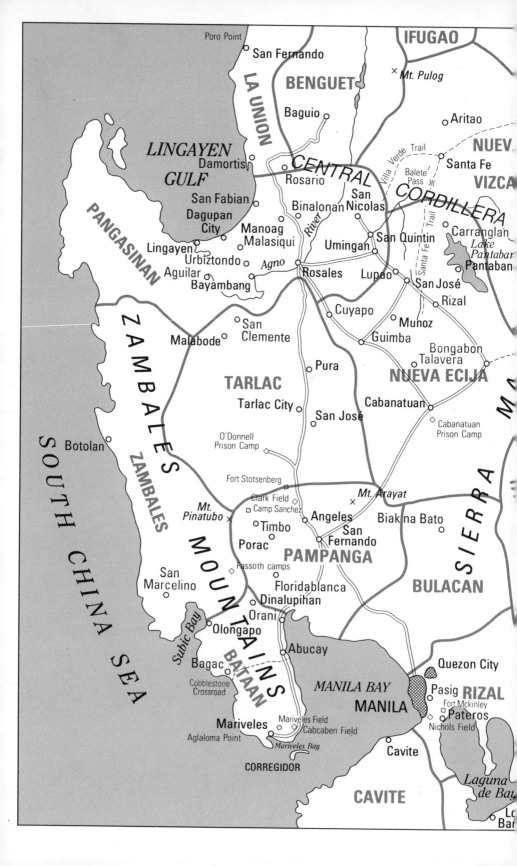